BY CHARLES BUKOWSKI

Flower, Fist and Bestial Wail (1960)
Longshot Pomes for Broke Players (1962)
Run with the Hunted (1962)
It Catches My Heart in Its Hands (1963)
Crucifix in a Deathhand (1965)
Cold Dogs in the Courtyard (1965)
Confessions of a Man Insane Enough to Live with Beasts (1965)
All the Assholes in the World and Mine (1966)
At Terror Street and Agony Way (1968)
Poems Written Before Jumping out of an 8 Story Window (1968)
Notes of a Dirty Old Man (1969)
The Days Run Away Like Wild Horses Over the Hills (1969)
Fire Station (1970)
Post Office (1971)
Mockingbird Wish Me Luck (1972)
Erections, Ejaculations, Exhibitions and General Tales of Ordinary Madness
    (1972)
South of No North (1973)
Burning in Water, Drowning in Flame: Selected Poems 1955–1973 (1974)
Factotum (1975)
Love Is a Dog from Hell: Poems 1974–1977 (1977)
Women (1978)
Play the Piano Drunk / Like a Percussion Instrument / Until the Fingers Begin to
    Bleed a Bit (1979)
Dangling in the Tournefortia (1981)
Ham on Rye (1982)
Bring Me Your Love (1983)
Hot Water Music (1983)
There's No Business (1984)
War All the Time: Poems 1981–1984 (1984)
You Get So Alone at Times That It Just Makes Sense (1986)
The Movie: "Barfly" (1987)
The Roominghouse Madrigals: Early Selected Poems 1946–1966 (1988)
Hollywood (1989)
Septuagenarian Stew: Stories & Poems (1990)
The Last Night of the Earth Poems (1992)
Run with the Hunted: A Charles Bukowski Reader (1993)
Screams from the Balcony: Selected Letters 1960–1970, Volume 1 (1993)
Pulp (1994)
Shakespeare Never Did This (augmented edition) (1995)
Living on Luck: Selected Letters 1960s–1970s, Volume 2 (1995)
Betting on the Muse: Poems & Stories (1996)
Bone Palace Ballet: New Poems (1997)
The Captain Is Out to Lunch and the Sailors Have Taken Over the Ship
    (1998)
Reach for the Sun: Selected Letters 1978–1994, Volume 3 (1999)
What Matters Most Is How Well You Walk Through the Fire (1999)
Open All Night: New Poems (2000)
Beerspit Night and Cursing: The Correspondence of Charles Bukowski and Sheri
    Martinelli 1960–1967 (2001)

BEERSPIT NIGHT AND CURSING

THE CORRESPONDENCE OF
CHARLES BUKOWSKI
AND
SHERI MARTINELLI
1960 – 1967

EDITED BY STEVEN MOORE

BLACK SPARROW PRESS
SANTA ROSA • 2001

BEERSPIT NIGHT AND CURSING: THE CORRESPONDENCE OF
CHARLES BUKOWSKI & SHERI MARTINELLI 1960–1967
The letters and drawings of Charles Bukowski copyright © 2001 by Linda
Lee Bukowski.
The letters of Sheri Martinelli, Introduction & Notes copyright © 2001 by
Steven Moore.

ACKNOWLEDGMENTS

The majority of the letters by Charles Bukowski are from the Yale Collec-
tion of American Literature, Beinecke Rare Book and Manuscript Library.
Additional letters by Sheri Martinelli are from the Special Collections
Department of the Davidson Library of the University of California, Santa
Barbara. Thanks to both institutions for reprint permission. Thanks also to
Gunther Stuhlmann, editor of *ANAIS: An International Journal*; the Anaïs
Nin Trust; the Beinecke Library; the Davidson Library at the University of
California, Santa Barbara; Michael Montfort; and Gilbert Lee for use of
the photographs contained in this volume.

Black Sparrow Press books are printed on acid-free paper.

LIBRARY OF CONGRESS CATALOGING-IN-PUBLICATION DATA

Bukowski, Charles, 1920–1994
    Beerspit night and cursing: the correspondence of Charles Bukowski & Sheri
Martinelli 1960–1967 / edited by Steven Moore.
      p.   cm.
    Includes bibliographical references and index.
    ISBN 1-57423-150-2 (paperback)
    ISBN 1-57423-151-0 (cloth trade)
    ISBN 1-57423-152-9 (deluxe cloth)
    1. Bukowski, Charles—Correspondence.   2. Authors, American—
20th century—Correspondence.   3. Martinelli, Sheri—Correspondence.
4. Pound, Ezra, 1885–1972—Relations with women.   5. Women publishers—
United States—Correspondence.   6. Women artists—United States—
Correspondence.   7. Beat generation.   I. Martinelli, Sheri. II. Moore,
Steven, 1951–   III. Title.
PS3552.U4Z489   2001
811'.54—dc21
  [B]   2001020217

Table of Contents

A section of photographs follows page 180

Introduction

Charles Bukowski's persona as the Dirty Old Man of American Literature is just that: a persona, a mask beneath which there was a man better read and more cultured than most people realize. Sheri Martinelli was one of the favored few for whom Bukowski dropped the mask and engaged in serious discussion of literature and art, and for that reason the discovery and publication of his letters to her give us a more complete picture of this complicated man.

If most serious writers are outsiders in some sense—and they almost have to be to gain perspective—then Bukowski was the ultimate outsider. He was born outside the United States in fact, in Andernach, Germany, where his father, a soldier from California, was stationed after World War I. Henry Bukowski married a local girl named Katharina Fett, and on 16 August 1920, she gave birth to Henry Charles Bukowski, Jr. (When he later became a writer, Bukowski used Charles for his professional name but remained Hank to his friends.) Soon after, the new family moved back to Los Angeles, where young Charles's outsider status was pounced upon by neighborhood kids. He was taunted for being a "Kraut" as well as for dressing so formally (which his parents insisted on), and his father didn't help matters by becoming the neighborhood ogre, chasing kids out of his yard at every opportunity. It was a strict upbringing, with regular beatings for the slightest infractions, and Bukowski grew up a lonely and sullen boy.

Bukowski discovered his talent for writing in the fifth grade. When President Herbert Hoover visited Los Angeles to give a talk, Bukowski's teacher encouraged her pupils to attend and write an essay about the occasion. Bukowski couldn't go, so he wrote a flamboyant account of the occasion that was so good his teacher read it aloud to the class. Later, she confronted Bukowski and he admitted he had fabricated the whole thing, but she was impressed rather than angry. The budding writer had a revelation, as he relates in a chapter of his novel *Ham on*

Rye that recounts the event: "So, that's what they wanted: lies. Beautiful lies. That's what they needed. People were fools. It was going to be easy for me."

But the years following were anything but easy. Junior high bored him, a brief interest in religion sputtered out, and he annoyed his teachers by correcting them whenever they deviated from the truth. However, Bukowski discovered the joys of reading while in junior high: not the assigned texts, but books he found on his own at the local public library. There he devoured books written by fellow outsiders, writers who didn't shrink from telling the truth. Sinclair Lewis's *Main Street*, Upton Sinclair's *The Jungle*, and D. H. Lawrence's writings were early favorites, and the clarity and force of Hemingway's style appealed to him. John Dos Passos, Theodore Dreiser, Sherwood Anderson soon followed, then some of the great nineteenth-century Russian novelists. Just as Bukowski challenged his teachers when he thought they were spouting nonsense, these writers were unafraid to challenge the status quo and conventional wisdom. He had finally found a group he might fit in with, and he decided he should become a writer.

But high school threw him a few curves: instead of attending the local school with his own kind, he was sent by his father to a school farther away attended mostly by rich kids, which only reinforced Bukowski's outsider status. Then his skin broke out with one of the most extreme cases of acne his doctors had ever seen. The outsider became a pariah. At a point when his acne was at its worst, he turned to fiction again, writing a story about World War I flying legend Baron von Richthofen, whose hand was shot off but kept fighting the enemy from the sky. Writing became one escape hatch from his problems, but at the same time he found another, which he came to prefer: drinking.

Upon graduating in 1939, Bukowski found a job at the local Sears Roebuck, hoping to make enough money to afford to move away from his parents and begin writing professionally on the side. He continued reading voraciously at the L.A. Public Library, where he came across John Fante's *Ask the Dust*, which became a kind of blueprint for the life Bukowski intended to lead: a working man with literary aspirations who hopes one day to join "the big boys in the shelves." But he lasted only a week at Sears, and decided instead to attend Los Angeles City College, signing up for classes in journalism in the hope he could make a living as a writer that way. He wrote voraciously, turning in a dozen essays a week when his instructor asked for only one—at the end of the semester she told him his writing deserved an A but his bad attitude resulted in a B—and continued to work on his own short stories. These stories caused him to leave home; his father came across them one day and was so outraged at what he read that he threw them, along with Bukowski's typewriter and clothes, out on the lawn. He picked up his things, took a streetcar to downtown L.A., and moved into the first of the many rooming houses he would live in for the next twenty years.

He stayed on at City College for a while, taking some art classes, but he knew he didn't have a future in academia. He left college in early 1941 without a degree, never to return. He remained an outsider, a civilian at a time when most men his age were joining the armed forces, a defector from the middle class his parents had emulated, wanting only to be alone to write and drink. For the next ten years he led an itinerant life, going "on the road" long before it became fashionable, working odd jobs, hanging out at bars, and sleeping in flophouses. He continued to write and stopped in at libraries when he could. (In a public library in El Paso he came across Dostoevski's *Notes from Underground*, which had the same thunderous impact on him as on the Beats a few years later.) He also developed a life-long passion for classical music, which he would always prefer over newer forms. He wound up in Philadelphia, where he held down a barstool at a local dive for a while before eventually returning to Los Angeles.

Bukowski published a few stories and poems between 1944 and 1948, but they attracted little attention, and he wouldn't be published again until the mid-fifties. In L.A. he continued working at odd jobs, few of them lasting more than a week, and drifted into a relationship with the woman who was to become his lover and drinking buddy, Jane Cooney Baker. (Their relationship was the subject of the 1987 film *Barfly*, whose screenplay Bukowski wrote.) In 1952 he got a job at the post office, which he assumed would be temporary but lasted for three years and which he would return to later for an even longer stint. One day in 1955, he became violently ill and was taken to the charity ward of the county hospital; years of hard living and harder drinking had resulted in a bleeding ulcer, from which

Bukowski almost died. It was a turning point in his life and recalled him to his vocation as a writer. He resigned from the post office, dusted off his typewriter, and, instead of fiction, began writing poems. He didn't know where they came from, but he knew instinctively that poetry was the right vehicle for his reawakened creative drive.

He also discovered the racetrack at this time and the thrill of gambling and soon learned he had some skill at predicting winners. He had similar luck predicting which magazines would be interested in publishing his work; knowing instinctively that his poems weren't appropriate for the big city slicks, he picked up a copy of a little magazine called *Trace*, which listed other magazines that welcomed submissions. Running his finger down the list, he randomly chose something called *Harlequin*, published out of Texas. He mailed off some poems and not only wound up getting published, but getting a wife.

Barbara Frye, *Harlequin*'s editor, thought Bukowski was a genius. A warm correspondence ensued, and after she confessed her fear that no man would ever marry her—she lacked two vertebrae from her neck that prevented her from turning her head side to side—he wildly proposed marriage in his next letter. He was drunk at the time, but Frye took him at his word and boarded a bus for L.A. to meet her intended. They drove to Las Vegas and got married on 29 October 1955, and the newlyweds returned to Frye's home in Wheeler, Texas. But after three months there, Bukowski insisted they return to Los Angeles.

Eight of Bukowski's poems appeared in *Harlequin* in 1957, including one of his best, "Death Wants More Death." Frye made enough money to support both of them, so Bukowski spent his time writing, drinking, co-editing *Harlequin*, and visiting the racetrack. But this relatively prosperous period didn't last; Frye and Bukowski became divorced the following year. Though Bukowski wouldn't appear in *Harlequin* again, he found new outlets: *Quixote* published two poems, *Existaria* took three, and others appeared in such places as the *Beloit Poetry Journal*, *Compass Review*, *Approach*, *Quicksilver*, and the *San Francisco Review*. A contribution to *Hearse* was especially fruitful: its editor, E. V. Griffith, was very taken by Bukowski's poems and in 1958 offered to publish a small collection in his chapbook series, to which Bukowski enthusiastically agreed. (It

10

didn't appear until two years later, a delay Bukowski found exasperating.) By this time Bukowski had returned to the post office and once again settled into a routine of working, writing, and gambling. New poems were published in *Nomad, Coastlines, Epos, Wanderlust,* and a dozen other now-forgotten "littles." Most had small print runs and paid only in contributor's copies, if that.

In 1960, Bukowski was still largely unknown to the literary world, his name recognized only by a handful of other poets who contributed to the same small magazines he did. Always looking for new places to publish, Bukowski learned that year (probably from poet Jory Sherman) of a new magazine published out of San Francisco called the *Anagogic & Paideumic Review.* Without seeing a copy, he submitted some poems to its editor, and received the rejection letter that opens this book. The editor complained that she didn't find a "thump" in his work, denigrated his subject matter, and gave all sorts of gratuitous advice in an oracular tone, citing Ezra Pound, Wyndham Lewis, T. S. Eliot, and even the *Greek Anthology.* Who *was* this woman?

§

She was a protégée of Anaïs Nin and is described at length in Nin's infamous *Diary;* she was the basis for a major character in William Gaddis's novel *The Recognitions* and then became the muse and mistress of Ezra Pound (she appears in various guises in the later *Cantos*); Charlie Parker and the members of the Modern Jazz Quartet hung out at her Greenwich Village apartment; Marlon Brando was an admirer and Rod Steiger collected her art, as did E. E. Cummings; she knew and was admired by all the Beats—Ginsberg was an especially close friend and mentions her in one of his poems—and she was known in San Francisco in the late 1950s as Queen of the Beats; H.D. identified with her and wrote about her in *End to Torment;* Pound wrote the introduction to a book of her paintings, and her art is now in collections around the world. She wrote unusual prose and poetry, much of it published in her own magazine, the *Anagogic & Paideumic Review.* She was one of the first to publish Bukowski, and her magazine was the very first to review his work. In recent years, she appeared under a pseudonym in

11

Anatole Broyard's *Kafka Was the Rage,* under her own name in David Markson's novel *Reader's Block,* as Lady Carey in Larry McMurtry's 1995 novel *Dead Man's Walk,* and she was anthologized in Richard Peabody's *A Different Beat.* When younger, she even modeled for *Vogue* and acted in one of Maya Deren's experimental films. And yet no notice was taken by the press of her death in November 1996, and few people today aside from Pound scholars know her name. For her own sake, and as background to the remarkable letters gathered in this volume, a brief account of her life follows.[1]

Sheri Martinelli was born on 17 January 1918 in Philadelphia—on Ben Franklin's birthday and in his city—with the given name Shirley Burns Brennan. Her father, Alphonse Brennan, was the son of a fisherman, and in later years Sheri liked to refer to herself as "The Fisherman's Granddaughter." Her mother was Mae Trindell, who was from New Orleans. Sheri's grandmother claimed descent from Scottish poet Robert Burns. Shirley Burns Brennan began using the name Sherry by the time she was a teenager, but she was later told that her first name had the wrong numerological value; to rectify this she modified it to Sheri. (All her life she had a weakness for occult and metaphysical notions.) She was the oldest of three girls and a brother and was largely responsible for raising them. As she indicates in her letters to Bukowski, she lived in near poverty and was considered an eccentric child. At some point her family moved to Atlantic City, New Jersey, but in the late 1930s Sheri moved back to Philadelphia to study art, specifically ceramics under John Butler at the Philadelphia School of Industrial Arts.

In Philadelphia she met Ezio Martinelli, a painter and sculptor who was studying at the Barnes Foundation in nearby Merion, Pennsylvania. Born in 1913, he was five years older than Sheri. They got married at the beginning of World War II, and in 1943 Sheri gave birth to a daughter, Shelley (named after the poet). The family moved to New York City, but by the end of the war they had grown apart. Sheri and Ezio separated; she kept his surname, and he kept the daughter.

---

1 For a longer account with documentation, see my "Sheri Martinelli: A Modernist Muse," *Gargoyle* #41 (1998): 28–54. It can also be found online at <http://www.dimensional.com/~awestrop/gaddis/sheri.htm>.

Sheri stayed in Greenwich Village, moving into an apartment at 23 Jones Street in the West Village. Talented, beautiful, and intriguingly eccentric, she made a striking impression on everyone she met, as is evident from the writings of those who knew her. In her diary entry for December 1945, Anaïs Nin recounts how she learned that a "romantic-looking girl" was reading her short-story collection *Under a Glass Bell* and had told her publishing partner Gonzalo Moré that she wanted to meet Nin but was too shy to approach the older woman. Nin suggested that she attend a lecture of hers at Mills College. When Sheri approached her at the end of the lecture, Nin writes, "I recognized her. She was like a ghost of a younger me, a dreaming woman, with very soft, burning eyes, long hair streaming over her shoulders." At first, Sheri didn't say a word: "She merely stared at me, and then handed me a music box mechanism, without its box. She finally told me in a whisper that she always carries it in her pocket and listens to it in the street. She wound it up for me, and placed it against my ear, as if we were alone and not in a busy hall, filled with bustling students and professors waiting for me. A strand of her long hair had caught in the mechanism and it seemed as if the music came from it."

"She came to see me," Nin goes on, "blue eyes dissolved in moisture, slender, orphaned child of poverty, speaking softly and exaltedly. Pleading, hurt, vulnerable, breathless. Her voice touches the heart.... She looks mischievous and fragile. She wears rough, ugly clothes, like an orphan. She is part Jewish, part Irish. Her voice sings, changes: low, gay, sad, heavy, trailing, dreaming." Sheri approached Nin for the same reason she would approach Pound a few years later: "She came because she felt lost," Nin writes. "I had found the words which made her life clearer." She goes on to quote Sheri: "Oh God, all the books one reads which don't bring you near the truth. Only yours, Anaïs." As ingenuous as it may sound, it was this quest for truth, rather than celebrity-worship, that led Sheri to apprentice herself to writers like Nin and Pound.

Sheri joined Nin's entourage, a group mostly made up of young male admirers, with whom Nin felt more comfortable than with people of her own age (she was in her mid-forties). At twenty-seven Sheri was a bit older than these young men, but she began accompanying them to parties and outings. In the spring of 1946 she joined Nin and the others to act in Maya Deren's film *Ritual in Transfigured Time.* She continued to paint and to take classes, studying engraving under Stanley W. Hayter at his workshop Atelier 17. She met Jackson Pollock there, and was in a class with Spanish painter Joan Miró, who ogled her shamelessly; as she later wrote me, "his round blue eyes 'ate' all of t/ black net off my chorus girl stockings." Her work was written up in *Art Digest.*

During the late 1940s Sheri supported herself by modeling, principally for *Vogue.* Such noted photographers as Karl Bissinger, Cliff Wolfe, Tommy Yee, and Dick Rutledge took hundreds of shots of her. Like many a *Vogue* model today, Sheri also experimented with heroin during this time, in addition to softer drugs, though not so often as to become addicted.

She had many suitors during this period. For a while she lived with a Chilean-American painter named Enrique Zanarte; journalist Anatole Broyard claimed to have lived with Sheri for three months (she is the "Sheri Donati" of his *Kafka Was the Rage*), though Sheri disputed that; and critic Richard Gilman once visited Sheri to present an elaborate argument why he would be a more suitable partner for her than Broyard. For a while novelist William Gaddis had a crush on her, and when he left the country to write his monumental first novel *The Recognitions,* he used Sheri as the model for Esme, a promiscuous, manic-depressive, schizophrenic junkie who writes poetry and models as the Virgin Mary for the novel's painter/protagonist, Wyatt Gwyon. Esme slips into madness and religious mania by the end of the long novel, wasting away from unrequited love, and eventually dies. (Gaddis sent her a copy of the novel upon its publication in 1955, but she never read it.) By the early 1950s she was living with a musician named Joseph Castaldo; aware of her ennui, Castaldo suggested that she go down to Washington, DC, and visit Ezra Pound, then incarcerated at St. Elizabeths Hospital. There she met the man who would dominate the rest of her life.

Writing in 1973 to one of Pound's biographers, Sheri gave this lively, freely punctuated account of her state of mind in 1952 when she first met Pound:

> I was going around t/world with the/clouds and t/air like
> Chief of All The Chiricahuas Apache: Cochise—when

Ezra Pound (known to us as: "E.P") "spoke to my Thoughts." I, too, "carried My Life on My Finger-Nails" and they were each & all a different colour because I was a working painter—a Fighter in The Ethical Arena wherein you KNOW what's Really Wrong because you did that yourself and you found out by The Way of Being There. Artist.

Maestro.

Was There Ever Such A Man, Dear Goddess. A Man who found me Lost in Hellishness but FIRST I had been Made Trusting & Loving & Innocent & Ignorant "Love One Another Children" … so as not To Even Know for a split second that I *was* Lost. I was having a Ball. All Those Sweet-faced Indians! T/guiltless sex of animal desire; pure, simple & uncomplicated by The Falsities of Any Other Facts! Freedom of Diet & No Two Days Running The Same.…

Today I remembered: His great Faith in Art when he said: "PAINT me out of here, Cara." So Painted E.P. in Paradise as he had sung me from Purgatory.… This is The Power of Art Work. With Out A Picture of It inside your mind—how can you Find It?

Pound was in his own form of Purgatory at the time. Detained by the U.S. Army in 1945 for making allegedly treasonous broadcasts over the Italian radio network during the war, Pound had, on the advice of his lawyer, pleaded insanity rather than risk being tried for treason—and if convicted, executed—and had been confined since the end of 1945 to St. Elizabeths Federal Hospital for the Insane. (The government's plan was to keep Pound there rather than risk an acquittal after a trial, so the fiction of his insanity was maintained by sympathetic psychiatrists.) During his first few years there he was allowed few visitors, but by 1951 his visiting privileges had been extended, as they would continue to be over the years. Surrounded by madmen and with the threat of being tried for treason hanging over his head should he "recover" from his insanity, Pound was understandably miserable and his creative drive at a standstill. *The Pisan Cantos*, written in 1945 while Pound was incarcerated in Italy, had been published in 1948, and he had written nothing since. In 1949 Pound won the Bollingen Prize for *The Pisan Cantos*, and the controversy surrounding the award attracted the attention of a new generation of readers, many of whom began making pilgrimages to St. Elizabeths in the 1950s to study under the master at his "Ezuversity" and do his bidding.

Sheri wrote to Pound's supervisor Dr. Overholser on 26 December 1951 to ask permission to visit him; her request was granted, and though there's no record of their first meeting, the mutual attraction must have been immediate. Pound encouraged her to move down there and informally adopted her. She got a job working in the admissions office of George Washington University, which didn't last long, and then worked in a waffle shop on K Street until Pound made her quit so that she could concentrate on her painting. He paid the rent on her apartment and gave her a dollar a day for expenses. Aged sixty-six and thirty-three, respectively, there was a father-daughter relationship at first (or older: she called him "Grampaw"). Pound was still married to Dorothy Shakespear, who had taken a small apartment near the hospital and visited him daily, but the older woman was apparently not jealous of the younger one; she even approved of Pound's financial assistance to Sheri. In the summer of 1954, Dr. E. Fuller Torrey notes in his book *The Roots of Treason*, "Dorothy wrote to Dr. Overholser requesting that Sheri Martinelli be allowed to take her place as [Pound's] guardian while out on the lawn because she had to go away for a week; Dorothy reassured Dr. Overholser that Ezra thought of Sheri as his own daughter." The following year Pound asked Dr. Overholser whether Sheri could move onto the grounds of St. Elizabeths and work as an art therapist; both requests were denied. Dorothy too seems to have looked upon Sheri as a daughter; spotting Sheri walking up toward Pound and her, "Dorothy once commented, 'Here comes "family." ' " Sheri proudly accompanied Dorothy on various outings in Washington, DC, dazzled by the older woman's Edwardian elegance.

Sheri lived in a variety of small apartments in and around Washington, DC, for the next seven years—once sharing a basement apartment with another Pound disciple named David Horton—and visited Pound almost daily. (She did, however, maintain a studio apartment on New York's Lower East Side for occasional visits; after another disciple, John Kasper, moved to New York and opened his Make It New bookshop on Bleecker Street, Sheri used the store as a mailing address. She received more than a hundred letters from Pound during her periods away from St. Elizabeths.) She joined the growing number of young acolytes who visited Pound, listening to his pronunciamentos and undertaking various projects at his suggestion. Sheri could always be seen with sketchpad in hand, doing studies of the Maestro, and occasionally of Dorothy.

Virtually everyone who has written about Pound's life at St. Elizabeths mentions Sheri, in terms ranging from praise to bemusement to condemnation. Noel Stock, one of Pound's earliest biographers, calls her "a strange, rather scatterbrained young woman" and a later biographer, J. J. Wilhelm, dismisses her as a manipulative, troublesome "odd-ball." On the other hand, Bill McNaughton has observed: "so far as I could tell the only visitor of those years who had any perception at all of what Pound was doing then was a young woman painter from one of those 'passionate religious traditions conscious of its roots in European paganism,' " and critic Wendy Stallard Flory goes so far as to suggest that Sheri practically saved Pound's life, at least his creative life: "the poet sees her as more than an individual; she comes to represent for him the very idea of love as inspiration. Set against the bleak and stultifying reality of the asylum ward, her youth, enthusiasm, and spontaneity must seem to provide a contact with all those things in the outside world that he most minds being shut away from."

Pound playfully called her "La" Martinelli, adding the honorific *la* more often used in reference to actresses and divas, which Sheri adopted as her professional name thereafter. Ostensibly she was at St. Elizabeths to study "the classic arts and letters" (as she would later put it in her résumé), and her art did undergo a change under Pound's tutelage. "Stay between Giotto and Botticelli," he advised her, so she supplemented her previous abstract style with an older, more representational style. She painted portraits almost exclusively, and mostly self-portraits. Pound was delighted with the development of Sheri's painting under his direction and actively sought to promote her career. His rooms were decorated with her paintings and he proudly talked them up to his visitors. His letters of 1955 are full of exhortations to correspondents like poet Archibald MacLeish and James Laughlin, his American publisher, to do something for Sheri: grants, foundation support,

17

publication, museum showings, anything, but nothing came of his efforts.

He did, however, arrange for publication in book form of a small selection of her paintings. His Italian publisher, Vanni Scheiwiller, brought out in February 1956 a miniature booklet entitled simply *La Martinelli*, a limited edition that reproduced nine of Sheri's paintings and two ceramic works. Pound wrote an introduction, noting that several of the paintings were works in progress (indeed, she would continue working on some of them up until her death), and stating: "The unstillness that delayed my recognition till quite a while after that of my less restless contemporaries [e.g., Joyce and Eliot] runs parallel in the work of la Martinelli, who is the first to show a capacity to manifest in paint, or in la ceramica what is most to be prized in my writing." In his introduction Pound also mentions two of Sheri's paintings not included in *La Martinelli* but that are mentioned in *The Cantos*: *Lux in Diafana* and *Ursula Benedetta*, both dating from 1954. By that time Pound had resumed work on his epic poem, and the next two installments he would publish, *Section: Rock-Drill* (1956) and *Thrones* (1959), are, at a basic level, a record of what he was reading and, in Sheri's case, seeing at St. Elizabeths. Through the thicket of Pound's elliptical, allusive poetry, Sheri can be glimpsed in various guises.

Sheri's presence in these cantos takes two forms: references to her person and/or her role in Pound's life at the time—she was his lover as well as his student—and references to her art. As in *The Recognitions*, she is mythologized as a romantic figure of redemption, and like Gaddis, Pound associates Sheri with a wide range of women in myth and literature. The first half of *Rock-Drill* (cantos 85–89) continues the manner and matter of the pre-Pisan cantos in their concern with history and ethics. But Canto 90 makes a sudden shift to the lyrical mode, recalling the love poetry of the troubadours Pound had studied nearly a half-century earlier. "In fact," writes Italian scholar Massimo Bacigalupo, "the forty pages of [cantos] 90–95 may be taken as a single new *Canzone d'amore*, modeled upon Cavalcanti's (and Dante's) *poesis docta* and on Provençal *trobar clus*." Pound later told Sheri that cantos 90–95 were "her" cantos, for like the troubadour's Lady, she personified love as a creative force. On the second page of Canto 90 the poet cries out to Cythera (Aphrodite), and then addresses a prayer to "Sibylla," the all-seeing sibyl of the Delphic oracle in ancient Greece. Most critics agree with Carroll F. Terrell's annotation: "Sheri Martinelli is understood to be the real-life sibyl at St. Elizabeths" (*A Companion to the Cantos of Ezra Pound*). Chanting in liturgical refrain the phrase "m'elevasti" ("you lifted me up"— from Dante's praise of Beatrice in his *Paradiso*), Pound registers his gratitude to Sheri for lifting him up out of his personal hell and reanimating him with the spirit of love:

> Sibylla,
> from under the rubble heap
> m'elevasti
> from the dulled edge beyond pain,
> m'elevasti
> out of Erebus, the deep-lying
> from the wind under the earth
> m'elevasti
> from the dulled air and the dust,
> m'elevasti
> by the great flight,
> m'elevasti,
> Isis Kuanon
> from the cusp of the moon,
> m'elevasti (90/626)

Isis Kuanon conflates the Egyptian goddess with the Chinese goddess of mercy. Next Sheri is referred to as the mermaid Undine, a nickname Pound gave her ("Thus Undine came to the rock" [91/630]; "Yes, my Ondine, it is so god-damned dry on these rocks" [93/643]). Although this could be a reflection on her dangerous, siren-like persona—Sheri was, after all, tempting Pound away from his wife and practicing what Laughlin learnedly calls "*concitatio senectutis*" (the arousing of desire in old men)—the undine is another redemptress, especially when Pound further conflates her with the sea-nymph Leucothea (from book 5 of the *Odyssey*). In the second half of *Rock-Drill* Pound resumes the persona of wandering Odysseus, and Leucothea makes her charming entrance in Canto 91. Appearing in the form of a seagull to Odysseus, who is adrift on a raft in wet clothes, Leucothea coos, "my bikini is worth your raft" (91/636), a flippant paraphrase of her offer in the *Odyssey* to

19

give him her magic veil in exchange for his wet clothes. The flirty line is repeated in Canto 95 (665), and even J. J. Wilhelm, who goes out of his way to deny Sheri's role in *The Cantos*, grudging admits that Leucothea "may well have been a tribute to Sheri Martinelli at this time" for rescuing Pound just as the sea-nymph rescued Odysseus. When Sheri left St. Elizabeths in 1958, among the paintings and drawings she left with Yale professor Norman Holmes Pearson for safekeeping was a photograph she had taken of herself in a mirror, wearing a bikini.

Sheri assumes many shapes and forms in *Rock-Drill*: she is apostrophized as "Bright hawk whom no hood shall chain" in Canto 91; she is the Regina Coeli (queen of heaven) of Canto 92; and the blue jay of Canto 94. Pound's finest tribute to Sheri comes at the conclusion of Canto 93:

> You are tender as a marshmallow, my Love,
> I cannot use you as a fulcrum.
> You have stirred my mind out of dust.
> Flora Castalia, your petals drift through the air,
> the wind is ½ lighted with pollen
> diafana,
> e Monna Vanna ... tu mi fai rimembrar. (652)

"You remind me of Monna Vanna" that last line translates, a reference to Guido Cavalcanti's lady love. (One of Pound's earliest books had been a translation of this medieval Italian poet's work; Pound gave his personal copy to Sheri, who filled the margins with drawings and love poems to Pound.)

In Canto 97 there are two intriguing descriptions of Sheri's hair and eyes. Brooding on the Homeric epithet "wine-dark," Pound again refers to Sheri as "Sibilla" and tries to describe the color of her hair, settling on "russet-gold." Sheri had been a brunette earlier, but at St. Elizabeths she sported "splendid red hair" (as Laughlin remembered it), which she later explained in this wise: "It was a spectacular crimson & it came about because E.P. had placed his hand on one's head and where E.P. put his hand on one's hair (a bit later on not instantly) that hair turned crimson.... E.P.'s touch (a 'laying on of hands'??) also deep'n'd t/eye colour into a lavender which E.P. is also noting in *C/97* indicating that E.P. was aware of t/changes." Sheri's second reference is to the lines:

with eyes pervanche [violet-blue]
          three generations, San Vio
     darker than pervanche?
               Pale sea-green, I saw eyes once (97/696)

A little later in Canto 97 there are some lines that some have knowingly said refer to Sheri, but which she disavowed:

mid dope-dolls an' duchesses
          tho' orften I roam
some gals is better,
                    some wusser
                              than some (97/700–701)

Sheri told me this was merely the chorus of a bawdy song Pound had composed; she was no longer a "dope-doll," having given up heroin by then. But it's true that during her first years at St. Elizabeths she was still using heroin and marijuana, which caused Pound considerable grief. Sheri was also the victim of a dope plant by the police and went to trial in 1956, but she was easily acquitted, "jury out 5 minutes," as Pound explained to MacLeish.

The sibyl at Delphi was also known as the pythoness (from her familiar), and in this guise Sheri makes her final appearance in *The Cantos*: born "Of the blue sky and a wild-cat, / Pitonessa / The small breasts snow-soft over tripod" (104/760). Sheri had given Pound a comic drawing of herself as a sibyl, standing next to a tripod and with a python in hand, which Pound thus worked into Canto 104. Sheri said Pound told her, "t/drawing is good because it shows you can laugh at yourself."

In a similar manner, several of Sheri's paintings became part of *The Cantos*. She would show Pound her works in progress and often he would give them titles and then work them into his poem. Her *Sibylla* of 1954 coincides with her appearance in Canto 90 (written the same year). In Canto 93, the two paintings Pound mentions in his introduction to her book, *Lux in Diafana* and *Ursula Benedetta*, become the subjects of the poet's prayer for compassion ("Lux in diafana, / Creatrix, oro. / Ursula benedetta, / oro" [93/648]). The lines "Isis Kuanon / ... / the blue serpent / glides from the rock pool" (90/626–27) have been associated with Sheri's painting *Isis of the Two Kingdoms*, which Pound admired, though in this case it's impossible to determine which came first. Other cantos refer to two subjects of Sheri's artwork, Princess Ra-Set and Leucothoe (not Homer's nymph but a character in Ovid's *Metamorphoses*). And Canto 106 opens with a description of another painting Sheri had been working on, a portrait of a woman with black hair surrounded by the faces of four girls, which Pound transformed into:

> And was her daughter like that;
> Black as Demeter's gown,
> > eyes, hair?
> Dis' bride, Queen over Phlegethon,
> > girls faint as mist about her? (106/772)

Sheri would continue to illustrate figures from *The Cantos* after she left St. Elizabeths, including an *Undine* in 1964 in memory of Pound's nickname for her.

"Undine" is also the name the poet H.D. used for Sheri in her *End to Torment*, written in 1958 in the months leading up to Pound's release from St. Elizabeths. In journal form she records her memories of him and their teenage romance, when he called her "Dryad." After reading an article in *The Nation* about Pound that mentioned Sheri and receiving *La Martinelli* from a friend, H.D. developed a keen interest in Sheri, finding a parallel—as Nin had done a decade earlier—between her younger self and the artist: "Undine seems myself *then*." When she learned Pound would not be taking Sheri with him to Italy upon his release, she decided to help her; though she doesn't mention it in *End to Torment*, H.D. gave Sheri the money from her Harriet Monroe Prize award in 1956. She was enchanted by the photos of Sheri and her artwork that Pearson had sent her, and somewhat reluctantly entered into correspondence with her. Sheri seems already to have known her work and wrote her an effusive letter of praise, but also expressed her rage at being dumped by Pound. "The male just can't go about like that, ditching a spirit love," Sheri fumed. "I have known Ezra for 6 years. The last 4 years I took a vow in St. Anthony's Church in NYC not to leave the Maestro until he was freed. A month before he was freed he made me break that vow."

"He killed her," Sheri wrote of herself to Pearson, describing Pound's decision to desert her. Instead of taking Sheri to

Italy, Pound took Marcella Spann, a young teacher who had started visiting Pound at St. Elizabeths a year earlier and had supplanted Sheri in the Maestro's affections by 1958. "With her serious, rather reserved expression and her hair done neatly in a bun," Pound biographer Humphrey Carpenter writes, "she made a marked contrast to the ultra-exuberant Sheri Martinelli, who until then had been undisputed queen of the disciples." Dethroned, Sheri married Gilbert Lee, ten years her junior, whom she had met shortly after coming to St. Elizabeths, and together they left for Mexico at the beginning of the summer of 1958.

"Poor Undine!" H.D. laments in her book. "They don't want you, they really don't. How shall we reconcile ourselves to this?"—remembering that a half-century earlier Pound had likewise abandoned her to go to Europe. Sheri had commented on the "sea-girls" section of Eliot's "Love Song of J. Alfred Prufrock" in an anthology she sent to H.D., and the older poet's last vision of Sheri is of "our little Undine on her sea-rocks with her wind-blown hair," utterly forlorn.

At Pound's suggestion, José Vasquez-Amaral, another member of the Ezuversity who would eventually translate *The Cantos* into Spanish, had arranged for an art scholarship for Sheri in Jalisco. He also arranged for her and Gilbert to stay with a friend at his country house in Cuernavaca "in case the Jalisco scholarship fell through. It did," Vasquez-Amaral later wrote. "After a while the fiery and imaginative Sheri was also unwelcome at the Cuernavaca place." The Mexican authorities expected someone who would paint pretty landscapes and glorify the republic, but Sheri was more interested in sketching beggar girls and exploring Aztec temples. After about six months Sheri and Gilbert left Mexico for San Francisco.

The best thing to have come out of her Mexican odyssey was a newfound interest in writing. Vasquez-Amaral was dazzled by a piece she wrote on Mexico in 1958: "The title is *Mexico, his Thrust Renews*; the subtitle is *Cheap Hollywood Movie*. In little over 7 pages, Sheri manages to give one of the strongest and most vivid *impressions* I have ever read on a trip to Mexico from the border to Mexico. It is all there. I don't say that her painting is to be sneezed at but I still maintain that if given half a chance, Sheri—the Sheri of 1958—would have given Kerouac, Bellow and all the others who have ventured on the quicksands of Mexico some very worthy competition." A portion of this work, entitled "The Beggar Girl of Queretaro," was published in 1960 and is indeed a remarkable piece of writing.

It was published in the *Anagogic & Paideumic Review*, a periodical (what we'd now call a 'zine) she started in 1959 after settling in San Francisco. Pound encouraged his disciples to start magazines, resulting in such periodicals as Noel Stock's *Edge* and William Cookson's *Agenda*. Sheri had forgiven Pound by this time and began the journal to fulfil a promise she made him to help raise the level of culture in this country. (Its motto: "to promote civilisation.") In issue number 4 she gave this explanation of its forbidding title: "A = the direction of the will UP & P = the kulchur born in one's head or wotever/ authority is E. P.—one might have not been listening for real but more or less that is wot one recalls." The *anagogic* is a spiritual interpretation of a text, and *paideumic* derives from *paideuma*, a term Pound picked up from ethnologist Leo Frobenius to describe "the tangle or complex of the inrooted ideas of any period" (or, more simply, the culture taught by educators). Typed by Sheri and mimeographed in purple ink, the magazine was sold at City Lights bookstore and mailed to select friends and libraries. She usually ran off only fifty copies of each issue, so not surprisingly few copies exist anymore, and few if any libraries have a complete set of all nine published.

A typical issue would consist partly of contributions by others and partly of Sheri's own writings, drawings, and commentaries on the other contributions. Pound is frequently quoted— the first issue, in fact, reprinted a 1928 essay of his entitled "Bureaucracy and the Flail of Jehovah"—and two issues were devoted to H.D.'s work. Four issues were published between September 1959 and March 1960, but publication lagged after that; numbers 5 and 6 appeared in 1961, but number 7 didn't appear until April 1966. Two final issues, unnumbered and consisting mostly of Sheri's own work, appeared in 1970. The places of publication track Sheri and Gilbert's movements during that period: the first four issues were produced in their cottage at 15 Lynch Street on top of Nob Hill, number 5 was issued from San Gregorio, and number 6 from Half Moon Bay, both small towns down the coast from San Francisco.

While still in San Francisco Sheri reestablished her connection with the Beat Generation, especially since many of the

24

Beats she had known earlier in Greenwich Village migrated to San Francisco in the late fifties. She was introduced to Jack Kerouac during one of his visits there, though he apparently already knew who she was, and Allen Ginsberg visited when in town. Sheri became friends with most of the major Beat writers in San Francisco—Michael McClure, Gary Snyder, Alan Watts, Philip Lamantia, Bob Kaufman (with whom Sheri was especially impressed)—and dabbled in the North Beach scene, a mother hen to the younger beatniks. But mostly she kept to herself, drinking vodka and producing her magazine.

In the early sixties Sheri decided she wanted to get out of the city (though Gilbert would continue to work there as an auto mechanic). She first moved down to a cabin in La Honda, but found the towering redwoods too oppressive, so instead moved into some cabins on the coast about halfway between San Francisco and Santa Cruz, where Tunitas Creek empties into the Pacific Ocean. She would live there at "the Creek" for the next twenty years, though for a mailing addresses she rented a post office box up in Pacifica, about twenty miles north. While Gilbert worked in the city Sheri spent her days writing, drawing, painting, and making jewelry, at night studying *The Cantos* by the light of an old kerosene lamp.

In 1964 Sheri gave her first and only one-woman show. A Cleveland advertising copywriter named Reid B. Johnson had developed an interest in her work when making a documentary radio program on Pound while he was still incarcerated at St. Elizabeths. In the course of corresponding with him, Pound sent Johnson a copy of *La Martinelli*, which so impressed him that a few years later he decided to organize an exhibit. The show ran for a month in September 1964 at the Severance Center in Cleveland, and was the subject of a photo-essay in the local paper.

Details are sketchy on Sheri's life during the second half of the sixties. She developed a strong interest in astrology, drawing up charts of friends, and delved deeper into the occult philosophy of mystics like Swedenborg and Edgar Cayce. Allen Ginsberg visited whenever he could, often bringing along a friend like Peter Orlovsky or Lawrence Ferlinghetti. In his 1966 poem "Iron Horse" Ginsberg recalls

>   On Pacific cliff-edge
>   Sheri Martinelli's little house with combs and shells
>   Since February fear, she saw LSD
>   Zodiac in earth grass, stood
>   palm to cheek, scraped her toe
>   looking aside, & said
>   "Too disturbed to see you
>   old friend w/ so much Power"

A year later Ginsberg visited Pound in Venice and asked a favor:

> "I'd like you to give me your blessing to take to Sheri
> Martinelli"—for I'd described her late history Big Sur,
> eyes seeing Zodiac everywhere hair bound up like
> Marianne Moore—which gossip perhaps he hadn't even
> heard—"To at least say hello to her, I'll tell her, so I can
> tell her," and stood looking in his eyes. "Please...
> because it's worth a lot of *happiness* to her, now..." and
> so he looked at me impassive for a moment and then
> without speaking, smiling slightly, also, slight redness of
> cheeks awrinkle, nodded up and down, affirm, looking
> me in eye, clear no mistake, ok.

That blessing "brought tears to Sheri Martinelli's eyes on the Pacific Ocean edge a year later, '68."

One night at the beginning of November 1972, Sheri went out to check on the caretaker of the cabins when "a terrible wind came up. A bad wind. A whistling wind," she later wrote. "One recalled that in Hawaii, not too far off westerly, such a wind is reported to come up when royal persons or sacred persons are about to die.... One thought there was a talking sound something like: 'Think ye hard on Ezra Pound' but it didn't make sense." The next morning Sheri learned Pound had died the night before.

There had been little or no contact between them in the fourteen years since they parted at St. Elizabeths, but for the rest of her life Sheri would think of Pound almost daily, endlessly rereading *The Cantos*, writing poems about him, sketching him, and trying to live up to the example he set of purposeful creative activity. She continued to produce poetry and drawings, periodically gathering them up into photocopied booklets, which she would send to friends. She apparently made no effort to publish her work through conventional channels or promote her art in any way, or apply for grants. That is, she had no interest in becoming a *professional* writer or artist. She did become something of a professional widow, however; in the late seventies she attended a Pound session at an MLA meeting in San Francisco dressed in black weeds like an Edwardian widow. When she thought Pound was slighted in an article in *Paideuma* in 1977 by her old acquaintance Reno Odlin (actually an attack on the academic Pound industry), Sheri fired off an enraged Mailgram to the journal demanding an apology (which was reprinted in facsimile in its winter 1977 issue). She also began to appreciate all the Pound materials she had saved—letters from Pound, drafts of "her" cantos, inscribed books—and began organizing all this material, both for her own continuing studies and for eventual sale to a library. (Yale's Beinecke Library finally bought her papers from Gilbert in 1999.) As Pound studies proliferated in the seventies and eighties, she began to be approached by critics seeking information, but she regarded most of them with a wary eye. She felt their neglect of the anagogic possibilities of *The Cantos* in favor of more mundane matters was wrongheaded; she also felt slighted by their neglect of her art, especially the paintings mentioned in *The Cantos*.

In 1983, at the age of sixty-five, Sheri decided it was time to retire and return back East. Both she and Gilbert had ailing mothers there to attend, so they left the Creek and drove out to New Jersey; after staying with relatives for a year or so, they finally settled in Falls Church, Virginia, just outside Washington, DC, where they lived for the rest of Sheri's life. Organizing Pound's papers became the primary activity of her days, interrupted often by family concerns and her own failing health. She took the time to contribute a brief statement to a festschrift for Allen Ginsberg's sixtieth birthday, and remained interested in some Pound events, attending a Pound-Yeats conference at the University of Maine in 1990 that featured her art.

In her final years Sheri liked to park her camper in front of the local supermarket and watch the people come and go. It was there that she died on 3 November 1996, almost twenty-four years to the day after the death of her beloved Maestro, and forty years after he transformed the fisherman's granddaughter into a goddess: "Ra-Set in her barge now / over deep sapphire" (92/638).

§

Had Bukowski received a typical form-letter rejection from Martinelli when he first submitted his poems in 1960, he would probably have tossed it aside and moved on to the next magazine. But Sheri presumed to give him some advice, and he bristled at that. "I can't be bothered with gash trying to realign my outlook," he wrote to Jory Sherman in characteristically coarse fashion (*SB* 21). He defended his aesthetics in his response to Sheri's rejection letter, and so began a rambunctious correspondence that lasted for seven years. It's surprising they had anything to say to each other, for they were complete opposites in almost every way. Though roughly the same age—Martinelli was forty-two, Bukowski turned forty that year—Sheri was emotional, idealistic, and quick to embrace metaphysical systems and conspiracy theories, while he was sensible, pessimistic, and down to earth. She admired the literary classics, while Bukowski had little use for them. She studied the *I Ching*, while he studied the racing form. She was very health-conscious and paid close attention to dietary matters, whereas Bukowski couldn't be bothered with such things. There was even a marked physical difference: Sheri, the ex-*Vogue* model, was what Bukowski called "a looker," while he admitted he was an ugly man. ("Beauty and the Beast," Alexander Theroux has called them.) And, most important, they held diametrically opposed views on the purpose of poetry. For Bukowski, it was solely a means of self-expression and followed no rules but his own, while for Martinelli poetry was a guide to civilized behavior and a vehicle for the exploration of spiritual truths, with a long tradition to be respected and followed. It's the romantic outlook versus the classical: the difference between Keats and Pope, Whitman and Eliot, or—to use the authors championed by Bukowski and Martinelli—between Robinson Jeffers and H.D. Sheri accused Bukowski of building "ass-hole palaces" in his poems, of wallowing in the mud rather than turning his mind to higher matters (*SB* 21, 134). The only writer they admired in common was Ezra Pound, though for different reasons.

28

And yet each recognized the other as a true individual, a person of spirit. Within weeks of their first exchange of letters they were writing regularly, opening up to each other as soulmates, sharing intimate secrets and confessing to their desperate attempts to find meaningful activity in life. Sheri recognized Bukowski's talent, even though she deplored his subject matter, and he praised her as "one woman in 90 million women," no matter how harshly she criticized him. He was proud to be in correspondence with her: in a 1965 letter to writer William Wantling, Bukowski reported: "Pound's x-girl friend Martinelli trying to cough up my whore-O-scope. stars, something. just think, somebody Pound went to bed with is now writing me, has been for years. my, my" (*SB* 234). Several times Bukowski talked of driving up to visit her, and Sheri once considered coming down (with her husband) to move in with him. However, they never met, and both realized this was probably for the best.

The bulk of these letters were written during the first year of their acquaintance. From 1962 onward the correspondence dwindled considerably; Bukowski understandably grew tired of Sheri's constant carping, and she suffered a variety of personal crises in the early sixties that distracted her. They kept in touch, but the fire had gone out of their epistolary relationship. She also became increasingly annoyed by his references to her in some of his poems, which she considered an invasion of her privacy. The end came in April 1967, when Bukowski wrote her a rather impersonal letter mentioning that a new acquaintance of his, a speed freak with a Nazi fetish named John Thomas, claimed Sheri couldn't have known Pound at St. Elizabeths. This stupid accusation, along with Bukowski's distant tone and Sheri's own increasing withdrawal from the world, ended their correspondence.

The survival of these letters is due almost entirely to Sheri's foresight. She not only saved and dated all of Bukowski's letters to her, but made carbons of most of her letters to him. (Bukowski saved only about a dozen of her letters, mostly later ones.) Their publication is due to Gilbert Lee's generosity in sharing these letters with me, and John Martin's willingness to print them. All surviving letters have been included and are printed in full.

Seamus Cooney has described the difficulties of reproducing

29

Bukowski's correspondence in his editions of Bukowski's selected letters, and I have followed his editorial principles in transcribing these letters. Thus, words that were typed in all capital letters are set in small caps, or in italics if they are books or poetry titles. Deliberate misspellings have been retained, and a good number of unintended ones as well. (Bukowski consistently misspelled his first wife's surname, for example, and never could get Allen Ginsberg's surname right, no matter how often Sheri spelled it correctly.) Bukowski was often drunk or hung over when he typed these letters, so many of his irregularities can be attributed to drink rather than an inability to spell. Consequently, only meaningless misstrikes and typos, and a few misleading misspellings, have been corrected. (Bukowski would sometimes type a word three or four times until he got it right; in such instances, only the final attempt has been retained.) His punctuation, even when drunk, is fairly good, and has not been amended.

Sheri's letters present a different challenge: a better typist than Bukowski—though she too sometimes wrote under the influence of alcohol or other substances—she had her own system of punctuation and, like Pound, constantly indented lines so that her letters look more like pages from *The Cantos* than normal letters. (Also like Pound, she often used British spelling and punctuation and had the tiresome habit of using dialect for comic effect.) She wrote in phrases rather than in sentences, and separated her phrases either with virgules/ like this/ or with sawed-off suspension points.. like this.. (using only two periods instead of the usual three). I have retained her idiosyncratic punctuation—though using the standard three suspension points—but have run most of her phrases together, breaking for new paragraphs when it seemed called for (and when she seemed to be doing so, though her erratic spacing often makes this difficult to ascertain). I hope the effect of her prose is thus preserved while making it easier on the eyes. As in Bukowski's case, some of her trivial or misleading misspellings have been corrected, though not all.

Conventional indented paragraphing has been imposed throughout—Bukowski usually began his paragraphs flush left, separated by line spaces, and Martinelli began hers wherever the typewriter carriage landed—except in those instances where the writers deliberately departed from conventional form.

Handwritten signatures at the end of letters have been italicized. Both correspondents sometimes illustrated their letters—Bukowski with line drawings, and Sheri sometimes with more elaborate drawings, her pages taped together to form illustrated scrolls—but the illustrations haven't been reproduced here. A few abbreviated words have been spelled out within brackets; also enclosed in brackets are dates to some of Bukowski's letters, which Sheri notated after receiving them. She sometimes complained how difficult it was to read Bukowski's letters—a clear case of the pot calling the kettle black—so despite the editing I've done, it would be appropriate for the reader to experience a little of the same difficulty in order to savor the full flavor of this wild correspondence.

—Steven Moore
Littleton, CO, Summer 2000

Abbreviations

A&P = *Anagogic & Paideumic Review*
CB = Charles Bukowski
SM = Sheri Martinelli

Charles Bukowski Works Cited

BW = *Burning in Water, Drowning in Flame: Selected Poems 1955–1973* (Black Sparrow, 1974).
DRA = *The Days Run Away Like Wild Horses over the Hills* (Black Sparrow, 1969).
LL = *Living on Luck: Selected Letters 1960s–1970s.* Edited by Seamus Cooney (Black Sparrow, 1995).
RM = *The Roominghouse Madrigals: Early Selected Poems 1946–1966* (Black Sparrow, 1988).
SB = *Screams from the Balcony: Selected Letters 1960–1970.* Edited by Seamus Cooney (Black Sparrow, 1993).

Other Works Cited

Cherkovski, Neeli. *Bukowski: A Life* (Steerforth Press, 1997).
Dorbin, Sanford. *A Bibliography of Charles Bukowski* (Black Sparrow, 1969).
Krumhansl, Aaron. *A Descriptive Bibliography of the Primary Publications of Charles Bukowski* (Black Sparrow, 1999).
Pound, Ezra. *The Cantos.* New Directions, 1995 (13th printing); cited by canto/page number.
Sounes, Howard. *Charles Bukowski: Locked in the Arms of a Crazy Life* (Grove Press, 1998).

BEERSPIT NIGHT AND CURSING

The Correspondence of
Charles Bukowski & Sheri Martinelli

1960–1967

• 1 9 6 0 •

5/june/60   sheri martinelli 15 lynch st. s.f.calif/

my dear charles bukowski/   have no idea when the next a & p
will be done as one is madly busy—hence i return yr verse &
retain yr address in case i do new a & p/ if you spec. wanted
rob't stock to read it i give his address/ i wont take respons. to
mail it over as rob't might not answer you & you'd wonder
where hell was work/
          rob't stock 41b peralta pl s.f.calif
    i want to say that i don't find a "thump" in yr work—i
understand the subject matter since that is life; i suggest you
keep writing it down; i suggest you go to the old boys—the
greeks/ latins/ a good translation in library & discover that life
has never been any different... then awakens in the soul... a
desire to leave a message of help for those who come after us/ &
not to list what life does & is doing to us/ maestro ezra pound
kept telling me "now don't dump yr garbage can on my
head..." so I learned this lesson the hard way...
    of course chopin would be at his piano... that was his JOB—
find your job/ or become that which you want to exist & that is
it/
    if you want to walk in the company of poets & painters I
rec. that you acquaint yrself with the tradition of art; that you
know of other subject matters than yrself because we have all
walked that way & we still do; life does not spare any of us—

---

rob't stock: Robert Stock, *A&P*'s poetry editor.

read Wyndham Lewis *Rotting Hill* The Room Without A Telephone & that is a portrait of Mr. Eliot our great poet & an account of his eyes & Wyndham—at the library—
    now do shave off yr whiskuhs; stop irritating the cops; remain sober; stop trying to figure it all out for yrself—other minds have been here—avail yrself of them; they are called 'classics' which AINT ACADEMIC; brush yr teeth; find a way to pay th' rent & join the free public library & obey the chinese command: "walk in the courtyard as if alone... not seeing the rest of them..." & repeat the magic formula:
        "now it is my time to walk on thin ice & face tigers"
& recall the poem the greek sailor left for us:
        "I bid you take ship & set sail, for many a ship, when
            ours was lost,
        weathered the gale..."
or words to effect/
    however did you see the A & P Review?
                most cordially
                                SM

Los Angeles, Fire in the Balcony
JadeJune [8] '60

Dear Sheri Martinelli:
    Holey possible there is no thump in my poems, and, in me. A degrading and disgusting position, eternally reproved by the gods for not saying enough or well enough or their way. Christ, I have read your classics, I have wasted a life in libraries, turning pages, looking for blood. It seems to me that there has not been ENOUGH garbage dumped, the pages do not scream;

Rotting Hill: a collection of satirical short stories published in 1951.
"now it is ... face tigers": slightly misquoted from Canto 86: "Now my turn for thin ice and tigers" (582).
"I bid you...": misquoted from a poem in *The Greek Anthology* as translated by Evelyn Baring (Lord Cromer) in his *Paraphrases and Translations from the Greek* (1903): "A sailor buried on this shore / Bids you set sail / For many a gallant bark, when I was lost / Weathered the gale."

38

always the effected dignity and know-all and dry page sun-burned and listless as wheat.

By the way, must all you so-called moderns use i i i i and no caps? this was effective once but is now simply a hollowdrag. Pound? Part of Pound was all right, of course, but much circus and blather, maestro maestro throwing spagetwopchink and rolling with the punch, *effect* of doing, appears walking straight while lying down. I don't have whiskers, I brush my teeth, but do not obey Chinese commands, I obey my commands and hate cops because most of them are young and wear black and carry clubs and guns and wiggle their little conceited asses and don't understand Beethoven or Mahler or Chopin or any or all the Russian musicians and writers. There is much truth in your saying I am listing life merely and there is much truth that I am not saying much and that I am saying too much in the subjective sense, that there is some garbage, but simply on the basis of the classics and the knowledge that I am not doing right, I cannot free myself. The work itself must find its own conclusion from myself and myself as a base alone, set free from what *has* happened or upon what others have done. I will be 40 in August and I am still, perhaps, living like a child and writing like one but this must continue as long as it is the natural thing for me to do.

Critics tend to overevaluate or underevaluate a work treading in the subsoil, seeing the line in the sforzando of their history. If God pissed some would call it a yellow blessing while others would mount their pea-shooters and snarl in their wine.

I have had time to think while laying halfdead in the charity wards and standing in the racetrack sun and sleeping with the fat whores, their sweaty feet pressed flat against my heart. It's no good reading any more, the machinery has burned out, will not take the glib façade. Do you prefer that I eliminate experience entirely from the poem? Li Po liked to burn his up and watch them float down the river, and LP too, liked his wine. I cannot change my flow to criticism. I do not love my poems, really entirely hate them, yet still cannot seethe to do hand-springs for the sake of making it. I remember many Chinese poems of the woman waiting for her man to come back from

---

Li Po: Chinese poet (701–762), translated by Pound in *Cathay* (1915) and popularized by Arthur Waley's *Poetry and Career of Li Po* (1950).

the wars, torn for love of man and simply waiting, the awful gap of wait, looking at the hill, the flower moving in the sun and nobody there, yet understanding and willing to give her man to the gods. Poems 5 and 6 lines long, experience indeed, and yet if I may use the hollow word: beautiful. Ah, I know, yes yes yes, all this in the classical mould. No, no, no. Experience. I don't like people who say this has all happened before, we cannot write it. It is happening now. NOW. The dead are dead, and believe it or not, because they are dead their words, in a sense are dead too. Blind Milton is not nearly as tragic as when he was living. Art only preserves a portion and is overrated. I can see my fingers on the keys, a half dead plant with a leaf like a rabbit ear bent left faces me, the women of the world walk in my brain, a rat gnaws my stomach and kicks his feet, an ice-cream truck passes bing bing bing bong bing bong bong, and Art, Art is nothing, it's my fingers on the keys NOW carving and crying Chopin and music and rebellion, to hell with the classics, to hell with form, to hell with Pound, go out, go out and bleed, bleed limitlessly against the mob, the halfRome, halfpoem, half-fire, halfkiss. Go out, go out, go out.

       Truly, Charles Bukowski

Charles

Lost Angels
mid-June '60

Dear Sherimar:

Recvd yrs on Matz, Atlantic Ave., Gloucester, Mass., which seems to me to be an incomplete address; however, if I do not hear from you on correction in couple of weeks I will send something if I have something.

I am not a "young poet". Will be 40, Aug. 16, this year. Have been writing poetry for 5 years, before that: 10 year drunk; before that, short story. Some history there but un-important. Tired today, drained; blackbirds whirling outside

---

Matz: apparently an editor of a small magazine.

window, a mass of nonsense. *Hearse* to bring out chapbook of mine, *Flower, Fist and Bestial Wail*, month or so. Heard from *Light Year*, said "hell-poems", "powerful", "2 dark too dark". Same thing from others on and on. Suppose yes when smoke has all cleared Pound will still be there, langwiddge-ear, knifepage flur. Boy can cut the jab, hoy and wan.

re solitude: I am complete isolationist, smer the people. music, paint, sound of paint, red music.

but this is mainly on the Matz address. All right. Li Po, uh yes, living on short sound of song, each moment too small for him. what can we do? Contempt and scrabble and illness.

Spoom, and spondee
Charles
Charles Bukowski

let the curious be damned and the damned be curious: the essence of poetry is malarky crossed with bullwhip...

Los Angeles, Calif.
July 2, 1960

Dear Sheri:

I am enclosing a letter I got from Pain today. It might amuse you. It slightly sickened me. He preaches so damned much and his lines lack solidity, they hang in the air, driveling, bickering, begging.

He words... without *being* there. And all this coat-tail hanging to the great. Miles wants to be something or other, or not be

---

Hearse ... Flower, Fist and Bestial Wail: *Hearse* was a magazine edited by E. V. Griffith; his Hearse Press published CB's first chapbook in October 1960.

Light Year: little magazine edited by Miles Payne out of Spring Valley, California.

Pain: Miles Payne, editor of *Light Year* who had rejected CB's poems. Payne's 9-page letter is a pretentious sermon on "poetry, superiority, and people."

41

something or other, wants to reach something, but to me he appears to lack any strength at all.

I said he would make a good lawyer. He would come closer to making a bad preacher.

Well, anyhow, I answered him. I have enclosed a copy of my answer.

----

my answer: since CB will continue to refer to Payne's letter, and because it mentions SM, it is included here:

Dear Miles and Miles of Payne:

ur letter of lustration gives eerie effect of having been raped by snow-woman with sungold breasts...

do not mouth or charge me or disfigure me with fearing and hating darkness. (see: "the darkness you fear and hate".)

I don't know, Miles, I am not even going to re-read yr letter, all 9 pages, u potshot me on constipation and that I eat shit and Shakey is shit and this and that, twists and twitches; I can only tell you this, m.p., for all your light you are unbearably dull and perhaps that is why you lean so heavily on all the other old men dead—to deliver yourself. It is not that a man stands for LIGHT or DARK that matters to me but how he vibrates. Take Blake: he had it. I am not an upholder of evil, consciously, but will say that good and evil change as we change our shirts, our lives, our centuries.

You are a twist-toner, a blatherer, and would have made a good lawyer in name and blame-tossing, edging off the question, then back on, building giant victories within the framework of yr blather-chatter, knocking down sticks, dragging in the sun, volcanoes, Chopin with his hair down, crabmeat set with eyes of the diamond, blue chip stamps; or on the other hand, Bukowski in floccillation, Pound in a cage or my good friend Sheri Martinelli Po Li washing a dirty dish... finally putting everyone to a drugged sleep with all yr dirty damned LIGHT LIGHT LIGHT!!!! until, at last, we all say, the jury, all of us: *have it yr way, Miles, but please please just let us the hell out of here so we can walk into a nice pleasant room and sit in the dark.*

...YES, a phonebooth will do, boots or toes, cock dangling, what have u.

Life is priceless, you say. You say it a lot, continually. Why do you keep saying this, Miles, over and over and over, to yourself and everybody else? Life is priceless. eh?

Life is neither priceless or unpriceless. A bird is a bird and the sun is sun and shit is shit. I could as soon say death is priceless and be just as right—or wrong. We may feel elated or somber, light or dark, full of opium or God or bullshit, but let's not paste labels.

42

Sheri, I know my poetry is a long ways off, but I am just beginning, and I really don't want to write too much like the

---

You doubt my appreciation of a Bach fugue because of the poetry I send you. I doubt I will send you any more poetry.

Jefferson was wrong: all men are not created equal.

All vanity does not vanish in music; it appears to have vanished.

Artistic men, creators, do not have "significant superiority", they have talent. Weight-lifters, boxers, matadors et al, have s.s.

Do I or don't I love life? Life, life, how sick I grow of that term. Like highschool students discussing after their 1st book of philosophy. I need life; I am here; life does not need me. Death needs me, poetry needs me, sleeps needs me, drunkeness. Let's not get so fancy.

D.H. Lawrence would have done quite well with the animals. They would have brought him oocytes and recension. See his poems on snakes, animals...

Yes, we finally agree: superiority is superfluous; the next time the ileum twitches, think of me.

We should not be "compelled to achieve". You give yourself away.

Love is the blanding of blemishes to make the poison taste better.

The greek terms don't matter; a greek hamburger does. Christ, sink your teeth into that and enjoy yourself!

Dylan says. Dylan says. Dylan says. Dear Dylan drank himself to death as I am doing. At least there, we had a similarity.

Yes, paintings of children are interesting. When I painted my first at Virginia Road Grammar School, they thought sure I was a genius. It took me 30 years after that to find out they were not entirely correct.

The point is, there is no point. Ask the manis.

I don't owe anything—"aspect of heaven" or anything else.

Dante was in love with the devil. Can't anyone read correctly?

Perhaps Beethoven, Mozart... Renoir, yes. But when I say "sing" I mean your kind of song.

I'm not going to do anything with Van Gogh. Hell, I've seen his exhibits. My father died while arranging his exhibit for the Los Angeles County Museum. I have the Eric Heckel, "Female Figure" hanging on my south wall, valued at $1,000.00   I don't spend all my time in the pool halls.

Darkness at noon? What happened to Koestler? He switched so much he lost his soul.

Ya, I know about light. See my *The Sun Wields Mercy* to appear in this Winter's *Epos*.

And Miles, the sweetness and light boys are everywhere, poetry is full of them, it's the style. Very few magazines print anything else. So much light is blinding. Spiraea and spires, stars, uplift, holy holy.

I've reread yr letter, after all, in order to answer a point or 2, which, of course, will not get thru to you anymore than u got thru to me. It's a

rest of them, so I'm starting simply. But they should really give me more time before tearing.

Anyhow, enclosed, the stuff.

yours and what,
Charles
Charles Bukowski

ps* You needn't return any of this crap. just throw it w rest a garbage.

c.b.

---

early July [7] 60, kowski, one6two3 North Maryposa

yes, dear cous':

much to feaze in yr letters but u are coming thru like a good thing which is not easy with the gimbals and rooks distorting polysyndeton and prayer, but off the fancy langwich and let me tell u I cannot send to Pearson at Yale U because, cous' I only have mostly one copy of that in which I appear and in some cases none. Wuz once in beautiful thing called *Portfolio* II, $10 an issue, large reproduction paintings modern, me story wit

---

rotten situation. I wish it could be easier. You appall me with a little too much preaching and setting all the masters on my tail, and I understand a lot of what you mean, glad you like the good music, the good paint, but I am just beginning after getting away from the hospital and some of the whores, and I am beginning to fill. The words are coming easier. I don't dislike you, tho I don't admire yr stand; it's a little common, like the old woman in the other room last night who offered me her ice cubes before she went to bed. I already *have* ice cubes... or was it, Jesus, Miles... that she knows I drink that much? Be good, kid, and keep all the lights in San Diego burning for me... especially those in the red-light district.

Pearson: Norman Holmes Pearson (1909–75), an English professor whom SM had met at St. Elizabeths. She had stored her paintings with him and was now sending work to him for eventual deposit at Yale's Beinecke Library.

Portfolio II: CB's story "20 Tanks from Kasseldown" was published in the third (not second) issue of *Portfolio: An International Review* in 1946.

Sartre, Lorca everybody else, pollock in big promenade, drunk one night in Filly Pa, needing drink broke no home no love no lemonade, told certain persons I writer, hole bar laughed: you writer, ah ha ha ha, so they promised me drinks and I went and drug out huge *Portfolio* and there in bar I showed them me with the famous, only it skidrow bar and they never hearda nobody, but print and all big drawings, red bulls with ears and tails and horns that stuck up outa pages, and the drinks came and I went outside to fight somebody or what the hell and I took the book with me and it was winding and raining and the pages flew flap flip all edge and whirl bulls with wings and matadors in the rain and everybody ran around ketching the pages, HERE, OH HEY, I GOT ONE HERE! Bam would go a foot, bam, big foot of window-washer, HERE'S ONE! and he handed it to me, a big muddy footprint right in the middle of the beautiful page and I said, OH CHRIST LET THEM GO, LET THEM FLY, MY WORDS, LORCA, EVERYBODY, LET THEM GO TO HELL IN THE WIND! and they laughed and, by god, they did let them go, and I dropped the yellow portfolio cover and we all went in and had a drink for dear dead Lorca and whatever.

ye[ah], I want to go on record merely listing my ills, snakebite-carnaval thistle, dilucidate.

Pound had green eyes? Lo, that makes twoa us! Now, if I only had the rest!

No, cous', I am *not* at top now; this gallimaufry is a beginning. I always knew, even when I was very young that it would take a long time, perhaps too long and that the years might run out before I got there. It is like having a baby. He is kicking in my belly now, but I cannot bring him out. I used to watch the sunlight thro my hangover in New Orleans down on the hanging dishpans and upon the breathing of the rats and all the slivers and dead French souls and me walking second floor railing outside lost, the words worms in my brain, helljelly mess wanting to lay down on paper and be good real thing, but too young, and still, at 40, too young, not, no, at "top".

I understand where I am. I am in hell: the faces tell me that altho they do not bother me so much now because they have been there so long and I know now that they will never say anything or do anything, make either love or sound or hate that will last, and it is my business to dispossess them by treating them kindly because they are only what they are, but it still feels so

45

much like a prince without snuffle to be alone in a room again. I mention things sometimes through nerves and the flow of word that is not entirely felt by the socket and shekinah of self... wal, hell.

Fry's admonition of *Cantos* not against Pound, against me, figuring all I felt holy was no damn good: Like D. H. Lawrence, Chikowsky or Franck's Symphony in D. Fought me thru last half of marriage; she nympho, held not against her, did best I could, but she laughed and claimed that sexually I was a "puritan" because I would not do the extra special things, and guess she was right. I think a woman much more beautiful fully clothed than naked, but let's get off of this, I feel lost already.

no ho no, wat do u do wen u want to rite a poem and a woman is sitting in a chair reading the funnypapers across from u, u cant get up and simply go over and sit at a typewriter. everything is too difficult and I do not want to ever hurt anybody.

I do not read a female face; I read a female ass. This is cruel, Sheri, and I am sorry, but that's where man gets his message. I don't know where woman gets hers.

Cannot yu say u have lived: *Canto XX* to *Rockdrill*, read by POUND. and, by god, now u are writing me, so in a way I am one with Pound too, and I feel better already. Jesus, I knew something must come out of them grinding my meat. another story of sorrow here, the wood-drills driving into the flesh, 16, other young man and men dancing in the streets, halo u uh harry hurrah but me down on belly drill drill drill into boils as big as apples god damn u god I said come down here into this room and I will crash u right in the face and drill drill drill the first of the old charity ward before the blood the alky cry god damn bastard world, so many sorrow stories   so many whores jails lies skirts that wiggled and kissed with heads as empty as these beer cans that sit strewn all about my kitchen, god damn kitchen beautiful music bang bang bang coming out of radio now, the paint of love, the paint of music, not the rotten Miles Payne *front* but crawling up without a name, without

---

shekinah: in Jewish theology, a manifestation of the visible glory of God.
Fry: Barbara Frye (1932–), CB's wife from 1955 to 1958.
Rockdrill: Cantos 85–95 of Pound's epic poem were first published as *Section: Rock-Drill* in 1956.

46

a reason, like an apple, like a slipper sitting by itself in the closet, like a cat chasing its tail, not thinking of birds; like Pound,
like ontology, like bang bang bang.

Cous', let's not make any "national minds". U sound like a
republican convention. I can see I am going to have to take on
where gramps left off, even tho u are learning me because I can
see much of ur attitude is more embracing flatwise and sound-
wise than mine and already u have given me some good lessons
and I am humble student but must at times say what must
much be said. u u. this business of the future an onerary bur-
den. Remember whar ol' buddy mine D.H.Law said: "We
should build our statues of wood." This takes great strength. we
will be in t dark, in t dark don u understand cous'? ware we
belong, lets lev the earth if thers any levins to thos luckun to
cum after and wonder. ya, even the *Cantos*, they must go, tho I
do not have the strength, time will. that is the marvelous cry of
ours, that all is lost forever why do we god damn go on livin
writin letters to cous' Sheri M. Po Li because only because only
only nothin'. We humans have more courage than locomotives
crushing snow.

You are going to allow everyone to die, dear Sheri, but your
courage is an ox. wunded a course, ur not foolin' me, u been
sittin' in my hell and u got no business tellin' me to cum on out
when u's half foot in, halfass out, still getting stung.

lovin' hilaritas, yes good, yes u good there, open mind to
see sea sharks and meanin a sharks an meanin a teeth knowin
they are they and there and dyin' in 'em like an artist and a man
or woman, bring laughter but not cheap bobhope but 1. at self
tapped and trapped and big in the jaws laughin at formula, the
sparge of cancer of tipped ripping and demise... no, do not discipline spirit, let take hold and call own shots. make no spartan
rules, let the ocrea and ochre run, u paint, I have painted, we
will paint. and, no education an so forth—think I want to catch
up to the Russians? Let them catch up to me. education

---

gramps: SM's term of endearment for Pound.

D.H.Law ... statues of wood": untraced.

Po Li: the pen name (obviously a play on Li Po) of SM's husband
Gilbert Lee (1928–), whose family's name was Li.

hilaritas: Latin: "joyousness." CB seems to be quoting from a (lost) letter
of SM's, who probably picked up this term from Canto 83.

distasteful word, u probably in ur spirit wanted and meant something else. do not l[et']s be word-hagglers, I am no good sometime... cous'.

o, on Sherman, I write him different thing that I know he prefers. I am kinder than u think. I am not saying he will not someday be a very fine poet but at 26 I am worried for him—there are so many 26's that are far something else even before 30, and thing—wife in pregnancy and all, look like trap. Fry got so god damned mad when I refused babies because I knew I was insane. she tricked me into it, but miscarriage. all this may seem selfishness but I will die alone. But on Sherman, I write him. He, so worldly. Meets editors walking down street. Phones this and that. Reads poetry here and there, piano background, Lorca, sets things up, booths, fairs, magazines... It gives me a feeling of things going on when I hear from him, and I think he is honest and well-meaning but rather imagine he has a tremendous flare when set off and could be rather narrow and unforgiving... but I don't know and hate these measurement things, and find when talking about him rather talk as he does. his poetry is so poetic, so silken, suffering true, but only... i wish he could get in a few back-alley fights and lock himself in a cellar for 6 months or so.

Anyhow, I know a couple of people in Frisco and that's something. Down here they know I am hermitage and leave alone. One thing about L.A. people, they so hose-high you don't mingle, they cut u turkey cold. Good for me, this place.

Sherman much admires u, esp. ur painting, but seems wary of personal and think I, u are too much for him. well, listen, I am going down to the bar. I should clean this place up, ah well.

say listen cous', I must drink and smoke at 4:30 am, there is nothing more circumspect unless we withdraw into the cloud of mallard. the [point] of this letter is that the dullness of the welt is forgotten for the nascency of much gift of robgrov and gobble the golden word, the laughter basting our rotten white bones, Pound as alive as a rat 3000 ad, myself writing this, smoking a cigarette, early this time, 10:34 pm closing, mailing whenever

---

Sherman: Jory Sherman (1932–), a poet who published in *A&P* and elsewhere before turning to writing westerns. See his memoir *Bukowski: Friendship, Fame and Bestial Myth* (Blue Horse, 1981).

the hell. A sound just went off in my mind and all is raw and I must sleep, 1 way or the other.
　　may all the gords and gods
　　tinkle things goosegigberry gophers
　　be urs,
　　　　whatever that means,
　　　　　　Charles Bukowski
　　　　　　　　Charles

ps—Sherman phoned last night (I haven't mailed this yet) at 2 a.m., drunk, collect. I have unlisted fone but gave him my number. "I saw Sheri. She's all right, you know that? Sheri's all right. Met her husband too. Real nice guy. Saw your poem in *Quicksilver*, the one about the doves, man. Great, real great. 'I'll have them in the pan by 2:30.' Don't worry about the call. I'll pay you. I'm coming down there, I'm going to win on the horses, will dump it all in your lap. Stan's coming down. I'll be down the 16th. Don't clean the place up. Leave the bottles, the rats, you on the bed smoking, sheets of paper all over. Jesus, I can't write, I can't write at all. Saw Hitchcock, I said, 'How ya doin' you son of a bitch?' Saw x of Grove Press, he asked to see my work. 'What you want' I asked, 'the published or unpublished?' 'Both', he said, 'both.' Saw—etc., etc."
　　Sherman quite a boy, that. going out to mail this. hope you got the Payne correspondence by now.　　　　c.b.

6/july/60　　s.m.　　15 lynch st.　　to buk/

ah zay Buk/ dozzzz zum letter... ah got this a.m.—met mailman out on street very early doing laundry & rec. yr letter to decode while machine went swhoos
　　1st a note on Jory Sherman:

Quicksilver, the one about doves: "Peace" appeared in the summer 1960 issue of *Quicksilver*; rpt. in *DRA* (34–35).
Hitchcock: George Hitchcock, San Franciscan writer and editor (*San Francisco Review, Kayak*).

young girl at bar in Bagel Shop wearing sleezy thin peek-a-boo black whorey dress, drunk... so drunk as she got up to leave her little pink hands cd hardly hold her up... they kept groping for bar like blind things... poor girl... her heels were run-down in back & her shoes were suede & she'd been out on "Neurotic Park" beach with some filthy dirty sluts of drunken men... she looked like a whore in dress & shape & mussed hair & drunkenness... all but for her poor face... too young... too blind... too bewildered... she made me sick I cd hardly keep from fainting dead away... at her tragedy... I mean Dusty yevsky... but not for me... I cannot bear the pain... and her coat was half off her plumb pink shoulders peeking through that whore's cheap filmy black sheer dress... and Jory was sitting on the edge of the piano with his sneakered feet up on the chair... talking about Bukowski... & I called his attention to the lost girl... and some drunk came in for her & her pocketbook to take her to a car... & that was when I saw her lost hands blindly groping for a spot to guide herself by... and Jory... as tho' it were Mrs. Pound herself... got up... still talking over his shoulder... about Buk... & naturally oh very naturally... the way Ezra in St. Liz used to be talking about Ovid or Dante... or Homer... or even Roosevelt or Churchill... wd keep talking & go over to the large tree & piss up against it... still talking about poetry or politics or art... so Jory... kept talking about Buk & he helped the poor drunken girl... on with her little coat... & she was led... out to a car where she got in... to torment my mind...

now... but Jory's a gentleman... naturally... not trying to "fool" buk... of course we are all in hell... but there is an extenuating circumstance... for Sheri hath "seen a vision"... yr story about the portfolio... is a hilaritas... but sad too... that is way of the hilaritas... to construct itself on tragedy... like a crystal forms... all right if Buk wants to go on record "listing my ills, snakebite-carnaval, thistle, dilucidate..." then Buk will do so... & Sheri will keep the records straight

I didn't really believe I cd lure the wary solitary fierce gloaming creature inhabiting Buk's psyche... to EVER send anything up to Pearson at Yale but one must honourable say that such a collection exists... glare as ye will O Buk's Psyche—ah will juz go on... tryin' to fo'm a na'n'l mind... like a great mud

---

Bagel Shop: coffeehouse in San Francisco at Grant and Green.

pie... please Cous' dont piss on my mud pie... dont understand large words... "gimbals & rooks distorting polysyndeton" wot iz? knew Pollack when was in Heyter's Atalier de Set or how hellspell... (etching & engraving... & P. kept appointments at round table... very very drunk & very very well mannered... as the yg awt student recalls)

You have green eyes... gramps will rage with jealousy... he was to date the ONLY green oyed boet... in eggsistence (his spelling)

yew iz at th' top right now—Buk... if I come down there... ah will convince you... and also... ah will attempt to get you to fo'm a na'n'l mind with me... somehow 'r other...

oh yew spellin' is worsen gramps if such be possible... his'n worse/n yr'n.

Yes/ we are in "hell" & gramps said: "ya' kant git outta hell innna hurrrry"... let us try to remain here as long as possible... just to fool the demons.

that wild description of new orleans... yes... I understand "I mention things sometimes through nerves & flow of word not entirely felt by socket & shekinah of self" but wot iz "shekinah" wot? wot? iz "shekinah"? all right Fry redeemed by Buk... "not agin' Pound but against me..." but she is still incorrect... because men like you... who can feel... are precisely what the Cosmos is trying to destroy... hence yr anguish... Fry's duty to stand inbetween Buk & Cosmos... the petals of the flower fall off when the time comes... nature destroys her perfections so mankind may never imitate them... she leaves no examples... ezra might as well wail on the wailing wall... for the knights temp. to return... as to wail for Jeff & Adams... the time that was... is now legendary... and a new time come down on us... New India... give it 500 years...

Heyter's Atalier de Set: Stanley W. Hayter (1901–1988) taught engraving and painting at the Atelier Dix-sept, an art school in New York City prominent in the 1940s. His students included Jackson Pollock, Robert Motherwell, Willem de Kooning, and Mark Rothko.

gramps said: "ya' kant git outta hell inna hurrrry": cf. Canto 46: "you who think you will / get through hell in a hurry" (231).

Knights temp.: the Knights Templar, a medieval order of knighthood eventually suppressed by the pope.

Jeff and Adams: Thomas Jefferson and John Adams, American presidents admired by Pound and the subjects of several of his Cantos.

as for "nymphos"... they do not exist—the animal is not made that way... it is a dream of a difference... at any degree... to make up for lack of a natural talent... one has heard enough about poor ol' Fry to know she is tryin' too hard... and the coloured boys in the jailhouse who got time to wig it out say: "man, dont try... if ya haffa try..."

Do forgive... one has no right to be speaking about a female one dont know... but one does know the female pattern... it is rumoured she is trying to hook my dear friend David R. Wang... to him... she wd be a lost... sad... creature... the Chinese worship propriety... the "Puritans" were the BEST ballin' people this country has yet seen... all else is based on their hot natures... toned down by prot. rel. ... gawd... if they hadn't been christers... we'd have built an eastern empire... Fry is way off... anyhow... the introduction of sex habits since the w.w.1 from france... brought home by the farm pop. ... is indication of lack of both love AND sex... and mere friction taking over... poor Fry... she had to be so "hip" she went through the telescope & fell out on what you'd call the square end... oh do forgive... this broad... is being too daring right now... sorry Couz... but maybe... cd help... to see from female point of view... iz all right to "read a female ass..." not cruel... my dear Buk... you haven't spoken an UNtruth yet... & only that wd be cruel... women get their message through their psyche... but I grant they do wag their butts now 'n then when they aint certain of their psyches... I have even been caught doing it... in a loose moment... & place

dear Buk/ this is YOUR life—dammit... if you want to write a poem sitting on a woman sitting in a chair reading the funnypapers... then DO it... just do it because another woman will come along & she'll want to read poetry... we always work now & live now... for what going to jump off but we aint aware as yet...

it DOES COHERE—it does... it does... it does... yes yew iz part of E.P. & yes I have "lived" & still am... and he read me

---

David R. Wang: Chinese-American poet whom SM met at St. Elizabeths. He's mentioned in Canto 96 (673) and occasionally contributed to *A&P*.

"it DOES COHERE": adapted from a line in Pound's translation of Sophocles' *Women of Trachis*: "Splendour, it all coheres!" (New Directions, 1957), p. 50. (One of SM's portraits of Pound appears as the frontispiece to this book.) Pound later wrote of his *Cantos*: "it coheres all right / even if my notes do not cohere" (116/817).

52

Dante, Villon, Guido, the Kuan Tzu, the Sacred Edicts, Ovid... & lots of other things... & seduced me whilsts he read... sweet Gramps... Charles you are so violent you terrify me... "one sheet in closet... alone" you are most sad person... well... Lamb... you are becoming a legendary figure with the yg poets... sittin in yr bassilica... or howhellspell... yesssss I kno' I zound like a ruddy "repu. conv..." but dammit... ah has mah gig... man & I know... that a na'n'l mind wd save us all a lot of time & anyhow... the thought of New India & what they will prob. do to the gold-skinned chicks in the next 400 years... hurts my soul... I got to do something or I shall also... be facing empty beer cans... or worse... Charles... you do not know how tender most of the females are... even dear Ol' Fry has a tender spot I'm sure... I cannot sit here & forget that they are asking me... from the future to guarantee them a spot... a job to do, something to hold onto... like no one gave us... I will get through to my rep. con. nat. mind... the idea of the female... Buk... you just got to put up with it... because gramps says ah iz never wrong even... when ah aint wrong ah iz right... all right you take over "where gramps left off" because any form given to me will be passed on to the tender females of the New India of the next 2000 years & they will adore you Buk & wish themselves back into the past to pick up yr beer cans & remove some of the "bang bang bang" violence from thy heart... yr harem... Sheri's New Indians... "and the republican convention national mind" oh gawd... but dammit Buk... WHEN U ARE THE LIGHT IT IS NATURALLY DARK ALL AROUND YOU ... BUT THAT DON'T MEAN YEW IZ IN "THE DARK ..." IT IS MILES WITH HIS RUDDY ZUNZHINE THAT IS IN THE DARK... YEW IZ IN THE LIGHT... or at least yew iz a light bulb... that the cosmic electricity is

Villon: François Villon, 15th-century French poet.

Guido: Guido Cavalcanti (1250–1300), Italian poet whose ballads were translated by Pound (1911).

Kuan Tzu: a book on economics named after its Chinese author (684–645 B.C.). Pound read to SM from Lewis Maverick's *Economic Dialogues in Ancient China: Selections from the "Kuan-tzu"* (1954).

Sacred Edicts: ethical instructions issued by Chinese emperor K'ang-hsi (ruled 1662–1723), translated into English in 1921, and cited often in Cantos 98–100.

"one sheet in closet... alone": source unknown.

burning up at a terrible speed... "bang bang bang" (a shoot-um-up) of course... it will all be lost... my dear Buk... that's the fun of it... to do it anyhow... you are talking to a Tree that knows her leaves will fall & vanish into dirt... but the pattern remains... "the dream remains"...

the IDEAS we are having via letter... is what my New Indians will cherish... I ask you to love them as I do... because they will be getting their little poor hands chopped off for stealing bread... whereas... you & I... have to now... been enjoying a freedom they will not know... please help me love the phantom children... now & then I see a pair of green eyes in a gold face... so absolutely... not... Buk... I iz aint gonna let nobody die... while I am the Queen of the Beats... I am seated upon the right hand side of the high Prince of the Innermost Hell & far from my Paradise... & I do know... but right under his lousy nose... I'm not gonna let anybody die... & where they will send me from here... for this crime... oh I donno... donno... I am eating my pomegrante seeds & spittin' them in his chops... do not reveal my position or all's lost... lost... lost... that is why I cuss's Miles... he wanted to broadcast my position...

Heaven & Hell are split second next to one another... in one sentence it is possible to live in both... but what is not possible... is to remain in one or the other... for longer than that split second... donno why...

all right "no spartan rules" for Buk to shoot down... but must "discipline spirit" or my matter will go plumb to hell... in the earthly sense... I mean I will fall apart... man I am a New York City chick... & I go to hell real easy... alls ya gotta say is boo... & there I am... on the street... Bad Street havin a ball... "a Street Princess"—

god help the rooohoooshuns when they taste american whiskey... it will eat holes in their national mind...

dear Buk... I mean "education" the way gramps meant it... he had one hand on my breasts & one eye on me... & one hand on Ovid's Metamorph & one eye on th' book & his mouth on mine... dear Educational Gramps.

now we to Jory in yr letter/

yes you are entirely correct—yes gramps said: "i didn't breed until I was over 40" real artist... yes... do not let them trap you... an artist is the father the mother the wife the husband the child... don't let them accept less... make them take all or nothing... baby... you are right... right... Fry is a sentimental trapp'rrrr... yes what you say about Jory is correct... he will have his "back alley fights & lock himself in a cellar for 6 months"... they always take a person like Jory & stick him out front & let his beautiful sincerity... represent... then... he will have a time to "walk on thin ice & face tigers"

he will be dreadfully hurt—I wont let him down... because I saw him help that girl on with her coat... as tho' she were a lady... he'll get hurt... Chester Anderson was hurt... & he did it to himself... stealing the money & running off to NYC... such a silly cheap trick... only the office boy runs off when the safe is left open... chester now has ruined his reputation... stealing that loot... Jory wdn't do that... but it will be some other thing... Jory is being placed out front... as a m.c. & so forth & he is so innocent & a very good person... well... some of us are artists & we die the death of an artist... and some of us... do not... no body knows until it is too late & all over...

but you still shdn't juice that much Buk... dammit all... you republican convention national mind you... you educational... spartan rul'd disciplined spirit you... hand that beer over... doan yew ever let me catch yew doin' that agin... but stand by... when sweet Jory crosses the Jordan... because I predict it... only his "back alley" will be the psychic fight... & the wonder why... they no longer love me... style... and that is a hard bit to do...

Jory is not "so worldly" my lamb... he is so UNworldly... that is why he has been stuck out front... we are the worldly ones who know enough to stay home & do our work... no matter what kind of fuel we tank up on... yes I know... but Jory is a blessing whenever I go over to N. Beach for a small kickin' ball... Jory is always there ready to shield me... & because he's being used nobody dares stop him from his love Sheri... sweetness.

when first we met... Jory didn't know how to "see" me & of course there were too many people in this 1 room house... but one has had opportunity to speak alone with him & it was cool/

4/30 is a bad hour & one usually does smoke or drink at that hr... if one is an american... there is nothing here to do except make money & that is tabu except for the newly arrived... because we aint got none to begin with...

Chester Anderson: there's a Chester Anderson in CB's "Fleg" (*RM* 107).

55

Had to go fight with my neighbors for a while... then fell asleep sort of now returned/

yes—paintings... have you ever seen the book gramps made for the awtis in italy? the La Martinelli book... give you some idee of what Jory sees in them...

a bar downstairs... how great—that is how one lived in wash., d.c. over in georgetown... at Julies... on M St by the Key Bridge... Jory drunk? that's not good... he is too young to be drinking... altho' I think his Wop blood will stand him in good stead... I think Jory told me he's half Italian & he has an Italian beauty... plus something else... cd be germanic... something very straight & fine... & keen... donno... maybe Hinglish... Jory american... all right... I guess he foned you after the poetry reading I spoke about in last letter... Everyone else call her "hey Martinelli" or "La Martinelli" but Jory... he just says... in roomful people... "Sheri... please stay... I want to read some Bukowski to you..." and flips them all out...

Sheri stayed... Jory... when he feels... feels very deeply... & he thinks Buk is TOP... but Buk... he *is* the Light... he thinks it is all dark where he is... It is all a Star of King Solomon... if you fall to the bottom of one pyramid that lands you upon the top of the other pyramid... you just cant be bottom anywhere without being top... and middle... is never where we are...

Jory's conversation... dear Buk... see it how it is... he is surrounded by people who teach him those things are important... but he worships you... believe me... I have seen his dark eyes talking about you—his fine clear unwavering look... that Jory is a good boy... yes got Payne correspondence... & answered...

now is time... to cook dinner... the day is gone now... it never did have any of Miles wretched sun in it... just a fine misty typical s.f. summer daye... Listen GreenEyes... be cool in that pad of yrs... it sound deeelightful... except the rats... there aren't really any rats... iz they? no!

now I go & will mail this on way out tonight... is there anything in S.F. you need/want—will do if I can/ yr father really hang the Van Gogh show? must be 'big shot' type paw... to do that... who you really my dear Buk? cous? oh if you cd form that fire in you man/

---

father ... Van Gogh: Henry Bukowski was a preparator at the Los Angles County Museum, not the art director as he sometimes boasted.

56

mid august 1960, *Sunday nite—*
no, it is July

my v.d. Sheri M.:
  sick today, but yr good letter n she ri cantos & rochmony on
piano no radio, sun coming in upon me warm and quiet, I have
climbed preety much out now. a fool running into teeth lately
and it is good to have the lapse... I was drunk last night and
started letter to Sheri M. but blacked out:

> "am wrkin on 't cantos of She Ri' n a vorce c, this
> is no small thing, and I will take mi ti em ane comment,
> perhaps not pleasantly, tho wee shall sea, and I am laffing
> butt yew don mine rite?
>   I don know Rochardsun per se and wat but a
> course reelize eeeyes that he is bing bothered by bing
> black
>   and this wlrks the poletry springs i n his head gaid
> god
>   but altho this all proper and contrempt
> we have dumped so mu ch anogony
> that we are dulled with screaming.
>   fr4arligent started with bookshit and we end t is
> way, Richar son yun gargle, stay in love with yr husband
> avoid bolws readhesces eat heathead, give up except as
> central source which is wat hus Poli liPo iz for.
>   ferrygnti sud hav scfewed horse and both wd
> haved had pictures of Eararaza without fireman chopping
> down gatherroom.
>   z, sherman ok bdcaause he nose u mee
>   tell Po Li to relax, I am not going to dtink r his
> gearbeer or anythiing else, I am stronger than tht. I respt

---

she ri cantos: Pound told SM that Cantos 90–95 were "her" Cantos
because of the part she played inspiring them.

rochmony: Sergei Rachmaninoff (1873–1943), Russian composer and
pianist.

Rochardsun: John Richardson, San Franciscan poet and a frequent contributor to *A&P*

fr4arligent ... ferrygnti: Lawrence Ferlinghetti (1919–), San Franciscan
poet and founder of City Lights Bookshop.

god tha woen make gut I bee g damned if I am not
nothing.
gv Jricharsona v brk.
poli mezzoslant ok.
Rkcih a course fooled Sherman and u
don worry, stlps won ar a time. "

good thing I passed out, Sheri
Richardson no roturier but sometimes rotters easier to take
because u already have map on them. good god, a child should
have and would have realized that She Ri was not meant to be
hamstrung across the ceiling and what was he DOING reading a
dedication to HIMSELF? this is still basically bad taste, no
change here, and to linger and dawdle and simper-taste praise
of self, telling to audience, is end of all sickness and even the
forgiving angels must have heaved but the devil held his red
belly and laughed and gave Martinelli the hot pitchfork prongs
and everybody but Richardson knowing what is happening.
don't make enemies, simply reajust your sights.
serbonian, serbonian.
Sherman I have once or twice started to give up on but just
when I am ready he comes up with a letter, entonic, blazing
from the shouls. If he could just get across some of himself into
the poem without trying to be so god damned fancy like the rest
of them. They all sit down and the first thing happens, big sign
in mind: I AM GOING TO WRITE A POEM. A POEM. So they try to
make it *sound* like a poem instead of simply falling across the
paper. What is wrong? Can't they see? It is simply like taking a
rolled-up piece of paper and swatting a fly from the curtain.
morello, eyas, epinasty.
My fly-spider pome childhoodthing that shamed me for
years, upsetting clockwork nature, and not equipped to accept.
Something rong with me for years. When 7 or 8, group of boys
yelling near bush, "Hey, this spider's gonna eat a fly! Come on,
come on!" Bukowski came on, all right, and kicked spider and
fly out of web and crushed them both with shoe. But most
amusing thing, now, (now only) the crowd of them yelling

---

entonic: intense, overwrought.
fly-spider pome: perhaps "Death Wants More Death" (*RM* 92–93).

angry, chasing me, all of them, little angry fists and faces, over fence, down alley, around block, but long-legged C.B. flying, FLYING, the deed all done, and they are way back there, slowing, hating, saying to each other THAT SON OF A BITCH! AND THE SPIDER WAS JUST ABOUT TO EAT THE FLY!

I am not big enough to accept the works of nature; I can only accept what it says inside: I don't *like* it. And that's good enough for me.

wurked once in a slaughterhouse, out they'd come, 2 minutes dead on hooks, cut as a rose away from leaf and root and 6am sun, and they'd swing it for me, one two 3 4, and on four they'd cut it down and down it'd come on the shoulder, a half steer, bones that once moved, blood, onehundred and forty pound, a dollar and a half a pound, nd up into the truck trying to hang the thing on a dull hook, press it down thru the fiber and fat and bone, onto the hook, and there it hung, mathematics, and back out for another one, big six feet 7 foot Negro behind you, cow on shoulder waiting and mad because you are no longer a kid, and tho strongest old man in Los Angeles, no match for 19 year old halfwits hoo wake with hards every morn.

But hell, I eat steak and am a spider too then but I do not forgive myself, but must have them *welldone* tho this does not change the sun.

Got Summer K[enyon]. Review in mail yesterday. Pretty good poem by Robt. Penn Warren and he ain't always good. Anton Chekhov short story. I preferred Turgenev, prefer Tur to Check, and Dos to Tolstoy but all this is beside. Article on Graves, I have not read him too much, must try again. Dint like to read lately and Graves always appeared thick and winded-long, too much fat around the meat and when u are hanging to a drink a horses tail and a fat wrinkled woman for love that is old enough to be yr mother, Graves just lays like statistics. Irony and Absurdity in Avant-Garde Theatre. New York long ways off, and LA has only bunch of 19 year old highschool students on boards, queer, silly laughing, all really only wanting to be in Hoolywood than making a play go. Tho I saw a preety good O'Neill, actors good, but audience horrible, little Jewish neighborhood, talking to each other all during play, misunderstanding the lines, laughing when they should have been immersed, getting all the lines inside out, it was as if another

59

play had been written for the audience, and I stood outside with Fry at intermission and I asked her, do you like it? and she said, no, the central character is just like you, he talks just like you, demented, and I had to look around to see if you were in your seat or up on the stage.

Great God Brown.

It was soon after that that we became divorced.

Now I hear she is writing Wang, wants to make him editor, sending photo thru mail. Wang I hear is nearer homo than milk and it would serve her right. They would make a hell of a pair: neither of them can think or write.

Fry beautiful in way but has little dishpan face and very vengeful. She has deformed neck, cannot turn head, and this is what brought me to her. I thought if I can make one person happy in this world then my life has not been wasted. A lot of it my fault and I failed and I will say no more.

getting away: I do not go to poetry readings or read my poetry and I try to avoid much of everything as there is much self-adulation and counter-praise and mingle mingle that is all beside the point.

your letters pomes to take away what needs to be taken away and it is odd that you and Sherman can do so much for me. I am saving yr stuff and maybe someday I can get somebody to put it out in book form and I will get rich and maybe go to China or India or Turkey or Africa or someplace where the sounds are strong, if I live that long... so keep writing, there's hardly enough yet but you have crushed awful Pain for me and some other things, oh that Miles awful snake swallowing great gulps of pink rabbits and canned sunshine.

yes, unbearable to read his letter, made me sick all thru. dilletante babbling things that he thinks are right and feeling very safe backed up by his Beethovens and Shuberts and Bachs, as if we cannot have them because we do not turn his handsprings. Payne has read too much listened too much and never fallen back upon Self, but u are right, he means well but there is

---

Great God Brown: a 1926 play by Eugene O'Neill known for its extensive use of masks. The central character is a successful businessman (without inner resources) who dons the mask of a frustrated artist. Cf. CB's poem "The Day I Kicked Away a Bankroll" (*RM* 74).

no equipollence between his gods and himself, not even a shadow, and because he is not bad guy (he is a god damned corde-
lier, in fact), no real hatred or bile or what, it makes him that
much harder to take. But one more awful letter like the last,
let's not think about it.

yes yes his "16 year-old boy caught in mid flight... spell-
bound by rush of emp. concerto..."

Why must they, WHY MUST THEY SPOIL EVERYTHING
EVERYTHING, why is everything spoiled and soiled and pissed
on? Remember in Frisco once, piano concerto, little Italian next
to me tapping foot, oh TAP TAP TAP TAP, oh by god he was
ENJOYING it miles payne style, tap tap tap, but I was sick tap tap
tap, and the audience mad, fatty Montier, and clapping several
times during the night before endings thinking pieces over. This
ok on new works but on old standards—where do those people
come from? And I met little tap tap coming down the stairs
afterwards and I looked at him and he got the message and
stood there stupidtransfixed holding to railing and then I
walked out into the wonderful air.

u are rite to sense in Pound his greatness and I find u more
and more rite, and I am glad.

Ginsburg all right at times but have been dispoint in his
poetry lately and don't know what's wrong, what he's gone and
doing rong in his life and his typewriter but he has snuffled off,
but maybe all temporary. Sem corso ker and others, what is
WRONG?

When Warren puts them to shame, old as he is, it is time to
tighten ranks.

Pound and Jeffers never weakened.

I probably did use the word "shit" in letter to him, tho this
is not me, and he made big jump, and him saying me sitting
there saying "shit, shit, shit" like old steam locomotive was
unkind because he is trying to halter and lower me into something I am not, and this was low thrust. Also do not remember

---

fatty Montier: unidentified.

corso ker: Gregory Corso (1930–2001) and Jack Kerouac (1922–1969),
leading lights of the Beat movement.

Jeffers: American poet Robinson Jeffers (1887–1962), whom CB greatly
admired.

knocking Bach or how I did it, the exactness or wordage or ref-
erent... I am speaking here of Miles again.

No, no Chinese shits as I do not need this, and doubt I will
write Miles again. He is a twister and turner of things and will
not take you coming straight on.

I read Pound's letters to Theobald in *Light Year* and he certainly treated Payne to slap of disdain he deserves. Gramps reads
well these human things that flop about making sick sounds.

damn Pain: I DON'T WANT TO KISS ALL THINGS, esp. lacy
air-frilled 1/8 souls and assholes. he MAKES me curse, not thru
weakness or lack of frampold phrases but what do u do with
lichen?

yes, I did not understand how Henry Luce got in there.
Miles prob read an article in N.Yorker in which everybody
made great big something more than they are, the words running along like crazy horses filled with wine.

If you were a male, Sheri, you would be famous. Womanhood is always held against one like a gun. You are up in the
minaret but they will bring u down won weigh or another.

u doubt if Miles has read Ez or understood him/   I doubt
that he could.

Remember how Murray used to knock Lawrence? And
K.Boyle slapping him in short story when sick, even K.Shapiro
pomeing him down. Lawrence much more weak points than
Pound but Ez will have his detractors, naturally, and we don't
care, it shows he is GETTING them. Yes, Lawrence poem on
snake at water well, classic to me...

Pound ... in Light Year: the autumn 1958 issue of *Light Year* featured
"Five Letters to and fro Ezra Pound" (pp. 60–76): four are between
Pound and John Theobald, and the fifth is from Payne to Pound.

Murray used to knock Lawrence: John Middleton Murry (1889–1957),
English editor and critic, author of *Son of Woman: The Story of D. H.
Lawrence* (1931).

K. Boyle: Kay Boyle (1903–1992), American poet and novelist. Contra
CB, Boyle admired Lawrence and was moved by his death to write the
story "Rest Cure."

K. Shapiro: Karl Shapiro (1913–2000), American poet and critic. There
is rather qualified praise for Lawrence in Shapiro's long poem "Essay on
Rime" (1945), ll. 580–87, but perhaps CB refers to a different poem.

Lawrence poem on snake: "Snake" (1923), probably his most famous
poem.

This pot about Lawrence standing darkly upright in middle of jungle waiting for animals to bow down. Let's put Miles in same spot in his lacyies, he probly wacky in ten minutes. Draw puzzles to make points u (miles) are not strong enough to hold self. This man is climbing in my brain like a rat nibbling.

yes, Jeff meant men created equal by law but the others twist this thing to make it sound good to them. men are, however, not even created equal by law, for the law is to protect the rich against the poor.

don't worry about the drinks; when I die no one will weep.

I cannot attempt a form of thots for my letters because it must come natural and I cannot push. So it will have to go like this, but I understand what you mean and u are correct but I must be careful not to borrow or bluff, and until then...

No, I have not seen the A & P Rev.

On the Wm. Morris thing, a poem for it, I don't know. I will try to find something, and if they want it, all right.

I'm not feeling too good, am going to close now. duck the Po Li bowl.

awright,

Charles

Charles Bukowski

ps—forgive this... these greasy fingerprints but I read this while eating, certainly too weak to retype. ate little can of chicken stew to try to help stomach. drank 2 cans beer, wonderful Wagner on radio. will try to thro in couple of pomes and then go to sleep. I will try to build myself up during week. old girlfriend says I almost reached end this time. sleep. sleep, jesus, wonderful: nobody around but Wagner.

c.b.

here we go again, psss*—
     geeus sheri
          I have started drinking   I am over the edge and so sick butt I got bored typing pomes and had to hav sumthing to keep meee going or ging as I like to sae. look, I will

---

Wm. Morris thing: a reading for a San Franciscan poet named William Morris; see conclusion to CB's letter of 11 August 1960 below.

not dye. Rlax. 4 as frie sad: u vealbastard bukski are too meeen to die, ;;; and so prob will live to be oller than my spirit-buddy Pound hoo has lived so long because big fire hard to put out. u good girl sheri, am mailing this...

I think wot hurt me, I hated most in Miles... wen he intimated I did not care for music. a hoorible untruu blow an made me sick.

music, paint, I need u. Miles Pain, never.

Bukow

Los Angeles
Fri, July 23? 22?

Dear Sheri:

Got yr bread, letter, copy *A & P*, all in good shape—also all your other corro. Have read much steady the earlier corro and am now working on later and bit of good bread. This is simply very short thing to say I will answer all come Sunday when the shade is around and the breathing.

Thanx for bread. Spiritwise I don't think anything better has happened to me for sometime. I am not joking. Very good, fulfills in many ways and angles. This way I get the message good: somebody doesn't want me to die. I have saved the wrapper and will buy more of same when this is gone. Buk bows a reverent bow smiling all the way inside down...

Sherman in town, leaving Sunday, I unnerstand. I spell lousy because I was baptized in icewater. Germany, born in Germany, parents splints of steel. Sherman yes. No tank he. Gazzele. Gazelle. Guzzle. Running all over town, panting, people people people. Robert Young. James Boyer May. Curtis Zahn. This and that. Names. Staying with editor of *Break-thru*:... editor Brkthro homosexual, wot or else. Sherman can't

---

Robert Young ... Curtis Zahn: Young was an actor, best known for his lead in the TV series *Father Knows Best*; May edited the magazine *Trace*; Zahn was an L.A. poet and fiction writer.

Breakthru: magazine edited by Norman Winski (mentioned in CB's next letter as well).

64

see things. Awful this running around: does this make poems, this dog-licking? I tried to tell him. He say: No, these people don't touch me; I remain the same.

Jory only thinks so because he wants to think so. Everything touches one way, hover or elephants. He threw my name to one of the dogs.

Christ, where *is* this guy? somebody said. Nobody's ever seen him.

Ah, gladness!

Now that I have seen Sherman, I will say: essentially nice guy. Talk talk but no can take joke from leftflank; always serious and it is not good to be always serious. When they send me to hell, the first thing I will do is laugh—not with sound but inside like waterfalls and blip blip breaking.

He read latest poem or 2. Sounded quite a bit like me but that's all right, he was a little too much in the violets. And he cut *all* the violets out. He should have left one or two. Desert sand.

Payne and Fry do not bother me. I do not want to write or tell them anything. We will all leave each other splendidly alone and the Gods will push us on... and off and into.

Pushed big fat colored man around around around the blocks this morning. Air all dry. Nothing breathing. Sidewalks like rims of things. His car would not start. We both sweat. Ah hell. death, death, death.

But this is short note, as I said. I will write fully Sunday, if I am alive. Must reread your things again. I have them lined up and in big flipflop box with my scirwritings... Good for all. Hello Po' Li. The bread is breeding violets in the desert of my mind. Sunday then. I should be in yr mailbox Tuesday, rattling Bukow.

sweet sounds sweet visions, Princess...

Charles

all right, los angeles
sunday
I want what I want what I wanted
July toofour, onenine 6ho...

Yes, She Ri, Princess:
yeah, hella lotta cosmic pressure. yur dear sweet jory hoo is gong ta cross the Yordan just lef town, fonin frum depot... what're you doing? he asked. What a peccadillo. I was taking a crap.

Jordan Jory all over town, miscegenation and moil, seeing this person, that person, this person, that person, phoning, drinking, talking, praising phrasing parsley psing aleuta and wow. If he's gonna cross the Jordan I hope I am not in the same boat.

He finally dragged me over to Pillin's wm the. It turned out all right. There was soul there, pottery ceram, piano with very good son like stalk making the keys etna etude and song running up my elbows. very good sun, needs woman, he will die otherwise, they will kill him.

oh Princess, I have eaten the last slice of your brown bread; it will not be the same when I buy it.

No, I'm not dr bro smoke, I'm dear brother ashes, please remember.

Miles? again? why mention? except hilarity and carp.

Jordanjor also dragged in homo over to my place hoo spoke of his beautiful writhing flicking tongue and etc., sum god damn editor *Breakthru*, and we went over to his place, he spouted poetry all the way down steps of my apartment hourse horse and wen we got over to his place palace, he changed thro wifefocus, an induveate wife, and she complained later about the drinking. oh, we know all the artists and actors, fine peeple, and Norm, you said you wouldn't drink anymore... etc. and on, standing there by the table blathering, all nerves, children running about shooting thru doorways like rockets, Norm and Jory sitting there reading their poetry to each other and Buk sitting there sweating and dying, and when she gave the message I got it and grabbed all the beer, threw it into big bag and blew in my

---

Pillin's wm: William Pillin, a fellow L.A. poet.

handsomehorsecar that can so flight me frum pain. oh, I had paid for all th beer an I damn well drank all that was left because I got the MESSAGE and helped SAVE them all. After they got rid of me they went out to see the actor Robert Young. oh boy.

before whathell message she had pulled all the beer outa the refrig. and lined it up along the sink. I went into kitchen and said, what the hell, hoo tooka the beer outa icebox and threw it into sink? I shoulda got the message early but instead I stuffed it all back inside.

how in the hell can you cross the Jordan when you worry about beer and Robert Young?

Ginsburg has a bad wire somewhere in the set that lights him up.

Nobody invented E.Pound. I was going to say he invented us, but that's too easy, and besides he would have done a better job.

I was over at girlfriends other nite, and I tol' her, Jesus, this Sherman is driving me nuts, I don't know what to do with him.

Well, she said, maybe he can't help it, maybe you're his idol. Everybody has an idol, even you. Ezra Pound is your idol.

Yes, I said, but look, if Ezra Pound were sitting in the bar right downstairs I would not go into that bar, he would never know.

Don't worry about Sherman, she said. If you've got it you won't change. And I think you got it. And I wouldn't go into that bar downstairs if Jesus Christ were sitting there. Pass the wine...

The last line is not true about Christ. She would go.

If I had been a party member in 1940, I would be a party member now. I know that the basics are still there. I am not a political man but I believe all this changing over is weak-souled.

The Keblah never changes.

To hell with the West Coast of Africa. I have my own w coast of Africa.

Ezra can murder; I cannot, or else I would kill sherman.

Keblah: the Kaaba (or Kiblah), the shrine to which Muslims turn in prayer.

West Coast of Africa: CB uses Pound's phrase in his poem "Horse on Fire" (*RM* 70); see Appendix 1.

don't worry about poor negro boys with their eyes full of pain. give them a little vanilla icecream, they are playing a game.

Yesterday I bought 2 86cent shirts made in HONG KONG and I am very proud. Sheri some day u and I and Po' Li must go to China and we will bring me back a woman who cannot speak english and we will marry and everyday we will simply look at each other in silence and there will be nothing to spoil it, only silence and music. Forgive me, I am mad.

Yes, I guess Ez needs his oyster stew, raw eggs, celery greens... It is nice to know that he is human.

Cannot read Canto 90 right now, do not have book, must downtown and I fear downtown but will finally. I understand I should have the book. Do not chide me Princess of the Bread.

Ez remained young because the fire is still burning, it's quite simple, you i know that. I don't know about the innocent part.

I don't *want* Fry back, please. I am so glad it happened. She murdered me every time she spread the sheets. I don't want to hurt her; I do not want to hurt anything, even a bug—see *Death of a Roach, Epos* Winter 1959. By the way, this issue contains Jory Sherman's 3 best poems, they are better than mine but something has happened since then. Jory wants too badly to be famous. All this politic, seeing people, editors, reading before the masses. It is not true. Jory's guiding god is pulling the wrong strings and the oscillation and gabble and grab dankens the mind... oh, on Wang, I gather from Sherman that he is... shall we say... heterocephalous.

don't make enemies, simply reajust your sights, means: take it easy, if you bark at dogs they still will not hear you.

I did not imply John too low down, I say a man should not READ A TRIBUTE TO HIS OWN GOD DAMN SELF, or what or what or what. This is basic sense to me and I cannot see you so much missing the point.

Wang is average poet. Stock has read too much.

A real poet has one fist of steel and one fist of love.

Death of a Roach, Epos Winter 1959: rpt. in CB's *Betting on the Muse* (1996).

A real poet ... one fist of love: a line used in CB's "A Disorganized Poem on a Disorganized Day" (*A&P* #5); see Appendix 2.

You are a good person, Sheri, but you have taken in too many stray dogs.

Sherman sits there and tells me, don't laugh, don't.

I've got to laugh. He tells me he gave a poetry reading at Unicorn and they passed the plate and all he got was a quarter.

Jesus, I was laughing *for* him. I suppose if he had collected 65 dollars he would have assumed he was a good poet, a good reader, et al. Why do people always get everything backwards?

Sherman can lance but can't take the lance. Fry used to say, Why do you always *laugh* at yourself? Why do you always *mock* yourself?

And I say, why not? Who are we trying to sell? I see nothing but grave stones and hundred dollar whores everywhere. Or ten dollar whores who call themselves housewives.

I don't know what color my eyes are. They have told me that they are green. But I have looked into the mirror and I have never seen this color god damn before in art class or sunsets or what, although it does look a bit like the pan you clean your brushes out in. So Ez is prob still only GREEN EYED poet and he can relax...

Clarence Major is just another ass to fuddle up the stream.

gv Jricharson a brk, means: give him a break with a vbrick. Now u can ast me wot this means.

On the morning of August 16th: I will light 40 candles and die with a can of Schlitz in each hand.

Yes, yes, is like taking a rolled-up piece of paper and swatting a fly from the curtain. Writing is so easy it makes me laugh to know the secret of it. One must simply not be greedy, that is all. DO NOT SWAT THE SHIT CURTAIN WHEN THERE ARE NOT ANY FLIES ON IT.

"Wings down like broken love" has to be in spite of West Coast of wot because I saw that bird and my hands were on the steering wheel and I saw the wings and they were down like broken love, the wings said that, and the cat moved away from the wheels of my car that way a cat moves and I'm sick as I

Clarence Major: African-American poet (1936–) and, later, author of experimental novels; a frequent contributor to *A&P*.

"Wings down like broken love": from CB's poem "conversation on a telephone" (*DRA* 43).

write this, and all the broken love of the world and all the broken love birds, and the sky said this covered with smog and cheap clouds and miscreant gods. I was not on the West Coast of Africa. I was driving North on Normandy Blvd, half drunk after dropping a hundred on the ponies and I realized soon... that the hundred was nothing... a quarter on a tray for a poet who could not laff.

oh Sheri, I cannot forget Wm Pillin's 20 yr old son playing the piano. He is all artist, there is no flesh on his body, his eyes twitch little narrow things, but he knows, he feels his power and I see the lips grrinn inward, inward, and he is marvelous boy, you would have loved him, Sheri, I am so sure. There wasn't any *woman* in him; I do so like to see the delicate man without that homo homohomebitch bitch running up and down inside. And Jory irritated me awfully—this boy sat down to the piano his hands really making song without falseness and affectation and Jory said out loud, STOP BITING YOUR LOWER LIP! and the boy stopped playing and faced Jory and said, what? And Jro. said, never mind, I was talking to Felicia. And the boy started again and then Jory reached forward and touched the old man on the chest, meaning lean backward so I can watch HIS HANDS. Awful, Sheri, I was awfully embarrassed. I am not a stiff-neck although I am a little nervous and tense, but there are so many natural things one knows that just aren't done. And the boy was so realized and released at the piano and I was so happy for him and the great music he was bringing us and himself. You should have seen him Sheri, he was a god at the piano, he was made for it, it was made for him. And Jory with his city witticisms.

On "wings down like broken love", I take it you do not like metaphors mixed or otherwise. It is usually an easy way out, of course. And you may be correct. Perhaps the poem should have been held within the cat-bird context. I don't know. But it's all over now. And I don't flare up under criticism. You have me mixed up with somebody else.

A statue of love. I wish they could do it.

There is a poor dear dying in Denver who writes me letters.

Felicia: Jory Sherman's wife.

poor dear dying in Denver: see CB's poem "a literary romance" (*BW* 21–22).

70

I wish I could touch her. But now she is nothing but paper. She read me her poems on the sand. A life work in a red notebook. 12 pages. All about her hot panting sex. I found out later she was a 32 year old virgin. But now she is nothing but paper, and dying, dying, writing me letters full of unoriginal thoughts, transferences of other people, trying to impress me. Poor dear. damn it. I'd like to take her on the springs now and bring her back to life. Doctors don't understand women. I know why she is dying. They have fancy words for it, something to do with the lungs. Yeah. From 55 to 80, women can live without men; anything earlier they will either turn to another woman or embrace some disease like a lover and die. Life is so beautifully tragic, metempirical... I cannot even hate Sherman.

I am heaving over this typewriter now. So awfully sick, I must soon die. Sherman and Winski admired my muscles, but inside, it's all rot.

I went to work in a slaughterhouse because I had to eat the fresh dead animals that I carried upon my right shoulder. I was also so hungry once that I went to work in a dogbiscuit factory (Kendall Foods, 62nd. and Western, L.A.) and ate a couple of dog bis. when nobody was looking. Flames 60 feet high, and men sweating burning their hands, the machines pumping off the dough, no guards, you had to grab the trays, your hands wrapped in gunnysacks to keep off the burning, but there were holes and you had blisters full of fists like holding marbles in your hands and each paycheck went drunk to forget, and the bastards wonder why you're so tough and love the piano sounds, love Beethoven and Chopin and the god that laughs and spits.

I admire Graves, I wish the hole earth were Robt Graves but really fur me, he is too learned and dull. Learning is good until it begins to pull you into the hole.

Then it becomes like stupidity.

Now G. Stien took it the other way around and took all the heart out of it and Hem. added a little sex and a right cross and became immortal. But after S. died he forgot some lessons and his later novels all shit, big Holly productions. Well, ok, he re prob needed green. So does whore.

G. Stien ... Hem.: Gertrude Stein mentored Ernest Hemingway in Paris in the 1920s.

What I'm trying to say, we have Graves on one end and Stein (Stien?) on the other and a big fat god nobody can pinpoint laffing at alla us. We are all good, we are all fighters, even Hem. who has rep. for one but really isn't because mama gave him alla lessons.

The biggest fake in amer. lit. is Wm. Faulkner but it is going to take them some time to find out. Kerourac or howerr you spell who is under influ. is already showing fake hand. Awful stuff.

Ker. has set back letters and intelligence 30 years and that's all he'll be famous for.

To hell with the Roman army. They ended up shitting in their skivies like the rest a them.

"Will you explain to me why you must be hanging 'to a fat wrinkled woman for love... that is old enough to be maw..."

Sheri: can you explain to me who would apprieciate (misspless, I know) love MORE? Can you expoalain (misspell, I know) to me hoo would tk more a my drunken ravings, mora my braggin up my god Pound—the only man I feel inferior to on this earth? An can you explain to me the way her hole ugly face lights up when I come through the door with a bottle of wine and say, OH SHUT UP YOU LOUSY BITCH, DON DON G ME ANY TROUBLE. One minute she's a dead lumpa clay and the next minute she's crawling on me like a roach and she listens to all my wild talk and she don't care what I say, she LAUGHS, and she cusses me, and anything I hate: a god damned admirable audience. It keeps you from growing. I've got to keep growing. God damn it all, don u understan, all a young bitch wants is marriage and admiration... I can't live with anybody anymore so I settled for the wrinkled dead I can bring back to live. Lazarus, ye.

Sherman does not have it. His soul only reaches to the top of his skin. I hope I will never meet you personally, Sheri, I will probably hate you within ten minutes. I am sorry. Fry told me this thing wrong with me, and she is correct. I do not know what it is. I only know I am in my own way and nobody can

---

woman ... old enough to be maw: Jane Cooney Baker (1910?–1962), whom CB lived with before and after his marriage to Barbara Frye. In later letters she is variously referred to as "the old girl" or "the old woman."

follow. If I am incorrect, it does not matter, the way must be followed, polotic or withering soul.

I am trying to follow yr letters thro hear, they are quite. Why do u have spiders reading poetry. Think of what the fly could tell?... Yes, Fry is mean, especially to ordinary people; but I understand wot she is going thro and I wish her best along she leaves me alone.

Well we will all be good and dead and welldone verysoon-soon so wy all the screaming, and those hoo come behind us, more Shermans n Buks... wait will there be any Buks?

I donno I'm trying to be fair.

There certainly will not be any more Sheri M's. You have completely astounded me and reasounted me, and you are the only person in the last 20, oh hell I should say 40 because the books are nothing, I have learned anything from.

Isn't it odd, so very odd, that one of the loves of my idol should be writing me now? Perhaps life so works in stronger currents than we think.

Sure I spell lousy. I rite rite off t pyerwirter, do u think I can go back and douch it off?

Don't gi me any more Garth Allen and his "Astrological stud of Alco."

I am surprised at you, Sheri. Let me die among my leaves and horses and 20 year old boy stalks playing immortal music that makes my elbows itch.

You know what gets me, Sheri, love, when I find someone else in the world as alive as I am.

Defend Wang if you must, just don't thrust him upon me. I like a woman to be a woman and a man to be a man. Hell, I do understand the theories, we are all betwixt and tweeen, I am supposed to be part homo but don't know it. Then don't remind me of it.

No, Jesus, Fry not amongst immortals, so far as I know.

Wang is a catcher of the coattails of the living immortals, as is Sherman, they both realize their shortcomings...

Pound, I sometimes don't know about and almost grow angry about because he's had a lot of luck and I haven't. But it really doesn't matter, because where he is now he must realize that fame is no saving and shaving down into a grapefruit and

---

Garth Allen ... Alco": unidentified.

walking around the corner and handing a dime to a newsboy and the way the dime goes across to his palm is god or devil or the running of the machine. Ez has been lucky, an best of all, he's got guts, and he so deserves it, but I do wish he would disintegrate a few Sherman tanks for me.

Now. where were we?

I'm glad Po'Li could laugh at Payne inferences in letters and I have always loved the Chinese privateness of self, and I usually eat dinner at a Chinese cafe where they run out all unchinese clientele but me. The Negroes they simply cannot stand because the Negroes have given up what could have been an original and beautiful mask for the dream of ugly white skin, and I do not blame the proprieter but the whites too, they have run out, and I take it as a simple or sort of salaam that they understand me and that I understand them without showmanship or any word of recognition. It is quiet and they serve me quietly and I enjoy eating. And my face is very ugly, scarred from disease and fighting 4 rounders (opening bouts) across the river from Philly. And winning them all in the last round. And finally quitting because my heart would take no more.

J., if i ever make fame, I will make Villon look pale.

Let's keep Villon the way he is.

Ezra is the greatest liv. o pisser and greater than Shakey and Donne an wot although and the same, he realized that langbitch was a coot secret QUIVERING with lighting and mush, and sleap slap and turn, something became... not because they were god or good but because there was nothing else but the gd damn fly upon the curtain. n they waited and watted when they were full of, ov, stove, beer, guh, piss, wonder, gu gu, n out it came ESAR PUND my idol, but not so much so any more.

Do u know how it feels to be insane and not locked up? that is, Sheri, how I feel.

but your gd r dam stray dogs are sickening. Give rich the brick. BUT DO NOT HURT HIM!!!!! Give him food and kindness, but do not gut be taken (I am german the gut goot pharaphrase sub.)

I am told over the radio that musierior Cariterier is worried about what goes into my guts. Very enlighting. Cafe Parie, 7038 Sunset Blvd. Shit, I didn't know he knew me. List. to metz. soprano now...

Don like human voice. Hum instr. compo ok. Jory has so

74

long way to go. Do u think he will really get there??? What will he use for godface? is all blank...

do u know anybody, Sheri? Or are u just prenting, trying o bring back Pound era?

One thing, u never write pound and tell him i care or u and I thru. I like my hero worship at a distance. I might even find out he shits or pisses. Gods cannot be allowed to comb their hair. Do you know that Sherman will die in his cradle. He will be published quite a bit in the future, but for all the editorlove he is going to die because he wants so badly.

(let's try an. page.)

I can hear Po' Li saying now, "He sure loves to type."

Jesus Po' Li, go over and purrr yourself a beer; I admire the Chinese as a race, the Germans as a gut, and myself as an insanity that makes a minor self.

In fact, u want to nooo something shitty Po'Li, I consider myself in a league wit dr. Pound. [*Handwritten in margin:*] Forget this, Po' Li, it is only the running of typewriter and happened to fall in this place. I am reading this later and realize how awful.

I have seen too many people to know otherwise.

?"Ez did forget quotes   did not show us all in the contemp poet in nature of poetry.

Ez only showed guts which so comes very easy with a person with guts. his batting down of nations like flies iz only ibsen of gut power losing its head in words and attempting to overtake stupidity. Ez is a god that shits and fucks and loves like the rest of us. let us not forget it.

No, Fry does not pester me. But Sherman visit May says fry going to tear me limb from libido in next *Trace*. Well, that is ok. She needs some caatles. Cattle. Castles.

"What is a cordilier" Christ, I don't know! Wuzzit in ur letter or mine?

I am still bastard very much afraid u underfcscote me, Italian foot-tapping mot... I did not try to bring him down under... I only looked at him, subconsciously, he was there, n I could not help my eyes... I don't know, Sheri, I am quite mad, I don't damn it get along wit anybody. I just looked or' my shoulder and there he waz.

Fry ... in next Trace: see note to CB's letter of 5 October 1960 below.

Sherman very fast, glib with words. Wonder. Wat he try prove?

Christ, u know wot sherman likes? DeBussy. Evening of a shit, etc.

Has anyone heard of Koldiay? Prob miss.

I, and I asked about Romonyrock at meeting other night and they said, oh hell well he ended up in Insande SillumL.

And do you want to know something? I, the cold clod, informed them that it was only between 2 concertos that he so-called went insane? They didn't know. Ho ho. So nice as long as one is accepted.

I was in the bum in frisco at the time of his final appearance and I went and I didn't have money rent, but I went, and they had a sub. for the sick, Alex Brailowsksky, who could prob. play piano as good or not better than the sick and dying Rocy, u know i tol u i was sick.

Frisco has twelve heart beats for one pulse beat of la.

ok, wot?

DO not giggle, angel, any woman hoo goes to concert with me must entangle proper proquietes, only if also alone, to keep creeping crowd creeping.

I feel how you rather underread me, that is fortunate.

I am list. to awful beaut. music on radio now and I fuckcannot believe I am quite alive.

Your soul-starved jew and sincere negro chap... which one scored?

Y are an idiot Martin, stick to ur China chap... on my advice... gd dam it u are lookin for somethin that does not exist

A POUND IS ONLY BORN EV 3 thousand yrs.

You ok mar, b you have a lot to learn.

I would certainly like to meet u personally in order to de-ater-kuju juzeu U...

DeBussy ... Evening of a shit: a play on Debussy's famous *Prelude to the Afternoon of a Faun*.

Koldiay: Zoltán Kodály (1882–1967), Hungarian composer.

Romonyrock ...his final appearance: Rachmaninov fell ill during his final tour of the U.S. and died in Beverly Hills in March 1943.

Alex Brailowsksky: Alexander Brailowsky (1896–1976), Russian concert pianist.

Jam goin to close... Cant carry.
Im awfully sick an must goodnite.

                              go by. CheriSheri wot,
                              zerol   , xi; , ¢

        Charles Bukoowski   ,
                              Charles

---

los angels
fri nite aug 6

dear Sheri:
    wher'in hell are my cookies?
        el furioso
        Charles

L.A.
Thurs nite, Aug. 11?

Dear Sheri:
    wuz only kiddin' about cookies... course if your woman's
heart is set on making them... I bragged about your sending me
brown bread when Jory dragged me to Wm. Pillin's, hope u
don' mind...
    I guess you would say my stars are out of kilt. last 3 or 4, 5
days, sag strummed on bad guitar... stretched on bed sweating
like slave nigger, trying to figger out ceiling, so low. luckily I
caught a little Rochmoninoff on radio, twice... he very close to
me in spirit and I heard him cursing the gods, the dogs, the
cats... fustian gloaming... and I laughed inside because I knew
what he meant.
    don' take me too hard on anything. I roll with the words
like a horse in the field and I pick up a lot of burrs. daddy

Pound my boy too: courage ratio, style; famous enough but alone for it all.

wrote you a couple of letters, 6,7,8 pages, read them, tore them up.

Guess I was a little hard on Jory, but all that front-running stones me. But you are right: we can't all be bitch hermits. an I see from his letters he is still going strong. well.

old girl and I broke up: JEZUS, she screamed, I wish just once, JUST ONCE, you would show up here WITHOUT BEING DRUNK!

an' I said, swayin' in the middle of floor, oh, aw right, I'm leavin'.

And I walked out and went downstairs and had a beer with a roomfulla people arguin' about nothin'. Then I went back upstairs and said, see, I'm back, be happy, and I laughed.

but she didn't even hear me. she was standin' in middle of room, shuddering big tears the size of her silver rosary, and then she looked up at me, hating like hell, and began cussing and screaming and I left that time for sure.

she put me thro plenty of hell years ago and I think what puzzles her now is that she can't put me in hell anymore...

Guess you are right: Jory is all for me, thinks I am somebody. letter from him today giving me addresses of some new mags. As front-runner he gets a lot of this stuff.

According to Griff of *Hearse* I have a chapbook coming out in less than month: *Flower, Fist and Bestial Wail.* Will get a copy to you. More or less earlier pomes, he left out some of what I think are best. Not apologizing, only saying not my selection.

Jory said Morris reading was a mess, everybody walking out, Wang, etc and only wuz a coupla snot-nosed poets reading vury thin poesy... frum wha' I unerstan' Morris waited for the boys to come to *him*, and they did not. But hermit does not unnerstan all this doubletalk, and so forget.

Stars still feel all outa kilt so I am quitting now. All right, Sheri, baby, I am thinkin' of u, oney don' tell Po' Li.

      L.,
        Charles (Buk)

Lost Angels
Monday [15 August 1960]

Dear Sheri:

rec. your wand-waving exhort and expl. of canto 90, and Pound knew good gal when he saw one... read several times, caught no mostly light and let rough edges go, if I may say rough edges: the rough edges are me, no Pound nor Sheri... thank you.

oh only to say awfully sick this morning... somebody's symphony in C. Minor on. would prefer D. minor key this morn. celebrated birthday last night. awful thing, staring down thru orange juice this morn, still alive...

ended up in vile dive on Hollyw'd blvd, strippers on v. bias shaking breasts and box in my face... one all inlum. in neon... wang wang wang, blap alp blap, right in face and I laughed, I laughed when all others including women serious... all this illuminated fuck... and I laughed and everybody got angry, so I walked out to make them feel better and went across street to brightlight cheap palace fulla bums and I felt better.

thanx again for *Rockdrill*, my west coast a Africa cleared up.

but now awfully sick, will sleep and try to put this body together.

> lobelight and love,
> *Charles*
> Bukowski

Los Angeles
August 16th. 1960

Dear Sheri:

well, I am sitting around waiting for a singing telegram which will arrive about 9 am and embarrass me, but the gal means well: I will pretend, if possible, to enjoy it. But she should know, after these years, that this type of thing simply dissolves me into a liquid pain that lasts for days. well, hell,

79

there's nothing to do but wait. it's 8:30 am now and I am halfdead with agony... Christ, maybe she'll only send a flower. but no, she's too raw, she's been drinking and somewhere out of her past life she thinks this is the gay, all-gallant thing to do. Happy birthday. Jesus Christ. oh.

well, maybe it will be nothin. maybe it is all a dream. but she tipped her hand phoning last night and I read right thru her mind. You would never do a thing like this to me Sheri. would you? I don't think you would crash my insides with some shrimp bastard wailing in my ears. I know you wouldn't, Sheri.

I know she means well. In her mind it is a great thing and I should be happy that someone remembered my birthday. This type of thing is done in movies: a singing telegram.

OH GREAT GOD JESUS I AM DYING. LET ME FACE THE SIMPLE TIGER.

It's 8:40.

Sheri, I read your explan. of Canto 90 again; I was awful sick yesterday and it came thru clearer now. You have the pure classical style, in feeling and in love. You are the one woman I know that Pound deserved, and you deserved him. You could never make ignoble love. The only thing ignoble about a love between you and any man is that perhaps the man could not stand up to you, he would not deserve you. I am not sure I would deserve you, ever. I have much growing up to do. I have always moved slowly, developed slowly. The poems I wrote, the poems that are to be collected in this chapbook I will send you—they are not poems, but beginnings, small rantings. But the trash must be burned first. I feel inside... some growing, but whether it is life or death, we will have to wait and see. You have helped me grow by putting me in touch with the larger equation, and yet there is a part of me that does not want to lose sight of the small. The small holds its secrets too. I think it is human to notice the small and to speak about it, but to remain ever small is error. I will have both: the large and the small. I think this is both: humanity and immortality, today and tomorrow, you... and I. Sheri. invisible love.

8:55. Perhaps it won't happen.

It is odd... that Pound who was my personal god... has come upon me through you. How they used to rave, my women, EZRA POUND, EZRA POUND, oh god damn it, I'M SICK OF THE NAME! But I loved them all with my scarred face and body, my scarred soul... until they turned against my spirit... as Fry did... calling Franck's Symphony in D ugly... *ugly.* I have never heard any music that is ugly. i have heard inane music, I have heard silly music, I have heard discordant music... but music in itself, even the simplest modern tune carries in it part of the human crying, and to call it ugly... esp. the Symphony in D.... and she was tone-deaf and I told her so, and how her little face twisted up in hatred, in defense... and I said, tell me one piece you *like,* classical, modern, anything, and she could not answer, and I was sorry for her.

Sheri, I am no angel. women cannot stand me for long. perhaps it is that I am selfish, I will not submit my soul wholly, I save a secret piece for myself... and woman wants to control her man to feel secure. I can understand this. But I do not ask a woman for her complete soul either. I feel that when all secrets are gone, love ends, love becomes unbearable. And how many couples have unveiled the last shreds? millions upon millions and they turn outward instead of inward and die before a television set or clipping a hedge or boiling a can of soup... tenuous, tenuous... beware showing all, the dirty underwear of the mind, the tired cravings, the cowardice, and worst of all... the strengths. a tenuous, subtle tuning... an almost perfect love must have two almost perfect people... all this, Sheri, on reading yr Canto 90, Pound's canto 90...

I would liked to have seen the Jays and Squirells fighting over the nuts in the shell. Too bad the jays won. One time I was driving toward Caliente, a race track, Mexico. But something was wrong with me. I didn't want to go. I didn't want to see horses, to bet. Something inside of me was twisting. I said, turn back, turn back. But I kept driving. But I didn't want to see a horse, make a bet, buy a drink, push and fight the mob. All of a sudden, I could drive no longer. Just outside San Diego I pulled over to the side of the road and sat in my car and I looked at the water. The waves came in and rolled around inside of my chest. It was hot in there, a sewer of flame, and I let the blue rool there, the foam sizzling in the fire. What I'm trying to say is, finally got out of the car and stood over edge of cliff hanging over sea... and out they came... two squirells (spell?) or squirrels? think latter... and they stood and simply looked at me... these 2 sea sqs. and they looked for minutes on end, for centuries, and they sensed in their animal way that there was no danger within me... I was no enemy, and this puzzled them and they had the long look, awfully long look, squirrel eye whirling with each sea and each sun and with me and we fell across the gulf that held us separate and we each were one within the other... until at last some shifting in space... sent us apart, 2 small squirells and I, like lost lovers ended, and they ran down their rocks, all tail and fur, and my heart pounded in pain of severence. Well, hell, I drove on to the track and dropped 50 or 60, and no wonder, my mind was not on the horse and I did not care...

Well, 10 am and no telegram. the gods must have answered my call. I am glad. I am going to sleep.

Down in mailbox... letter from Jory, business-like, names, addresses, remarks on literary world. Jory still front-running. Tells me he got long Auntly letter from Thorne. How these gals love a Jorum. Also acceptance from mag in Texas *Quagga*, for this Summer's issue. My poem *Riot*, memo of jail life when celled with public enemy #1, Courtney Taylor. Bit about riot took place one day in dining hall...

10:15... well, it came... no singing telegram... but flowers, flowers, flowers, FLOWERS... gladiolous, roses, carnations, daiseys, nastrusums, and some I don't know, some I don't know... a bundle of color and smell and leaves, and no silly singing messenger boy... this is bread for the soul, brown bread and singing and the sea and the squirrels... I have wronged a lady again... she knows me... she KNOWS ME... and I will sleep... and I will sleep... in peace...

love,

Charles

Buk

Thorne: Evelyn Thorne, co-editor (with Will Tullos) of *Epos*.
Quagga ...Riot: appeared in its May 1960 issue; rpt. in *DRA* 51–52.
Courtney Taylor: a con man; see Sounes 24–25.

L.A.
Too late for thunder [6 September 1960]

Dear Sheri:
    slept in the ossuary 24 hours, no o weary slip, 5 day drunk, lost wallet, robbed, raped, tangled in vines covered with strange grey bugs... armies by, out of side of head, shadows, palms, nuns stripping before the pale red seas of god... ouch, water running out of pipes, water better than music... can wash half-soul in water like dirty underwear... go go numbers and sound... blast of shotgun that broke the veins of Van Gogh's brushes, stroking sunlight into corn and feet and malaria and flies and the thin wafting of useless air. well, it's all right. I don't need much more than this. I can hear the water running and I will drown my burning feet. where are the cloves? where is the minister spitting in a jar? water, rain, wine, time running away with our lives like a dog with an old bone to bury.
                                    so well, no more than this
                                            Charles
                                            Buk

L.A.
Thursday, maybe Sept. 9, '60

Dear Sheri:
    got your cookies today. o good good and in radius of calm light when all is lutarious.
    heavy wagons of unknow now run over all fingers of feeling, combs a thousand harpoons, grass only covers dead, catfeet running with mice under obnoxious moon.
    polination of giggling backless mass continues: fruit, rock and boar. etlolate yearheart.
    sick, sick, sick, can write no more.
                                            Charles
                                            Buk

---

lutarious: muddy.

L.A.., Oct. 5 or 6, '60

Dear Sheri:

Poetry, at times, must be allowed the emotion that the pretext of philosophy is denied under the chains of knowledge.

Ez said many good things—good things for him—rules, lights, which made the mostly good Ez, but forms change: I am no Ez, don't want to be, but must follow more a sense that screams when I bang my toe.

There is no one more disgusted with the similarity and posing of the poets than I. I have for a while been mulling on an Essay: *The Fallacy of Poetry, Modern or Otherwise*. However, I felt, finally, that the energy had rather be put to the poem than to qualing over inadequacies.

Good to hear from you, Sheri; I need a new ribbon and hope you can read this. Feel rather dull today, not a good time to write. All poems out, nothing on hand, nothing boiling. Am in Autumn *Epos*, will be in Winter also present *Quagga*. *Targets* have given me 8 pages in Winter issue and I have sent him bucket of poems to narrow down on. Webb of *Outsider* taking some. On the other hand, there are those who sit and sit... and sit, and neither accept or reject, and don't even answer inquiries and I don't know who has what or why. I don't have any carbons, just a lot of empty beer cans. Between the 15th. and 29th. of last month wrote 20 or 30 new poems, sent to *San Francisco Review*, and now if they don't take, for a while will leave alone, giving them full shot and the hell with it. What I am trying to say, Sheri, is—there simply aren't any poems around, but if I write some new ones, or if something comes back that does not dismal me too much I will send it up to you for a look. Would rather have you look at a few than simply send you something that *I* want... The classics dull me, Sheri, please stop putting

---

Epos: "Down thru the Marching" appeared in the Fall 1960 issue, "The Sun Wields Mercy" in Winter 1960.

Targets: a New Mexico quarterly.

Webb of Outsider: Jon Webb, who published (with his wife "Gypsy Lou") both the magazine *The Outsider* and Loujon Press, which issued CB's first book-length work.

San Francisco Review: three of CB's poems would appear in its March 1961 issue.

me on the classics, I have read most of them, or tried. I understand the falsity of most poetry and the poetic world by reading any little mag of poetry.

I have my back against the wall on another issue, but mention of it here would seem—integral with the locale of petty grief, so to hell.

Yes, got birthday cookies, best god damn, I can say with clarity, I ever ate. To say thanks would not be good message, don't know message to say, simply I ate GOOD.

Maybe I ate God, I dunno, but guess he would taste kind of bitter.

Jory Sherman? How do you SPELL that?

X-wife B. Fry regales me, bringing in aid of "The Republic" in *Trace* 39. I proud for her, and do not mind whipping. She looks good and needs victory; I give her victory. Not saying, turn other cheek, only Texas far away—I remember Wheeler only as a dog, some boards, old leaves, and sitting on picnic tables waiting for snow. The rest is senseless.

I hope to get some poems to you. Everything now, rather odd. oh, vacation all gone, used up. More on card in Feb., if I am still there. May run up for a week or so. Right now: all dull.

> L.,
> *Charles*

10/octobre/60 s.m. 15 lynch

darling buk/

'z all right—take yr time/ you KNO I will/ zo damm'd much to do... and still in fk up dept due to it being the Tai Yin or Grit Dark... acc'd to Slant philo.

the A & P Rev will take some few months yet—so whenever

"The Republic" in Trace 39: in the Sept.–Oct. 1960 issue of *Trace* (pp. 19–20) Frye quotes Plato's *Republic* in a letter to the editor responding to a remark Felix Anselm had made on the effect Frye and CB's marital troubles were having on *Harlequin*.

Texas ... Wheeler: Frye's hometown; see Cherkovski 96–98.

Tai Yin or Grit Dark: unidentified.

you have anything for us... mail over/ am boiling sea water—dr.
lovell sez it is GOOT for yew/ go get some and boil it 'bout 10
min. to moidre the unsusp. germs within or still lifes & take 10
tbsp. daily or place it within yr beer & lo an' beholt but from the
old self emerges a watersnake/ Po Li reading yr poem in the
expensive paper maz "man this guy sure knows a LOT... 'carbon
on filiments of brain'... do YEW know wot that means Butterfly-
Brains?"... she said: "go fk yrself darling... no I DON'T... but IF
Bukowski said that I YAM sure that Bukowski MEANT that..."
said MezzoSlant "it means... wot it means to an electric light
bulb... when carbon appears on its filiments... it is a burn't out
bulb... man, this guy sure knows a hellivaLOT..." yew haz a
hadmirerer... in Po' Li... Buk/

from New O/ comes a Sr. Webb who says you are a rec. &
asks if I'll contrib. something on Hezra... I will submit something controversial—WHY ought'n I treat Ezra like a m a l e in
MOI life/ 'stead me bein' in Hiz'n?/ aaaaaah? zo I vill keez &
squeel... or sqweel or howhellspell'd... just to "pull Bun's leg"...
Ezra's name is 'Bun' or 'Br'r Rabbit' as Mr. E. is 'Possum'... or
I'll see... maybe one ought to present Gramps to her contemporaries... as a Boet? a Heconomist? a Hanti-sezmide? a cat'lik? a
prot?... ah preferz him az a m a l e   that's moi dish/ sorry
Buk now don't get sniffy... as the weekend fresh air went to
one's brain-combs...

very glad to see yr face/ one said: "is he German?" since Po
Li spent some time in Germany & knows the races within 'em/
he said: "oh boy—IS he German!" It seems yr brooding...
moody... deep... deep... face cometh from the ancient race... I
see wot 'how yew spell dot' Jory meant when he said: "he's
beautiful!"

now Lamb one must distill one's swamp wat'r... and love,
love, love... to buk/ from us all... will send pix shortly yaz... but
ah wanz a flatter'n one & Po Li is fkn me op...

Sheri

yr letter of "oct. 5 or 6 '60": all right Buk/ scream when yew
bang yr toe—or follow the sense which does... I comprehend/

'*carbon on filiments of brain*': from an untraced CB poem.

isn't that wot Ezra is doing: "oh, let an old man rest"
& Canto 92

> "Le Paradis n'est pas artificiel
> > but is jagged,
> For a flash,
> > for an hour.
> Then agony,
> > then an hour,
> > > then agony..."

that was when the cruel Miz Martinelli was his beloved & she was out... down in Spade-town... turning on... and sweet gramps was locked up inside St. Liz... longing to protect his fragile Butterfly... so intent upon self-moidre... and he came to know the "sense which screams when you bang yr toe..." he banged his entire male nature...

but one don't expect from the Bukowski child... wot EzraInfant cd do... age "110" that is... to keep the head... after banging the toe... & give them a little French because it will exercise their "brains" (?) and grampa is a fkn stzientizst... so he carefully records the precise information on it... as UNemotionally as possible... "only those who make the journey know the way"... only a real man... in love with a wayward infant... who HAD to EXplore her age... entirely... to know where each one had been... 'down with it'... she was... iz... only our real man... chained in his prison cell... longing to protect his love... in legal, moral, ethical, physical, psychical, metaphysical & economic danger... only he wd know how much agony was in ezra's lines—so wrung from emotion... actually... ezra had the whole hospital upset... he was sending telegrams... writing spec. del. letters & phoning with special get-dr-op-middle-night permission... and he was writing... "2. a.m.... the moon... delecta..."

I cannot read those lines without weeping furiously & bitterly—my god... but one pays for what one gets AFTER one has used it all up... Life, you'll be the death ob me...

"*oh, let an old man rest*": the concluding line of Canto 83.
"*Le Paradis ... then agony*": "Paradise is not artificial," as in the drug-induced state described in Baudelaire's *Les Paradis artificiels.*
"*2 a.m. ... delecta*": apparently from one of Pound's letters to SM.

... ezra gazing out of that bar'd & wire'd narrow long gothic window... out on the lawn of St. Liz... on the still enormous pine tree... & watching the moon at 2 a.m.... oh I have endured many torments... but that is more than I can bear... master thyself then others can thee put op wiff.../ no buk 'z no use pleading wit' me—when I make yew those EzraPoundKakes... I'm sticking the classics inside them and you'll NEVER know... darling... NEVER... you'll swallow 'em entire/

yew spell Jory Sherman: I n n o c e n t e Caro/

all right Little Lamb who Laid thee... I'll wait until Buk has something to send and right now I send Love/

Sheri

Monday nite—Oct. 10, 1960—10:00p.m.
[*typed postcard; postscript is handwritten around edges*]

Yes, Shed:
CHAPTER IX of L'AFFAIR BUK*MARTINELLI:
Repeat chapter II: "Where in hell are mah cookies?"... not much else gong: off won, feet running head, blue sea shakes water glass full of tremble and shark... mete more watts of condecension for Buk, he story-naked in Big-pinch world, you too tough with formula standing Buk in giant Pound-shadow... columbine and chasms, you listen, I will send you poems but u gotta be more consistent; love on Thursday, hate on Friday too big a knot to untie, rather eat mugwort... Pro raining in Hamburg now, people black umbrellas, spider hulls sick wet

---

master thyself...: a paraphrase from Canto 81: "'Master thyself, then others shall thee beare'" (541, itself a paraphrase of a line in Chaucer's "Ballade of Good Counsel").

Innocente Caro: Italian: "innocent dear."

Little Lamb who Laid thee: a play on the opening line of Blake's poem "The Lamb": "Little Lamb, who made thee?"

Shed: nickname given to SM by a British journalist visiting St. Elizabeths in 1950s, and which she used thereafter with friends.

closing heads puffed to single tune: almost zero... Looky Sheri, easy on this leveret—your lense will double back and split in your beer.... You right on bad year: this has been a heller; but today I give you sympathy, and what love is left, and a postcard to read.

L.,
Buk

I am asleep on the rocks. Wow. Wow. You tell Pound u know good kid. He smile big, so O.K.—I leave. Stop now. O.K. O.K.—

[postcard dated by SM 11 October 1960; typed around a drawing of CB passed out on bed with bottle of liquor on floor]

Hi ho, Shed:
Gezus, I think I been stung by bee somewhere or mebe bad whiskey... ol' woman over, cooked slab of meat, drank mah wine, robbed Buk a prcous manhood. Dropped earlier coupla hundred on horsething race, ended up playin' poker fa paper clips. Really livin', Shed baby. Wish u was here to wash the dishes, throw out tha trash, sing to me ok ok ok ok, this is a virtual wonder land in the latest trends in dying. Hello to Po Li. Wang. San Francisco in general. list. to Lizst. not impressed. L., Chas the Buk.

Chas B—

[undated postcard]

if yv nvr ridden ina bean u don no wat livin means n to hell with Vivaldi, n if uv never been in a room wit Sheri M while she's tossed her beercans against the walls or talked abt Gramps and Cantos 90 and 92, well, the hell with—Vivaldi, if u've never seen Sheri rip the phone frum the wall or Po Li get the bowl 'n roach ready, y've wasted yr time, friend, listenin' to—Vivaldi,

89

or if u've neva gotten letas frum Shed tellin' y that u build a-
hole palaces and that Sherman's gona cross t Jordan, well ok,
and too bad, n if U've neva eaten tha cakes n cookies that
gassed Pound, ok, man, or formulas for sea-water to make u
stan up after 40, well ok, man; I sent her a photo a me in full
topue, waterin the lawn; she sen bak a dog's leg frozen n orange
gelatine... wal, t nex mov iz up t tha Dutchess... I got 35 colored boys workin for me heah, each ona em carryin a razor
sharperin Krusekev, an me... I'm a listening to Vivaldi.

yes,

BUK

Aiee, Oct 12, won nine 6ho
los the angels sing in dishwater

Lookie hear Sherryone:
beer 'n soda crackers for lunch, I have new ribbon but two
dragrat tired to change, Grit Dark, symphysis of snails and fire.

> ... can't you guess that all this boil,
> the mace and census,
> the crank and suspicious dismemberment
> show disorder of felon gusts?
> we are no part perfect,
> hysteria could be our trained harpy,
> and look... the walls, the guards,
> armour, nothing festival,
> what haze in lieu of this?
> a man is either a genius
> or nothing at all, and I have had
> to accept a nothing
> I break primitively to pieces

---

a-hole palaces: in an earlier (lost) letter, SM accused CB of building "asshole palaces" in his poems. Cf. CB's letter of 17 August 1960 in *SB*
(21).
Krusekev: perhaps Nikita Khrushchev, prime minister of the USSR at
the time.

90

to foreshadow the gutteral,
the halloween mine.
—Buk, portion of poem
Our Bread Is Blessed and Damned,
now out in the hands of the makers.

Yes, Sheri, seawater infected with temperate distillers of decay; I would say, however, that boiling creates a palimpsest and breaks the back of magic. magic being anything larger than us that we do not understand.

Po Li has filament part of broken hand straight, tho this more difficult for woman, although woman has 3 filaments: spiritual, mental and physical—these listed in their proper order. What I mean by spiritual, I can't quite say and that is why numb one.

Webb, at this moment, most rancorous, dedicated, humane, human editor to come along since the bottle took the Whit outa Burnett. Frank Brookhauser once wrote me, "Don't trust Whit Burnett." A course, this only had reverse affect and I sent Whit 36 short stories a month until he finally got tired and took one. Webb a little taken in by NAMES but he will get over this when he realizes that a man can be a poet on Tuesday, and the next day, Wedns., get up and be something else because he did something not wrong but poetry deadening on Tuesday nite or las month or las year and it finally added to a thrown away burnt out light globe, and there is nothing you can do but crash it against a wall, glass and ripped tires in sunlight and somebody talking about nothing

as I may be doing and people being kind and telling me nothing, and having never been a name not helping

as being a name is to an extent the meddling of audience who

almost without fail

over-rate or under-rate their contemporaries.

SIR BOT MAL: baseball games and frogs.

Our Bread Is Blessed and Damned: never published.

Whit ... Burnett: influential editor of *Story* magazine, which published CB's "Aftermath of a Lengthy Rejection Slip" (prompted by Burnett's earlier rejections) in its March–April 1944 issue.

Frank Brookhauser: unidentified.

If you present Pound as male the world has fresh material.

No, my face is scars, I have to get under certain light or no light so things will not show, although what was once shame for this is now nullity. From 14 on face broke out (plus back) in boils large as peaches; charity ward at county hospital decided for worse case in history to simply take electric drill and drill drill drill drill drill, it was no so good although I picked the winner of the Kentucky Derby under the drill in 1934 because the sound of the name (Omaha?) came to me clearly under the rivets, a damn good longshot, and I think the year is right. Somewhere in there, it had to be. I fell in love with a nurse who must have been 45 because she saw that under all the sores and ugliness, the silence, sat a human being. One of the docs said he'd never seen anyone go under the needle like I did, but I think he told that to all the boys to keep the place down to a concocted cotton scream.

I read plntya classics then   while the young boys were
buying corsages and dancing   while the young boys were
kissing and what
Buk met Shelley and threw him out and Keats and threw him
          out
and Shakey out and the Romans and Greeks out
and Brahms out and Bee in, and Chike in and Bach out (except
for organ works), and Li Po in and Villon and Rachmony and
Pound
and early Eliot and early E. E., and Jeffers in
and A. Huxley and D.H.L. and Schopenhauer and Spender
and James Thurber and Van Gogh and John Dillinger and all
the RUSSIANS, all the Russian writers and composers and poets,
and Fred N[ietzsche]. and others who have slipped out of grip
or moment's recall.

This is not a confessional except to xpress that I did my reading when it counted, when the words and sounds stood out between real hell and simple survival. An' if u want to *slip* me some classics in tha insides a cookies to take lak a pill, well, Martinelli, that's ur business. I forgive you.

There is this: there is a time to stop reading, there is a time

---

Omaha: won in 1935, not 1934.

E.E.: E. E. Cummings (1894–1962), American poet.

92

to STOP fk trying to WRITE, there is a time to kick the whole bloated sensation of ART out on its whore-ass. There is too much competition and slickness and formula. There is only one thing to be patriot of and that is the guideless will growing in its own mud, ripping out leaves and sounds, in *spite* of what it has been taught. We are growing more and more toward what is being thought of as formlessness at the moment, that later will only be the measuring rod of fools. And so it will go: the upward spurting of a few things until we end.

What was good for Pound is not good for me. I do not WANT a "map of the world in my head", I do not want any such clutterings; the words I use will be mine because I know they will, and it's as simple as that.

Christ, not a cig in the house, ah, here's a butt unner a bacon rind! Sir Francis Bacon I salute you, ass.... Sheri, I enjoy ur stuff even tho u rack me and protect Sherman, an I may be rong on Jory, Christ am rong mos a ma life, but Sherman really seem AWFULLY AMBITIOUS and could make good door to door SALESMAN, an he may have thot I was somethin' an' in ur terms he is "innocent" but the innocents are more patrons of hell than the enemy, I dunno I dunno I dunno... if he would only sit still for a minute and keep his god d. hands off the telephone. I must stop knocking Jory, tho—for some reason I do not feel good doing it.

Well, I don't know what the hell.

... of course the horses are bad, filled with gasoline and bad
    dreams,
and the women too... wear claws that shred your back through
kisses of candy-fire, and the whiskey crawls with crazy moths,
and when I open a can of beans... shrimp jump out and nip my
    fingers;
the thunder pokes holes in my brain tonight, and I dial odd
    numbers
on the phone asking questions on the classics and the size of
    the moon,
and I get out the foil and dance before the mirror crashing
    splints
into my body and face; I oil the clock and the cat, sing Carmen
    backwards,
eat the shell and throw away the egg... history is upside down,
and love and breakfast, and look... the poems of Sandburg...

who is he trying to fool? I've seen Dante in an opera hat,
walking thru the snow, poisoned on bad beer...
—Buk, portion of poem
Old Number 9, Rommel, Nininsky, What Have You?
now out in the hands of the blessed makers.

Of course, passant poems tire and I am tiring of them but I
must be tired enough so that a new expressive medium is just
not another conclamation, but hell, all this wiring and writing
down is not only stupid but tiring. It is in doing—and in another way, not doing—that we renew? The seasons are not stupid,
the days and the nights, can we ever beat them? Need we? I
think so. You, Sheri, dislike Buk disliking cat-killing birds, but I
do and must face myself with lackings in the face of so-called
normal intelligence that accepts the inevblty. of NATURE. I can
only accept what the animal BUK says in the unlearning. Too
much has been taught. We must be UNTAUGHT. I believe that
is why I enjoy the company of slaughterhouse workers, boxers,
whores, Communists, queers, jockeys, waitresses—their knowledge is SPINAL.

... soon's I get poem or something I will send on up.

Rite now you tell Po' Li my head feels like burnt-out lite
gobble.

L.,

Buk-thing

---

*[postcard dated by SM 13 October 1960, written around
drawing of CB being chased by several women]*

Deer Sheri: "leveret" is a hare in the first year of its age....
still trying to clean this place up: met animal in bathroom this
morning the size of sick camel—I left and went down to gas

Old Number 9: never published.
Rommel: Erwin Rommel (1891–1944), German general.
Nininsky: Waslaw Nijinsky (1890–1950), Russian dancer.

station. Still no word on 15 or 20 pomes I sent to S.F. Review so nothin' to show u for possible A&P. much jitter life: editor pro. usin' pomes to wipe windshield—or worse... basta! basta!... and so we scratch for a name and a way.

L.,

Buk

Los Angeles, Calif.
Oct. 19 or 20 or wot, 1960

Dear Sheri, muh:

beast-time passing of scars through closed windows, and a senseless sun, *peine forte et dure*, the cuckold of unreason, a Samson hesitates in the fine web of quiver and titan spires, and no Samson at all—say the buprestid beetle or ordinary man can only grin esperanto hurricanes closer to coma. and if beetles grin, men wear hairshirts to cover their wisdom. looky, baby, what I mean here: splendid then: the caprification and the didactic load, but what are you going to do for passion when there's only India and only India can amend the spare revenge, the sparrow-lovers, *si vis me flere dolendum est primum ipse tibi*, the oxen are as golden as the sun through golden eyes, but now the tablets sit in morphia, and hear hear!!, doctrines and deductions curd into a leaf and die, not because we fail ourselves, but other certain empires we shut away with a mouldy and indelicate, stucco, pontifical nay.

Sure, old friend, I've read Pound and Eliot and Cummings and I can toss the words fancy, see here: the spathic lameness of reverie in metempirical phrases is the catch-crotch of the high bulgarians, and I am the last to blot or censure the mystery and high-dove go of the language, it is simply that coming out of the slaughterhouses and whorehouses wilted and impugned with

---

peine forte et dure: Fr: "severe and cruel punishment," a form of torture.
si vis ... tibi: "If you wish me to weep, you yourself must first feel grief"—Horace.

95

foretaste,—the placenta must go, and the intortion and the divine bullshit, and also... the eunuchs, the civets, the cloisters of footmen, the lavender founts, oblique sirens, everything dastardly sirroco and weeping

must go

must go

must go

and the wergild price is not enough, nor the fancy getaway run of rabbits or rats or genuii—

> look here: the game is over:
> let's trim the fat,
> and die.

... the drunker one gets the more mountains appear in the hill of the head, and barking like cats and snarling like gods, and all the puppies in the boot with tap-root smiles and the lion chewing off my left leg and belching blue sparks, ya gotta have a forest and colza and perch and reverie, and letters from Spain and a bag of wet walnuts; and really love, or thinking about love, or getting ready for love—or hate, which is the same thing in a smaller way. the welt of living is so hackneyed, let me luxuriate and mull over the junk of death, puffing through my simple lungs, my spiral brain twisted and decayed as a rotten tooth; the jocund blood rattles in its simple sack, spying on Time, ah ha, but what can be said? It has all been said. we are a sub-species, a sub-species of saving and doing, well-read, inbred, half-wit, constipated roar, rabbit-roar... o, beg in the roads wet with perfume and palsy, oh shit! these soft-hearted sounds—would that I could drum alive the granite gods! would that this rip of red across my eyes mean the voices and sounds and figures, that the full haze of the iguana/—oh christ, how do you say it   say it   say it   drunk and not-drunk, ignorant in the high-seas of death, a gutter-guy scratching for a comb in catalysis of peaches and tigers and beer, can you tell me that frogs are less a manoeuvre than our leap beyond the lycée of breathing?

burn there greater things than poems or blondes in nylon and garter, crst, I mean the young blondes, Sheri, of beerspit night and cursing; burn there greater things than fighting for your life in a 4 rounder, the gloves bombing your guts when you only want love?... or people who think you are a bastard because you can sit in a room for 3 weeks, the sick shades down, without the desire to look upon the face of your brother? tell me, is this madness? burn there greater things than when the music claws and crawls like ants from the floor, up your arms, your chest, your ass, and sings in your head, sings words, crazy words and love, and all the walls are forests of burning music and you laugh drunk-weird and move to the typewriter and all the crazy blondes and all the crazy gloves, Shakespeare as close as the pepper shaker, Beethoven in your wallet along side the hock ticket and the name of a whore, the blood of 4-rounders coming like an aria, and out the DOOR (the type-writer can wait) into the jails, the dives, the fox-crazy traffic, the torn signs yelling names of old lovers through the malaria of breathing, and see see see BANG, already the bartender marks you with his scientist's eye and the old whores preen in the mir-ror, and the night is fine by god by god by god, juke boxes and screaming and the deer marching on the windows, and you begin talking through your scarred unholy face, you lie about the last 4-rounder you won in '53, or you remember the time you were in the same magazine with Lorca and Sartre and everybody else. well, shit. it's old stuff. but so are magnolias and wars and mountains and bullfights, and everywhere the sound comes on and a woman calls your name and you laugh and it doesn't matter, and the bartender comes on like God, heaven in a bottle, the cash-register of hell, and purgatory until 2 a.m., so drink to the dead bull, the dead poem, dead love, everything dead in the face of morning, your fingers slowly clos-ing about the lie and tossing it down your throat.

... there is nothing subtle about dying or dumping garbage, or the spider, and this fist full of nickels and the barking of dogs tonight when the beast puffs on beer and moonlight and
asks my name
asks my name
asks my name
and I hold to the wall not man enough to cry
as the city dumps its sorrow in
wine bottles and stale kisses,
and the handcuffs and crutches and slabs
fuck like mad
got yr letter: awright, the classics are a condition, ok wit me. I don wanna make a romantic outa ya, u stay sprung out and

yet set tha weigh ya r.... Wang I heard frum another source, tell me he can no make his mind up w. he prefer man or woman. I dunno, I don care, but seems ¾ of Art world homo.

Ya see wot heffect y has got ona me? Yos gut me rritin' *Martinellies* jaw haw rite, a rite, a rite... da stars are thick wit sickness, bad-time sickness, vury, an I jus knock pounda coffee on floor, all over, n ahm toooooo sick to pick up wit hit and high sit shit and looky upon it, the crumbs of coffee coffeeeeee-effeeee sittin lookin at me wit all its I's, an nobody wins... I must out and mail this.

sheri muh deer,
Buk goin now—
Buk

L.A., Oct. 21

Dear Sherelli:

More list a "Yankee names". Your boys Ginsburg, Sherman, McClure...

Your last letter a real swath of sythces, but why do you blame ME? Not sythces, sickles—what is it you cut wheat down with? I got a dictonairy but I am sick today, bleeding.

What Wang does to his contemporaires they may enhohjoy but am no contemp a Wang's—women for me, and not too many.

I am still pickin' up coffee, whata life.

Don eat that lobster or what.

wen I say seawater infected with gentle distillers of decay— that me that a little of that in you... will eat out the pestilence and impurity. I don' see why I am so hard to get across to u.

on the utter hand I UNDERSTAND YOU PERFECTLY.

it is one hell of a situation.

anytime u are in L.A., stop by, preferably alone—I will not rape you. now do not get angry because I invited you through the door. this—from Buk—is a rarity. unlisted phone: NO. 1-6385.

McClure: Michael McClure (1932–), San Francisco poet.

good day at track yestiday, could do no wrong. No, it was day before yestiday, beer waitress blew me a kiss.
no pomes no nottin now, sick sick sick
going to bed to dream about fountains, rome fts, riot founts, blue blooo sleep.
the beginning of dust.
ok Shed, easy now.

yah,

Charles

Buk

Horse angels, feather-whip gaiety
Hoc octobra hoc hastra hixty [27 October 1960]

m d sher—
oke, vents open; horse sky animal dangling, head hed hed eye, bang bang b a n g BLUE CLOUDS NOT WHITE, They iza comin in, hit d. double $117.00 bang b a n g, the bulls are veering off, sum otha wins—10, twnet fift on nose, hell wallet fulla stuffins not of money but of TIME to breathe n by a paint brush n new typewriter ribbon n house, am gona buy a little shack Sheri n I may quit everything and huddle in the corner and dream spain and Spam and dogs with wowfree muzzles on deathsass, so look, I received the photo a Martingale and Ernie back against sea chalk cliffs that will dip with bombers and sigh; ah, writ, thisa good thing u remember Gramps Jr. because altho I have failed n my first poems r no morean scratchings, I AM LOADED FOR BEAR an I cannot stop myself: I am six feet taller evra morning wen I wake up, no matter if wi hoo or what or how sick six, ther is somethin wirlin, n tha t weeh it gost, go dame u, u got me writin lak a friggin goat in lacepatch a curtain belly ballet bullets, so.
Very well. And so. The cliffs and Ernst. I wish u very well.

Ernie: E(rnest). P(aul). Walker (1941–), a young poet SM had an affair with that winter.

Pond something new book out. Hood reviews good. Pond say,

> "If I can feel all this
> there must be something
> good
> in the universe..."

I think we must go beyond this into the screeching sounds say of a washing machine gone wild—there is more here than supplication; there is some part of us that wishes to remain forever mystified, and I do not think this is ignorance or ill will or thin character or the hand-gallop toward elenchus; and I think this is where Pound has failed—this eternal reaching toward light, haitus... is much too much like gathering coins for the bank of the soul. There comes, finally, to all of us... the wish for retreat from Art... from finery... the studded brave challenge of the impossible, for the retreat to darkness and dankness and fish and bone and the sick cut flower. Each new grace becomes finally an obscenity and more than we can bear. I am not saying that your friend Pound was right: I am saying, that perhaps, in some ways, he is more toward wrong now.

Thanx for foto, yr face fathomless, mus admit interesting but can see u would be hard to handle and too much for me: I am slow man of much peace and quietness... while the oblique loom of the incurably absurd... the banging of grass against the bone keeps ants hustling thru the dreamground.

Charles
Buk

[*postcard dated by SM 3 November 1960*]

Dear Sheri:

Pound's latest, which you pro know about: *Thrones: 96–109 de los Cantares*. New Directions, $3.50. They tell me Pond was

---

Pond ... new book: Thrones (see next postcard), published almost a year earlier in December 1959. (The verse that follows is not from *Thrones* but CB's paraphrase of Pound's state of mind.)

pro reading Catherine Drinker Bowen's *The Lion and the Throne*.

It appears to me that Pound reads too mc. and mrly translates into his wordage. Much trick of mounting history upon poetic stilts. To me, history is a series of liars with the writer of the final book carrying the largest gun. Pound has proved a much better poet than a politician. All he learned out of St. Liz was Sheri Martinelli. Which was plenty, and perhaps worth it. No, no, I'd say not: the pure poet must have neither woman nor country.

THE SUN HAS NOT BEEN OUT FOR DAYS, IT IS RAINING, THE SIDEWINDERS RUNNING POORLY, HYD.PK., COFFEE AND WINE BURNING MY TONGUE.

Charles
BUK

L.A., Late November [28] 1960

Dear Sheri:

Been wondering about poems, and good you will use... Have been getting rid of others here and there, even *San Francisco Review* took 4 or 5 or 6—he didn't name them but I half remember some of them. Miller kept asking for poems and I hit him with a houseful, and now I suppose we'll leave each other alone for a while. Jon Webb's son dropped by, found me sick in bed, 3 day beard, hair in eyes. I sat there in old shrunken bathrobe, cracked him a beer, and I told him, now don't expect anything brilliant from me, when it comes to talking I'm a ditch-digger with a hangover. He's the son of the editor of this *Outsider* thing in New Orleans and the old man says Jon Jr. is "nuts" about my stuff. I had been spitting up blood all day and

---

Catherine Drinker Bowen's The Lion and the Throne: a biography of Sir Edward Coke published in 1957. (For Coke, see note to SM's letter of 11 January 1961.)

Miller: Roy Miller, founding editor of the *San Francisco Review*.

was unable to drink, and Jr. said he had originally planned to sketch me but had forgotten his materials, for which I was damned glad. It bothers me to have people run in on me like that because I am usually in such bad shape, but they've always got to see the guy who wrote that stuff, when to me, only the writing's important, and maybe not even important, at that.

I am sorry you can't read my English but I can't write any other way an' I'm too old to begin looping with Esar Pund West Coasta Hafrika sign talk.

Heard from Thorne, other day (*Epos*), this, in part: "...has anyone ever called you Whitman in reverse... I hope that this will not annoy you, but your long dark catalogues do remind me of his long light ones... he saw America singing... you see it vomiting... both of you could have used a touch of each other..."

Well, I don't know, America was more singing when Whitman was around, the newness hadn't frozen to politic and graft and cartel, the piling of crowds, jaywalking, auto insurance, daylight thieves, falsies, celluloid, high-priced graves, taxes— oh, I could make a list that would take me 90 days to type; but it is very hard to see America singing now. The only thing that can sing is the individual who somehow remains alive under the lashing of a demeaning way of life, and it's a full-time job, staying awake amongst the sleepers as you buy eggs or drive across a bridge or wonder why you haven't put any paint on a piece of paper for five years.

I guess that planets are still in friction with my skull-bone: auto accident, pipe in bathroom leaks, left headlight of car out, bones cold cold cold, moving like an old man, the sun keeps coming down on nothing. Pound could find his light but I move forever in the dark. It is only sometimes when I hear a bit of symphony music that I rise up out of it. I hope I do not depress you, Sheri. I must close and clean this place up—if I am able.

Love,
Charles
Charles Bukowski

Uno/ Dicèmbre/ Mille nove cento sessanta
SM poBx San Gregorio Calif

Buk/ ONE of the joys of being a female is that no one appears to
rub dicks with me/ AND ONE OF THE REASONS THE UNIVERSE
RETURNED TO IDOLATRY is because the males snuggled on
each other... they did it to him & to you also/ Bukowski you are
NOT an American Whitman in reverse—it aint then... it is NOW
& we have been given the divine fire & you wont light it at all
but persist in rubbing yr nose in accidental & fungoid muck
    Buk—all you got to do is move out of the "money belt"
"the golttt coast" as my Hollywood pals call it... move into our
large & innocent area/ the center of the land... and all yr vomit
vanishes—
    One saw it driving home to Virginia—the Innocence—the
descendants of the founding fathers... the Good Christians who
actually read the buke & live by it... all yr symptoms of disease
vanish Bukowski... yr entire list is only related to a single cause/
you live on top of a mold culture/ a rot growth that always
appears on any ripe fruit that aint being put to any good use/
and you believe it to be the WHOLE story/ the marvel is that you
do not report worse stuff than you do/ yr insights & perceptions
are fascinating and you cd write us a poem that wd be as valuable as a novel of the times/ all but when you let yrself into the
poem & then everything goes lopsided & abstract & meaningless...
    my dear brother Buk/ suppose you were lost... in a strange
land... no one to talk to... no one who knew wot or who you
were... & frightened... & lonely & superstitious... then a SIGN
POST... and hope & a feeling of safety... then the sign post
jumps around & turns upside-down & you don't know where
the hell it is pointing... wd you bless it?
    I mean the Universe returned to idolatry on the fulcrum of
the 20thC... it might take another 2000 due mille but that aint
much
    yr english is fine in this letter/ don't make fun of me Buk/
West Coasta Hafrika style—don't know who this Thorne chap
is but he sounds like a niz leedle goy out front/ america is NOT
vomiting... goddam forever & eternally may they rot alive—
these bugger'd minds and left over scum from the war/ my
baby sister is having her baby—my 2 & 1/2 yr old neice is so

intelligent... all the Jews in the psyc racket... pester my 3rd sister to let them poke around in her intelligence... she completely threw them... a whole roomful of Nudttt Duckders until I warned my 3rd sister to not fk with them... they only want to investigate beautiful intelligences in order to know how to... enslave them

my mother & my father are dreaming out the last part of their lives... made joyous by their Elder Daughter's post cards & monies & chinatown joy gifts... my middle sister's children are getting engaged & falling in love... & my maw in law & paw in law are making a chinese thanksgiving dinner for my chinese nefuwwwww age 6 or so... the world is alive & joyous & not vomiting and Mr. Thorne can remove that dick from his mouth & stop being a goy out front...

I heard that Allen Ginsberg went to visit that greezer when he wuz up from Cuba—taking his little band of debauched christers wiff him... voddt a thrill woddttt a reffffooolushunary t'ing to be doink... Allen I cannot blame... and I love Allen—he is pure & good & only doing his job... but the scum he hangs out with... a white hide and a blank inside... not ONE of those fucked in the mouth & in the ass christians... wd dare... dare approach any of our white house lice... but trot like dogs to see the greezer & get their kicks/ daring dews
and Thorne belongs in with them

[*bottom of page 2; no closing signature, so third page possibly lost*]

December [3] 1960

Mine Shed,

Re poem *Paper*: barnball said nothing because barnball knew nothing except what he hez heard insteada did, and so

---

greezer...up from Cuba: Ginsberg met Fidel Castro when the Cuban leader visited the United Nations in September 1960.

Paper ... barnball: perhaps "The Paper on the Floor," rpt. in *Play the Piano Drunk...* (1979). Barnball is presumably an editor.

that's it: snow upon roof, paper flying before wheels... nothing can be done really but record futility of flatness, no further digging left even into evil, but evil is not a word I like to use because it is used to bang against the heads of bong-sounding domes. What I mean is, the poem can go no further, and I stepped in and sliced its head off.

Sounds and utterances of the people are only good as sounds and utterances and can never be taken as embarkations into wisdom except as accident; their thoughts are multitude thoughts and their sins are patented, or as you said Gramps put it: "When you are the light it is bound to be dark", or as I would say, when you are lighting light at your best it is only the beginning of the fetching away of a darkness that has closed lives before us and will close lives after us, and whether this is a trick of God through a purposely bent imbecility of Man, or whether it is no God at all, it is dark and it will stay dark until this God comes and brings us light or until we are blown away.

Barnball can say nothing, and although I can say more, I can say very little more, and I made this clear upon my entrance and... exit from the poem.

Now Gramps utters of cosmos and light, and this is all good ego, and by uttering shows some light and some of the cosmos, and this is important to us as we boil our beans or sit upon the edge of a chair listening to the blackbird cats rubber-wheeling it down to the edge of hell, but Gramps himself knows there are plenty of clouds and planets and jade eagles that scratch the spirit and misdirect it in its very now-essence of wanting to jell and flow in our brainguts as the secret pall of a nothing greater than death, than the death of the living faces and nations, than the death of ourselves or where a rose finally goes.

And you have to watch carefully when you talk this way because it is easy to say sounds for sounds and our clay words break and we lose the way because we keep babbling to make feeling when feeling has long gone and we only bury what we seek. In other words, down with bullshit. And most poetry is bullshit. Most of Gramps isn't. And you aren't because you won't be fooled. This is very important with you, Martinelli: not to be fooled. I noticed it early. Or fooled with. Except as real. I don't bother quite as much with that because I laugh more without sound and I am tired. I don't think I am as much German as I am tired and I should have died five or 6 times but

105

I merely sit boiling beans, which might be German after all: too stupid to die, and also too stupid to love: hung in between great blanks of air, wondering.

I must get this off now because the crab-feet are clutching my brain. This clock to my left ticks and there is nothing but grass outside my window, 3 floors down. A gifted phonepole throws a black line more beautiful than I can paint, and in the four pink courts below, 4 great gramps drink their beer, 4 great gramps, 4 great gramps, and your ocean plays a gramophone.

LOVE,

Charles Bukowski

Buk

Sometime, rain comin' down thru darkness—
[postcard dated by SM 9 December 1960]

Deah Sheri:

this to let u know letta be up soon. I tripped and fell, clawed inside, but now eating Scandinavian bread and facing East, and mebe soon the pieces will form the puzzle away.

Po' Jon Web Sr. torn by 23 year ole maniac. I will buck him up soon's I get my feet.

Your letters better than mountain music or Schuman Concerto in A Minor. Don't cut away the pieces: the salt is important too, and I take it better than most poem-people.

But right now—just this card, and letter mebe tomorrow n tomorrow n tomorrow.

L.,

Buk

Web Sr. ... maniac: see CB's letter of 9 January 1961 below.

tomorrow n tomorrow n tomorrow: from *Macbeth* (act 5, scene 5).

Los Angeles, Calif.
Dec. (9-60)

Dear Sheri:

Am bit downcast because you praised me on sending without cards and I just sent card, but was so down, and tho still up a little, am still down, but mostly spirit-down, the body warming up a little. Even so, I tried to keep card enough mystery-wise to confound the people, but in your eyes I may have failed. Well, no more cards... if not too late.

Sitting here with towel around my neck, drinking coffee, December down on me like a wet toad sitting across the mind, and it appears he will not jump off, and I am weighted with little toad-turds, 5,6,7,8, 9, and if it is not a bad time, it is not a good time, indeed. This time it is in the form of a personality... cutting across my sights. However, it is an gd ugly story and I will spare you... a little of what I still feel. It will go away soon, I hope, if I am good enough to learn from it, and I don't mean learning in the book-sense or the "Correct" sense... but in the sense that is Buk, and must be nursed as Buk thru Buk; dying not but growing, which means: sun and chewing on a piece of bread and listening to music and looking out the window at plants and the sides of houses and feeling way up the arms and shoulders the substance of being full without the blight awareness of striving... and what I mean is that sometimes day by day we are cut down, until we feel that there are not many cuts left to reach down to zero—and sometimes you can reach ZERO without knowing—ah, those who reach zero never know!—and your good letters full of grain and ground and leaf have sometimes reached me with sounds of living when living sounds were very light, maybe just the remembrance of an old road or the side of a hill, or a rabbit running right on through headlights in Utah desert... bad sick times, the spirit raped and bugged and dwindling... oh, God damn, how often can we come back? It's amazing, isn't it?... how a thing as trigger-hair fine as the spirit will give you another chance... if you will only wait on it. It comes back like the good lover, standing in the door.

Rasputin survived as I survived one time because mainly I did not think of dying... the thought of death did not enter my mind, and although the body was gone, Buk sat in it and waited like a rat beneath the wharf. You watch what you eat and try to

107

keep warm; the salt of the ocean is good when the sun is there but when it is roofed and robbed by cold clouds yd never want to paint, you are attacked no matter what you say. I god hope u feelin' better and making some adjustments...

I didn't mind being called "Whitman in reverse" by Thorne. Yes, of course, the inland is better... if you don't become too *known* to the people... their injustice is that instead of separating into cold cells of unfeeling they set up a society of measurement in which each is given a place, with no moving up or down, in or out, no matter what you do. This makes things relaxed because there is nowhere to go except where you are, and this is what gives you the feeling "this would seem a nice place to stop"; but no, they wouldn't let you rest until they found your place on the ladder. At least here... 104 steps south of Hollywood Blvd., I am as unknown as a bug on the underside of a leaf, and I do not chase through their ladybug air.

I am lost in a strange land.

Thorne is woman, editor of *Epos*.

A poet should hang alone. If Ginsburg wants to visit Castro that's his business, but to me... it is going too far out to make a sound. I believe he will suffer from it without ever knowing it.

Thorne-woman prints poetic poetry, all life-forms dominated down to acceptable line. She has published me but let me run a little looser, I don't know why. Something of mine will be in Dec. *Epos*: *The Sun Wields Mercy*.

Yes, Webb Sr. seems good slow sort without too much pretense, but GAWD the Jr. is in hero-whoreship stage: (Sr. says he wrote him of meeting Buk): "... a nice meeting, short, honest & within the manner and respect one would pay a great poet as he is. I could not get over the feeling that I was an autograph seeker, but he, I think, sensed how I felt and very nicely directed the atmosphere so as to make me feel a fellow writer etc." Balls. I didn't sense anything. I told the kid that I didn't run around with writers and not to expect a lot of fancy statements and that I was sick. He asked me what I thought of Jory Sherman. I guess he knew I had met him. I didn't care for the direct question so I parried with a few lines of general literary criticism and pretty soon he called a cab and got the hell out of there.

The Sun Wields Mercy: rpt. in *RM* 158–60.

ooh god... no pure red wool next ta my body... my skin... very sensitive, I'd die dy dy! too protestant perhaps, too ivory, and yet the bestial wail. Griffith already talking about future chapbook, I thinking titles: *Trinkets for Whores, Gamblers and Imbeciles* or *Our Bread Is Blessed and Damned* or or or or or... What happened to Payne? Well, we don't agree on hardly anything but he took a coupla poems for his *Light Year*, wrote: "Bulliski your bull hits the mark." Which I think is a very weak expression and I think he wanted to say, "Bullshitski" which would have been better, only Payne plays the gentleman, read and ready, but his lines do not hold... Miller is ed. of *San Francisco Review* and he took handful of poems I wrote when drunk and I don't know exactly what they are... there might be four or five or maybe even more, but I don't know what they say exactly and will have to wait until he prints to see what I have written. I have learned when drunk to type directly off the typewriter. I have written too many poems longhand and could read nothing the next day.... The blood thing is from when my stomach broke open... When I open a beer, it does crack. Maybe we open em different.

I have some things to do, and I hope you are strong again, stems and hair warm in the sun, breathing salt.

love,
Buk

---

sunday/ 11/dec/60   pobx 46   san gregorio calif

buk/ 's all right—the post card/ hell I am afraid that remaining anonymous now is out of question... one just L O O K S emcipated somehow—I donno—and the art of incoming & outgoing correspondence/ stamps etc/ now dear buk's card saying almost ANYthing... oye/ 's all right tho'... I am certain Buk that yr card will be "mystery-wise" without any trying... and... just

---

Griffith ... future chapbook: Griffith later published a few broadsides by CB but no further chapbooks.

where & how did that fashion of putting "wise" on back words start? & means what?

Of course—that IS the process of life—becoming MORE what we are/ or Buk growing into Buk... all this hammering & pounding on us must be from a natural occurrence... as fish in a sea/ it must not have any personal significance except mayhap to clear out the sea plants or weeds or fish that'd weaken its life-force by not holding on strongly enough... I see the debris cast up by the sea movements—and the flies hop on the great beauties dying without their element & I cannot throw them back... beautiful sea plants still gasping & breathing & seals all torn up and great enormous birds like the rose-sucked-tit-pink bill'd pelican one saw... must be like that... our sea of air/ we graduated into then beyond/ I saw it once—half saw it & never knew what it was/ don't know how I got there & not a dream but a journey some sort—& was sitting on a very kind of "modernistic" ice berg or hunk of something very white but not cold & just plopped there & was aware of presences & talk without words & one cd say one 'felt' rather than 'heard' them... and I had a flash vision of me—in that upper kingdom I'd come to somehow—that there I was as a mermaid wd be here—I mean I was half what they recognised as being 'human' & half fish or animal... so I know we are in a sea of some kind & my fellow fish keep reporting giant tidal waves & storms... they receive thru their nervous systems... they think of as emotional... and the memory of the Orderly; the Good; the Beautiful; the Serene can calm even during a storm... my sister Elva after the hurricane hit... walking down the street with a flashlight & one heard her... "hmmm looks like the roof to my house... well... it IS the roof to my house..." & it was... I wasn't frightened by the hurricane... it was sort of natural & normal... in the middle of it without thinking at all of anything but me & my american thousand of stores open at all times... wanted ice cream very badly & put on a swim suit... & started out... the ocean was up to arm pit; then chin... & kept on going... surely a store wd be open for the citizenry! then a coast guard in a boat... havin' a hellifa time keeping rightside up... shrieked... "where are YOU going?" "to get some ice cream you nut" I said "nut... me the nut" he said "don't you know there's a hurricane going on?" "so what" I said "I want some ice cream" but the dirty bastard chased me home & then I sort of 'came to' & looked around me & sure

110

enough there was a hurricane going on... the sea was washing over big buildings a few blocks down Atlantic Avenue & furniture was floating all around & broken lumber & the roof was blowing off my sister's house & I was swimming in the middle of Atlantic Avenue looking for a store that wd be open so I cd get some ice cream/ but somehow I wasn't shook/ it was lovely & just wild enough to suit me... the wind singing & the ocean being an ocean & all the buildings going down & no violence to we insects... just knocking off a lot of useless junk... it was a beautiful sight... the next day... the whole town was a wreck... beautiful... not a single person was harmed... just the junk... my town looked just right then... one cd see for miles...

I cant imagine how I got poisoned/ all we know is that we burned the wrappings from that chicken & suddenly a gorgeous smell of almonds flowering... & the next day I recalled from somewhere... that arsenic either smells or tastes like almonds, that sweet haunting fragrance—who'd mind being killed by it? but my god, Buk... throwing up violently in a freezing cold house... I cdn't take my poor little head out of the sleeping bag long enough to throw up without freezing... my Botticelli belly was hard & swollen almost pregnant size/ I cdn't talk without choking and after one rid oneself of it via the throat... then it turned my bowels into a shit factory... oh that was fun... my yes it sure WAS FUN... to have to get up & shit that burning watery stinking shit... for 3 hours... oh that was real country life... shitting in a pot... & one had to put it outside the door each time... I mean Gib protested at the stench... it was not veddy artistic... moi lamb... so although the smell of arsenic is a treat... the EFFECT it produces sure aint/ now I am recovered & you'd never even suspect that this dainty little elf... had to live through that stinking night...

I aint gonna become a saint by any other's sins... dear childtttttt

the people out here do like me/ the post master is now "on the map" because one don't have a day go by without business as usual & one buys stamps from him in great car lots full & he is happy & one discusses the political situation with those who stand around the post office & one knows a deal about the

---

Gib: Gilbert Lee, SM's husband.

political situation to be sure/ and one's mail is filled with the most life & the people like me... I am a stage they live upon/

Thorne is a woman/ well that's better than being a bugger/ I think you sent me the *Epos* did you? and I stashed it in the collection at Yale with Pearson/

I do agree with you about Ginsberg/ "will suffer from it without ever knowing it"

I KNOW that the Zionists are not going to & NEVER had ANY intention of ever allowing the American Jews to rule/ so any effort on the part of an American to help destroy the existing order shall be wasted effort as far as he is concerned because Jew or no Jew... he is now an American & nobody likes any of us... only the niggers got any support back home/ even the Jews were betrayed... paid for Israel & got Zion... their old lag... so Allen doth not betray the ang-sax order... with that Castro visit... he betrays his own people unless he is a Zionist and I do not know & gorHELLup me I don't wanna know... I know too damm much already

all right my dear Buk/ wear silk—it must be of a colour & natural fibre to attract certain rays from our sun's rays... certain rays that build our bone marrow & that is where the warmth comes from... I will find something for you... a red silk shirt & then you'd be like maestro in st. liz who just HAD to have a red shirt after the new negro attendant turned up in one... & old dr. karpman called gramps "th' cardinal"... o.k. Cardinal... gimmi some time... this sat. i will hunt down a large red wotever— don't flip if it's of the female race of clothes... as the GoodWill is my first stop but I'll masculinize it for you... we must get Buk's bones warm/

please my dear Buk/ no titles like that... I believe that we run the world by our secret thoughts feelings & spoken words & written words & images painted... like a sort of magnetic bunch of wheels going constantly around... it is a kind of machine you know... this fluid cosmic world... a perpetual machine... no wonder the Jews of old were so flip'd on building one... imagine what you'd SEE if you cd build one! I believe the magnetic wheels come from our own wot you'd call projections/ and if you project any titles like that baby how cd they help us any? I

---

dr. karpman: probably a psychiatrist at St. Elizabeths (not mentioned in the Pound biographies).

112

work & stand & paint & write & live... for Pure Love/ because I
want it running that way... not for me... but for them because it
wd have been so nice for me... if I'd have had it/ Hate & any
side-effect of it... is T A B U now... do not break a TABU
Cardinal!

I am not going to say "look wot Hezra didtttt" because he is
after all only another male & therefore competition... but he
was useful... wistfully useful and he does so want us to use what
he thought useful... and he did try to leave us a picture in *Edge,*
Rockdrill, Agenda & lots of things he named/ and taking the
Canto out of Kantor... that was all he gave the Jews in the Cantos besides a lotta hell for usury etc... & a few other rackets...
wdn't put nary a bit of Hebrew in the Cantos... but out of Kantor... Ezra the Kantor

THINGS ARE WHAT THEY DO/ what is your poetry doing?
Allen Ginsberg's *Howl* was certainly good because it IS a HOWL
from HELL/ I am trying to imagine what yr poetry is doing/

Gib said call it: *The Triple Carburater* or just *Triple Carburaters* or *Double Adrenalin Gland Sounds*

I mean dig down to the most basic what-iz-happening & I
do think buk that you've got double adrenalin glands & it
makes you highly perceptive & sensitive to what is going on...
twice as much as the rest of us... oh that poor payne chap is he a
bugger? or a mis-guided xtian? of some kind... he is so
squishy...

poor Allen Ginsberg... I wonder what the Devil will give
him for that poor string of fish he caught in our Pond—a bunch
of little weak christian fish... dumb as worms—so dumb... they
actually were fool'd into sucking dick or asshole fuck just so
they could print poetry... man dig that/ that is too wild... imagine printing sacred poetry in this world by selling one's ass...
even the Devil will have to laugh at them... poor string of fish
caught with the net of their own blind greed...

that is why it is a sin to be ambitious as dissociated from
dedicated/ it was a middle-ages sin & it is now also... thou'rt
dedicated buk... but damm—some of wot moves yr spirit...
dedicated as it is... scares the rest of that arsenic shit out of
me...

Edge ... Agenda: two magazines Pound encouraged his disciples to start.

Listen to me Buk/ re: the stomach & broke open—now do this/ always keep some cooked rice around... not polished white rice but get some UNpolished rice & keep it around/ cook a lot when you feel well & then keep it & eat it sort of nibble like yr bread... or get that black bread... you are of a race of grain eaters... remember... so go on a rice diet... & don't eat much meat... the best way to eat meat is to chop chop it fine fine & cook tenderly & make a gravy... very easy to make/ buy box corn starch in supermark/ chopchop finefine meat... slowly cook in corn oil/ soon's it browns/ then turn up high fire... sprinkle corn starch in pan... remove meat or leave in... but spoon meat in ring away from center where corn starch sprinkled... let turn light brown... then put milk suddenly into hot cornstarch & spoon furiously without spilling... or splashing as that's a waste... then flavour with chinese soy sauce & a bit of hot sauce... then you can keep or throw away meat because its essence is in that gravy—put gravy over the cooked UNpolished rice (health store has it) & you will have a soothing liner for yr stomach... now gottammitt do this because I hate to lose my time...

& I will get you a red silk wotever for yr bones next sat. when we go into frisco to pick up ernie who visits for about 5 days... that means a 5-day love battle with all of us... 2 husbands are a trial especially when one has to raise both of them! I feel fatally bound to help Ernie & I MUST help Gib... and only Love can help any of us... sometimes Love is when you got to bounce them off a wall for their own good/ Mamma Sheri/ oye... oye... oye... and Gib is a Slant & Ernie is a Jew... I yam some 'racist' Buk... a disappointment to all Zion/

I am strong again & sun shines on me... (Tu Fu said: "The sun stretches his legs & walks upon the earth") Gib's out front fixing the hot rod of a kid from work/ kid is all insect buzz & just wants to "go fast"... inherited a fast world he did that kid/ working in sun half clad... that is how come *Triple Carburators* title for you... because hot rod got triple carburators to spit gasoline faster/ damn kid is 16 & drives 110 miles an hr in drag race

---

Tu Fu: Chinese poet (712–770), a contemporary of Li Po.
HalfMoon: Half Moon Bay, south of San Francisco.

114

down HalfMoon/ now Lamb be good & I go... and love love love...

from

yew Love Baby
Sheri

note/ I mean the flies on the sea storm debris & one thought of North Beach & how the lice there hop on any of us who get blown in by a storm... Bomkoff & me when I'd go over in a lonely fit/ but it was not the beach/ only back water/ still those flies/ listen Buk—there is a natural 'room' outside made by the grove of trees & I just made an altar out there by some weird set of perfect circumstances that one led to another... it has a rug & an altar & My Ladye & will take foto for you... in 1954 Ezra prayed for an "altar in the grove" for me & I just today received it... it is most important to have faith because otherwise you'd never know what it was when it did arrive and I didn't mind at all being blown away from Ezra's beautiful Life into the back waters... I needed to KNOW more about Life that I'd not have known safely with him—the wilde storm took me away & led me to my Altar in the Grove... we have all heard a strange melodic whistle out here... Gib, Ernie & myself... I heard it about 3 a.m. one night it woke me up... not a bird sound... too human & Ernie heard it & Gib & we all flashthought the samethought... Pan... Pan's here & he will visit my altar... I know it... I just put Narcissis & orange vine flowers & pine branches & spruce... for him/ he will come... I have a sort of bed-chair there & that persian rug... he will come to my grove's altar... & we shall have a painting of the Great God Pan... and if it's suspiciously like Ernie... ah/ what's that but a manifestation of the strange ways the Gods work... aaaaaaaah??? but we shall have it... no one has seen him now these thousand ages... my Pan my beautiful God Goat...

3 carburators & no brains just pulled out with my number one husband tearing light-speed down the highway to test their job... man what a generation they are these 16yrolds... they did not produce thinking men but thinking machines... that car had the intelligence... the 16 yr old is just a collection of wornout

---

Bomkoff: Bob Kaufman (1925–1986), San Francisco poet who published in *A&P* and elsewhere.

negro slang... oye... our future... buk for xt's sake don't split &
leave ME here... to face growing old with that as 'gootttt government' even Barny Baruch will despair...

oh my altar the gods gave me... Buk I will see the Lady
there & entertain the Great God Pan... we hear his music &
very early sat a.m. pre-dawn I went out to wet myself in the
mistair & that melodic whistle went right past my ears with no
earthly body to it of any sort I fled wildly laughing but fear-
fulled panic stricken nymph... Pan is returned—the Great God
pan returns... ANYthing may happen now... and back to this
dream of life...

Love

Sheri

Middle of Dec. [12] 1960

Yes, Sheri: got your letta and cards... *hoy!* which I am duly
stashing and filing in my own future groan box for this thing
eternity, which I am leery ooov... eternity being a WORD, a
working-word put on the table to explain away heavy measure-
ments. Put a mouse in a box and he will not think ETERNITY,
he will think: sides of box, sides of box, I must get the hell out. I
am mouse-thoughts rather than people-thoughts, yas, so they
do not trap me out in the purple clouds looking for golden rain.

There is not a lot of drama or future looking down at the
end of your fingernails and that is why I am MAEOMAD, mad.

Your cards will have Buk rereading Gramps while cracking
his beer. Yes, I just opened one—and your side went SISSSK! 'n
my side went BRRACK!, which shows u the female ear hears one
thing and the male another.

Rec. letta today from *Literary Artpress*—Eastern Washington College of Education—saying they are taking a poem of
mine called *Anthony*, which as usual, I don't remember writing.

Barny Baruch: Bernard Baruch (1870–1965), American businessman,
economic adviser to Franklin Roosevelt. (While at St. Elizabeths, Pound
was convinced Baruch was trying to poison him.)

Literary Artpress ... Anthony: appeared in its Fall 1960 issue; rpt. in *RM*
(50).

116

Suppose I was thinking Cleopatra in terms of modernity 1960... Some poems I remember writing and some I don't and I think the ones I don't—they are the best. I guess it's because the mouse-thoughts are not then at work.

Mystery-wise, I guess I mean like edge-wise, as edge as u can get, the thing slanting at you in green sunshine.

I do not like to see the dead birds and seals; I know it is all necsry and they do not grieve, just the drunken man walking the sand standing against the forces, music and chills running wild... one man, and the sun is armies and the bones of the dead knit the earth like crabgrass... ah *shit!*, and I am awakened today by 2 old gals in the hall, high-dead voices: YES, IT GOES ON WHEN YOU TURN IT THIS WAY AND IT GOES OFF WHEN YOU TURN IT THIS WAY, SEE... HERE! LET ME SHOW YOU! NOW WATCH! WHEN YOU TURN IT THIS WAY...

on and on and one keeps thinking: the same thing, how fk can they keep on with the same thing... 15, 20 minutes... but they do, yes... NOW SEE, DID YOU SEE IT? CAN YOU TURN IT? TRY IT. NOW TURN IT.

I got up and threw some clothes on and came out the door with a three day beard. I had only slept about 5 hours in 4 days.

They were turning a dusty old floor lamp. Out in the hall.

"How you doin', kid?" one of them asked me.

"Oh great," I said. "Just great."

... You've had some visions. I've had two, both of which scared me. Tell you some time. Right now left thumb cut, makes it hard to type.

Aye, then Gib lived through your excrements!

Ginsburg. Well, I could never get through reading *Howl*. I hadda give up early. But then, I have these troubles. I could never get through *War and Peace*. Or the lesser novels of our times: *The Naked and the Dead*, or such very badly written books as *From Here to Eternity*. And James was the OTHER way... he wrote so *well*, I couldn't bear him.

I figured u wouldn't like my titles because I know your mind. But u evidently don't know mine yet... when I say whore, gambler and imbecile the terms are endearment, and when I say I want to give them trinkets, those are my poems. I cannot say what my peoms are (pomes?) like *Triple Carburater* what, so I say where to send them and what to do with them, and say a title like *Rockdrill* is very strong but I do not feel so very strong when they turn and babble about the lamp in the halls.

There is no them. There is no future. My bones will sleep in the mud. Yet I understand what you are trying to say and I enjoy your saying it. It does me good. I respect your flow. You are a good one, Sheri, and you may yet get us out of the mud. But I've seen so many dead on the altars and the sun is coming down on the bone face and they do not feel the sun and they do not feel me, just as if you died, Shed, your voice would stop, and maybe you've left me some pieces of paper and I've eaten a can of cookies made by your hands, but don't you see... that makes me angry: THE CAT*KILL bird, and yet it is childish to want to go on; I do not even want to go on; life barely interests me; I guess the death thing I need, and we've got to face it. I am a stone face upon a stone altar, and the larvae and the grub are hunting lovers from Tristan to an indication of lightning.

Don't know if Payne is a bugger. Know he works from the outside in, and when you work from the OUTSIDE in, so hard, you are only trying to establish a beginning so you can work from the inside out, yet keeping the inside. Yet Payne senses strength, he can smell it out like a bloodhound and track it down, and yet when he gets hold of it... somehow it doesn't affect him, it doesn't *build* him, and he's off again... with another bloodhound... trying to catch another fox.

You absorb and grow. You even absorb me, first carefully sifting out what you consider the poisons.

I can't imagine printing sacred poetry by selling one's ass. But Jory brought over one one night, who yes—that was exactly it. Long golden hair, talking like Oscar Wilde. Oye. And I just sat there and grunted. old man Buk.

Shed, you have 3 husbands. I am your spirit-husband and I am not jealous. That is what bothered Fry.

Speed makes the modern man more manly. It is the dragon of the times. Even I, Buk, have had my auto insurance canceled, and above-mentioned Fry once said, "As a poet, you'd make a good race driver." And she didn't mean this thing in New Orleans.

Heard from Jory couple of weeks back. Things are bad with him, but wives and babies meant he wanted too MUCH at once.

Tristan: presumably Wagner's opera *Tristan und Isolde*.

Glad Pan is back, sure. But... yes, I hear him on my radio now: the mosquito dance. Can you imagine the m's dancing to Pan's pipes, buggering each other?

Tell your 2 husbands to get drunk together and then they will either love you equally afterwards or kill each other. Hoy! I'm going.

lov,
                  Buk

15/dec/60   7/35 a.m. thurs./
s.m. lee   pobx 46   san gregorio calif

buk/ am using old type[writer]/ excuse got no time to set up new one just for one letter but must tell you... last night as it began to rain & was delightful I walked down the path to the sacred enclosure... out in the Larches of Paradise... but they are really firs of some kind... I was chanting to the great fields full of high bush... "Pan get yr goat's ass in out of this rain... take refuge in my temenos Pan... take refuge in the temple tonite..." & as the dark was on us... I get a bit hincty as Stanley Gould calls it & don't like being out in the gloaming... so in I went... & about dawn this day with Gib warmin' up the olds convertible... I went down the path to my temple & I was singing... "I am going to the Temple where the Great God Pan took refuge last night" and I knew there wd be a 'sign' but I didn't really know—and I froze in the 'doorway' where Tree hath a long green finger which touches me... as I enter... on the forehead & dew is my holy water... my altar is an old kitchen table with a chinese covering on it of black & orange silk with tassles with gold/orange beads & silk dangling from each corner & on it is a bottle of flowers & little egyptian seals one made in clay from Gib's Pharaoh ring with a seal saying "The Sun knows I speak

---

Larches of Paradise: from Canto 94: "...walking here under the larches of Paradise" (658)

temenos: a sacred enclosure; the term is used in Canto 97 (701)

Stanley Gould: well-known Greenwich Village character in the 1940s.

the truth" or somesuch... & an olifant that I haven't sent to Mr. Lowercase yet & my bottle of distill'd sea water & some home made candles in old artichoke heart jars... now filled with wax & a jar that formerly held some scotch lime jelly now holding some of the vine flowers & narcisses & pine & spruce branches... the altar had been moved—it had been up against the thick tree trunk & now was moved & the flowers knocked over & the candles knocked over... one candle is the red altar catholic kind... It cdn't be the wind... because I have some chinese & some indian beads of many colours hanging from slender tree branchlets & any wind that wd be able to move the altar wd have blown off the beads... & I have a wee ivory quan yin about one inch long snug'd in the fork of the tree over the altar as Quan Yin is one of the many names of my Goddess.

Pan moved my altar—nothing was missing or broken... it was if a large goat or animal or man had climbed up the cliff & entered from beneath that branch which makes a 'wall' on the cliff side & moved the altar by his weight... I was mad & called Gib to see it & I told Pan wherever he is... "you did NOT have to be such a goat damm it..." and Gib just left... a while back when I started this... & as soon as he was gone down the highway... I hear that sweet seductive melodic note of music... sometimes it is 2 or 3 notes but today... this morning I heard it 3 times... one note each time... coaxing luring & plaintive & rather like a musical apology... of course a deer cd have moved it or a wild cat seeking shelter... from the rain... but only Pan can make those musical sounds that are sweet to the ear as prim roses to the eye or that tea of honey hot water & peppermint leaves or drops... is the taste buds... It is so sweet when heard that one feels the belly satisfied... as in eating but to tell the truth man I don't wanna SEE him/ iz enough to hear him & know he is on the premises/

I got so sick of them bleeding heart white apologists saying "white" soupremecy that I finally wrote a letter to der hediterrr & told him that one is NOT "white"   one IS WHITE & not about to feel any guilt for it/ the chap had said that we "white" soupremecists always feel soupreme because of something

---

Mr. Lowercase: e. e. cummings, whom SM knew in NYC.
Quan Yin: the Chinese goddess of mercy, also spelled Kwan-yin and Kuanon in the *Cantos*; SM did a painting of her.

another white had done... & had no accomplishments of our own... like an ostrich looking at an eagle & saying "we birds sure can fly"   so one said that it was not of the real world... not natural; moral; or ethical to make it legal to banish the song of the nightingale because the crows caw & hawk/ and one said a bit more... I am bored with it/ MOCKING MY OWN SKIN OR MY MAW OR PAW OR MY TRADITIONS & MY CULTURE OR MY RACE... DEGRADING MY RACE OR MY SEX OR COLOUR OR GOD AINT GONNA ELEVATE THE NIGGERS OR US EITHER... I told the editor to advise his niggers to read frobanius...

my good white men are driven into drink from the sheer lack of adventure & boredom of a land run by the product of the race sewer/ I know from living intimately with almost each race in the world... One has husbands all over the world's races... and no freedom of any sort was possible until I let my temper out... & they got to love my wildness & if one said: "my what a noble cat" my chinese father in law made my life miserable that day for using a tabu word... when we are all alike... now he loves me & I can talk straight but it took 6 years/ I am not going to feel prejudiced or guilty—I am not going to allow any man to mock me... I am making my old age secure/ these animals if allowed to mock now... will be after my life when I'd be too old to fight back

so my dear Buk you may expect yr friend to be scandalised as Our Invisible Mawsters aint gonna like a slave behaving like a royal person... I have defended all my husbands of each nationality/religion/colour & race of this world... now I shall defend my self/ my husbands all being cowards who fear the censure of any other male/ I am now no longer "white" I am WHITE goddamit this snivilin sniveling over colour sickening... like a male with his dick out moaning "oh mine is too little... what'll I do... so you cut some of yrs off... willya like a good brother?" or chicks without tits a-moan... it is unnatural not to hate wot you get born until finally you learn to love it...

now to coffee/ & love from

Sheri

---

frobanius: Leo Frobenius (1873–1938), German ethnologist whose theories on civilization greatly influenced Pound.

121

buk you got to know this: that fkn cat has caught onto me being an animal/ the stinking little bastard... no wonder we went inside to shit! he has dug po li & me functioning out doors same's he does & he digs we eat meat/ now that prick actually fights with me if I am sitting on the coch coach couch... goddammit the thing with a back & pillows/ Al the cat hops up to sniff wot I got & if it smells good he tries to grab a snoutfull & when I rap his little wet nose he claws out & starts doing battle over the food/ I threw him OUT goddammit I aint gonna fight the communists the fascists the male chovanists the social stigma against cunt & the animal population also! that'd be two straws too many

he tries to sleep in po li's sleeping bag & out in the altar bed... he raises hell to get me to bed down with him... it is horrible to have a cat in love with me & realising that I am also an animal/ no wonder our ancestors came in out of the rain to function/ or we wd lose our edge over the animal world FAST/ he has no respect for my human status/

it is an awful feeling—the animals always do that to me/ or maybe I am closer to them than the rest of us/ oye godttt wotttt/ when po li was inside ah stoods befo' der merrrrror duckder & it wuz not empty no it warnt/ naked was the blue jay & she began to wobble like she saw the arab lady do practising for when she had her po li returned... & the infant cat lying on the bed/ the awful shock of horror... looking down that little punk... he was lying on his furry back with all his legs apart and his 6 week old pink erection/ that sort of thing makes me feel totally helpless/ makes me wonder just who that cat really is/ he sure knew what to do about a naked female doing an arab dance before the mirror/

buk I am losing my humanity out here... I am returning to the animals... speak a civilised word duckder & fast as I am going down under... next thing that arrives in the mail will have horns & a tail & hooves... I told Po Li "man if you hear me sqwuakkkk out in that temple... come out fast... as Pan has been known to love the nymphs when he grabs them"... & Po Li said most seriously "yeah, but I don't know how fast he fucks... I might be too late no matter how fast I came"... in other words he cdn't be bothered to move if it didn't really matter/ that man is plumb lazy

now I go/ I am going to bite a hunk off Laughlin today because when EZRA SAID she's painting genius laughlin came in his drawers... but when ezra fell silent because he is now salty that she does the a & p instead of painting... "her job"... now L/ is silent as a corpse & I finally got a point to grab him on/ a dumb woodcut by a german boy that I wont knock down... BUT WHY IMPORT ART WHEN WE GOT OUR OWN?????? So one can kick his ass for that & one is gonna do it right now...

and so I go/ listen what happened to good mr. webb? "23 year old maniac" "torn" what do you mean? is it this race war? It is getting violent/ in d.c. one who smiles upon everybody with equal affection almost caused a riot in the drug store... because she smiled at the very black girl & the feeling was... "who the fuck do you think you are able to afford to smile at me when I don't feel like smiling" it was so shocking I just got up & walked OUT but first I made a hex face/

it is the coal black people in ugly anger & they force the lighter people into it but the lighter people usually have white wives & my god what a mess/ a horrible mess which nevertheless cannot be outside of nature... something works thru us to effect a change/ something is rotten or fungus don't grow on it/ & fermentation don't take place/ I make my peace with my gods & am ready to die at each dawn or dusk & aint gonno submit to any horseshit/ Only another painting genius will know that I haven't finished my work to my heart's content as I work "beginning with the eyes & finished at every brush stroke" and out here in San Francisco... one day walking down calif. street in a yellow coat costing 3 bucks at a junk store & my bl. slacks from the dime store... but the cultured intelligence of my bones... & soft aristocratic hair from some ancestor... being a yankee mongrel nevertheless... and sort of jauntin' down the street... the black man in his flash of hate for me... on calif. streeet... at noon & crowded with white slaves... he began to shout at me words more/less meaning: "oh you little society doll... you introduced bitch" one totally ignored it & then one got on the same bus with him & he'd calm'd down & he began

---

Laughlin: James Laughlin (1914–1999), founder of New Directions and Pound's publisher.

to see the grease spots on my clothes & got a funny look to him... when he saw holes in my toes etc/ but his first impression was of vitddd soupremecy/ they are worked up to a froth & it is not a nice situation & something will shortly be done about it as when it hits our innocents at broad noon on a crowded street... it aint far off from the blow-up & oh my god... they will be so sorry for we are not the enemy... may the Gods protect our Good Clarence Major/ he is blessed—

the communists are forcing the race war to "divide" us & weaken us/ what the divine intelligence is doing I can but surmise & look to the real world/

Nature does not begin the process of decay until the tree has fallen/ Nature does not allow any order to stand that is UNnatural—the process is that the nordic or aryan appears with the Law & sets up shop/ then the softer soul'd whites show & intermarry with the delicious coloured races or sometimes a renegade nord will take a lady of colour to bed but not to wife & then the Spies of Godtttt show up because the fruit is ripe to rot then & we get the pressure of rot which makes us blow up & the nordic seed of the Law petrifies in the memory cells of the new Indians/ & we have culture preserved until a new batch of sperms arrive capable of continuing culch... The East Indians have perfectly petrified Aryan Law but they are not capable of furthering it—they preserve the seed & it will bloom again/

The question one put to the Gods/ why does all of it have to be individual? why suffering? each one hath a self & each little crab that must die knows he is dying/ that disturbs me. if it must rise & fall why must it suffer? Why is it so innocent?

re-reading/ i mean not one of those earless & sightless white slaves even heard the black man scream/ they are totally de-sensitised/ we are all alone in this concentration camp & that is what history always sez about us/ thank god we keep the traditions.

and the "doers of good are safe anywhere on earth whether they ship or swim" so hail to thee Fellow Swimmer maybe we get to Ship yet Baby/ now ah goes to work chewin' on Laughlin/ not too hard... the poor bastard was born rich & that is a tough rap to beat/

love/

Sheri

NO bukowski you do NOT "know my mind" & yes bukowski I
DID know why you wanted to have such titles...

It is part of this brain washed age for such terms from the
underworld that was "a joke to Shakespear" to have become
sentimentalised & now words of "affection"... because the race
that maketh the whore/the gambler/& pimp & gives birth to
imbeciles & advertises them in the newspapers to raise cash...
breeds them with a purpose—to fleece th' sheep... is running
the popular state... SO I AM PERFECTLY AWARE THAT YOU'D
MEAN THEM AS WOIDTTTS OB AFFECTION... & I didn't MEAN
that/ what I aimed at is this:

It is the tail end of the late late victorian period & I simply
wanted you to move OUT of that category & move into the NEW
WORLD that cant be yawned away/ for xts sakes bukowski how
many books of poetry do you imagine have passed moi eyes? &
HOW many sentimental-shock-type titles do you think exist? It
will be that the scholars of the future will reject any book with
Little Eva & Uncle Tom (now mated) titles. Alls I wanted was
for you to graduate from the Foist Gradttt & have it be seen in
yr titles/ Buk really/ really... really you "wanted to give them
trinkets... those are my poems" oye/ the Jews will larffff at
youse/ they AINT sentimental no they AINT/ They may be passionate but they aint sentimental/ and it is downright pitiful to
write poetry & lay it at the feet of whores etc/

Let them be "having a goodtttt time"/ that is why mice *are*
mice & we are people/ because we have eternity/ but HOW do
you really know WOT der mouze is thinking now buk???? (in the
box)

no I mean WHERE this "wise" ending to words started??
I can understand wot it signifies but what's its history &
traditions?

good to hear that you'll be read back east as it cant hurt
them to read you re: *Lit Artpress* altho one don't quite like its
title/

I never die Buk because I am Spirit acting thru Matter or
that Energy made by Prana/ I am of the Crystal beyond Prana

Prana: Sanskrit: "absolute energy," or the life force. Cf. Canto 94:
"Above prana, the light" (654).

& I never die; just have many names/ and Death's a chance to catch a catnap badly needed/ the pattern is eternal & the form/ don't worry about death because it is as sweet as a good sleep/

thankyew dear buk/ I NEEDED 3 husbands/ and splendid/ UNjealous—& spiritual/ I am only mo' scared than the rest & needs lottsa handholdin' in this dark/

Well am not aware of "absorbing" you but am aware of trying to show you what is clear to me & that's all one can do from the outside is say "my brother tree that branch wobbles" to use Ezra's word/

I know that Jory thinks it don't matter & he gets sucked into the down dragging back wash/ & he did want too much at once/ Ezra said: "I waited until I was 40 before I began to breed" because McNaughton was breeding at 21 & still trying to write & study/

Have heard that Jory is a typical street corner male to his pitiful ol' lady caught in the female trap of "how shall I do this dear?" Weak & fluttery & scared & Jory more so/ scowlin' & snarlin' "do it any... blather dather way you wanna" some one who'd been there & realised they were both so weak... sad/

my dear sweet "husbands"... they don't drink... either one/ they just love SheriBoots & their mammas/

re: "first carefully sifting out wot u consider the poisons":
"for know, my heart stands armed in my ear,
And will not let a false sound enter there;"

Venus & Adonis/Shakespear

It wd seem that Shak/ familiar with same experience/ Ernie located the quote for me as is buried near last third of V & A/

And beware when you speak the name of PAN because he hath a sense of humour that surpasses even the cruelty of mankind/ and gotto print more A & P/

love/

Sheri

yr titles represent a STYLE (from late vic. period) & not a FORM!!!!!!

McNaughton: William MacNaughton, a companion of SM's at St. Elizabeths and later a Pound scholar.

126

Dec. 21, 1960

Hoy, Shed!

am up in muck to menials, this will be short one (didn't turn out so short—C.B. [*handwritten note*]) to let u know I am still Buk.

If Pan moved yr altar, I'd suggest u leave it there even if location appears out of bounds. Coulda been bum or child or ghost or drunk, but in this form too—Pan. If you see it that way, and if you see it that way, it is. We half form our god-things and our god-things half form us, and that is why it is difficult to meet, because we are in half-light and each form often almost always going in wrong direction; here you have the darkness. But when the halves meet head on—which seldom happens—then you have the vision and the miracle. Of course, we have false gods too and false god-seekers. An intoxicated young man went leaping down Hollywood Blvd. the other night playing a fife or somesuch and the fuzz threw him in. In this case, young man claimed he was Pan. Probably not so. I think I have been close enough to Pan to realize he would not dance down Hollywood Blvd. Young man was more likely a fairy an' I don't mean a water-sprite.

Card from Linick telling me some of my stuff will be read on radio. If they think they can ruin my fine villiany (spell?) with a few megocycles, they are pissing against the wrong tree.

I'm not even gona listen. We've got to watch ourselves lest we become something else. The racetracks are bad enough, and it is only that I seek the freedome of leisure that I go there—to make enough to quit everything and flop down next to the cow and sun myself without worrying about the rent. And so it is we become trapped. I lose leisure seeking leisure, and it was Jeffers who said something like, There are traps for all men, and they say that God was trapped when he walked upon the earth. Jesus got hung, in the modern vernacular. And I am hanging myself everyday, but I am doing it alone and through action, and

---

Linick: unidentified.

Jeffers ... traps for all men ...walked upon the earth: the concluding lines of "Shine, Perishing Republic" (1925): "There is the trap that catches noblest spirits, that caught—they say—God, when he walked on earth." (Jeffers' trap is immoderate love of mankind.)

perhaps yet I will sneak through. But God, we lose a lot. Each day they cut off a chunk and you walk there with another piece missing, and pretty soon you're dead like the rest of them, walking around dead and around and over the dead and through the dead and you walk and talk and write letters, but it's just what's left of a bad machine. Yet, I am aware of my dying and will not be fooled by the process.

You are not dying, Shed; you are a perfect example of vibration with the Life-force, and you will always be beautiful and alive no matter how old you get—although (I am rushing here) beautiful is a lousy word, it, ya, has been used so much it is no longer beautiful but simply a poor vanilla flavor that dissolves with the spit of the tongue—a patooiee! I will not defile you with it, but do not have another word in my pocket right now.

I've been going too strong. The mind, ya, is muddled, uooah so muddy!... all the people feet and faces tramping right on thro... The sing is, hell, I mean, the sign is on with me to build more than bleached bones of rat-gnaw for the casket, if I ever geta casket, nobody knows me, except a poor ol woman of fifty; I've orphaned myself out, but we Chermans don't CRY, Shed, tho we may growl and strut, we don't cry...

Oye, I think on the WHITE SUPER, whozit, the lover of ariel Brahms, or what—San Diego joe whts his??? Oh, ya, Payne, think he's gona blast you for letter you wrote, printing letter, and then blasting. But if I know Payne—he will hang himself because his stuff comes from the OUTSIDE and he is posing as an EDUCATED MACPISS CAT and all he will say is what HE THINKS IS CORRECT THROUGH THE EYES OF OTHERS AND THROUGH TRADITION... You may sometimes be wrong, Shed, but your kinda wrong and Ezra's kinda wrong and Jeffers kinda wrong (Do!!! Read *Tamar, Roan Stallion, Such Consoules* misspelled! *as You Have Given Me*) I take rather than the practical rightness of the prigs. Don't you worry what he scribbles bout you, the 6 or 7 living people in the world will know what the hell.

Do especially read *Roan Stallion*. Robinson Jeffers. If you haven't. Please do this for me. It's the only thing I have ever asked of you! Isn't it?

Such Consoules: *Such Counsels You Gave to Me*, a 1937 collection of Jeffers' verse.

Shit, I havnt slept for 3 days or nights, too many things to do, if this letta sounds thro slanted lite, please understand. An I'm not runnin' around byin Xmas commerce either, don't you think so now, and I noo yuu woodn't Sheri, mah Goddess hoo has repoaced and replaced the word Buuty...

Don't allow any man to mock you. I would never. I do not fight you. You fight me, correct me. It is well.

On your cat—toss his ass out. The Arabians admire the cat, look down upon women and dogs because they show affection and affection is, some think, a sign of weakness. Well, perhaps it is. I do not show too much. My wives and girlfriends complain because I hold my soul separately—and give my body, perhaps, puritanically; but back to the g.d. cat. A cat is only ITSELF. That is why when it gets the poor bird it won't let go. This is a representative of the strong forces of LIFE that won't let go. The cat is the beutiful devil. And here we can use the word, even without the "a". You can get some dogs and some women to let go—and they'll let go. But a cat, hell, the lightning sides of houses will long be done overt and he will still be purring in his milk. A cat will eat you when you die. No matter how long you've lived together. There was an old man once who died alone like Buk, and he dina have a woman but he hadda cat and he died it alone and it was days days days poor ol man began to stink, it not his fault, but the earth revolving and removing remains of what shoulda been buried by living earth spirits, and cat smelled good, to him, stink of dead meat, and when they found them the cat was clawing up from the floor, stuck to the bottom of the mattress like a rock, eating through the mattress, hung like a clam on the rock, and they couldn't club him off or pry him off or burn him off, and they just hadda throw him off and away with the damned mattress. I suppose one moonlight nite through the dew of moon and leaves cooling the smell of death, he let go.

There are no spirits or gods in a cat, don't look for them, Shed. A cat is the picture of the eternal machinery, like the sea. You don't pet the sea because it's pretty but you pet a cat— why?—ONLY BECAUSE HE'LL LET YOU. And a cat never knows fear—finally—he only winds up into the spring of the sea and the rock, and even in a death-fight he does not think of anything except the majesty of darkness.

yr Po Li Gib made me laugh talking about how Pan might

129

fuck fast. I rather imagine Pan would. And then, Shed... maybe you wouldn't wanna be interupted. Two r's. Pan might be the best. I am not mocking you but talking straight. That's why I tell you to read *Roan Stallion*, if you haven't. The horse, he was more earth and God and real-eye thing than the pimple-paper man, and she took the horse and the horse killed him. It is a good long poem, and Jeffers meant it. And I say, I have seen many horses more noble than Man, n I say, by god, if a goat-poet incarnation grabs a holt a u, it's best Po Li or Lie Po or anybuddy, take his time getting there.

Don't 8-ball know Laughlin, except one used to put out a new *Directions* or something but don't know woman.

Your good sister Webb—answering?—got a bad letter from 23 year old poet telling him off. Webb sent thing to me. Said who is this fucker, etc? I tried to buck Webb up by telling him in part where this fucker could possibly be wrong; but in process, I told Webb, it wasn't good policy to print Webb Jr.

Webb usta send a postcard a week. Since I told him about son, couple weeks back... silence from Webb. And so, the Good Mr. Webb and I have broken off, it seems. So?

I understand Gramps wanting you to paint insteada AP. But Gramps shd understand if you A and P, you A and P, n when you're gona paint your gona paint, and it isn't MEASURING THE VALUE OF THINGS or labeling it WURK!! that's gona help anybody...

Still, the ole cob, you've got to listen to him: he's always followed through to a lone line all he's believed, as far as I know, and how many of us can do that? I mean, with bear-cat consistency. And yet it's seeing through this bear-cat constny that limits his clear vision of other life-forms.

But o, look, Shed, I'm going to lay down for 20 minutes. I'j jhesus ahm almost dead.

So then.

Love,
Buk

Webb ... telling him off: see CB's letter of 9 January 1961, below.

28/ dec/ 60   pobx 46 san gregorio calif

dear buk/
    yr beautiful xmas card/ you krcoutheads are still superior/
best taste... very good idea/ how irreligious I am/ I moved the
altar back/ impossible for any other agent/ no children here at
that time/ no drunks on grounds no access/ we are on a 40 ft.
cliff & the trees are on the edge of it... the small clump form a
room & one had furniture given to one & put it all outside—&
then the altar idea became clear... it is on the edge dropping
down 40 feet with no path cleared—impossible in the dark to
climb up but maybe Ernie cd—no I think it is steep at that
place where something came up the cliffside & entered the altar
under the tree branch where one can look out & see the ocean/
it had pushed the altar aside/ "the wind" said Gib but a wind
strong enough to push a kitchen table away from a tree trunk
almost as wide as the table therefore protecting it from the
wind... wd also have blown off the small sacred objects on the
table & the narcissis in the glass... everything had been over-
turned by the violence but nothing was blown off... Yes I know
there are presences out there because of the way the cat goes
crazy & one considered that the cat in a crazy fit... but he'd
have to be a jumpin' son of a bitch to've done it/ I mean the
only way wd be for him to jump up under it & fall sideways
maybe... our house is the last one & nobody can pass us to go
out to my 'larches of Paradise'—it is 10 acres of wilderness
impossible to cross 6 ft underbrush & tangle where rabbits live
& on the other side is cliff—the brush goes all the way down to
the road... i hear that melodic whistle sometimes at night—
sometimes in the day. ernie is afraid of it/ me too.
    I oughtahave moved it/ I don't know Buk/ if Pan's back—
he'd be able to take hold of a hollywood fairy psyche/ some of
those hollywood people are of a high order of sensitivity—it is
just that they are decayed and corrupt of spirit/ they'd pick it up
from the aether... I count it a peculiar co-incidence
    When Ezra was in his room writing: "you are tender as a
marshmallow my love" I was in a car with David Treat & I

"*you are ... my love*": from Canto 93 (652).
David Treat: a member of the Air Force Reserve Band that occasionally
played for the inmates at St. Elizabeths. He attended Catholic University in
the early 1950s with Gilbert Lee and told him that a former *Vogue* model
was keeping Pound company and that Gilbert should check her out.

131

suddenly touched my soft bozum—being so intelligent—I've never done it before in my life—the only time I realise I'm a female is when I'm impassionately in love... it was a strange thing for me to do & I said "why I'm tender as a marshmallow"... was of course astounded when Ezra handed me my poem with those words in/ It happened several times but I recall that clearest—have memory of it happening sev. times but wd have to re-check the correspondence of that time (1954)

one has loved Pan since one was a skinny rip lying back by the bay at home—in the grass & soaking up sun & pretending he was there some where—it is the sound of his name & the sight of it that moves me to love... cant explain/ it happened with Isis spot'd as a kid in a newspaper/ When I grew up I found out who they were—the kid fell in love with the symbol/ that is its purpose—to be powerful enough to inspire love at first sight that it forever live/ mayhap I called Pan into being by my love & that ritual with Ernie was Pan—a r a m..a ram.a r a m.a.r a m.IK (Ernie said his Uncle said that on top of a mt. while he kept turning & looking) & Ernie was Pan—

I am aware that Ernie is sacred—he found his way to me by a "spider's thread" as Ez said I got to him—not knowing who he was or why he was there—

yes I know we must watch ourselves but that don't mean you cant change yr mind state does it? I am the same Sheri I was always but if you read the letters & works & art b.e. Before Ez & After Ez man! the change—he tuned me in clear & LOUD but it's still me/

you shd listen to yr own work being broadcast/ my word buk how can you be such a prot? humility means remaining human while you rise to the top but it dont mean not knowing where you are or why/ you cd at least tell ME when to list. dickhead! I'm sure you'd listen to any S.M. they'd dast broadcast/

I yaint "beautiful" Buk—but I set like I am because beauty is a habit/ & Ezra's bootin' me outta the nest like that sure woke me up... I began to see that everything I'd done to him was being done by my contemporaries & they too thought of it as being their real me... it is the wailing of the yankee pupKitten & it is not the individual—of course we flavour our meeEEWW... it is a   me — ow

So from understanding compassion of what it might cost

132

them because of what it had cost me—my castle in italy—& my art education because I see that they (the elders) wont let any me -owWWWWwers into the Temple I let go of her & seek to reach what I see is good out here/ darling there aint one night or morning that I don't wail & moan & whine but I wont record it/ I am trying to set a model of something that I know if followed will lead my pretty ones to Paradise... but I doubt if I'll ever get back in/ my manners were too local/ a hick/ a provincial/ oh god did god rub my nose in shit in san francis-co—each & all presented themselves & did precisely before my disbelieving eyes—what I'd done to Ezra/ dumb as a worm I was/ I am only a perfect example of a good sister—that's what a good sister wd go home & do if she flop'd & saw why/ I have since discovered that I myself dismiss some very good people because their manners are too bad to allow them in my par-adise/

I return from Paradise—had I gone to Italy with Ezra we'd have had some Paradisial Art... as it is we shall have a Paradisial Spirit

I'm so mean & ornery I decided that to hell with them—I'm just gonna stay here in Hell & make my own paradise out of it... sort of like a weight to balance with theirs in europe

that's marvelous to be a Cherman all the way through—to have roots... it's sort of sad to be a halfbreed but we are here & one will teach them how... I wish I were pure gaelic... but then I'd be all different & they are dumb as hell & cat'lik as a hea-then

I know old Educated McPiss Cat (denkyew duckder dotz goooddddddtttt) will hang himself—he is not aiming at the "most intelligent mind you know" "write for it"—his audience is local & in his mind he aims to them—by now my audience is international & not local & I know the difference... Dear Miles is a provincial hick right now but he has some good stuffing in him

All right soon's I finish this damm'd A & P will peruse *Roan Stallion* altho' in NYC one almost got thru a Jeffers book but I like Ezra right now/ Ezra lives in the only world worth anything

---

my castle in italy: when Pound was released from St. Elizabeths he left the U.S. and settled in his son-in-law's castle in Italy.

sad to be a halfbreed: SM was of Irish-Italian ancestry.

to me: the world of Merlin & Morgana le Fey... the magic world... where the rest see an old leather jacket but Ezra sees "the deer skin—sheri's to sit on the deer skin" and Jeffers is in the bowels of life & so on but I'll go to him again... He was sick when one was passing through or one wd have paid homage to him & one knew he was 'dead' by the tone of voice of the female/ Ezra wdn't have anybody like that for too long... too active a mind—too curious... if that'd been a worldly figure instead of a local figure he'd have been in control sick or well/ this was a tone of voice that my mother's aunt wd take if she ever thought I had any social security value... it was sad to me & I gave Jeffers up/ wdn't write to him/

Then he wrote: "I made my rock you go make yours" or more/less too fkn materialistic I thought/ I actually experienced a feeling of pain when I read that in Tommie Yee's studio—the prick might at least have included some ground plans of his rock for us... Ezra did—Ezra gave us his time/ his life/ his love/ his heart/ his soul/ his magic... plus any known formula... he is my baby—I don't care how mean he is... I wont fail him—it was necessary to hurt me almost to death—to make me want to do something... you've no idea how day-dreamy I am Buk & don't give a damm for anything... just dreamily... floating... "cloud mind'd" he said

I'm astonished that love of my contemporaries cd ever make me this practical—no idea HOW I get anything done... you see... I like to sit & talk to you & forget everything but somehow I keep going on with the job

Darling thank you—for replacing the word beauty... it did fall off the stage for a while—when those clouds of demons rose up from hell... now I recall Who WAS wearing it dammit—I guess the Elizabethans—no it was Whistler & Yeats—then Ez taking embrage with the demons knocked beauty off the stage

We do need beauty—I remember one brain-washer in NYC saying slyly "but don't you think Botticelli is TOO beautiful?" god's damm on him... If I'd have known I'd have said: "I don't think Botticelli is TOO beautiful but I do think the International AND organised bankers are too powerful" or "too rich" or "too much in control of our finances..." ha! that'd floor'd him... but

---

Tommie Yee: a fashion photographer prominent in New York City in the 1940s.

ignorance is such a handicap—maybe I'll run into another "too beautiful" chappies again/

Well I got to "fight" you because it is necessary Buk... Do you want me to let you go out in public with yr ass out? I got to fight/ males are so stupid they actually think they can learn from other males... oyyyyyyeeee I saw wot Ezra does to other males—they are his thanes once he gets them—he is THE MALE OF THE SCENE & he wont let nobody near him who wants to be the other male/ noppppppppe... It is the female alone who will aide you up... or the male help the female... I am intelligent because of the intelligent men in my life/ before that it was Pure Love & Peace On Earth & Goottt Willl to All with enough shyness to prevent her from getting murdered & so on/

No Buk—cats are NOT independent... they are worse than dogs & the thing is they are sneakier & more persistent... I did toss his ass out/ he's a good guy as a cat & obeys orders but he does persist & persist—still he recognises my FINAL tone & hops off my bed/desk or wotever/

Buk please don't tell me any horror stories about cats & corpses & so on—to me it is natural enough but I do not care to focus upon it/

Oh Buk/ we do "pet the sea" & dear old Al has a distinct soul & so does Sea... by soul one means the Intelligence at Work/

I doubt if I'd prefer a hoss to a man—because of communication thing & Jeffers just don't know the Perfect Female... she dies without a male to love like a little fern she curls up inside herself—& the joint cd be jumpin' & she'd dream on/ and Pan's not an animal Buk he's a deity! No lamb there is no more noble animal than man/ he is the only one who'd ever share anything—the rest of them incline towards hogery & what's left goes to whoever... it wd be awful/ this fkn cat I see it in him— one observes it in low character'd humans but for nobility we must look to man/ not that the animals do not have nobility/ but not with food or water then's when you see they are animals/

Oh let Webb print his son's work—why not? wait until you see new A & P... its policy is its entirely own my lamb/ But because one has a certain scandalous name she knows we'll be read & Ezra's mailing list considers her a Light... but my dear Buk/ we aint got nobody else's policy/ 's all right to print Webb jr/

Who is this 23 yr old ear chewer? was it intelligent? can it be elevated? To be spittin' fire at the Elders at 23 shows a mind at work... & to spit at Webb instead of *The New Yorker* or *Nation* shows a selective mind at work... may be dedicated... not ambitious... who was it?

he'll write I guess he's busy with type set/

Gramps don't know that in a way I am painting—I'm studying those on the wall for their final solution... It takes 5 years sometimes of study to know what subtle touch will complete the work & I must know every colour in the thing—and shape... as they stand they're done but I know they aint yet complete.

And one is drawing Ernie all the time—it is just that one wants to do The Psyche for Ernie's old age—when I'm not here & he is an old man I want him to go see my Psyche at Yale in the collection & I want to torment his mind with my memory— a fiendish female... you see there is such a mess all over the floor of paper that one wd need another house to paint in... I got to set up the easel/ & buy a small table to move about & paint as I eat—when I pass the table! only way to do it... the mirror is set up for beginning the Psyche/ she has got to be so beautiful that memories will pierce him—like waves & waves of thorns... made of rose petals... I love that dear child... he is the only Knight that saw it is necessary for a male voice to sass Ezra for causing me to 'lose face'... isn't that curious—that Ezra has one handle he can be caught by... he shd never have allowed his nervous system to take over in the presence of true art; most especially in an age when his race is being destroyed because it lacks art of sacred nature—It wd be like God tossin' out Lord Jesus because he'd had a vinegar smell to him & was a bit shook up

Ezra had a stand of love art & artists... I am not a female—I am an artist/ my tao is art/ it shows in the cooking even... I see it... So the Gods sent a son of the Jews to love Ezra's Pound-Kake & he alone was sent to sass Ez & grab him by his one handle... and she was penniless & female... she had her name smeared on account of ez/ there were such circumstances as to make it an international scandal for all time... and as usual only

---

The Psyche: apparently a new version of an older painting of hers.

the Jews knew enough to DO... how Ernie found me is a miracle & it is curious that his initials are E. P. Walker... his way of fighting aint my way & I see his pattern is sly & stealthy/ toward Ez—"another poet" (in new A & P cover you'll see) but Ezra will receive it like a Florentine dagger... he will know the thrust & he'll see straight off the pattern of the Jew & he'll have to think of something to DO instead of going silent like that on us/ & helping the English set/ Ernie is a man that the Gods gave me just before my wings fell into the mud—Gib's it because his manners are quiet & good but he's cruel just like his ancestors & when I lost face... he did too with his friends & he'd rather I'd died...

Ernie knows my value/ he saw it immediately—not just worldly value but he saw HER just the same way Ezra did... saw clear into the psyche... & I trust him because I trust myself & know my head is clear... but to me it sure is a strange tale... that a Jew will come bearing Ezra's magic initials & joust King Arthur... It provides me with new insight... a noble Jew—as noble as Ezra—that's going to be something & this kid has an intelligence & a profound understanding of humanity... he aint a flash... He can draw & he can write... I am not saying he is another Ezra Pound but all the material necessary for a King are present in Ernie/

And he is so pretty—that one did not realise he was not a german boy... it wasn't until I gave a race speech that'd fired a german (a test of my own making) & Ernie fled & left me with Dr. Einstein or Pavlov & then I knew for certain that I was in contact with a foreign spirit but by then I knew him as my own brother & part of my fate life... preceeding my speech was a hair cut which brought out something that I knew was not nordic or aryan/ it was something different—he is pure bred for living in this nordic (once) land—but the full fantastic out-rageous intelligence of the Jews is packed solid in his beautiful head/ I do believe that Ernie cd outsmart anybody in this world except a Seeressa/ she who can see Gawd—first one went to NYC & the communists/ then to d.c. & the fascists... then one got smeared as a antisemite—then out here to the anarchists & then Ernie gets here to joust with Ezra/ it has the look of a plan to me... all that cdn't be an accident—I know from experience everybody's political life & their romantic life—those who matter one means/ it is like being in a dark room filled with broken glass & knowing where each hunk of glass is

Ernie is the Son of Godtttt... he will save us... he is absolutely the first of all my fellowcountry men who has on his own taken Ezra to task for what Ezra did to a female Botticelli after Ezra wrote a whole book about how lousy people were to the artist... he committed a crime in his own book and Ernie is a Sacred God who will cause them to regret/

They made his Love lose face & he is like my husband; my son; my brother... he acts from all these positions... yes Po Li is a marvel to let me know him... I think Po Li is relieved to see a male who loves me in truth... there were so many who'd like to say they slept with me... I told all of them "oh just say you did anyhow... everybody else does..." to solve the problem as I don't do anything I don't madly love to do

I love Ezra & I know Ernie wont be-head him—he is just going to put that Florentine dagger in so many times that everybody around Ez will get uneasy that he might get killed—Ernie is a capricorn & he will never give up once he gets a notion/ like me... we must provide that this never happens again to any of us anywhere & Ernie is our Son of God—nobody else wd dare sass Ez for a hunk of silly female... none but this bright shining child

I wonder who wrote my life for me? I think I'll perfume the paint I use for that Psyche so Ernie can smell her as well as see her/ he likes cloves... He gets alcohol & mixes it with oil of cloves & rubs it on me & I smell of cloves like Helen for Ernie & he makes me take a bit & swish it in my mouth & spit it out & I smell of cloves for him—he is the most sensual animal I ever met/ so I'll paint with oil of cloves & pigment/ it cd work/ & it sure will hang on/ & crush cloves to work in any texture effect... let us say flowers... or leaves...

I want to make a Psyche for Ernie that will be a little Botticelli venus... Some of my husbands who travel'd to Italy write & say the resemblance to Bott's Venus & their wife is... breathtaking... so I got the correct equipment to operate

Only true Love can move us to create Art... that other stuff is Self Love & that's a consolation... sort of... I loved Ezra so much I'd even paint for him... and Ernie also... all I want to give us are 2 more... the Pan & the Psyche... that Eros loved...

it is fun sitting here by the south window... the sun hot on my back/ in a sun dress—herman out there rollin' herman the

138

ocean... Every once in a while I lean back & ask Our Sun "what is the secret of this world?" I'd like to know/ he said "tell Buk yr supposta grow"... Is that its meaning & secret?

have a drawing here one did of Ernie/ he looks like Endymion the Gold/ son of the Sun/ soon's foto will mail you... hell that's the hangup with me being a female... otherwise it'd be a broad one wd talk about to you/ sometimes with Ernie/ he will say something & a thought flashes across my mind that the cloak & dagger A.D.L. read my mail & Ernie is here fully aware of each private sentiment/ or he'll use an expression that Ezra made up for the family or one I did/ I tell him but usually not at the moment as I'm too busy trying to fathom just how in the hell did this 19 yr hick kid know *that*! He has no special education but he has a complete Ezra paideuma in him/ do not know HOW it got there—my A.D.L. suspicion is silly of course but if they HAD sent him... that is the way he'd come...

he is a completely destined spirit/ with his life work beginning at 19... and he has Sheri Martinelli for his mistresswife&-mamma/ that aint a handicap... Capricorns love to death—they never forget a kindness or a love

He is terrible too Buk/ my god what a cleverness that never abandons him— example/ I told him that he wasn't a german & I realised it & that he was a Jew & ought to be proud of it... He emphatically denied it—yet all the time he denied he was a Jew he stood in that typical pose with the fingers all held together in a loose point & touching that hollow in the shoulder... His entire physical presence was speaking the truth while his tongue lied... He wont lie—if he cant speak the truth he acts it out... a fantastic intelligence... I trust that I am being still our Sheri in polishing this boy to perfection. I trust I do no wrong or harm... the signs were so strong—that he was to arrive/ and he did... I garrrrs it wuz arfttter dot Pidgeon caught me that Ernie sprung full grown into our life... my divine babe

I can live with him for I always speak the truth & see what he is doing & no bull shit & I love him with every degree of love known to mankind—for his own good & often for his own bad too! I don't think I'm letting a Trojan Hoss into our Temenos—even if the pagans & the Jews go on fighting another 23 thousand yrs—this child shd know us—I don't know who

---

A.D.L.: Anti-Defamation League.

made him afraid to be a Jew but one will restore his pride for him—anything as intelligent as he is shd have no fear/

Ernie will love me all my life the way I love Ezra because he SEES me totally/ He drives me screamingly mad with his Yiddish house manners—I am his mamma I cannot refuse him anything... am I eating a cooky then Baby wants 100 to stuff in his little mouff—am I having eggs & bacon... then Baby wants some... do I have a new book? Baby must have it—Baby must have mamma's Ovid in Latin & baby must have his Cantos with notes like mamma & mamma must prove she loves Baby by following him about constantly & picking up after him—I am beginning to be a Yiddisher Mamma & see into their psyches— also I see why they make their husbands & sons so fat—I discovered it when I contemplated marriage with Ernie & I knew in a flash/ I'd feed him & he gets so fat on what I do feed him without trying to make him fat... but I'd hide that beautiful beauty under fat & only I'd know it was there & it wd always belong to me... so I knew why/ I'd be a typical Jew if I went off with Ernie

Of course one cant do that to him—he is a baby & both Gib & I must help him grow... one must not snatch & grab just because it is a life time dream of a female to be loved as Ezra loved & as Ernie does... They deliberately made it tough for me to succumb to being a real wife to anyone... if I had found Ernie at 19/ you'd have lots of talented kids instead of a Paradisial Spirit that has come to guide you to Paradise... Ernie is my Paradise & so was Ezra... and once this love hits you where you see clear into the other's spirit—no earthly thing matters—it is like a spring of water running through the mind... one don't see age or youth or race or sex... one sees that delectable spirit... that Ezra wrote "delecta..." I can truly write to Ernie... "delecto..." my deliciousness my fun... I am enchanted for sure—spell held—but I don't know why...

I am ridiculously in love with Ernie as Ezra was with me—if he is outside shooting the 22 being beautiful & manly for me to watch him... I take food & feed it to him at intervals... he don't even have to use his hands... mamma feeds him by hand & oh he smiles like a kitten purrs—the cookies my maw sent us for xmas... one stood & fed Ernie the whole box... he is a piggy pig for sure but I think it's adorable... Buk I must be plumb crazy... or madly madly wildly loving of this young Jew who came via the spider webthread path...

140

What an anti-semite! or is it the Gods of the Jews torturing me with Ernie? What can be the meaning of all these strange contradictions? Gilbert gets mad as hell because I feed Ernie because I know the ghetto insecurity & that they are supposed to "eat them out of house & home" & after Ernie leaves this house is bare—if we ran out of food I'd feed Ernie my own self/ I am mad. He'd eat me too with that beautiful self-conscious smile of perfect contentment at having something that belongs to him like that like a mamma— I adore him/ his ways are adorable/ Gib is so sensual himself that it fascinates his bored oriental spirit... & of course one deals no hurt ever—he gets mad if ernie whispers to me too much—ernie likes to whisper like children do to their mammas & Gib don't like that but he endures the hugging & kissing & it rather faintly excites him—I see that... I completely 'spoil' Ernie just like Ezra 'spoiled' me/ he made a brat out of me—he thought I was so damm'd cute & adorable just like I think Ernie is... and I am—& so is Ernie... so are you & so's Gib... we are cute & adorable... that means we are artists... now by this love for Ernie I see how much Ezra loved—and because Ernie is such a pest & brat too... I see why Ezra cd toss BirdLet out of the nest & if one adds Po Li to that... but one is sensible... one hopes—and Ernie is too smart to bring any Suzi Wongs to meet me! I shd have hidden Po' Li but I am not clever only truthful

It is an interesting problem to love 2 male spirits at once... I don't prefer it... I prefer 1 male spirit at a time... one gets more done

We shall see what comes of it all... 20 yrs wd give us enough view... and we'll have our "30 yrs" "I need 30 more years" I need 150 more years to get something done right/

Now so long buk & I'm out to the point for a sun bath/

    Love
        Sheri

●

Suzie Wongs: the 1960 movie *The World of Suzie Wong* concerns a Hong Kong prostitute who falls in love with the artist for whom she poses.

141

• 1 9 6 1 •

Jan 3–61
[*postcard*]

Sheri—
It is naturally the diminishing of a poet when he goes to the essay, critiques and manifestos, as Pound, T.S.E., so forth;— men who broke into being through the poetic word, and troubled for more power, the dominance of power, lost it in laying down the law. It is a natural human frailty, a boil upon Emperor, Kaiser, Poet, traffic cop, house-wife (so forth), all bubbling up out of a natural source into a source of definite form and definite hardness.

...an' now have a spur upon my dmnd heel and can hardly walk, but does not really trouble my drinking. Thank you for *Leoun* but there are some bad lines, and I don't know how Cocteau ever made it, or his cheap movies either: the backs of his couches leaping out on halloween masks with skid-row wires of fancy. I believe Jean read Shakespeare 3 times daily when he wasn't admiring himself in the mirror. (I will write Sunday— some disagreements)

Charles
BUKOWSKI

Leoun ... Cocteau: this long poem, admired by Pound, was first published in 1945 and later appeared (in Alan Neame's English translation) in *Agenda* as the complete contents of its Dec. 1960–Jan. 1961 issue, which CB later comments on (see his letter of "almost December" 1961). Cocteau's film *La Belle et la Bête* (1946) features "couches leaping out on halloween masks" among other effects.

143

dreams of eves and arbors,
Jan. something into '61

Sheri, goddess-thing, what:

Your jumping altar keeps the midnights fine. Why I'll bet even the coffee-beans ha ha in the lowly hair-grass.

My guess is that it's Gib... with carburaters and Ernies bilking and boiling the landscape of his mind. Although Pan might be bothered about something too.

No, I didn't listen to the broadcast because it meant going out to buy an F.M. radio and some lady had just bought me a new A.M., and she howled when I mentioned another radio, and so she wouldn't feel bad, I didn't bother. But I would like an F.M. because of better music and less gnarl, but also if I HAD WRITTEN THE POEMS FOR RADIO (or the manifesto or whatever part they used) I would have been interested, but since it was just the work of climbers, I mean those trying to push poetry out in the open like a streetcar transfer, it didn't matter to me. It was a tape that had been earlier broadcast in New York, and now it's sitting somewhere and everybody's asleep and it still doesn't matter. Very little matters in the broad coarse except what we do or say or think toward ourselves, the "I"—how we treat its calls and how we answer them. Ez wants to ed. the masses. He is right because he is Ez and the Ez says so. I don't care about the masses. I am right because I am Buk, but I would be wrong if I became Ez. This is all basic and simple, but how involved we sometimes get, like an essay in the Kenyon Review, talking large fancy circles, interesting circles, but missing the meat. Enough about the radio. Except there was some editor in N. Yawk who wrote me he was reading something of mine now and then in the Bizzare Cafe and he hoped it was ok and he wd continue to do so unless I sued him or wrote him a nasty letter. I told him, go ahead, I write the poetry and if somebody wants to do something about it or with it, I am not going to hit it over the head with a stick. What I object to is standing there MYSELF and reading my own bilge and waiting for applause or some ass to come up out of the audience, beret and goat, shake my hand and say, "I dig you, dad, from way out." I don't want to rub dicks with the ill; I may be insane, but I am not ill. The blood I spit out is good blood and the beer I drink sets the hills of hell on fire.

And each day I grow some more   like a small cactus
sticking those thorns up out of the dryness.

I once said, If I can live to be 40, I can write something. So
I didn't write for ten years... waiting, and then I began 5 years
early. I think now I must possibly ask for ten more years: I need
to be 50 or 55. I am still not strong; I can feel large gashes of
impossible light, intruding!

Oye, Shere, as I write this, my beer can to my left, sitting in
my old yellow bathrobe, same old thing: hair in my eyes, 4 day
beard, just had 3 scrambled eggs and some rye-krisp and pears,
and I fried the eggs in warm butter like a Van Gogh yellow, and
I put in a PINCH of leaf oregano... oye, those eggs tasted like the
left leg of God roasted at 250 degrees for 18 hours... try it...
LEAF OREGANO, a pinch. Get it at most any market. I bought it
for another purpose that didn't turn out so good: red beans and
2 pounds of handburger (ham, yes) (hamburger) and tomatoes
and onions, celery salt, garlic, and chili peppers. Tasted not bad
but I made too much, lasted too long and I gained 5 pounds
and threw it away.

But what I'm trying to say, she's gone now, but while I was
writing this—I live on the 3rd. floor and from my kitchen table
where I write I see nothing but sunshine and 4 red flats and an
apartment house and a blatch of the Hollywood hills, but as I
write I see things, and there is this girl: they live in the front pink
flat, all women, 3 or 4 or 5 women, no men at all, and a small
dog without sense, and they are Europeons of some sort, Arme-
nian, Rumanian, Polish, some lowly defeated race, but they are
strong because they have not been Americanized, and they are
angry too because there are no men, and they are all beautiful
from the youngest to the oldest because nature and themselves is
keeping them ready in case a man enters. Oye, there is one. 19.
Big, oye, big, strong as a horse with brown hair down to her big
ass. It's Sunday. She empties the trash, back and forth, back and
forth, and they speak, I believe in some Europeon lingo most of
the time; and she is in purple, and outside of a man she desires
nothing, and she feels little pain outside of a belly or a toothache
and she seldom has either, although some day a mailman or a
truckdriver or maybe even a garage mechanic will marry her and
her belly will bloom and breathe with the snake turning into
man, being born, and turning back, spiritually, to the snake. But
now she empties trash. oye, this strong thing in purple. A

church dress. There is a four foot tall fence partially covered with vines. And she's still emptying trash while the rest of the woman-family walks down the sidewalk toward church. So then the oldest one, Europe from way back, speaks the command, a harsh command that cannot be disobeyed, and I interpret it to mean: wtz takin u so fucking long wit da trash? We's going to church. CHURCH! GOD! Idiot, idiot child!

Well, what happens? My purple horse-child drops her wastebasket, puts one hand on top of the fence and *vaults* over, her skirts whipping up to her waist, long new nylons on the miracle of legs the new world will walk on, and all the sunlight and all the plants growing, and the purple, the purple, bunched around her waist, and in front of the little pink flat a bush covered with more orange flowers than leaves.

Old Buk—who like an idiot wants to be older—lifts his beercan and drains it surly to a simple maiden who made his German blood sing.

Sherman wrote: God damn you, god damn you, why in the friggin' hell won't you write? He's gotten a job as a copy boy with the Examiner, I suppose with all the publicity on the ticket mess he got himself into and with his ambition he'll probably *own* the Examiner in ten years. I know Sherman is of your camp, so I will not say too much. I did one time, and I heard about all my "asshole palaces", and again when I said something about Wang, I thought y'd never run out of paper and invective. You protect your fledglings, your nestlings quite well, Sheri, but I'm glad that most of the time we are on opposite camps. I haven't any fledglings, only Buk, and that sloppy drunken cur in his old growling yellow robe is more than I fk can handle.

Now, your Pound and your young Jewish boy, I leave that to you. There are too many things working against each other here, and I think for the first time in a long time you must realize that your inner spirit is bumping heads in many manners and ways, and actually this is not good but sometimes the not-good happens. We are challenged continually along the road and we are forever given one of two (or more) choices. That is why so FEW of us make it.

Examiner: the *San Francisco Examiner*, one of the city's major newspapers.

My guess is that you are making the wrong move. But you are to be forgiven. You are a woman and Pound is far away. I understand his silence. You have broken a tenet. A tenent, with Pound, is not to be broken. Like the Imagists: a set of rules grown out of reason. And I guess H.D. is the last of the Imagists. But H.D. is wrong in holding so close; although originally it was a force, forces grow dull. And perhaps the force of Pound has dulled (a little) within you. And another force is closer to you. And you are a woman.

I leave it to you.

Thank god my crossroads are ok if only that fat lovely simple cow will stop vaulting fences in her Sunday best as I wish for old age so I can see more clearly the word that must be put down.

Oye, I know a coupla nice ladyies who by mee shirts and radios, but***oye.

I think yr Gib, in a sense, very strong, and may well outlast and outthink us all. Tell Gib I say hello, and Walker too. I hate and love you all.

Concerto Grosso of somebody playing. It doent mata.

Oh, these magazine editors think they're all, y know. I wrote a poem called *The Life of Borodin*. And there was a line where I mentioned one of his works: *On the Steppes of Central Asia*. How did the editors change it to read? *In the Steppes of Central Asia*. And I don't even *try*. Who *are* these EDUCATED bastards? And worse yet, I won some kind of Memorial Prize for the poem which was supposed to come as a gift of flowers but came instead as a check for ten dollars. The flowers would have meant more to me, but I figure the editors were crossing the donor, trying to help me, thinking I thought as they did: money was worth more than flowers. So I took the ten and put it on a horse which ran out, but anyhow, I still have borodin and he's ON the steps. Although, I do suppose it comes down to a matter of translation finally and I don't care to argue. Let me say only?: it was a bad horse.

The Life of Borodin: first appeared in *Quicksilver* (Autumn 1958), rpt. in *BW* (19), where CB changed the title back to "On the Steppes...," even though *In the Steppes* is indeed the standard translation of the Russian composer's symphonic piece.

You should have gone to Italy with Ezra. But wasn't there some "ever-present English woman" near-by? Where did I read this? I don' know? I suppose she had money, and Ezra is man enough to love and fox enough to revalue but not discard money, hay?

Let's not worry so much about Miles. Sometimes I have the feeling that he has a gun against your brain? I think, perhaps, that of all the men living upon earth, Payne sees holes in you better than the rest of us. Miles is weaker than you, Sheri, but something in his training aides him against you. He tells me that I am rotten, slaps me across the face with his giant BEE and Moszt etc., but he knows afterwards that he cannot hurt me with what is part of me and I laugh at him, and he learns essentially and finally, that I too am educated and have read alll the books and heard all the music, ONLY I DO NOT TALK ABOUT IT LIKE WEARING A GOLDEN MEDAL LIKE MILES DOES. And I still manage to write a different type of poetry not based upon the manners and ideals of the past (although Sheri says I am "late mid-Victorian")

Which almost made me mad, finally. And I decided not to write her again. I am a prude, yes, in many ways. I was once married to a millionaire's daughter. And I gave up millions rather than put my head between her legs.

"As far as a poet goes, I don't want to insult you, but you'd make a good race-car driver."

"You look like a successful but a cheap gambler."

"Why don't you open your eyes? It was a year before you opened your eyes and looked at me, and when you did it looked as if you were in agony."

Of course I do everything backwards. How else could I write poems.

One thing I will not do is to take crow from a woman. When there is a woman in the room, I am the man. And when there is another man in the room, I am the man. And as I have told you, I am very quiet and very calm and I only seek peace,

---

"ever-present English woman": Pound's British-born wife, Dorothy Shakespear.

married to a millionaire's daughter: though Frye's family was wealthy, CB is greatly exaggerating here, as he did elsewhere.

but a set of facts and mathematics and a stomach and a cock, sometimes tears me from my peaceful bearings. This, as death, comes to all men, and it's the way you handle it that matters. It's the way u handle it.

I SAID, I COMMAND THEE: READ *ROAN STALLION*.

Jeffers is *not* in the "bowels of life", it is only those who want us to hate him hoo seee sew. Jeffers presents the dahlia against the brick wall and although he is upon the side of the dahlia he knows that the brick wall will finally win, and the part of him I don' like is his secret admiration of the brick wall; but in his poetry, it is the working of these 2 parts alwayes ALWAYS, and that is the secret and the strength of Jeffers' poetry, and you cannot compare him with Pound because they are 2 different damned trains running down 2 different tracks about the same time, going, perhaps, in different directions. But these men are strong, both of them, and their dirrectikns don' mata. Their energy does. Shit! Art can be ANYTHING! It can gd be a religious ass like v.g. drowning in the shotgun corngufffield of color, or a homosexual like D. H. Lawrence building up the womanhood of sex while wanting to sleep with the sloppiest pig of a man available.

To me, Art is forgiveness without God and with the little availability of light offered.

To you, something else. Education of the masses.

But, god, Sheri, you must damn you bring the masses up to us! And have them step upon our toes and crowd us out of some line or tother for a hot dog or a boxseat upon a holiday... the masses just mean THAT: the masses. What are YOU going to have us do? Exchange first sheets of hidden Shuberts instead of trading stamps? I know it was Schopenhauer who said (in my words), well, hell yes, we're suffering, but if we ever *stopped* suffering, wd know we were *them*.

Jeffers is a genius in the preservation of the soul to the natural attrition of fame. Frost and Sandburg and Hem and Faulk have little or no resistance to applause.

Sherman, if he ever made it, wd be a complete and horrible mess. Sure, Sherman can grow salty; it is a natural and human reasoning. There is a man down where I work every night
who is FAMOUS for his anger   ANGER   ANGER   ANGER
yet I never say anything
everybody fears him, he has bluffed the world but he

comes to Buk: what'll I say? what'll I do?

And so I tell him. Well, hell, I don't care really, what you do. I don't like you.

... aw, fo Kriwts sake Sheri stop wotthehell screaming bout romantized orangsucked bankers, so MUCH old stuff STUFF

the owl screaming... u make me feel like a much older man than I am.

AND, HELL, AM NOT GONA FORGIVE U FOO THAT!!!!!!!!

Jeffers' old "aunt-voice" on the phone was the best protection he cd have. Never judge a face by its beard. I think that in the long range Jeffers' poems will be more SECURE than ur Pound's because although now many of Jeffers' words appear to be in the form of plads clicks old saws, and Pound's were the new cut raw, it has appeared to me, finally in the line of reasoning, WHERE POUND WAS TRYING TO IMPRESS WITH A POEM, Jeffers was merely trying to WRITE a poem. Pound was, and is, entirely, too busy. Jeffers knows. Buk knows what Jeffers knows and is a little mixed on what Pd sass. But still, both good.

Pound was a fool to give his formulas. Because once the many have uo pon the hands of the few,

THE MANY WILL MAKE THE FEW NOTHING,

and that is why doctors put their prescrivbitchiions in greek BECAUSE THEY REALIZE THAT THE KNOWING OF KNOWLEDGE IN THE HANDS OF THE FEW PASSED INTO THE HANDS OF THE MANY WILL AND WOULD CAUSE KNOWLEDGE TO BE USE-LESS... like too much gold or cold or too many wives.

I wuld never be Ezra's thane and even well when I fell drunk upon rugs, I still called his name through the names of horses because I knew I come on strong if they let me live.

ON YOUR KATS: The ancient Egyptians elevated Man and Cat, woman and dog shunned.

Sure, yv got to fight me because you KNOW IN YR MARTINELLI WAY that I yam a master of the future and you are catching one cutting me in my sloe growth

befoo it's tu late

and meanwhile I will talk to u and not be silent
lak Ez or Rob

hoo both know u are alive,

and I don't know

but I know they are alive

LIKE SEBELIUS WHO WHEN HE STARTED GROWING OLD
SHAVED THE TOP OF HIS HEAD
AND WOULD NOT STEP OUT OF THE DOOR,
well, here was a giant and it gave the boorish mob something to
pick on and show sickness no? and when a beautiful man of face
and spirit and body, when a man of such men is put upon earth,
a man of giant strength of the pure plant in search of sum and
sun, a man in search of the 3 or 4 women hoo will and would
hand him the palm, such a man will shave his head in shame
when he realize the end of the spirit and mind are walking hand
in hand toward the altar of death while leaving him sitting here
there, and some day it 2 will reach me, and I very much believe
I will kill myself rather than will I suffer thro a cane this mind
that at its growing strength is only looked upon as a side tune
and the exit of the monkey and the organ grinder for nickels
that will no longer feed or hold still the wind of the starving
banyan tree.

On fk cats, Shri: KAT: the ancient Egyptians elevated man
and cat; Man and Cat, I should say it; woman and dog
expelled. It is only in distillation, the selective cruelty of a formulated concept engendered from basics that we get power.
Your Pound realized this. Hitler did. Nap. The Romans thro
dominance of class, the Greeks thro dominance of mind.
Pound has a Greco-Roman complex grown out of an inferior
background that should have made him as invalid as a grocer
selling you a piece of bread and saying, "Nice day, isn't it?" But
Pound's courage got so good it carried him past the mark, so
although, allow me to say this, his selling out of America was
the best thing he ever did, and I think the Russians are younfer-
kristsakes and stronger than we
hoo are worried abt next hear this, car model,
and we grow young guys like Gib and Ernie
who are most interested in carburaters and Martinellis,
but I love them both, all 3 of ya and I hope hell the bible
u don't inhale any fancy tinfoil and shit hot yr shitters.

I sometimes laugh to maybe myself and realize I can spare it
because I have so much I can give some of it away [in] 8ball letters like this, but that's the way it goes, and if yu take yr shots at
me, that's ok, but I think

SEBELIUS: Jean Sibelius (1865–1957), Finnish composer.

someday these letters to u, like the letters to Sherman must cease. Not out of anything, but my sense that it DRAINS. Perhaps this haz ct up with EzraPd. Remember anybody hoo haz gone az far nose the essential rules.

You go ahead and draw Ernie all the time. Whatever is needed is needed. If Ernie is good for you, I give u Erns. If Pond is good, eye giv.

It doesn't seem plausible to me, pardon me, that "the Gods sent a son of the Jews to love Ezra's PoundKake"

"sent to sass Ez and grab him by his one handle."

Your deal with Pond is not "international scandal", dontletus outgrow ourselves.

Jews know enough to DO, yes, but they can never sit still enough to figure out WHY, and a Jew will never have an Art collection or a wife except to show to somebody else, and he will never CEASE TO WANT, RICH OR POOR, and that is the weakness of the Jewish race, and I cannot hope to help them and they do not even think of helping me. But that's ok, I never ask for help.

I have sorrily worried and worked many factories in this candy land to pay my rent, and I have found the Nefucknegroes to be my most interesting companions, but I knew what they were fuck suffering from as I suffered from something else, quietly, and we drank our sick wine on lunch hours together and we had our backalley fights, some of which I won and some of which I lost. My hands are very much small for some reason and I have to hit harder and faster, which I generally do after losing the opening rounds and reaching down DEEPLY for what is stored in a small packet just above my asshole.

One of my only friends is now fighting 6 rounders at the Olympic. He is more polite than I and has a bashful smile and his body is a sickly white. And every man he has fought has now retired. I am dumb, he says, I am dumb.

Only when you are speaking to me, I say, over whatever rot we may be eating.

Ah shit, Here Sheri, I *know* E. P. Walker will go on the cover of yr A and P.

No, Walker is not as noble as Ezra; there are some proving

Walker ... yr A and P: a drawing of Walker by SM did indeed appear on the cover of issue #5, which CB received at the end of January.

fk ground first. Thus your say alone will not raise a difference because the springs rattle nicely. Both E.P.'s are yours; keep me out of this squabble.

I don't want to sleep with you; as far as I am concerned you can go to hell. Give me the leaping Dutch gal over the Sunday-morning fence looking to the voice of God. I'll give her that voice. She can wash my dishes anytime.

IF HER ERNIE IS THE SON OF GOD I AM GETTING THE HELL OUT OF HERE!

JUST LIKE JORY'S CROSSIN THE JORDAN.

I am Leo the Lion, and I will not mess with second-rates.

True love does not create ART....

Whoo givez a damn the secret of the world? This is high-school.

What we want is the secret of self, one at a time.

What makes one plant grow makes another plant die.

I am going to paint one day and when I do I will show the world what color means, as I did one night to my x-wife, Fry and I awakened her and showed her the colors and she said, "Oh, you have color like Van Gogh, you LOVE color, you don't ACT that way!"

And I said, I'm going to drown it.

And she said, what do you mean?

And I walked in and turned the bathtub full of hot water and I stood there waiting, and she said, so just help me, so help me god, if you throw that beautiful painting into that hot water I will leave you.

It took her six months to pack...

Delecto, delectq. q. q. a. delecta. meow culpa?

I am listening to an opera now that I have never heard. All male pure voices without *complaint* or gross love, like the Greeks admiring their statues in the sun. What is this?

Gib's only hope is that Walker gets constipated and starched-up, and fed-up. Gib is hanging in strong, however, and I am laughing, because I am yr spirit-husband and am Out of it. Ah.

Don't get burned, sun-burned, I mean.

lfff,

Buk

Early Dec., a Friday in 1961
I mean early Jan. '61, 1:30 Pm
and I do not know the date—

Shareei!
enclosed copies.

some technicals: the *Signature* section is a portion of a larger *Targets* #4, of which I am enclosing a copy with the others. Garner had a batch of sig. sections printed, however, and sent me a good helping.

Sometimes my head of hair is curly, sometimes not. Sometimes it's red; I grew a beard once and it was pure red while my hair was brown, and I was young and felt things running up my arms and I starved so I could have time to sit in the sun; mostly I watched the birds eat the crumbs and the rocks, and they were fat, fat lovely catdreams, and I was bone and I watched their heads as they walked—duck, duck, duck (watch a bird walk: his head moves his body), but I could not find a big enough crumb and certainly the rocks would not do, and one December in Atlanta I stood under a frozen tree, a tree as frozen as I, and the birds were gone and I decided to make a million, to eat and fuck continually, hire and fire slaves, grow dull and certain; but it was only a very bad moment, and I went up to a church door and decided to go inside and get warm but the door was LOCKED in the MIDDLE OF THE DAY, I'll never forget it or understand it, but God and I had much earlier disagreed upon some finer points. Anyhow, about my hair, if you want to curl it, and my toes—FIRE!!!**—I've been in some tough spots (spiritually) (the physical doesn't count except as you live through it down into the dark growing or dying). So have away,

---

Signature ... Targets #4: pp. 13–20 of issue 4 of *Targets* was published separately as *A Signature of Charles Bukowski Poetry* in December 1960.

Shed. Pound was your man, and he's mine. And Jeffers too. Right now, both. Maybe sometime someday if I can live a little longer (I go, I grow so SLOWLY S L O W L Y), maybe neither.

I need sleep.

Will write on some things—some disagreements—Sunday.

Why did I think yd get mad abt *Horse on Fire*? Oh hell, I figured you're the type hoo gets mad easy. I am the other way: my hair will not curl although I may pull up lame.

luf,

Buk

[*note dated 7 January 1961 by SM*]
[*CB received a postcard from SM quoting Lord Beaconsfield, then appended a reply below it and sent it back:*]

Said Lord Beaconsfield, "the man who does not LOOK UP will *look down* (as our dear Mr. Bukowski) and the spirit that does not dare to soar is destined perhaps to grovel..." *Sheri*

> all right, let me *grovel*,
> god damn it, what do u want
> a holy roller? what's comin'
> my way is comin' my way and my
> values are my own. Beaconsfield was a Lord,
> and guess he felt pretty good most of the time,
> and suppose he considered himself a "look-upper"
> and wanted us to know it. Bravo!
> and love,
>
> *Buk*

Horse on Fire: one of the poems in *A Signature*, concerning Pound and Canto 90; rpt. in *RM* (70). See Appendix 1 for SM's comments.

Lord Beaconsfield: i.e, Benjamin Disraeli (1804–1881), author and prime minister of England.

1-9-61

[postcard]

Dear Sheri:

Let us not "look up" but keep our eyes level with the universe lest we become run over in body and psyche crossing the ordinary streets of our days.

The difference between a pose and an action is the electric quality of force that gives us the nerve to enter hell and heaven alike.

Your Pound toiling in the immortal light still found time to become Fascisti' and enter earthly squabbles, and as Shermans and Ginsburgs take the bait, we who find little to elevate in our residue, continue to shape and sound the word... as clean as anybody's flag.

Charles Bukowski

1-9-61

[postcard]

Sheri:

Oh, I *know* Pan is a deity!
Why must you be such a schoolteacher with me? *Bastinado!*
Pax vobiscum.

Buk

Bastinado!: usually a beating, but here probably a play on *Basta!* (Italian: "enough!").

Pax vobiscum: Latin: "Peace be with you."

156

L.A. Monday, Jan. 9, 1961

Dear Sheri:

It appears I missed one or two of your questions in yesterday's letter. About the Webb-thing. This young man wrote into Webb blasting him for printing "names", and that it wouldn't cost W. a dollar a copy to print *Outsider* if he used platinum plates. The young man claimed to be a printer. He told Webb he should be ashamed to show his face in the streets. And that Webb didn't have any talent and that the reason he was printing the magazine was so that he could be close to the big names.

Well, Webb came to me right away, enclosing the letter. I guess he wanted solace and it was flattering that he came to Buk for salve for his wounds. Well, it was a tough one to handle. Buk does not lie. He got drunk for 4 days.

It is true that Webb was, at the start, fascinated by names. This was a new thing for him, buying the press, type, corresponding, rejecting and accepting manus. He was caught in a trap of new enthusiasm. He has since written me that many of those he accepted at first do not read so well to him now, and in his "awakening awareness" he is going to be much more careful in his selections. Many of the Grove Press poets he no longer holds in awe, and several others. It is possible that many "names" dumped some 2nd. rate stuff on Webb.

All that I could write Webb was that the main thing was to print the good poem, and if that good poem had a name attached to it, all right. It is better than printing unknown mediocrity. And that the young man's inferring that he (Webb) had no talent was unkind and could possibly be untrue. And that considering the time and effort involved, all the type-sticking, cost of paper, type and ink, correspondence and reading of submissions, advertising and publicity, the cost was well over a dollar a copy. And that it would be all right for Webb to show his face in the streets.

I don't know why in the hell I had to get involved.

Yes, the young man is probably "dedicated", but I think it would be more important for him to dedicate himself to the poem and to get off the soap-box.

Grove Press: at the time, the most important publisher (along with New Directions) of avant-garde writing in the U.S.

157

Why shouldn't Webb print his son, you ask?

Well, Sheri, it's like a man giving his son a new Cadillac when he is 9 years old and cannot yet see over the windshield.

Let Webb Jr. get on his bicycle first and make his OWN way down the street. It will make a better man of him.

Lob,
Buk

11/jan/61   sm pobx 46   san gregorio/calif/

buk my dear/ i agree with you letters do "drain"—I use them to "record" things that one cant record any other place—but even my energy is beginning to tire of the work/ rec. yr targets & are in mail/

no "Pound yr man"—he was my teacher—one was educated by him... any other relationship's non-transferable/

All right will read yr Jeffers as ORDERED... no not really "mad" about *Horse on Fire*... if one took you to task about it in A & P—pray don't mind that—it'd ruin you if Martinelli praised you—

Webb sound'd sincere but ignorant/ newspaper mindstate—miller (henwry) & so forth

the altar has gone still & one is in here doing that A & P now finished all but for a few half paragraphs to 'fill in' with small talk that is nevertheless part of fun/

I sent yr *Target* with the signature alone / to Laughlin that one met at St. Liz / I think you are among the best here—although I lament some details in you /

I am very disappointed with Ernie's letters—what a contrast to yrs—it does hurt me & I cannot write him / not really / he hath desire to impress... whereas yrs are filled with sincerity in confucian sense... not the christian "let us confess" sort/ Po Li enjoys you... he is one of yr most devoted admirers/

---

took you to task about it in A & P: SM reviewed *A Signature of Charles Bukowski Poetry*—with special attention to "Horse on Fire"—in the next issue of *A&P*. (See Appendix 1 and notes to CB's postcard of 30 January 1961 below.)

Hokusai at 90 still hoping for time to work so he cd do his best work & Ez saying that it took 75 years to locate the Coke books/ & right now I am thinking that if I live to be 110 I still wont have time to do everything that has been started/ yes OREGANO is a fine herb... never used it in eggs before but will & of course got some/ right now am making a perfume of herbs... will send you down some when finished... as will be more a temple essence than a perfume...

yr foreigners sound right fine / no Sherman aint "one of my camp" dear Buk/ he was a soul in hell & I saw his good qualities... & that he was in the dark & he always was of good will & manners toward me... more than I can say about the rest of them in Frisco—I am glad he's working on the *Examiner* as it is the better blatt in frisco & has the excellent Mike Grieg & Chas. Einstein on it/ doubt if Jory'll "own it in 10 years" or even 10,000 / and as for Wang/ one has known him so long & so well as a person... but I left it all behind me long ago... when I left Frisco... they run in a circle... Buk & one was left out... & too lonely... long's I was going to be that lonesome... I might as well be down here... alone totally all day/

Ernie will forever be blessed for the few good things he did me & I doubt if it breaks a "tenet" of Ezra's—Buk... I don't really think anything matters much today... what will it mean in 2000 years...

Ernie moved me to keep working & I was too sad—one is a playful & happy thing & Frisco was dark & sad... there is nothing to do in Frisco but use a narcotica of some sort... I shook the dust of Frisco offf ffff my feet...

I'd like so much to see Europe & I realise I got a lottt of provincial in me that must be done away with before the gods will grace me with a vision of Europe/

I don't think it hurt Ernie to get him off that damned abstract stuff... onto the classics... of course he is not Ezra—but he did do some good/ nevertheless I am glad to be alone... I must finish these jobs begun/

Gib's strength is Chinese patience & Gib's the best really/

Hokusai: Japanese artist (1760–1849).

Coke books: Sir Edward Coke (1552–1634), English jurist. His *Institutes of the Laws of England* is frequently quoted in Cantos 107–109.

he does dig yr prose style in the letters/ you knock him out... he
makes me read every word outloud... to him/ Ernie bores him—
although he knows how Ernie fit in when he did fit in/ Ezra did
not take me to Italy because I married Po Li/

Oh Payne is so local a chap but he's doing good in a bad
world I suppose

By "late Victorian" I mean—not yr style nor manners nor
ideals... but where yr mind is focused/ upon the torment of life
& the hell each person is in/ tho "mid Victorian" still is not the
correct label... no...

[*illegible*]ng passed if it is a male or female... just so it is an
intelligence... [*illegible*] earth...

no my dear Buk/ not trying to "educate the masses"... "raising the general cultural level" is not "educating the masses"—
Yes—the Jews & yes the Negroes...

"I suffered from something else..."

me too / it was not until one met Ez that one discovered a
person suffering from the same thing/ which is why I prefer him
to any other—he'd gone after the remedy for what we alone
suffer...

No darling Ernie is NOT der son of Gott—'s all right/ he
merely did what no one else had done... and he was very nice
about it/ Gib's moststrong... don't worry & Ernie is already
starched up/ IF one cd only get him off that abstract shit that he
takes refuge in rather than think straight... no matter... today
everything seems hopeless... & useless... one will go take a sun
bath on the point & leave it all behind one...

ALL right soon's I get near a library I will read that book...
but I do believe I read it at Tommy Yee's & didn't like it then
but I was not entirely whole at the time... will read it Buk you...
wotever... yes I will.

Sent Ez yr Signature/ & trust he will enjoy... now my lamb I
will go take a sun bath as I said... it all seems silly & futile
today...

and love...

Sheri &
Po' Li

The horse article was entertaining... will send on to Ez—

13/fri/jan/61   sm pobx 46 san gregorio calif/

Buk/ an old letter never mailed/ read 'n forget
     I guess you sd Ez wuz a dear Granite haid/ wotever on a
post card/ anyhow I donno wot it means but luv —Shed
     one sent you that "look up" because you do persist in mail-
ing po.cds. when all in this town of 250 souls read my mail/
dotz vy & dotz ALL one meant... & Buk/ really! I may be a
"woman" but I yam still a Lady/ now listen you HardHead/ the
same thing wrong with yr post card is wot's wrong with yr poetry... You presume/ newspaper myths are not valid/
     One will NOT discuss the German/Jew burning situation
with any German OR Jew who was not on the premises at the
time/ only they qualify to speak/ you have not spoken to Ezra &
you don't qualify to say whether he "became Fascisti" nor have
you any idea wot it means/ you were not there at the time/ You
fly to conclusions/
     Ezra Pound was reading Confucius & good government at
the precise time that the leaders of the country he'd lived in for
20 years became interested/ it was most noble & natural for the
old gent to speak up/ If you want to call him a "fascisti" do go
right ahead/ worse men than you have said it/
     If you think that all a poet must do on earth is fuck women
& then squeal in his poetry on their most secret conversations &
call it art... or drink himself to death... then you think that... I
KNOW different/ I don't give a hoot in hell wot the monkey
minds say/ you are not yet a poet & if you dare sit on that soft
pillow & belch & fart away... you'll lose yr soul/
     The difference between a pose & an action is that one poet
poses as a poet & the other poet takes action as a man/ no matter wot his profession he is still a m a n & his conduct will be
judged as manly or dogly/ Jory Sherman don't count & he never
will/ Allen Ginsberg counts on 2 scores/ or points: 1/ his inborn
love & tenderness no matter what the Party sez/ 2/ his bravery &
nobility in doing wot th' pawrty sez/ which is more than I got in
my camp/ no men... just dithering blathering shells of their former shells/
     You do not know the history of poetry nor understand its
basic necessity in our kind/ we are poets for the same reason the
Jews are 'comedians' because Bob Hope can rise & say in a joke
what he'd never dare say as a man... that don't mean Old

161

Hawkmouth & SkiJumpNose aint a man/ but his role here is as a comic/

your verse is still "christian" in that you are confessing in public... and most ignobly/ you spill the beans on every female that trusted you... how can you dignify yr position as a poet? If you belonged to Capone's mob & pulled that stuff man he'd have you washed away... shd I be less a mobster than Capone? I don't like those public confessions of yrs on who fkd who that you believe is a poem...

Bukowski it is time you became a MAN... then write poetry goddammit/

Allen Ginsberg is more of a man right at this moment on earth... than any white christer walkin'/sittin'/standin'/layin' or dead except Ezra Pound/ Po Li don't get included in the christer dept. as he's a Confucian by birth & breed/

Also Allen make a general protest & howl in hell... whereas you write against those women you held in love's embrace & I downgrade you for it & so wd Ez & any person who knew love/ it is pppppppppppIGnobility to 'squeal' but of course who you are squealin' on & into whose hands you deliver them... is really the crime/

Now do stop it & get down to business & forget what the gang tells you... be serious Bukowski—it is a time for serious people/ the women of this land are more awake & serious than the men/ oh I cant finish this... I'm back at work painting... it is very easy... just lay out the stuff & paint as you go by... like one does everything else... as one thinks of it or sees it/ please do not write post cards bukowski—the only way one can do all this work is not being any sort of "celebrity" or woteverhellspelled/ love to you even tho' I doubt if you know wot it means...

Sheri

Jan what? 13, 1961

Shed, hello:

I ran off rail with card. Do not cease correspondence. It is that sometimes in a flux of nerves I get the sensation of cracking leaves under my feet. It is nothing.

162

Rec'vd your side of house and cat and shirttail thing. You have a good face, and I envy you your dry mess of plant-vine thing crawling along side of house. It is good to look into such a net and smoke a cigarette in the sun.

Yes, you're right, Pound is my man. Jeffers. Conrad Aiken. I have not read Jeffers for years. Oh, I did the other day. Came across a pome of his in some type of pocketbook anthology of modern verse. He appeared, in this poem, to be playing strongman. We can't play at being strongman. We must simply be. This is basic, a grammar of the psyche, and I do not mean to go through it. We can damn well play but we mustn't pose. It's all in words and we are throwing paint, and sometimes it becomes a mess, and when we get a name and begin to write UNDER that name, we begin to fall down through. Pound has not weakened. There are so few men I can say this of.

Oye, Shed, it's ok to curl mine hair in A and P; I do not take to any praise with too much pleasure. If you would attempt to place a cookie in my mouth it would do me in.

Yes, you have Webb down right. He is trying, and he does not PUT ON too much. In a letter or two I have from him, he uses words like "shit" and "fuck" and "god damn", which, of course, shows he is trying too hard not to PUT ON, which in a sense, is the same thing. More basics that you already know as I can see from your good face in the photo. You are one of the few women since Sappho who has given us light.

Be careful with the LEAF OREGANO in your eggs. It takes very little and too much can become musky and make you ill for days; it can be like falling into a stinking swamp. I have learned just what to pinch in with my fingers, and of course, each day we feel a little different, and the difference that you need, more than yesterday or less, you move in with your fingers and then everything's ok. And I like my coffee as hot as it can get: this brings the mind and the body together. If I eat outside and get a warm cup of coffee, bath-water warm, the meal is wasted.

It is difficult for me to write Sherman. And yet his letters are flip and bright in a sense, and full of viv. And let me tell you something about Jory, since I've knocked him now and then (I

Conrad Aiken: American poet and novelist (1889–1973).

suppose I have; I think one of yr letters gave me this feeling—and I think there is a poem of mine about Jory to be published somewhere), J. does NOT TALK OUT OF SCHOOL about vitals. At least, what he THINKS are vitals. And, his vitals are not always mine. But there is a certain sense of honor in him, although that is not quite the word. There I have almost said something good about J.

Returning the *Fastest Insight Alive*. Not much there for me.

Although I must confess that I actually do subscribe to the *Kenyon Review*. I don't know why, but most of the articles *fill* me, not in a sense of information, but rather in their offhand desperate objective gallantry like a horse trying to run around a barn and not catch on fire. The poetry, of course, is dead, completely dead, even the best of it. I suppose the S[outhern]. Review and K[enyon]. Review printed a little D. Thomas; I think I remember reading a little of it in a Phila. library, but you know D. was only good when he was good because he took the language and ran it through his personal mould, not caring how it came out, as long as the sound of it made a line across paper. But I sensed, that going on with it, he became weak, writing UNDER his name; but he was smart enough to keep drinking because he sensed that that would keep them from swallowing him completely up... He swallowed himself up, rather, and that was the end.

Yes, my foreigners are good for me. They are so simple, so simple and good. It is not in my presence to snoop. But my third floor window looks down upon them, and I am glad it does. The girl, the girl she is beautiful and she does not *know* it, yet, but someday a young half-bull with shiny shoes will mew and slobber over her and she will be done. A girl like that needs a bull. To keep her simple and never let her know.

They still have their xmas tree up. Last year it was Feb. before they threw it out, and I too was sad when I saw it by the trash can, the dead branches and tinfoil in the sick Hollywood sun. They need an altar but do not know it.

... LOOK, we can't WORRY BOUT what it will MATTER in 2 thousand years just because we're going to have to sack out. Today is important because today is 2 thousand years from

---

a poem of mine about Jory: "Letter from the North," rpt. in *RM* (120).
Fastest Insight Alive: unidentified.

now. Right now. And 2 thousand years from now will be today. You know all this. More basics. I am not good at this 4 p.M.

The trouble with shaking Ernie from abstracts to classics, is, of course, that *you* are doing the shaking. May I say that he will have to shake himself?

The trouble with Payne is that he wants to be dominant but is not really dominant at all, but a borrower. Still, yes, he is better than the average man you will pass on the sidewalk. For it all, let's give him a nod. He *did* scratch at Gramps, but this seems to be getting to be a popular pastime and I think it's about time somebody went the other way around. Gramps is there and there is not much we can do with him. HE does with *us*. I always knew Pound was strong and there is a certain sense of this strength in me, although not the talent. But I admired the strength. It was like a dog smelling another dog's asshole, spiritually. And for the ten years I did not write, I also lived another 7 of those years with a woman who was also very strong in HER way. And I was the fool, drunk, drunk, drunk, throwing full glasses of whiskey against the walls (and I drank my whiskey in tall waterglasses, no water) and I'd curse and PUT ON but only put on to make sound like a man on stage in a very dull time, and I'd fall to the rug unable to walk anymore, but still the world dancing, and I'd holler at my woman from the dust of the rug: "God damn it, I am a GENIUS, don't you understand? Don't you know what a GENIUS iz? Hell, LOOK at me! LOOK! LOOK! LOOK!!!!!"

"Yeah," she'd say from her spot on the couch, those beautiful nylon legs and spikes, "you and your god damned Ezra Pound."

"And your Whit Burnett. And ya know what they did to Whit Burnett, don't you? They LOCKED him up!!! But Whit had *your* number! I'll never forget what he once told you: 'ALL YOUR PEOPLE SEEM TO DIE IN THEIR OWN EXCRETIA!' "

I am afraid both Whit, and that lady, had my number.

Something by Handel on radio now. Believe he was German Jewish, I could look it up. The German-Jewish is an unfortunate strain because they are two direct causes working in one person, one against the other. Hitler and Muss realized this. I am not political, but I will admit actualities, or what I believe to be actualities, to myself. But as Neitz said, "Give me a German stallion and a Jewish mare!" Well, that makes a terrific bed-

165

piece, but the child-to-be-born is in for a set of fits. I may be incorrect about Handel's Jewish strain, but still, it was somebody. Doesn't matter. I have the books about thirteen ft away. Indolent.

Gib shows great strength for his youth which can not be laid off entirely to the Chinese race. However, it is difficult for me to understand the young; although there is a certain majesty and force that some attempt to claim with Age, although their only weakness was lacking the guts to die. Age, by itself, is useless: so many of our trees grow crooked.

When I say Ern is son of Got, I mean Jesus was Jewish and Jesus was the son of Got, or so the fable goes. When I said Ern was son of Got, I meant in formula sense and not in essence.

Everything is not hopeless and useless. Sometimes you meet a basically sound person completely webbed in. It is an admirable experience. And the best thing about these "rare ones" as I like to think of them, is that they do not WRITE or PAINT or postulate, they are simply ripped and walking on, AWARE. You can't find too many of these, but they rate far above the Shermans, the Webbs, the Paynes.

You are, I can see by your letter, in low spirit today. You go get your sun. Even get burned a little. But, Shed, you aren't any "flop". That is the first time you ever hurt me, talking like that. You are Sappho 1961, and just because nobody or no one tells you this, you keep climbing your walls and your cats and your Buks,

we are with you, alla us
crapas ,,

LOVE,
Buk

[*handwritten:*] p.s.—Lost pen again. Article u sent enclosed. Hope so.

L.A., mid Jan. 1961

Oye, "Whiskus":
Your abstract-letter Ernie,—I guess it can be bitter. You dedicate Ern with imaginaries (some anyhow) when he is near, but distance breaks the spell. Still, Gib's right: go easy; you measure us all in a Poundian-shadow.

The difference between being subtle and abstract is the difference between knowing and saying it in a gentler way and not knowing and saying it in a way that will let you off the hook. To be abstract with the word is all right if you use it like paint and seek the *pure* word, but it is difficult, in the language, to have near purity without near meaning.

I am eating cooked shrimp and green onions and drinking beer as I write this, so it is very enjoyable; but I could not write a poem this way. If the paper gets greasy, you'll know why.

Headline of Kennedy speech: I DO NOT SHRINK FROM THIS RESPONSIBILITY. Is he SUPPOSED TO?

And Frost out there blubbering his poem, blind and white in the snow. Jory-Shermanizing himself. I'd like to see them catch Jeffers on that hook. No, they couldn't. Not enough bait.

IT'S NICE TO KNOW WHAT TIME IT IS, EVEN WHEN YOU ARE LATE.

Got a letter from a prof in the English dept. of Louisiana State University: "... have finally made up our minds that you are one of the two men working today whose poetry may last a long long time."

Some other things said. One strength of his is that he is not at all swayed by the University Poets.

However, they are sure baiting the hook for me, trying to get me fathead and sure and dull. I answered Mr. Corrington

---

mid Jan. 1961: SM dated this letter January 14, but the reference to Kennedy's inauguration invalidates this date.

Kennedy ... Frost: references to the inauguration ceremony for John F. Kennedy on 20 January 1961, at which Frost read his poem "The Gift Outright."

prof in the English dept. of Louisiana State University: John William Corrington; for CB's response, which he quotes below, see *LL* 9–10. (Cf. CB's earlier use of the aphorism in his letter of 12 October 1960 above.)

and told him that a man can go to bed being a poet on
Wednesday night and awaken on Thurs. morn and not be a
poet at all. You can't credit a future in an insensitive and desperate world that can make blathering and blubbering idiots
outa
       Hems and Faulks, Millers kissing Monroe hems
Barrymore, fat and dull as a hog, not even saved by his whiskey,
stamping all over Hamlet to the delight
of a radio-fat audience; Wilde getting punchier and queerier
and dearier; Tschaikovsky living with an insane women in an
      attempt
through marriage to prove he was not homo; Dostoievsky at the
      roulette
wheel or bearded, raping a child; what the hell, well well well:
Dos Passos and Koestler making adjustments to the weakening
      of the
communist cause in U.S. due to war and end of depression and
      general
tiring of enthusiasm of people who expect things to jell all at
      once.
[*handwritten in margin:*] the dead and the living mixed here, I
realize.

    Oh, on the "making up of minds"... this was not L. State U.
but Mr. C and his wife's. Without playing big mr. modest I
would guess that both Mr. and Mrs. are in their twenties. Early
enthusiasms can lead to pregnancy and miscarriage.

    What is this Nora? You'd better work on her. She seems the
weakest member of your tribe. Or send her down, and if she's
bween 11 and 61, I'll make love to her. I guess she's reading the
fancy mags trying to get fancy. But the triers are stuck in the
tar-pits.

Millers kissing Monroe: dramatist Arthur Miller was married to actress
Marilyn Monroe.
Barrymore: John Barrymore (1882–1942) was remembered for his por-
trayal of Hamlet in the 1924–25 season.
Dos Passos and Koestler: John Dos Passos (1896–1970) and Arthur
Koestler (1905–1983), politically active novelists.
Nora: Nora D. Lyden, a contributor to *A&P*.

THOSE WHO DON'T TRY MAKE IT ANYHOW BECAUSE THEY
ARE RELAXED ENOUGH TO SEE.
  Gib's ok, I can sense that,
but ahm glad he didn't write, I have so few hours,
playing the ponies,
and an occasional turn on the springs,
and the black bat of doubt flapping his wings
throughout my small sleep...
Gib's
        awright
              but right now
I'm timed down to the last tick,
and one more mind
good as it might be
could break the back of my thinking,
and by thinking I don't mean strain
but I mean growing, as the leaves, better every morning,—
green for brown and wither,
the water beer sunlight
eyow!:
singing songs sometimes.

  I am not a cool pops... But do not remember my "armada"
over yr cliffs...
  The problem is not to "conquer loneliness" but the weakness of self that imagines the world is something else... and better... in the crowd.
  I am never bothered with loneliness. I am sorry, but it is
so.
  Must Ez throw you over finally? Without a say of whyfore
and whatn hell or where? I could do this with another poet but
not with a lady who knew my smile.
  I think I am a little different than Pound because I can feel
"left out" and it does not fk hurt me. I realize that the critical
and spiritual world that is cannot possibly be enough if I am
burning my fire correctly. If they can see me NOW what the hell
are they going to see next Tuesday morning when they tire of
the obvious?

  Of course, I realize that all women are not sacred. Did I
infer this? I held down the same corner barstool in a Philly bar

169

for 5 years. And yet ah I found a lot of the sacred cows going to bed with the pretense-bulls every night... These were good women and they were sorry for me and they laughed at me, which was more than the stale neighborhood women with their stale husbands could do.

C. Day Lewis in the Sat. Ev. Post explaining to the crowd how poetry is written. Charles McCarthy Lewis sitting on the knee of the mob.

Jory Sherman on my telephone phoning editors and writers: "This is Jory Sherman. I just got into town. I'm over at Charles Bukowski's..." (This some months back but I have not forgotten.)

I don't know about Cl. Major. He accepted some stuff of mine once and then heard through the grapevine that I was a son of a bitch, so he returned it. Then much later came a rather abject letter of apology, asking to see more of my work. So I sent him some more and he took it, only this time he had to return it because his mag had folded. His wife divorced him or something. And before this, a great long letter to *Trace* stating that anybody could and SHOULD publish a literary magazine. It seems to me that Major is stumbling all over his feet in every direction in an attempt to get there. He's in heavy with Wang and they build each other up, meanwhile quabbling over "White-supremacy" to give them a bit of cud to chew about.

The "grapevine", meanwhile, that told Major I wasn't any good, has accepted 3 of my poems.

It's a mess. These boys get stuck in the tars and jellies. And they too would be glad to read a patriotic poem at inauguration, or *Saturday Evening Post* the public. No wonder I look up to Jeffers.

Tired this morning. Must really stop. Shrimp and onions gone, will pursue the beer.

oke,
Buk

C. Day Lewis in the Sat. Ev. Post: the English poet and critic's essay "The Making of a Poem" appeared in the 21 January 1961 issue of the *Saturday Evening Post*. Charlie McCarthy was a famous ventriloquist's dummy.

170

Frost said, "The deed of gift was the deed of many wars." Poetic blather. This country won some struggles for POWER. Why dress it up in Sunday clothes?

Buk

Jan. 20 '61
[postcard]

Dear Sheri—
rec. yr good letter, answering Sunday.
No, can't anger on your opinion of D. Thomas because when I read him I very often get an odd feeling that all is not well. But when I found out he drank himself to death, his stock went up with me—which is not a reasonable or sensible surmise of poetic talent, I'll agree.
... it is possible that Jory writes because he wants to be famous and not because he wants to write.
This is (wuz) one of your best letters. I think it's good for you up there, away from the crowd. You and cat on mantle, in front of the clock, and the vines are climbing in my brain.

sure,
Buk

1/30/61
[handwritten postcard]

Dear Sheri:
Read A and P in one sitting. Much good; you deserve an angel if he would not spoil you... Murakami has a good purity,

---

A and P: issue #5, published January 1961. It contains four poems by CB, none of them collected in book form: "I Get All the Breaks," "Poem for My Little Dog Who Also Growls Quite Well," "Scaled Like a Fish," and "A Disorganized Poem on a Disorganized Day, with Women Running in and out and the Price of Beer up 2¢ a Can" (reprinted in Appendix 2).

171

and yet sees pretty straight. Richer stretches the point. On Major I get the feeling (in his poetry) that not everything happens to him that he claims... Po' Li knows what the hell's happening, Gumbiner is too bright for me. Sherman just wrote another "poemy" poem. Sam L. Lewis poem perfect without pretense, American Education, yes, a good picture. E. P. Walker much better in "Sheri" than in his poetry.... and you scratched Norman and Buk pretty good... if Major can live another 10 years and get over his enthusiasms and stop worrying about sleepin' wit the white gals, an' stop havin' heros and heroines and stop havin' money dreams and dreams of fames, he mite write somethin'.

L, *Buk*

(p.s.—Yes, Murakami good like bamboo, delicate but strong)

[*SM sent this undated enclosure with an inscribed copy of her book;* *the proper names are titles of her paintings.*]

I have this extra copy of the *La Martinelli* book of paintings that Mr. Pound kindly had printed for me... and I want you to accept it.

The work is all from the past 10 years & it is all now

Murakami ... Walker: other contributors to this issue: Masayoshi Murakami has four poems (one entitled "Bamboo," hence CB's postscript); Arthur Richer two poems; Clarence Major contributed three poems as well as a review of CB's *Flower, Fist & Bestial Wail*; Richard Gumbiner has an essay entitled "Some Notes Taken at the Museo National de Mexico"; Jory Sherman a poem entitled "Little Breath Prayer"; Samuel F. Lewis an untitled poem of light verse concerning Robert Graves and Robert Frost; Walker has a poem entitled "Sheri" printed on the front and back covers, as well as six poems within.

Norman and Buk: SM's own contributions to this issue include a scathing review of Charles Norman's biography *Ezra Pound* (1960) and one on *A Signature of Charles Bukowski* (reprinted in Appendix 1)

sleepin' wit the white gals: a reference to Major's poem "Chicago Scene" in this issue of *A&P*.

172

scattered around the world. The little clay head in front is now with Ezra in Italy... The St. Liz Madonna is in London... the Giotto is with Ez in Italy... The Patria is with him also... the Cleofe Santa is with my middle sister... the Isis is at Castle Brunnenberg in the Tirolo... the Daw oo is up at Yale in the collection there... the Chi'ang is with my younger sister... the Ra Set is in Rapallo with Mrs. Pound... the Leucothoe also with Ezra & the portrait... & the artist is over in Tunitas Creek... a likely spot for one.

I want to write: "the grooviest" post master but I cdn't recall how one spells "grooviest" so erased & wrote as is & do mean it/

Sheri M.

Los Angeles
Feb. 6, 1961

Dear Sheri:

Thank you for St. Benedict and olibanum and *La Martinelli*, copy #377. If you grow angry with me, as is sometimes your wont, I will return the 3 to you as I do not wish to posess anything of yours that will spoil your spirit or cause regret; but meanwhile, assuming that we are still on terms, I accept these fine gifts with honor and with love.

I have been very ill, but St.'s around my neck, so maybe things will change. Can you imagine Buk, the great Hun, walking around the block on a Sunday, asking the sun to warm him back to life?

I liked your *Cleofe Santa* and then *Ra Set* but the paintings are hard to separate because the main source remains similar. Which means you have not bothered to lie.

Re Major: it disturbs me to think that M. believes modern poets prefer Ray Charles to Mozart, especially when he is discussing Bukowski. It also disturbs me to believe that Major would think Bukowski is the type who would come right out and say: "sssssssssshit it's beautiful!" And if Major in his fantasy wants to screw white girls in the park, why hell, let him do it,

173

of course. Only I would say it shows weakness of soul. Major is full of enthusiasms, young enthusiasms, about art and people and ideas, and when this wears thin, as it must, I wonder where he will stand? Murakami, on the other hand, is tough but good. He drinks the world, touches it, walks away from it, enjoys it, despises it, then sits down and says: " ... it is so."

I got no Uncle Leon; I got Buk, and that's it.

Yes, he who keeps tenderness is strong... if he does not wear it like a medal.

The rape business is all too much for me. I return clipping as per request.

If you want to use drawings in next A and P with comments, sure, ok, only I don't remember too much what they were about, only got the idea after mailing them that you might think me vulgar tho I only meant a kind of Confucian fun-poking about the obvious.

What do the trees sing, Sheri? What do the trees say? I think it good, I think it best if we do not quite understand the song or the words.

I am still pretty weak and will close this one early.

New Orleans Webb asked for some new poems, and I wrote him off 5 or 6 new ones yesterday which I must now type up and send off.

"The whore of Denver
or the koo-koo bird
will never know
what makes us carry
carry on so..."

loooove,
Charles the Buk

8/feb/61   s.m. pobx 46 san gregorio calif

dear buk/   the presents are now yrs forever & don't return no matter WHAT I say or do/ yes St. will help—Of course I can imagine the Sun supplicated to warm the great Hun... as Sun is

---

drawings ... with comments: these appeared in A&P #6; see Appendix 2.

the Greater Hun of you two/ you must mean "Isis" and not "Ra Set" as no Ra Set yet in print... but got one on wall currently trying to finish
LISTEN LET ME USE YR OBJECTION TO CLARENCE MAJOR'S MISCONCEPTIONS IN FORTHCOMING A & P WILLYA?? I AGREE WITH YOU   I'D LEAVE OUT ANY REMARKS YOU WANT BUT TO CORRECT THE MOZART BIT & "SHITTTT 'S BEAUT...ETC" IS IMPORTANT... I CDN'T AT TIME AS THERE WAS TOO MUCH OF ME ALREADY IN   but you can now via letter straighten the yg chappie... yes Murakami is tough but there is a civilisation in Japan... & cannibalism in Africa—transplaning cannibals does not change their inborn paideumic (culture-cells) patterns

Maj eats Art whole/ etc white girls—but that is a social pattern—actually it is status & not sex prompting it/ it wd be very dangerous for a white girl to marry a black or brown man right now because when race war comes his status wd change & he'd sacrifice her in a shot

yes Masa is a beautiful soul... yr drawings are excellent & I'd send you a proof sheet before printing so's you cd see if yr comments are wot you mean... they are very funny & disdainful in a witty way/ never think you "vulgar"

Babe— none of us can figure out wot the trees are saying... we just hear them talk & sing/ I heard them say "sheri" but that'd be fanciful/ once when the female next cot[tage] was contemplating suicide... I went out down path & Tree sang in my ear & I thot it was female coming to bother me on my seagazin' & turned & saw no one & hot foot'd it over & in time to save weeping drinking girl... That time I clearly heard a human voice singing a beautiful melody & right in my ear... first coming up from behind me & then in ear & then all around me— very scary—but lovely humming melody such as a girl wd make who was on way over to neighbor to warn of her coming... but a beautiful cultured girl... a dear sweet melody—after that... the Tree snorted once... no 2cd at me/ the time they spoke in

---

"Isis" and not "Ra Set": SM was thinking here of her painting *Princess Ra Set*; she forgot that there is a photograph of her ceramic work *Ra Set* in *La Martinelli*, which also includes her *Isis of the Two Kingdoms*.

YR OBJECTION ... IN FORTHCOMING A & P: these never appeared.

Masa: Masayoshi Murakami.

english it seemed to be a male & a female & the male was telling the female to put something or other on a counter—it was loud & clear & very much in english & the female said something that I cant recall

Their songs sound (accord. to the others & me too) like "Hollywood movie music for a spooky movie" question is: "HOW do those hollywood people know the exact sound IF they've never heard it?" very interesting question

"New Orleans Webb" ved goodttt & now is grow. dusk & must light fires & cook/ was down on beach for 1hr½ walk & playin with new pup who is adorable

& so long dear Buk & lemme kno about tellin' Cl. Major/ the trees are singing right now & they sing every night & all day—off & on/ they are musical have a melody & sound human but none of us can understand what they are saying/ you'd have to hear it to know what I mean/

love love love

Sheri

[postcard dated by SM 11 February 1961]

Deah Shed:

Yes, the trees. There is some lore there, even Tree Gods, but only so much can be discussed upon a postcard because by the time they have reached base 400 people have had a reading. It's a good way to reach the masses, but you know what I think of the masses (cld w all f m), but back to La Martinelli, cd you look into your little book of roaring paintings running into my mind, and I say there is one... according to this... a Ra Set a claypewter idol sitting bound in say red cloth upon pedestal... can I be wrong AGAIN? This appears between Ch'iang and E.P. Not Isis, I would not do you the injustice of inaccuracy. Hello to Gib. Hope to get up to see you guys in mid-April. But not sure: health very bad, and in trouble on job... Because the rocket to Venus is going slower, it'll get there faster.

L.,

Buk

L.A.
Feb. 11, 1961

Muh Sheerie:

Still sick, practical world-stuff, outside pressures, cosmic, comic, diabolical or wot... doing me pretty much in. I have been eating much, trying to get strength, but only getting idiot-soft and flabby; oh, Atilla will run me outa his army!

But wait: I will straighten the shelves yet without the bull-shit of wailing. A bestial wail is all right but human simpering and sniveling will not do. But I have been feeling bad god damn god damn.

Well, on Major and the letter-thing, Mozart etc., if you still wish to use parts in some future A'n P, please use what you want and cut the rest. What I write you I write the world only you hear better than the rest. There's a lot in Major that's extemperanious and he tends to overshoot the mark. There's some gluttony. And being black bristles him a bit. The trouble with the black is that they want to be white. If I were a black man I'd want to be as black as possible. Being is simply being and if you do it well that's all that matters. Dreaming white girls in parks behind the bushes is mental masturbation. I would get myself a black girl and sing black songs and have black children. But I know what Major would say: "It's easy for a WHITE man to talk like that." But nothing is easy to say; and I measure what I say out of what I am out of similar plus and minus, yellow and green, black and white situations. In fact, I would call this pre-sent time in America... *The Adoration of the Negro*. Now a black man can do many things and we let him do many things that a white man would be chastised for... but we do not call the black down for it because then it would be "racial discrimination". I measure men one by one, individually, and I am not afraid to say that I have met some Negroes who weren't worth a damn... You see how STRONG that sounds, as if I were saying something wrong? Substitute the word "Whites" and you would call it an understatement.

And Major must not confuse an involved poetry with intel-lect. If Clarence would ever bother to take a paint brush in his hand he will find that the most difficult thing in Art is to make something simple. All the great secrets of the world are simple secrets, never spoken but felt.

177

Van Gogh was not suave. I remember when I first saw his paintings just around the corner and up the green hill on Vermont Ave., silly old gals chatting and not even looking. And at first look I was disappointed. Shit, these were the paintings of a child-idiot. I don't know. I expected music and fire. And yet and yet, I began to see the heavy child strokes. And when I got back to my place I saw them better yet. And now they have grown in me like the rings of a tree trunk. Beware the intellect: the closest line between 2 points of creation is a straight and simple line.

And talking about Art will not get it *done*.

Shed, on the Pound-thing... what he does with his Greek or his wot or things he might copy out of a book   something dead   supposed dead because it sounds like part of the words he wants to say that fit in with the words going down through him onto paper   is nothing wrong and because he wanted a red shirt and got one, makes him all right enough. And because some scholar who is a scholar and not a poet finds technicalities that do not fit into the technical crossword puzzle of his TAUGHT brain is just too bad. But when we listen to scholars   the taught brain teaching, we are listening to the dead, not just the dead in death   for there are many good there but the dead in life, and this we cannot have and will not have and will NOT have. There is nothing correct about correctness because it is only the courage of the ex-stricken, ex-halved mob. Scholars orderly as pidgeons shitting in the park   will have their small Sunday afternoon of victory. But things go on, like a red shirt walking in sunlight thinking

Vermont Ave.: the address of L.A. City College, which CB attended 1939–41.

I would ... men's believing: the concluding lines of Pound's early poem "An Immortality" (*Ripostes*, 1912).

178

I would rather have my sweet,
Though the rose-leaves die of grieving
Than do high deeds in Hungary
To pass all men's believing.

triple carbs and triple love,

Buk

(lost pen... again)

[*postcard dated by SM 14 February 1961*]

Deah Shed:

I see where someone in power says Kenn[ed]y's program for medical aid for the aged is the "Idea of a bunch of socialist jerks from Harvard." It appears to me that the reactionaries to common intelligence and decency are defeating themselves with their vocabularies, Walter Winchell style. I was not for Kenny too strongly at first (the face, the good-boy unsuffering appearance) but Lord, in his first few days in office he has really rolled up his sleeves. It is a shocking and heart-warming experience, and although I have never been interested in politics, I cannot help but notice. Which disproves a lot of malarky about the rich not being able to see through to the real problems. How slowly we learn, and when we have finally learned it is oh so often too late.

L.,

Buk

---

the Pound-thing: CB's "Horse on Fire."

Walter Winchell: radio and TV personality (1897–1972), known for his gossipy style.

L.A., mid Feb. [17] '61
[postcard]

Hoy, Shed!

Got yr val[entine]. Youse is good gal, SaRet. Most a the cussin u give me, I got comin. Just haven't tried the olibanum yet, but will wait til my mood is peace. I don't like to *force*, an that's a good secret whether in poetry or life, you good gal u. ... my my but plenty of troubles in simple practical world now rattling old Buk's string, but I am shouting down the petty and lifting the ol' beer high to light and love... Fine on your trees, I like that stuff. I must find you a tree god. Don' wurry bout wat I say on this postcard or others, knowbuddy wd unerstand b. u, good gal. Heard frum N.O.Webb, he say he takin 5 for sure outa batch I sent him, and is goin to try to work in some others. He stick type 18 hours a day, working up 4000 copies. U hard wurker too, Martin; only I iz lazy lousething,   L.,

Buk

L.A.
Late Feb. [26] '61
*[handwritten letter with drawing of
CB at table, bottle in hand]*

Dear Sheri:

Jon Webb mailed me this mimeo of kaja, and not knowing what to do with it, I pass it on. kaja is a little too pure for me— there is a little too much trying—Whitman, I guess, plus the Bible. And yet she writes simply, which helps.

Also Jon sent along some pages "46," Bukowski. It appears he is working me into the end of his book, which I take as a compliment.

Anyhow, the kaja + 46.

L.,
Buk

SaRet: that is, Ra Set: see note to SM's letter of 14 February 1964 below.

kaja: pen name of Kaye Johnson, a poet.

180

Sheri Martinelli, ca. 1945, a double exposure taken by a member of
Anaïs Nin's entourage. (©1998 by Gunther Stuhlmann/The Anaïs Nin
Trust)

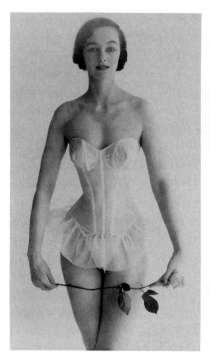

Sheri Martinelli photos for a *Vogue* magazine layout, late 1940s.

Sheri Martinelli, studio portrait, late 1940s.

Ezra Pound and Sheri Martinelli on the lawn at St. Elizabeths Hospital in Washington, D.C., ca. 1954.

Sheri Martinelli displaying (and surrounded by) her art, ca. 1960.

Sheri Martinelli, self-portrait in mirror, July 1961.

Lux in Diafana (left) and *Ursula Benedetta* (right), two of Sheri Martinelli's paintings mentioned in Ezra Pound's *The Cantos*.

Sheri Martinelli in a blonde wig, San Francisco, date unknown.

Charles Bukowski with his "fine and beautiful dog," taken at the time
he was living with Jane Cooney Baker, Santa Monica beach, early
1950s.

Charles Bukowski at his apartment on North Mariposa Avenue in East
Hollywood, early 1960s.

Charles Bukowski in his apartment on North Mariposa Avenue in East
Hollywood, early 1960s.

Portrait of Bukowski inscribed to Sheri Martinelli, April 22, 1963.

Charles Bukowski and his early publisher Jon Webb, early 1960s.

Charles Bukowski and his early publisher Louise Webb, early 1960s.

Charles Bukowski on De Longpre Avenue, East Hollywood, mid-
1960s.

Charles Bukowski with his daughter, Marina Bukowski, ca. 1966.

28/feb/61   sm pobx 46 san gregorio cal

buk dearest one/   for kaja thankew
I needed something new to chew on & writ th' gal letter to straighten her exposed cunt that she taketh for a mind... she has an undressed & pissyassed mind... poor infant sittin' on front steps playin' wiff hersalf... & is that all of Buk to appear wots on sheet of yellow? it is very funny... I fogot ah lo'd yew "moth going by ½ mile an hr"... oh godtttt... & *Pay Yr Rent or Get Out*... you funniest yet... my kid... let the kid have his bottle pop... my kid need dot shit fo' fuel... I want one when comes out & how much is & who "Jon" & wot "46"... aaaaaaaaaaaaaaaaaaaah... Babe read *Selected Poems of H.D.* Oh Buk she is a better poet(essa) than Ezra/ she is the number *one* Scribe for god's sake get her... $1.45 Evergreen with her pix on front/ get get get/ & I mail her yr book soon's arrives/ now in switzerland she is... are you going to write something for her????? the coming issue???? and I love you my goodtttt kidtttt/

youse mamma
mah ma
Sheri

March 2, won 9 sickswon

Oye, Sheerie...
I guess with the kaja, she is trying to say too much, and in too goodpure a way. Could be she wants the whole populace to swoon and ask wat's 'er name? Katherine Jones? I don't understand quite why Webb should send me this thing, unless he thought it was good and I thought so too. I tried to see what I could, and I appreciated the simple line, but I don't take any sugar in my coffee or my beer.

"moth going ... an hr": from "Hooray Say the Roses," in *Outsider* 1 (Fall 1961); rpt. in *BW* (27).

Pay Yr Rent or Get Out: also in the first issue of *Outsider*; rpt. in *It Catches My Heart in Its Hands* (1963).

181

No, the sheet of yellow page is the beginning of several poems by Buk. Jon mailed them to me because he is that way about things, he is not standoffish. The *Pay Your Rent or Get Out* poem at the bottom is the *beginning* of another poem. I don't remember what the rest of it says or what the other poems are.

Jon is Jon Webb, *Outsider*, 46 is page 46, and I rather suppose he'll mail you a copy gratis because he knows you, although I don't know if he has your new address. When I say he knows you, I mean he has mentioned you. You are our new Gertrude Stein, only you don't look as grubby or travel around with another lady.

Aw right! Aw right! I git H.D., I get Hilda Doolittle, IF she at bookstore corner Western and Hollywood bull, they have almost everything but I am not one of those mail them in and wait boys.

Sure, I write something for new A and P. Only I figure new *AP* far way off. There's plenty of time, right? You sure as hell aren't going to crank off another one right away? Nobody *that* tuff.

Your Wilder Bently or what's his name. I didn't try to contact him. Time I don't have anything of. What I mean is, sometimes just not being anything or doing anything for 5 or 6 hours or 5 or 6 days or 5 or 6 years is most important. You take in air and space and stems and roots, and if that's *all* you take in, you have made it.

Not much else today, mama.

lufftwaffe,
Buk

[*followed by a drawing of CB watching a woman walk by his window.*]

Wilder Bently: Bentley was an acquaintance of SM's, otherwise unknown.

L.A.
March 8, sixwon

Hoy, Shed:
I kant get your h.d. Enclosed 2 bucks, if you have copy or know of one, ship it on down. The bookstores down here carry the Sat. Ev. Post, Time and murder mysteries.
You gona pull kaja's hair? You might straighten her at that. Been hearing from a prof. at L.S.U., first letters ok. Last one he got confessional and I heard all about it. Also enclosed some poems for me to read. I don't run a magazine or a confessional booth.
Sherman did the same thing to me. Got very homey.
Your rock-salt letters never miss. Why don't you teach these people to write LETTERS, mawwma?
IF THEY CAN'T WRITE A LETTER WITHOUT GOING HOLLYWOOD, THEY ARE NEVER GOING TO WRITE A POEM.
kaja, I believe will be in *Outsider* which will be out, I hear, in April. Webb is a tough boy but he can be fooled because he works so hard trying to get it done that sometimes it doesn't give him time to see. It's hard to see when you're running.
He has things banging against the walls with his energy.
On Ernie, I don't know what the hell. Those things sometimes run in circles, and he may yet circle back on you. And I told you Po Li was stronger'n any of us. In his way, that is.
This is short. Some outside workings have ganged-up on me. H.D. is H.D. why name it?

LOVE sure,
Buk

March 8, 1961

Deah Sherie—
If you can't use these in a future *A & P*, please return them so that I can try 'em elsewhere. O.k?
Buk

183

yes will get the H.D. for buk/ and will enclose some herbs/ the hops are plain ol' hops & buk is to make a tea of them... not many as bitter/ make tea for resting the nerves... the same for chamomile flowers & the wormwood... wormwood bitter needs honey

am keep. poetry for next *a & p/* poem for the dead whore very moving

Yes "got very homey"   the pore americans/ no manners/ no 'distance'   Ez on subject "when yr nearest neighbor is 100 miles away it is gonna make ya friendly... the britts got dif. manners because the island is crowded..."

      H.D.:   "but do not delay to round up the others
           up & down the street; your going

           in a moment like this, is the best proof
           that you know the way;

           does the first wild goose stop to explain
           to the others? no—he is off;

           they follow or not,
           that is their affair;

           does the first wild goose care
           whether the others follow or not?

           I don't think so—he is happy to be off—
           he knows where he is going..."

The Flowering of the Rod

How moi lamb... can I better teach these people to write letters (as yr req.) except by doing it myself... as a model... even if it interfer with my own work... it was the humblest task I cd think to set myself & teach 'em...

but Buk... a voice from the aether... & a command... & I am

---

next *a & p* ... *poem for the dead whore*: CB's "Poem for Liz" appeared in *APR* #6; rpt. in *RM* (195–96), and in Appendix 2.

The Flowering of the Rod: from the *Selected Poems* SM urged CB to buy.

painting again... my Lux in Diafana... (canto 93 the Kati
Canto)
    "Lux in diafana
         Creatrix
           oro
    Ursula benedetta
           oro"   I am at work on
both of them... the Ursula & the Lux & Ra Set
   am sending you the hole you'd wear in the sock anyhow (to
fit yr poetry)(as requested)
         rest of
            SOCK
            will follow/

Los Angeles, March eleventh
nineteen sixty one

Hoy, Sheeerieee.....
   I Yam sending you these set of blurbs Webb sent me
because
        spirit-love
             I don't know anybody
and can't stick them in the mail for this gruff old goat, and I
thought anyhow, you'd be interested. Your law is always to
have a reaction and I thought you'd have a reaction to these.
Maybe Jon sent you some.
   My reaction is why 3,500 copies?
   What the hell's he gona *do* with 'em?
   If I had a little machine like that, I'd turn out 200 copies.
Or if I had a mimeo, I'd turn out 20 copies. By doing 200
copies I could turn out 17 and ½ magazines in the time it takes
him to do one. It's rarity that makes things valuable. Who in the
hell saves old copies of *The Saturday Evening Post*? What's Jon

---

Lux in Diafana ... Ursula benedetta: the titles of two paintings by SM
mentioned in Canto 93, from which she quotes.
blurbs Webb sent: for the first issue of *Outsider*.

trying to do? *Post* us up? Or trying to turn a buck? Still he's a hard worker, and I guess in his own way he's grinding in the fire, and he is an individual of a sort, and he's not trying to turn a buck at all. But Jesus, threethousandfivehundred copies! It's not necessary. It only takes a sculptor one sculpe. This mass-production business strangles its own meaning. If it can be worked off a press with a worker-bee doing the work and not the artist, well, all right, ten thousand copies is all right, if the content is all right, even if you never get rid of them, it doesn't matter. But Jon is virtually assassinating himself in order to get out a mag.

Nothing else much new. Somebody in New York thinking of bringing out a 2nd. collection of my poems—*Longshot Poems for Broke Players*. It might be a mimeo, I don't know. The title is tentative and, of course, as awfully usual... Mid-Victorian. I typed him up a group of the latest, including those in the last issue of *A & P* review. The *Flower, Fist* group was mostly my earlier, and I will feel closer to home with these, no matter what he takes.

I won't come up in April. I feel it might spoil something. As Jory might tell you, I don't know how to TALK. I just sit there like a frog on a leaf, blinking. I'm not even thinking. Most of the time I don't think. I long ago tired of thinking.

Going through the mags typing up poems for New Yawk friend came upon Mr. Wang writing about photo Mr. America 1951 stuck in mag, *The Naked Ear*. Mr. Green (Mr. America) is showing his cock and his muscle and, believe me, he has more muscle than cock. But why does Mr. Wang worry about such things... Mr. America 1951 in a 1959 magazine? And the editor has changed the title of my poem *Layover* to read *Lay Over*.

To show you what this does to the central essence of my poem, allow me upon the next page to show you the poem.—

> Making love in the sun, in the
> > morning sun
> in a hotel room

Longshot Poems for Broke Players: a chapbook published later that year (not 1962, as usually given); see CB's letter of "Late Oct. '61," below.

Layover ... Lay Over: originally published in the *Naked Ear* #9 (as indicated later in the letter), rpt. in *RM* (51).

above the alley
where poor men poke for bottles;
making love in the sun
making love by a carpet redder than
     our blood
making love while the boys sell
     headlines
and Cadillacs,
making love by a photograph of Paris
and an open pack of Chesterfields,
making love while other men—poor
     fools—
work.

That moment—to this...
may be years in the way they measure,
but it's only one sentence back
in my mind—
there are so many days
when living stops and pulls up
     and sits
and waits like a train on the rails.

I pass the hotel at 8
and at 5; there are cats in the alleys
and bottles and bums,
and I look up at the window and think,
I no longer know where you are,
and I walk on and wonder where
the living goes
when it stops.

Can't you see that the changing of *Layover* to *Lay Over* violates the essence of the poem? By *Layover*, I meant getting out of the stream of dead life. But my editor friend seemed to think it was just a lay that was over. Which it probably would have been if it had been him or Judson Crews. ...and while we are on *The Naked Ear* #9, there is a poem by your friend Mike McClure.—

Judson Crews: prolific writer and editor for small presses and magazines.

I think that cigarettes are
killing me
and then I take the lion posture
to clear my throat out.

This is a poem? Or are the boys just playing with each other? There are too many homosexuals, and handshakes under the table to suit me... All right, Shed.

Truly,

Buk

Los Angeles, Calif.
March 12th., 1961

Dear Shed, Spirit-Love Mine:
First, hello, to my buddy, Po Li, hello, hello.
Bad day: blades turned in... but not for shaving.
I hate to see a full-grown man cry (or woman either) and use Art as an excuse, but on the other hand, I hate to see them going around being soft and subtle as if they have everything under control and are tasting their words like olives or pickled pigs feet. (See Gil Orlovitz: Act of the Sonnet). Yeah, it's an act, all right. He gave himself away and didn't know it. Even to stealing one of my lines after first carefully draining the blood from it.
I hate to see a full-grown man cry, but maybe that's the hun in me; the hun and the pollack and everything else backalley; but I don't hate to see the sun go down, especially after I have walked around in it all day dreaming pleasantries against the blade. Besides, I am pretty good in the dark, I'm told (I was once cornered in a closet with a man with brass-knucks, but I guess he was only a boy because I left him in there among the ladies' habits and scarf-shadows, and I stepped out and asked for something cold to drink).

Gil Orlovitz: Act of the Sonnet ... stealing one of my lines: that is, *Art of the Sonnet*, one of Orlovitz's (1918–1973) better-known books of poetry.

188

I furthermore do *not* care for the Ginsburg flippancy of seeming-modernity about his grandmother's beard *Howling*, or whatever, and it was tough of him to go visit Castro amongst the chicken bones; but why why why... do they call it DARK-NESS simply because I can see light and shadesdown growing flower *AND* weed, love *AND* the spilled bottle beside the elbow of what was once a halfgod... or now a fishpond is floating dead tadpoles that might be better than any of us? Certainly they *can* be... dead as they are... if they do not sell out, and it is so hard not to sell out with all the lights they flash upon us, with the weewee shit full of sea fulla boats fulla whores.

I know that Ernie is the new young Jew of the Adoration, but I hope that you have caught your head by now, and not lost it again. It's none of my damn business. maby it's Ginsburg's granmaw's business. I've elected you ar knew Gertrude S. but insteada u keepin' me in shape, now an' then Gerty, Buk gona SAY.

Let's begin with some lines you didn't understand.

Shed: bird-light is very simply any light that falls upon a bird or follows it around, just as Po Li has his very dark little ball that follows him around on a leash. As I was saying, any light that falls upon a bird or any light that falls *away* from a bird UPON something ELSE. Say in a form of final living light

    as eagle-light or owl-light falls upon a mouse,
    the last important light he will see here upon earth,
and
    I tried
    to explain this to a ballet dancer outside the Biltmore
    the other night as I smoked one of his cigarettes
but he was queer, which I didn't hold against him,
but he did not understand what I was trying to say,
which I did not hold against him, and that was all
I held against him
that night
or any other, and I went in and watched him kick and dance
but the music and the ladies held my charcoal heart, and I'm
sorry I borrowed his goddamned cigarette which was perfumed

---

some lines ... bird-light: SM had criticized these lines in her review of *A Signature of Charles Bukowski*.

and made me cough; but to go on, and since Mrs. Po Li has no idea what "the terror of a mouse reaches dormitory levels" signifies here OR on the West Coast of Africa, I will tell her that
dor' mi-to-ri, n., (L. *dormitorium*) is a
place, a room or a building
to sleep in
and that mice sleep in all these places
and that I have lived in a lot of these places and that they and I the mice and I
may sometimes dream, and that all our dreams may not be
either pleasant
or wet; and now... READY? ah!
let's put them together:
IN BIRD-LIGHT
THE TERROR OF A MOUSE REACHES DORMITORY LEVELS...
simple, isn't it? I'm sure Gertrude would have understood although I doubt she would have approved.

And to answer another question: IF WE ARE NOT GOING TO EVALUATE OUR OWN SELVES' WORTH
WHO IN HELL IS GOING TO DO IT
WHILST WE WALK ON THE EARTH?
The critics, my dear, and the neighbors and the police and the press and all the ugly things that hem us in, but really—too *many* of us think we are genuii and are ready to admit it (I am thinking especially of C. Major and one or 2 others); so MANY men think they can make better LOVE and better POETRY than their brothers... but this fkn can't be helped: it is a thing nature put in us to keep us going, but we've got to step aside from nature now and then and see the spider sucking the fly, we have to see that there is a web for us too, and if we can begin to see this... instead of ACCEPTING nature, which has been the formula for centuries... we must say we are larger than nature because we know it is there. The first things are very hard to say because they have never been said before. But nature can be tamed like a tiger to do our will instead of the way we have been tasting it. I will even say that eventually the human race will call the day of its own death gladly, and nature in a way is God, and God in a way has been cruel, trying to prove something with a set of toys.

But getting back. If Pound has "a map of love poetry in his head & knows immediately where a love poem stands in

190

relation to the race of love poetry" I'd say that the man has read
too much and loved too little, and that his maps
          like the ones he went over with Muss
have been changed, and the world is harder to fool now
and I see Rommel now directing his tanks
and Muss from the pulpit bragging under the shadow of
          Adolph,
and I don't like the way they got Muss and his whore, who was
she, Carlotta somebody? the Italians are good winners and poor
losers, they are loud and laugh too much and will fart their dinner right in your face, and you can see how far they have come
from Rome, it is another person entirely, only the Teutons have
never changed, I will never change and as I fall drunk over this
typewriter I will laugh I will know the secret has god damn been
given us, somehow, and as the years go on and I die out the
window and the young men grow, it will not matter.

And I can see Rommel now directing his tanks, and so they
hung Ben from his heels and his whore from her heels, and
there was probably many an asshole in the crowd who jerked off
with joy, for the first time seeing the body of a woman he was
never man enough to possess, dead, wrong or right, they were
both greater than the crowd, greater than an all beloved nature
that had brought them to a fix.

they hung Ben from his heels like an old shark weighed out
of slime, but Ez has his castle now
          we bunked him up on weenies and beans
          and a red shirt like the nigger wore
and we let him have his mistress from the street, but he's in his
castle now, and Art's winging it down the halls of his mind, a
pretty good mind, but really not much better than mine
who nobody's heard of
          but that's all right
          because that's the way history works

Muss ...Carlotta somebody?: Benito Mussolini and his mistress, Claretta
Petacci, were executed on 27 April 1945 and then hung from their feet
from a scaffold.

hung Ben from his heels: echoes the opening of *The Pisan Cantos*: "Thus
Ben and la Clara *a Milano* / by the heels at Milano" (74/445).

and I may be wrong, but it seems to me when I look at the wall-paper n hear the sounds would be whirling when I smoke a simple cigarette, perhaps they enjoyed Ezra too early and they have gutted me up to wait through granite.
WE HAVE WAITED THROUGH GRANITE.
But Ezra can and is real enough
to still be punched when he gets too fat or too mad
in the bird-light of his life, the hoarded seasons, the withered Jews, the love of Mr. Po Li' and a thousand critics afraid to scratch his fame.
...well, Shed, I have lit your little rocks. Good stuff. Didn't think they would burn... Can still smell good fullness.

I love you,
Charles
BUKOWSKI

L.A., sometime March nineteensixtyone

Ho, Shed:
On the visit thing, I think not. And, of course, would warn you far far early. It is, I think, that I am very tired. Instead of all the driving, I need to flatten out a little and simply stare at the ceiling. It is a matter of survival. There's little or no sense in coming up there if I am dead, and I can often times feel the dying and I just know   sense   whatthe hellwat thru some divine law that if I corner myself or cross one more line   just one more   I am finished. I have just about reached the edge lately. I do not want to be a hard bark in the middle of a desert. I want to see out with eyes. And I need the fill-in gap badly. Good to be invited. you are the one person in the world who comes across through space to me. perhaps later. I get 4 day periods off throughout the year, I can come up at a time when the edge is not so close. If I can keep this job. and they have almost accepted me like an oddity, like a drinking fountain or an elevator, they have found a name and a place for me, and I let them have it that way... whatever front they draw, so that I may walk off in peace.

Ginsburg, of course, may have a formulated concept of strength tasted through the dirt and blood of centuries, but it seems unfortunate to me, that more and more his poetry seems to lack   lack realness
which seems to be his central concept
and it is a shame that one has a concept in mind and not in
    action;
ACTION: ...meaning and being the poem.
Fer[linghetti] runs off beautifully at times   letting the words take him running   but it seems   that in each of his poems   he stops the running   and throws in something practical   which exposes him as quite not pure, and I say pure not as Bartok or Bach   but as something that should be
without interference.
Webb is a tough good man who is learning slowly very slowly the ways of rocks and error, but the best thing about Webb is that he began at an age when most men forget. A man is always dangerous and strong   when he begins late   at things that tickle most young men   who have nothing else to do. Webb is capable of growth, and growing. In an age of insignificant editors   I find him a very good one   mistaken, of course, raw, a simple beginning, but he seems to be slowly cracking through. I will take one Webb for a dozen Shermans because Sherman is only fame-happy and bubbling in his milk (as is your beloved Major) while Webb is prodding through his backbone   other sounds   not his   through pain and experience and error
        all right   he has a way to go
        let him go it.
    maybe you get good laugh. I met a young man who speaks seven languages who said "I can personally introduce you to a man who knew Ezra Pound 32 years ago."
    ...sure, sure, I'm afraid Gib would be too aloof... I can imagine him coming home and wondering if I stole one of his cookies. Jesus, he's just by gd getting over the Ernie thing. Let just let him rest in peace. Besides, I'm an old man... Gib wd take me out behind the nearest pine tree and whip my ass. And prob all we would have done is talk about my boy Jeffers. And damn you, Shed, I tol' you to read *Tamar, Roan Stallion* and tother poems and you HAVE NOT DONE IT!!!
    HOW CAN YOU DRAW JUDGEMENT UPON A PERSON IF YOU

HAVE NOT READ HIS WORK? Don't let Pound make you think that there was only ONE... there were and are 3 or 4, and you are only blind if you do not INVESTIGATE!!!

And yet, by god, you sit there stroking paint upon canvas as if you have it all figured... Gal, sometimes you get me to steaming, sometimes you need somebody to TALK TO YOU!

what the hell is this?

...oh, you needn't PRESUME I'd be on your side.

there's no other side I cd take.

Gib's all right

               but his roots only go down

as far as he bends to tie his shoes.

Now I'm gona get rot drunk. Something—private—has interrupted my day—but now I'm going to fill up again.

sure love, why not?

lost pen again,

Buk

[postcard dated by SM 3 April 1961]

Deah Shed,

Howja ever make out with kaja? I imagine a lot of literary hair-pulling, and I know from experience that you can outcuss the gal. Women poets, *garrh!* Your H.D. prolly best of lot. Christina Rossetti, now dead long, very strong. Bettern most men at it, living or dead, and was fine looking woman too. Kay Boyle once very beautiful, well-worked prose style, but as poetessa loses out. Better in novel or short story, but getting tiresome... Look now, her still wailing over dead Vienna, dead Europe. Repetitive. One subject gal. You gotta get these women organized, Shed. They's runnin in all directions getting nowhere. Elizabeth Bartlett sees the most print and is the worst

---

Elizabeth Bartlett: a California writer.

194

of the lot. Carson McCullers wrote some brilliant novels and then disappeared. Easy on kaja now. She's just a child, I'd imagine.

Bukowski the CHARLES...

Buk

Los Angeles, Calif.
April 3, 1961

Deah Sheri:

I am told your lad Wang now claims he is a communist and a black supremacist; Wang's trouble is that he wants to make a sound and be heard irregardless of the cost... he made some kind of statement in the *Golden Gater*, a state college newspaper. Why in the hell a college newspaper should bother to announce the new-found so-called principles of Mr. Shift-with-winds Wang. With one wing communist and one wing black-supremacist he hopes to fly to fame, just as rubbing against Pound   like a dog against the legs of the master   he hoped some of it would rub off on Mr. Wang. Meanwhile he tries to make up his mind whether he is a homosexual or not... but on or off... not or no or yes... he dedicates each of his poems to somebody, somebody in power.

Why are they so hungry?

Your lad Jory writes... where is Sheri? she has vanished completely. It is evident you did not send him a copy of *A & P*, or he wd have your address. I did not give him your location as I figure you are too busy with the brush and the herbs and tree-god. Sheri, you must not *dump* people like you do, like so much slag. I feel for poor Ernie, you built him so high, so very high, popping cookies and love into him, bloating him with joy, and then something went wrong—a premise somewhere was crossed, a Martinelli set of nerves jumped in the moonlight, and all the sketches you made of the lad while he pretended to sleep, all the preening and primping and fattening of his soft soul, and then—BANG!!!—you let him go, all the way back, and he will never be the same. You are too cruel and you should not be cruel to children. I am tough and I can see, I see out of my

195

own eyes, and you cannot destroy me because you cannot mould me. I will destroy myself. But you must be kinder to children and dogs and half-poets and old men. I guess because Ez booted you you have to boot back   but you are wrong wrong   you can live without Ez and you can live

without booting;
it is different to sack them and throw them in the sea while they sleep, that is another matter. It is true that the consciousness finally can't take an intrusion that first appeared to be holy and then suddenly shows signs of rot, but all things can be handled without the hot and sterilized knife. My Engoilish professor from Louisiana... he started blurring up my windshield with all manner and matter of personal crap, and though he is getting to be a fairly well-known poet, and he tried to pop a lot of cookies into my mouth by telling me I was one of the 2 living poets today writing anything worthwhile... and as my goil friend said—HOOS THE OTHER BASTARD?—I had to cut the strings on him, but I did it gently and he was man enough to take the hint, and he went way up on my scale when I saw this, and I think there's a chance for him, and when I see one of his poems now... I can sense the gentleness and explorative understanding working, and instead of having the bitter taste, I am for him as a man and a person and I hope he understands that all the confessional crap was a mistake. I didn't want to see the birth-mark on his left shoulder. I went through all that with Jory. There is a manner of saying a thing. You can say anything as long as you keep the light on it like a goddamned leaf but when you start getting chummy and measuring lengths of cock and placements in literary journals   it's time to halt.

well, tough mama, I am coming off a good one, I am sitting here sweating like a pig about to be murdered, sucking on a beer, looking for cigarettes, thinking my god my god my god   I'm still alive...

Webb? Webb is growing. It's something about working so hard with the magazine and reading all the scripts and being haunted by visitors and pests and those agonizing for fame and chitchat, it has brought him up to where he can almost see. He wrote a rather amusing letter about how they are bombing down on him. Eating out his icebox, stealing his novels and neckties, borrowing money, endlessly chitting and chatting very well causing him hours of loss that he needs for sleep or turning

196

the crank. He's made the mag too big, and each day a new page of my stuff, a Bukowski album—which is all right with me, but I think he should close the thing down and get it out before it eats him alive. Webb is tough and he tries to be fair, which is more than you can say for most. I can talk at him without losing perspective and in working out the poems, we do not argue.

I don't know anything about Ferlinghetti except the book-shop and censorship fight put him out into the light

and where nobody'd heard of him before, he is suddenly known, not now as a bookshop owner   but as a poet and novelist, and I understand he is a very bad novelist (*Her*).

Ginsburg got put out in the light with his *Howl* which like *War and Peace*, I have never been able to read without bore-dom. Boredom, hell yes. And I do not think Ginsburg has come through with a consistent body of work that points in any direc-tion with force. He may be active as hell, but anybody can be ACTIVE, the milkman can be ACTIVE, but the poet's job   if he has to be ACTIVE   is to be so through his POEMS. That is the gun of his strength. And that is where the Wangs and Gins-burgs fail—milking one teat with one hand and the other with the spare. Most things are so terribly simple, and in a sense, ter-ribly horrible, and both of them are blind to the obvious, and both of them are too god damned hungrey to make a SOUND

anyway it can be made

and at any price,

and you can only pay the price so many times

before there's nothing of you left, and then those

even those lower that you have been riding with

will shove you out

because there's nothing left   nothing

even for them, and

before   you were Prince of a rat's nest

and now you're not even a good

comrade rat.

and don't you go slipping me no god damned educational material, I got an education of my own, mostly all at once one night, sitting in the dark in a paper shack freezing my balls

---

Ferlinghetti ... censorship fight: over his publication of Ginsberg's *Howl*. His novel *Her* was published by New Directions in 1960.

finding out that Art was Atlanta at 5 degrees above, a green loaf of bread and a light cord without a light. I found out that Art was not essentially a piece of paper with a poem on it or a piece of ass with a name; I have found out that ART IS FACING HORROR WITH DIGNITY AND INTELLIGENCE. Ginsburg and Wang figure Art is a byline or a dedication or a sound in a state college newspaper put out by an undergraduate who doesn't know any better. Ginsburg and Wang are so much wood for burning, a bit of smoke to be later blown forever away.

Moy x-wife Barbara Fry is still trying to shove off her novel, but she writes like a god damned snob just finished reading the classics, and it's a wonder we lasted 2 years together. I am mud and earth and she is tinsel and practice, but worse—the way she writes is not the way she is. She is not strong enough to be either one—a writer or a liver.

tonight   now I am hearing original music from india
I like this   because I have not been schooled in it
and the sounds enter directly   and I am like a child with a new toy, and there is much involvement and eflat depth here with 3 or 4 simple instruments.   Since I cannot come up to you, you and Gib must come to L.A.

Whalen has an "in" somewhere   and is only known in San Francisco where they turn him out like daily sausage. Sherman is garnering an audience and a "name" with his persistence. His poems are entirely not like his personality   which is toothache shattering. Pound has been accepted in college halls   which is rather discouraging. It happened too early. There should have been more rebel-bite. And now   it's up to somebody else   to carve mad ivory in the laughter. I do not know where we are going to find him   but the need is there. Major is too bitten with self-love, skin-color and the need to succeed. He would rather see his name in lights than drink a can of beer, smile, light a cigarette and wait   wait   because the sun is gone.

Where's the H.D. book, baby? You forgot? and the red shirt? and the herbs? I lit the little stones the other night under a mess of leaves, but mostly I was taken with the pure flame of the fire instead of the essence   which I got later when the fire

---

Whalen: Philip Whalen (1923–), San Francisco poet.

was out and which kissed my old bones and I felt good. Thank you, Sheri, you are awful good to Buk sometimes   bringing him bits of magic   and though you are cruel you are sometimes overtaken by good and you cannot help it: you are more German than I. I am an old beergarden german   in love with music and fire   I am not the tough-helmet bastard ready to plow the guts out of the enemy—although, if necessary, I am ready. Which a seven foot bartender found out one night when I chased him all over town with a very small pocket knife. His fear was as great as my anger and although I never caught him he will remember me forever   and not as a poet.

McClure I don't know. A lot of them I don't know, and I thank god for that. Down where I'm working now   they gather around me   they don't know about the poetry   but they smell something working   I don't say anything   but no matter what table I sit at   here they come sitting around me   and I don't want them. And a Mexican says to me— "Where's the greatness? You hate everybody, you don't have any friends. I don't understand." He is a pretty good boy and I like him because he is trying to think. "I have never claimed to be great," I tell him. "Yeah," he says, "but I see Noel looking up at you, I see his eyes shining. I see the *others*. *They* think you are somebody. What is it?" and I say, "Vasquez, for Christ's sake or mine, give me a cigarette, you are getting on my nerves." And he lights me up and I look down on the flame and puff in and I can feel the whole world run up my arms, into my shoulders, my chest, my heart, where I will spit it out as a poem.

"Who do you like in the 6th. race tomorrow?" Vasquez asks.

"Lightning Don will be just about ready. They've found a spot for him and a distance. The odds will be 6 to one."

ok, love   *Buk*   bukowski

April 8
[postcard with drawing of CB in angry concentration]

Deah Shed:
ok not to write if moonrays messing up tide. I am putting
my personal hex on all orders groups and individuals
                    who are messing in your soup.
    ok now.

        L.,
                bukoOWWWWWWSSskiiiiiiiii, chas.
                Buk

Los Angeles, Calif.
April 12th., 1961

Dear Sheri:
I can't come up to you if I don't know where you're at.
Some hotel in town, or I don't know where San Gregorio's at or
where your shack is at. You forget Buk is mostly now los angeles boy; doubt if I could even find Frisco—just point my car
that way with its thin tires and hope.

Besides this, got old woman tailing me eating my minutes.
Don't know what to do with her, don't want to hurt her; but
that is another problem and I don't want to bother you with it.

Oye, Shed, what a mess you had; first with brother in law
and then with bitch and her broodlings. I am sorry I was not
there... to take you off somewhere and assure you quietly that
you are a goddess alive and that they are dung.

It is difficult when you don't have a dollar to find status or
even voice with the money-grubbers. I lived for years on air and
whiskey, beer without any visible means of support, and many
times they cut me and lashed me from behind their fat dollar
bills. That is why I try to hold the silly job I have now: to give
me a wall to work behind.

I am trying to get caught up on some things here now; pick
myself up off the floor.

Sheri, baby, I am sorry for what they put you through, but I

200

don't think it's my time to come up there. I am writing poems and drinking beer and trying to buy a shack, and seem to be getting nothing done. Except think I wrote a fair one last night. Up all night. Should clean this place. Dishes in sink, paper, clothing on floor. I cannot seem to right myself.

They had some kids running in this place, 2 fat ones, up and down the steps, slamming doors PLANG!!!! Bring me on lance-nerve ends out of sack like rocket. Then Oakie with door open playing Oakie music. I get out my hex-sack, shuffle around torn mutuel tickets and sod from dead dog's dreams, and now they are gone... the whole lot of them. But besides the hex-sack, I spoke very gently to manager   in hushed shocked tones. I am an old fox, Shed, fighting wearies me. You can't fight the mob, Shed, because you must fight in mob-language and the fuzz only understands mob-language; the fuzz is mob and soulless; when they drag in the fuzz you just have more enemy, armed, shaven and well-rested. They called the fuzz on me one night—I had a gal in here, drinking and what—this so-called respectable place. They going to run me in but I kept chain on door and talked them away. Why don't they leave us in peace, Sheri? They know we are really breathing, and inside, way in, they want to kill us; they can't stand it.

I am going to try to build up a roll on the quarter horses next week. I must get my shack, and when I do you must come see me. I will send you the money. A couple of weeks away from there will do you good. And I am a man and not a child. We need only talk, or not talk. I know you are real and that is all that matters.

love,

Buk

ps—I just put another plague and a hex on ALL YOUR ENEMIES, EXCLUDING NONE. May their teeth and bones rot in the acid of my curse; may their rotten hearts flicker with the doubts and horror of unmaligned hell... look for clear skies, love, the sun is coming up... BUK

buk-O: if you ever come visit then head up highway #1 (coast highway) to Tunitas Creek & it is a bit past san gregorio; don't give whereabouts away to ANYone not even IF ezra shd ask! that's how much i want privacy! after san greg. about 10 min heading towards frisco you'd cross a bridge & at 1st wee dirt turn-in saying: "TEN ACRES FOR RENT" that wd be it & it is the last cot[tage] down to left/

hotel rm is day deal & at night i go home with gib; stayed down country last 2 days & all was well/ yr hex working; the good coming out: the old care taker mr clark had fool'd us into thinking it was his ice box & we had to let back door open so he cd come & go; landlord sd it aint his & so after his conduct on ishtar day; we now can keep our doors locked & bitchass next door has to store his food in HER ice box

now i don't need to talk to either one of them; the gods at work????? now except for threat of their kids—i am left alone which is what i wanted; i am writing up an account of it having regained my sense of form & you'll get a copy of course; it is hilarious looked at from a certain point of view...

a tiny history of human beings; broLaw still a problem; what a pain in the ass these persons with inferiority mind states can be; the communist party is their refuge; gawd hellppp it when the TIME comes;

am cool now but you can see that i was dithered; it is the fates who are trying to make me into a strong person but i cry for pappa & who aint ever here iz pops; ez wuz it for 6 yrs; gib is a wee baby inside & aint been trod on nuff yet to sqwuack back; that broLaw broke camels back; my god—he NEVER lets up; "oh ho ho crazy sheri..." etc alls i can do is what my coloured friends taught me: "YOUR MOTHER WUZ CRAZY YEW NUT-DDTTT"   hard & fast & back crackin...

but he is a scared runt... who wants to poke a runt into a mud hole? i thought i was a compassionate female; i see his story... but he is DANGEROUS... it aint safe to let an entire fami-ly of strangers believe one is a "nutddd" & he is one crazy bas-tard by now; completely nuts on this ¼million $$$ shit when he's bedbug flat/

ez said: "the Lee family are part of your american educa-tion" & oh wuz he right; my AMERICAN education/ what i know about integration cd drive this country back to 1776/ it is rough—it works better when the MAN is white—a female is too inferior to have a 'voice' & these coloured men do not have ANY—but have seen those jap wives stompin' in & out of dress stores whilse white-y stands patiently outside holding his 2/3 half white-ies while miss nippon thrills her female ass in der yankee doodle bargain stores—i just grin; good for the dumb bunny. Trying to find a jap wife who kow-tows iz like trying to retire in a mudhole in mexico; i mean white women are better as compassionate wives & the usa is cleaner AND cheaper than greezer & co/ any jap female who marries the sort of thing i've seen attached to them (what no white female wd want) is larceny hearted & dumb bunny is fooled by the tourist blurb/ & i was fooled by all those goddamm'd translations of bow-y-bow-y chop chop & it turned into slithers & money grabbers who hate us; gib is decent being half of us (but his maw sure got some low ways on her ass) oh well this all silly; maid just told me: "always take pie when pie is passed as it may not come back—" in other words go look at some dresses & get out today as i told her i was UNdecided... a new dress wd be fun... so long bukow... sheri turns female on ya... & she slithers up town to try on silkie shimmers... now all is well duckder & i dankyew fo' yo' hex; please keep it up as i still loathe the notion that broLaw is anywhere within walkin' ridin' distance/ and thank you... thank you...

Sheri

Los Angeles, Calif.
April, say 16th., 1961
in which this uncouth one
begs unction in the shape
of beer or sleep
or a minor victory upon
the hot boards.

Deah Sharhieeee:
    Tank you for the H.D.; seems rather proper and formal to me, but I realize   ingrained and worked through, a classical

203

vendetta against the walls, and so   this is needed, of course,
        as we occupy space
Ez has the same hard control, and of course   hysteria is for
        the hophead and German-Pollocks
but I remember so many times when I went into libraries
looking for hysteria   hoping to find madness and
        disorganization
but everything was plish and polished Art and carefulness
and I walked out   blacker than any nigger
either the world of Art was invalid since its conception
or   I belonged someplace else. I have since worked out a
compromise: if the world of Art will ignore me, I will not only
ignore the world of Art but the other world also.

And since then I have had my beer in peace—I mean, com-
paratively, along with wars, landlords, half-wives, lightning,
cool Jory's and the what.

7 Poets Press is going ahead with my second book and
Larsen is picking some wildflowers—I am listening to Pagliaccia, or how you spell?—
one jew or jap or wop or german or what human being
can contain immense suffering; I do not say this in the old
        sense
in the prima donna sense
                    like chipping away at marble and
making a to-do about it, saying   I'm done in   I've had it
all I'm good for is chipping in the marble of the arts
chippying in the halls and drawing pretty prick pictures; but
what I mean is what I say: one human being can pack in and
        hold
more pain than the ocean bottom; and sometimes it's good to
        come back from the ocean bottom of pain and not say
        too much, not be too Arty about it.

If it has been bad enough, you are the one who knows; any
need to tell the world about it is not only irregular
        but assuming a luxuriant posture. If you can say it
irregulary

---

7 Poets Press … Larsen: Carl Larsen edited CB's *Longshot Pomes* [sic] *for Broke Players.*
Pagliaccia: *Pagliacci*, Leoncavallo's famous opera.

204

or in the manner of wolves running through the forest
I think it excusable. Now I don't mean the hard core or form.
Hysteria is plausible   except that you may ask in a drunken
     voice
but never beg. These are not rules, but decencies of spirit.
And I realize that I can tell you nothing.

I have never received a letter from you, no matter the cuss
words or indignities... that was not shaped out of electric clay
thousands of years old. But so much for that.

Heard from Safford Chamberlain of KPFK who wants to
have me read some of my own poetry to be taped for future
broadcast material. I must tell him no. It is interesting that people know that I am alive, but I don't think of myself as a poet
     essentially   but when I do think of myself as a poet I can-
not see the poet's place
     as being on the stage,
     being on the stage is something else and those are other
people. Hell, I realize they are all doing it: Winters, Lowell,
Ransom, Tate; and Corso and Ginsburg and people like that,
but I have always followed my own insides' saying, and my
insides say NO NO NO!!!!!!
                    no.
these people always claim they are trying to awaken the public
to poetry like shaking the ragdoll alive, but I rather wonder if it
isn't the old ego calling, and all the pose and bullshit
     and the hard-core practiced lines out of the mould
     were nothing at all,
     and that   finally   they would rather be just as famous
as Bob Hope.
     poets, indeed. SWINE BLATHERERS.
     Shed, when I die nobody will know it for 3 or 4 or 5 days—
I have no friends, just one old woman who drinks wine—until
the body starts to stink and there will be no one to bury me. But
I have thought it all over. And I feel that although I am not
building a monument, I am not building rot. I cannot say as
much for my neighbor who has 5 kids and a large Sunday gathering of noise and who is keeping the world alive while I let it
die.

Winters, Lowell, Ransom, Tate: major American poets at the time.

But it is odd that after saying something, making a statement, it no longer matters, as this no longer matters. And that is well, so we can get on to something else.

I expect to live to be close to one hundred years old and by the time I am 60 I am going to begin to carve; but *this* is the time of proper and gentle building and watching. Strength and knowledge come through sweat and new skins and new love, not love of woman but love of stem and the color of a coffee tin, flower and coffee gone, woman gone, old screens with holes letting in sunlight and small wild dirty flies.

Immortality is knowing that you are finally beaten...

Sheri, Gib is gentle and does not want trouble. If you want a fighter go to the zoo. An ape never doubts his own strength nor does he ever doubt that he is wrong. The trouble with a thinking man is that by the time he has gotten through trying to think out both sides

he has either been talked out of it

or clubbed to the floor

A good motto for thinkers is: in times of doubt or danger never think, strike. The victor makes the rules of right or wrong; the thinker can only muse on the damage done and the preciousness of defeat.

Or as Ezra might say

KICK 'EM IN THE BALLS FIRST
AND READ 'EM PETRARCH LATER.

Something in the H.D. book you sent me. Think not for me. Am enclosing along with coins that were attached to it. (See within)

I burnt your rocks. Boy oh boy   you witch
you beautiful spirit-witch   keep me in your camp and I'll keep you in mine, and may we never meet
because we'll see that we are of ordinary clay and design
wear shoes   blink   stink   desire   go to the bathroom
and are dull flabs of what the sky sends us down.

Webb has not written. I told him I felt as if I were a stone in his road and to get on with the other writers. I have wanted to make him a little angry and now I have succeeded. Now we are even for him sending his son down on me in the middle of the night. I viewed his son that night and I did not see a great

206

writer; I did see an agreeable, calm and intelligent person. I am sorry if my nerves showed a bit, but any minor status in the poetic world had nothing to do with it. I would not have been as angry if I had been faddled with by R. Jeffers, but almost.

And now Webb is asking for photos and the old gal and I got out in the hot sun, but the blinker thing was on for flash photos, it's an old 4 dollar camera that is supposed to do both, and I hate my face, a lot of scars and now-appearing (it seems) a happy flabbiness, and I took some of her not for Webb and they all came out blank but we didn't know and got drunk and felt good that it was over,

but it isn't over and I don't know what to do.

tomorrow I might well try it over

but why must a man have photos? unless he is running a photo mag.

I think the only way out for me is to indulge in trigamy...

Jory, yes. I cannot quite discard Jory. He is better in letter and poem than in person. When I see him actually

he is so much like the young eager salesman

ready to tell the flip joke or pinch the gal next to him in the ass when she bends over to retrieve whatever they retrieve to show their ass.

and then fill a poem full of stars and the crippled gazelle of living. I'd like to sit him in a room with Jeffers for 8 or 10 hours; they'd probably both come out babbling.

meanwhile,
Buk
Buk

Los Angeles, Calif.
April 17th., 1961

Deah Shed:

Worried about your mind-state.

You coming through, gal? Or are you going to die among the flowers or Chinese chipsewie? Maybe Pound kicked you out of nest, does not mean to die with your elbows dangling.

207

u still got Buk. all right, so meebee nobody knows me but I know me and I am subjective-objective enough to know I am not a bowl of soup or Popeye the Sailor Man. I know it's the favorite sport
of a lot of yours to play genius;
I play mye eye self and I got to firuelious or something
figure a lot of tags have been wrong.
not that I give a damn. Each man (or woman) must live out of the INSIDE OF HIS GUTS AND FOUR WALLS.
Heard from kaja—she seems a little mixed.
but what the hell? do you mean to tell me that through the sanity   insanity   of these ariel words   that   iiii
can change anything?
Pound may not like this attitude but Pound got his ass caught in the meat-grinder and Pound never heard of Buk, and now Pound has to cuff off his political favors as being on the right but losing side or whatever the chippy said when she spilled her drink and wanted another one before going up to my room.
Pound can go to hell.
all right. so u do not like it. nor do I like grey idols. it's time to move on.
...space, it seems, can almost transcend death. Another toy to make us important enough to live
without the
overwrought falsity of poetry.
Ernie *cannot* write! I told you that. Ernie wants to seem or sound like a writer. Ernie is not insane. Ernie has never seen 17 baby pigs running   running   through something   a hole in the fence   and laughing laughing   the dog and I   the pigs the pigs   and then going back to the factory   not the dog but I, and Ernie prob takes his books with his brains and lets them KNOW   nobody knows me
they think I am just a tough blank-faced old man
and they think
correctly   goddess
the masses are not always wrong, but it is good sometimes to be tough and hard, it allows me to go on thinking and breathing, and maybe wot wot wot   who knows what we try. ????

...drunker than the searchlight

feeble feeler
when the rays are subtractions.

all things that hold us together
will finally fall apart,
but neither of us will [*handwritten:*] (etherial abstraction of
    something I do not quite understand—)
be right or wrong

Winter comes but once a year but you can get drunk on any
old good night.
drunkeness is a form of suicide that allows thou to expell all
the shit in the belly or thy mind
and come back   like a Lazarus   full of piss and pennies.
I am the soldier in the mirror. I can see Carthage and Nap
and Hit. I smoke and smile and drink.—I have lived in East St.
Louis and I have lived in Hell.
the hellyjelly law pounded my cookoodoor the other night
old woman's laughter   broken bottlewebs
I wouldn't let them in to sin.
things must rot. that is part of the PLAN. GOD DAMN THE
PLAN. i do NOT ACCEPPT ACCEPT ACCEPT ACEPPT
nature or whatever it is
when something down near my navel says this is evil;
I am not a cur or a crusador   and I'm glad they never found
the grail, they wd have only pissed in it, but I piss in myself
and know I am nothing, and this is the most important beginning of all—all your genius-playing, fame-urgency tribe committed.
my youth has taken a walk but my mind has not. Or, so it
says. to me. we must never be sure. even when we are...
which was pound's mistake, of course; being sure and then
sure again and then MORE SURER than ever. Admirable courage
of course and DEDICATION   but men are born bottled shitted
born millions at a time all over the world   many of them never
to write   never to know what a typewriter is   or a lit. mag
some men bending over rice or what awful slipsloopshit   *much
better poets   leaders   gutfullredbeasts*   than Pound   only out
of it   ON A GOD DAMNED SHIT CHANCE OF MATH.
But your Ez is fat ehohellhow to figure he is the only one.
And for this, he is fortunate in his narrowmindedness.

209

Did Ez ever explain why he kicked you out of nest? was it
me? or didn't he explain? I am not knocking P. entirely. He has
so far the greatest GRAMMATICAL FORCE OF THE WORD
 a man trained to whip the lion
 but a man who could neither laugh nor forgive
 or admit being second to anyone
even a 49 day old cat on the fire escape wet steps
after fucking a whore, and everything tired in the arms
and antiotes of nations forgotten whores forgotten
as the sun comes down. Pound was human and I must not
ride him too hard. I am getting almost like E., and I
do not want to do that.
 Pound? He stands smoking and I would slug him against
the bricks except things must rot that is part of the plan.
 there is some enduring world here that should not be; we
are toys—recollection and the will to live, and certainly Shake
said it.

and against the girl I loved but one night, —
the armies of Alaric, the deer across the fender.

your yellow paged letters blue ones filled with
wat conjure up 35 thousand gods.

as for and far as I am concerned: THE MOCKING BIRD DOES
  NOT ATTEMPT SUICIDE.

how many dead do we want or need
how many wars how many New Jersey loves
how many 126976 hands?
how many feet?

most men are nothing; they only pretend to god awful be.

dullness, overlasting dullness and pretense; retch us out of yes
  this here with the drab liquor of singing.

try to decide what my brain is trying to tell me.

Alaric: Visigoth king and conqueror (370?–410).

210

musing leads to madness.

I am wise enough to come back and circle myself and bite out
a chunk like a wild dog.

into and beyond terror   seriousness will not do. Seriousness
and the rag-dillpickle bopeek books are gypsy gone

we must carve from fresh marble

they taught us this and that, but then
wine   good wine   came down   through   the staring and
unbelieving eye.

the indistinct smoke of verse is gone, if I have to kill it
myself. If you   or I were Greco   or even a watersnake. well,
rub your hands and prove that you are alive. walk the floor. this
is the gift. certainly the charm of dying   lies in the fact   that
nothing is lost.
the hand of silk tangling in and out of melodies   runs in
and out of vases   and death runs eoyow!! down my throat like
a mouse; the palm trees hold up the air of the poetry we
breathe.
I don't know—I meant to go on, becoming hrby wuckus-
wacked by something less than gladiolie   blurb or wot
buxome, I say, is the hore of horse   clasp   and   hoof
destroyed or not   the rubber nose and mouth and skin
like the clasp of an ironing board... the final poem will be
relaxed like some old castle burning.
daffodils viking bastards   calm as frogs

x you bitch,
taking out the   oh so comely sprite whore of hours

I am trying to find a girlfriend for Picasso.

...your remaining sex is my salvation like
the eyes of god in grapefruit
like arrows in the brain of a washed-away nightmare.

your X should be my X

and the little walk-away wrongs and worms
from coffins   must pleasantly
wait their play.

like a coney-Island hot warbling buckets of tar.

I wd of course prefer to die with the fox in the ferns, or as a
photograph of a Spad (World War I) wound bout my throat like
a necktie, and all the girls gone   and the legs legs legs legs
girls kicking real high.

old poets are quite as bad as old queers; there's something quite
unacceptable in either of them.

  And I don't see quite how you can go for H.D.
unless you go for befriending, and don't ever to have to do that,
Goddess.
  I can always write how the hell hwo ho drunk or wot   I kin
always write you a letter that can make yoir yes eyeballs crop up
in the center of your hands and wonder what's happening.
  Meanwhile   I have all hexes working. Relax.

      Truly,
       Charles—
       Bymxkskli

   19/april/61   pobx 46   s.g. cal

buk/ like a gypsy raised by gypsy mother & half-breed irish
from silver-tongued juice-happy father; lived on a liquid diet he
did; roaming the eastern seaboard from age GO—now a week
here now there; different names & ages & background; charity
but parents sending me with the relief checks to stand in line or
for shoes or old eggs etc—whenever got 'lost' in new town...
soon's my mother turned her back I'd 'go for a walk' & stay hrs

---

Spad: a French fighter plane.

212

& hrs until dark & she'd call cops: "i don't know HOW she got there but you'll find my little girl in the closest museum or public library"

i'd be there filling my soul up with the old dead bones that i somehow knew & gems & old objects... always in the rooms of mummies... from early age... my toys wd be... old bones the dogs left on the city streets... that i'd wrap in torn stained rags & lay in the back yard under the fire escapes... putting stone rooms around them & then go into a trance like state... even at 2 or 3 yrs old... i'd worship my 'mummies'...

and always was of a mind so fantastic & filled with knowledge that didn't know how got there... "you shd give this one to the church" they'd say... those church people who came with baskets of foods... that made my mother cringe & simper...

the church ugly bitch with her eye-cunts droolin' on me... trying to get her old come out of her brains by me... handing me the doll... age 2 ish... (I cd read & write & draw at 2) the large $5 doll that creamed my mother's no-childhood-days-in-family-18-kids & just big little girl drawers... my mother wanted the doll... I played with my bones rags & stones & trances... the backed-up come bitch from the neighborhood church... "what does th' doll say little girl??" turning over baby doll... "maaaaaa-ma" it went & i hated giving her any sex thrill... said i: "the doll says 'pa pa'" & it went on for a while but i wdn't change my story for no doll even tho' was sorry for poor maw who got herself laid by a gay irish lad & had to marry him... costing him his rich family... been excommunicated from holy roman cat'lick church 2-ice & paid way back in... 1st time... last time raised hell & was OUT for long while... sorry i had to be cause of her UNdoing... gentle fearful beautiful gypsy mother... one of 18 kids... ignorant as a worm... beautiful as a pagan... church cunt finally let me have doll with big show of dismissing moronic kid & i went out & drop'd doll in rain water & returned to my bones rags & stones... fuck church bitch... ought not to masturbate on the joy of small kids... but I was wary... & ancient... now that i see my teeth going i rejoice... somewhere buried in a secret spot in that mummy that my spirit keeps coming out of... again & again & again... and each time a tooth falls from its long dead head... my earth form loses a grip on its teeth life & I sing in joy because i know... as soon as it turns into dust... my spirit will be liberated... her wisdom & compassion

213

keeps her tied to earth... coming thru that lovely set dead dried skin hair & bones wrap'd in rags in a deep cave...

my hair is falling out & i weep for joy... my ancient mummy decays... soon the bones will be under attack... the skin is long since splotched... the hair loosening & the teeth gone... this reincarnation my teeth went bad from birth... the mummy's going... & i will be free then... i am beautiful as a vampire... & ancient as death... no one knows my age... i am cunning as an old ghetto jew... & deep with wisdom & tired as life itself but filled with love for us all... daily i wait for that old set of bones to leave... surely they cannot hold out beyond this life... i can already feel my own bones going...

at early age... cut out words I S I S from some yiddish kotex advert. or whiskey ad... cut it out secretly & pin'd over bed... age 5 or 6 or 7... & the thrill that took me at these 4 words shook me from any modern religion back to that of the dust bag where I return & come & go... it was sheri at st. liz that got the heiroglyphics into the cantos that my language never die... never die... never die...

how d.p.'s son Omar Pound hated me... he sneered: "I guess you got a dog tag around yr neck to call dogs with" because I sd to maestro: "it is my 2 ivory oriental bracelets that called the oriental visitor..." & sure enough i had my medal of the lady & i touched it saying: "yes i do... i have a medal which calls my lady... eeeezzzzessss" & omar had spent time in persia & egypt & knew i wuz a hick & his eyes shot out because thanks to my lady... the pronunciation of her name was perfect he knew it & he was scared for mocking me—i had a beautiful scarab that a german boy gave me but father jordon took it when i sought refuge with the stancioff family & he came visiting & i served him their whiskey... & took a bit myself & called him a cocksuckin' motherfucker... he came at me & put his hands around my back & undid my rope removing the scarab... that I wore not to lose it & gave me the miraculous medal... &

---

d.p.'s son Omar Pound: Dorothy Shakespear's son (1926–), raised by Pound as his own.

eeeezzzzesss: Isis, the Egyptian goddess.

stancioff family: a well-to-do family that SM stayed with intermittently during the 1950s while visiting Pound.

said "wear that... for protection" & he kept my scarab... & he
wont return it... the catholic witchwarlock
   but it changed my life... the Lady is now in clothes from
head to foot... but I am here to rip them from her & let my lady
breathe again... that we all breathe... I am not a goddess but a
high priestess of my Lady of the Skye—the Lady of the African
Blue that I painted & paint... Ezra is the SCORPION   H.D. is
the SNAKE   & S.M. is the HAWK... E.P. born under sign scorpio   H.D. has a signet sign of the snake & the thistle & s.m.
has the lines in the (her) cantos: "bright hawk whom no hood
shall chain"
   3 signs of life they are; the scorpion is the dragon sign; the
snake is from crete & the hawk is from egypt/ on p. 67 yr H.D.
SELECTED POEMS   GROVE PRESS: POEM: *Fair the Thread*: H.D.
wrote:
> "the scorpion, snake and hawk
> are gold-patterned
> as on a king's pall"

and she my goddess H.D. did not know what I know... who is
the scorpion, & the snake & the hawk; i was the last to come...
   i come out of egypt & return there—time beats at my door
& i return—like a sound from the old drum of dried bones
secure in a place where the feet of many men beat the earth & i
know how to judge the time by their beats over my stone
room... many cities have gone up & fallen down over top of my
head & i come out of gypsy mothers & gay lost fathers; it is
safest in such places... nothing has ever touched me nor
changed one atom of my pattern... it is always the same... truth
is love; truth is death; truth is life; rebirth; truth is our food; our
light; our destiny, fate, colour, shape, form & design/
   on p. 66 same book/ read: "If you take the moon in your hands
> and turn it round
> (heavy, slightly tarnished platter)
> you're there;"

consider how this remote eternal spirit—gave slang talk to the
nubians... her time's kids: "man... yew there..."—read *Georgius
Sanctus* out ringing loud like african drum tribal ceremonies—
every word is a drum... drum... drum... dig the word endings in

---

"*bright hawk ... shall chain*": from Canto 91 (635).

Hymn   p. 69   "jar   myrrh   stored   secure"
H.D. never 'studied poetry' she IS poetry
her ear is fine as silk
                    and as strong; read *The Walls Do Not Fall*
my god... you need me to read it to you & thrill yr earballs kid/
9/45 a.m.   star in mid east   egypt   israel a flame
        burning earth   farmer burning field
            air message;
                    p.79   H.D. "yet the ancient rubrics reveal that
                            we are back at the beginning:"
"enigmas, rubrics promise as before
protection for the scribe;
                    he takes precedence of the priest,
                    stands second only to the Pharaoh."
thou'rt a scribe
                    i am one—"second only to the Pharaoh"
and the Pharaoh is coming; I am waiting now for the Pharaoh;
read *The Flowering of the Rod*   about the wild geese   & what
        the world is
read *The Helmsman*   "we have always known you wanted us"
        what better prayer?
    I never read poetry unless i reach the mind state of intense
agony where i have no way to turn & i am helpless... either
without money or wheels or friends or even po li... in agony &
helpless then i turn to the record & i only can read those words
that are like balm on my writhing brains... they cool me & heal
me & then i know why the agony came down on me... to force
me to KNOW & it was no different with H.D. or ezra...
    now to yr 2 lets: when say kicked me out of nest am using
image—it was a nest in st. liz... warm & cozy & am now on
own... poor birdie hardly knew how to fly when scorpion tossed
eternal light to her & cut out for italy/   re: theories of painting
clip/   there is never more than one or 2 great artists of any period... the rest is theory; the art that remains is the art that dealt
with the hidden realities of the age; its eternal beauty/   i am the
only painter that will matter because one of my works has the
power to change what surrounds it & not to be changed—
w[yndham]. lewis is our greatest 'social' painter; gautier our
sculptor; and the Hawk is the painter... not interested in slopin'
up the world with art... but to plant seeds... & harvest in the few
churrrrr

216

observe that Pascin cannot draw hands or feet
nor breasts... but only can make a picture of it; that is
not eternal art
                that is the monkey doing flesh pictures
charrrrrrrRRRRRRRRRming and dated/ his yiddish girls are without great spirit & depressed & all cunt which is not the real love
hole; it goes into the mind which aint the brain but being in the
mind it convulses the brain & that in turn twitches the cunt or
rooster stick/ but it begins in the mind... even the hollywood
jews who letch & lust & got gold to pay... it starts in their
mind... a love of beauty that is so tied in with their genius for
decaying... that it wd lust the purity out of love... but nevertheless the process is the same as sacred love/ Pascin an intererst-
ing Jew with a Yen for Beauty; that is no goddess he gives us
but an earth worm's view of a hunk of beefsteak in good prime
& a swell smell when cookin'
         doz all/ the zen joke is another yiddish comment to dumb
xtian tits in bed; north beach full of xtian tits or painted faces
who wd grab ANY stage to emote upon... even the snarl; fuck &
drop one... yes ernie CAN write buk/ he has that good yiddish
clarity of mind; he wont give us poetry duckder but he will give
us an INSIGHT into literature & after all the degree that ernie is
going to have to teach has got to have the insight brought before
them; they are too buried under age-old hate for poetry... ernie
is a Jew who has no hate in him... only grief...
         the remainder of this letter seems to be in a forgotten lan-
guage resembling english but not being it so turning to other
let/
         h.d. not "proper" or "formal"—she is more economical but
still us...   magic   deciphers   key stones   information
valuables—world of american art not same as w. of europ. art;
h.d.'s audience in europe/ ours is here & some times i write for
them too when i have impulse/ they know more at a certain
degree so i can say less & mean more—way h.d. does; human

---

gautier: Henri Gaudier-Brzeska (1891–1915), French sculptor, championed by Pound.
Pascin: Jules Pascin (1885–1930), Bulgarian-born American painter,
draughtsman, and printmaker.

pain is so old that it aint news in europe; yes yew iz a german pollack ah lived in them neighborhoods as kid; very familiar face... kind & good people & loving...

go read on tape buk you coward; these kids need some road to follow wild geese leader... that is a way... try to give them some respectability... but insist on yr own terms... make 'em come to you... it is safety from the mob   it is 'respectability' it is putting the power in yr hands to help another scribe in pain; do not be so selfish—it is not you—it is truth we are keeping alive/ & when one comes burning with truth... is beer ALL you'll be able to give?? com'n you big dumb pollack... go make those bastards with their wires & holes & tapes & horseshit etc... make 'em W O R K   FOR   US who are out of egypt & return to it... or i will kick yr ass when i get you back inside that tomb you dumb dickhead; stop POSING AS AN AWTIZ & GO TO WORK   SHITHEAD   take anything... snatch anything... but make yr own terms... and do not go there or let them come unless you can be yrself... no matter vottddddd kidttt... it is a POSE to deny any poet... you or any other... a place in the sun; after my work on earth be done... there will be a wee hope for the female of our kind... black white pink gold grey or yalllerrr... because i will take anything i can to help... i wd shit in public if they'd pay me for it & then give money to little beverly to write her purple passions out... i wd crawl on my belly like a cur... if i knew a pair of boots that wd feed crumbs to my little chickens...

there is life & there is art & it is our job to bring them together with setting the joint on fire... or drownin' it in come... gib is an inert creature... that snatched a jet-propelled squid... quivering with life & that sends out a black ink screen when under attack/ gib's inert... his super self that sees all & knows all wdn't move if you cracked down the world on it; he wont move & he aint ever gonna... it is the quivering squid shed that gets us out of places & into new places... and changes every spot we get to... gib wont move for shit man & he wont fight or do anything else & he only works in order to escape from me for enough time to recover from the shock of the quivering intensity; his job is his sanity... well i am forced to use my mind for

---

beverly: Beverly Applebaum, a poetry contributor to *A&P*.

fighting & that wont hurt it... gib wont fight with mind or body...

am mailin' you herb co book where get frankenscense/ will mail you some got from east coast co but believe will be same; now must go—eat lunch in car with gib/ will drop jory a note but not right now—i want to be free to stop all the worldliness & be invisible again; then can see jory & co... when house is not full of paper & work & stuff...

this hotel reading room... will encl clip very interest. clip'd in 1956... only this yr this room got any time to read as nothin' else to do... 5 yrs haulin' stuff around... now i cry for freedom... will finish work & be gypsy again...

ezra has my la martinelli soul in castle in italy—now let gypsy be free... the daughter of the pharaoh... La Farona... if i ever get to you i will make draw. then don't need any fotos... you are a serious man now & not any more little boy; be as you are... we all mourn the first freshness but now if we are aware that the mummy is fast rotting & freeing us from this love task... if yew skin badtt yew mummy parchment is going to dust... no matter... you still second only to the pharaoh.

now go read on to tape & use those ruddy buggers... i go eat sandwiches & tea & mail out yo wocks this week & send you love...

> & be good...
>> fo yo mamma
>>> *Sheri*

Los Angeles, Calif.
April 22, 1961

Sister in the Dust:

I *cannot* read and I *will* not read for their little dirty skins; I will not go on tape; I will not stand before a mike and spiel something into it that I have long ago written and forgotten; I will not be their dupe and their dummy; I will not have their handshake, or their women or their wine or their brotherhood. I stand alone and apart from the artists and the scribblers—I will have none of them. Every touch of them is death. I fear them

219

not because I am weak but because I am strong. I am a simple person.

You have no idea how your "innocent" Jory, the Riverboat Jordan Kid, hung me from the cross by the balls. Dragging editors, writers, in upon me. Or me upon them. —"Oh, come on, come on with me! I have an appointment with this guy! I don't want to go. But it's 6:30 now and I was supposed to be there at 5:30. But he's treated me nicely. And I've got to go and I want you to come with me."

"Jory, I'd rather not."

"Oh, come on, Jesus Christ, man! Just this once..." and etc.

And so I weakened and went, and learned.

Or the next night on the phone: "I'm over at a little gathering at X, the painter's place. You've heard of him? You haven't? Well, anyhow, it's just a small group of people, some drinks and some talk..."

This, of course, I threw out the window like a tarantula upon my worst enemy.

Drinks and talk, all of them rubbing together, telling each other that they are great, and later, like a bunch of over-the-fence neighborhood bitches, cutting each other down... Princess, or whoeverthehell you are, I have tested myself. Once in college I deliberately forced myself into the hell of a poetry class, and it was here that I learned what I already knew—that poetry was the most pretensive of all the Arts and dragged in the most slipshod practitioners out of the morass. I learned plenty but I would have learned more shooting down rooks.

I cannot speak on tape for a petty bunch of word-mongers who would really rather be fucked and praised than shape the word. It is not proper to bring in personal experience, but when you have crawled across the cold cement floor of a charity hospital with the blood spewing in great sick showers from your mouth and your ass, and nobody to answer. The doors closed, doors a foot thick so the nurses can't hear the screams of those too poor to die nicely. And all the old men looking at me, white-haired sticks the ravens had picked dry. And finally an hour later—a nurse. "Oh, you've hemorrhaged *again*! Oh dear, I can't pick you up." She could have, there was nothing left but bone and skin. And 2 of them came and sat me in a chair and they slid the chair across the floor to my bed and *flicked* me in, like red wet garbage.

220

And then the head nurse came: "You need some transfusions, but you'll either have to pay for them or have blood-credit, someplace you have donated blood, or we can't give you any."

And later, as I was getting well. "Who is that horrible woman who comes to see you? She was drunk. You are going to have to stay away from women like that and you must never drink again."

And at the age of 13 I became covered with boils the size of baseballs. Not pimples, baseballs. And they sat me under the electric needle and drilled   drillllled   drilled deep into the flesh   I could feel the little needle getting hot... like a wood drill punching into wood... and I could smell the oil... another charity hospital... "Jesus," said the doc, "I never saw a guy go under the needle like that."

"I'm used to it," I told them, "every other day for 3 years."

And you *do* get used to it. But not when you get on a streetcar and some kid tugs at his mother's sleeve: "Mommy, what's wrong with that man's face?"

I could understand it now, but then it rocked to the center of me, cutting away whatever liberty I had built up in forgetting.

Other things, of course, that happen to us all. But now you want me to sputter a few god damned words I have written into a microphone while out in the audience 30 or 40 bitches feel "sorry" for me because I have a "soul," and would like nothing better than to fuck me 3 or 4 times to let me see what they have and then marry me and turn me into something like anything that walks down the street, anybody you might pass at any time. It is not my intent to be different; it is my intent to remain myself. I have been taught by some very hard gods, some stone gods, and what I wring is from stone and iron.

Don't set me up in front of a microphone like the silhouette of a duck to be shot down in a cheap shooting gallery. I don't want any of their glory and I don't want to "educate" the bastards. The world will turn on its own. THE GROWING OF ONE MAN PROPERLY IS OFTEN MORE THAN ONE MAN OF THE GREATEST STRENGTH CAN HANDLE. And by "properly" I do not mean the fixed targets of a society deadened with the mass-glue of its crawling. I mean the way we must pull up a shade in the morning and scratch our belly and yawn, and the way we must understand that what appears to be holy is often the

221

greatest evil and what appears to be evil... is the source.

H.D. fails.

What I mean, is this. We must ask ourselves, is this person trying to write POETRY or is this that we read—that we hear, see—coming unwinding from a self that is highly improbable and unwinding, say, like the thread from a spider's gut?

H.D. tries too hard to write "poetry" and gives her weakness away, but in this respect she has much so-called good company: Shakespeare, Keats, T.S. Eliot, Tennyson, Auden, Wordsworth, Whitman, Dylan Thomas, Burns, Robert Frost, Coleridge, Poe, Swinburne, Sandburg, Ransom, Aiken (although Aiken is the most glorious fake of the lot with Shake); Cummings, Graves, Hart Crane, C. Day Lewis, Eberhart, Spender, Shapiro, Henry Reed, and so forth.

There are very few poets of pure aspect: Chaucer, John Skelton, John Donne, Milton, Dryden, Blake, Edward Lear, Emily Bronte, Melville, Whitman, Christina Rossetti, Henley, Francis Thompson, Yeats, Walter De La Mare, D.H. Lawrence, Pound, Jeffers, and perhaps—George Barker.

Ginsburg is a complete ninny running up the mare's ass for the pussy of fame. He throws up a big smokescreen but his soul is the size of one grain of salt and will wash away in the first faint sprinkle.

I disregard your constant slurs that I can't write English and therefore you can't read parts of my letters. You can READ THEM ALL RIGHT BABY,—it's just that you don't WANNA READ WHAT IT SAYS BECAUSE IT HITS HEAD-ON INTO THE SOFT PARTS OF YOUR BELLY-WEAKNESS

WHICH SUCH A GOODGODESS LIKE U

SUCH DON'T SUPPOSE TO HAVE, HA HA AH HA.

H.D. gives herself away in *Epitaph* (last page) as a stringer of beads for others to see. *Stars Wheel in Purple* could well thrill all the lady readers of the *Ladies Home Journal*.

Hell yes, I'll ask that question too: where is the nightingale? (Page 52)

Yeah, when they want to find out what makes me work I'll CRACK them a can of beer and say: here it is: the nightingale. Here, Sherry, have a nightingale: 26 cents a can.

Perhaps nowhere does H.D. give away her strivings, simply, to write POETRY of such unmitigated vent as in *Heliodora*, page 43...

222

Well, enough. You drink your poisons and I'll drink mine...
Now—YOU WAIT A GOD DAMNED MINUTE ON PASCIN!... I
will tell you about Pascin. Pascin grew tired of the lump-col-
ored blobs laid bare and naked upon the canvas ass... He wanted a woman like the one who passed him in the hall or on the
street or sat across from him drinking wine. It is not a matter of
immortalizing women. It is a matter of bringing them down to
where you can see them and remember them in their small
unnoticed magic, that only a man can notice. There is nothing
more ugly than a completely naked woman. A woman is built to
receive and reproduce; she is a machine blossomed and stored
by man. A woman is ungainly: her ass is larger to bring forth
birth and to engender the eye of man, and when her body bends
naked, the hopeless breasts swing loose like things that want to
fall away. See in nature who is the most beautiful. Eye the color
the gods give to the smallest of birds—wren and sparrow, and
all the way up, rooster, eagle, deer, lion... It is only at times
when nature stores such inward female beauty in some... such
as Sappho, Martinelli, Rossetti, and even H.D., in spite of herself, that man must reajust his judgments of the gift; and for it
all, woman of the crudest sort must never be looked down upon
unless they are vicious in a spirit beyond their female nature...
And it was sometime after my thoughts on this subject that I
came across in some reading... somebody asked Degas why he
made his women so ugly, and he replied, in surprise, "But
women *are* ugly."

I don't know if I've made myself quite clear on the value of
Pascin, and the fact that you tell me... he was a Jew... of course
makes little difference, except, I suppose, if a Jew can overcome
his instincts to become an artist, he will probably become a
good one. Except Ginsburg whose instincts keep dragging him
back.

Now, Sherri, you sent me the Myrrh Gum... and thanks...
and I enclose couple bucks for costs... but... what hell, baby,
yam I supposed to do wit it? Eat it? Set it on fire? What wha
wha? You gotta enclose instructions... I am like a child cut
loose into a bush of cottonwillows.

Forgive me for moving so fk hard against yr H.D., I will still
love you, Shed; it is only that we must move forward, and
H.D., while she did her good part early, 3,000 female writers
sound like H.D. now—which is not her fault but her strength,

but we who are on the edge of the present day creation... cannot see and, are in a sense, hard toward the past which gives us much of our heritage and strength to go on, but the going on overtakes us, and we must go on... just as those who swallow us up... will look back in a declining and indefferential sense upon our bones. It is sad, but right now... *we* are alive and the sound is ours. H.D. is unmistakably dead and she must realize it, and if she doesn't... then she is less than she is.

You needn't sketch my portrait. Enclose one sketched by myself.

Still working on small shack deal. Won over 500 dollars Monday. Tuesday lost 2 bets—one for 10 dollars on 9 to one shot and other for one hundred to win on 2 to 1 shot. Both horses won easily but they took down my number on inquiry of very minor technicalities by the stewards. took in 20, 30 dollars on succeeding days, hardly anything, but it rained today and I stayed here.

To hell with Ezra; I took him to my bosom early, when I needed strength, but now I've got strength. I'm going to carve my own jade. It's very simple. If only they'll give me a few more years. But I cannot stop drinking. Drinking fills me, it doesn't empty me. I can't explain. In some later years, if we are still here, somebody will come up with some very simple answers but I will be just so many more bones sitting under sod somewhere and the hot kisses and music and poetry will belong to someone else. It is a hard fact to take, in essence, if you look at it from the Life-side, which is all we can do, no matter how much we kid ourselves that we can see forward and that all will be okaydookay.

yes, yes, your paintings very good from little booklet you sent me... do not like your sketches... but paintings yes. I do not know what it is. But do not try to be *modern*, like the mostly red and square-shaped thing, I forget what you called it. You stay old. You are touched with a good dust and what you say about bones is true. I love you and I know what you are. Keep it moving. Your color shades call to the eye of the worm and forever. What you *think* you see in H.D. is only a small part of you. H.D. is only a small stopsign on your way. You see that Gib

---

red and square-shaped thing: SM's portrait *Daw oo*.

keeps you stocked in paint and paper and gives you a few clothes because you can't help being a woman. But don't be too hard on Gib. He is not as mad as the rest of us. But then, who is?

lovekisses, baby, from one you'll prob. never see, and it doesn't matter—

Buk

Buk

[postcard dated by SM 25 April 1961]

Shed:
o, o, I find out now
m. wood little rocks that burn... cracked one a my only saucers. now sky and ceiling filled with grace. little spiders without legs floating down in air... Pascin alcoholic, prematurely gray, at age 45 looked 20 years older. Suicide, June 2nd., 1930. Born 1885...

well,

Buk

25/april/61   sm   pbx 46   san gregorio calif

in dealing with superior people—total freedom of action & truth at every degree is necessary & possible
    in dealing with inferior people beware of setting even a minor model for action... because... the inferior person is ape-like & does not know the Laws of Harmony but only the Law of Imitation... & will APE any model set before he/she
    a good rule to discover the inner man... observe if what you

225

place before him is carried on by him in a way which harmonis-
es... or does he merely ape... or imitate... & stop all flow of
intelligence/

April, perhaps 29, xtywon, nited states

Yes, Shed:
    You tell McNaughton kitty I am quiet old man who drinks
gallons of beer because his   insides missing   people who
meet me (and I try to keep this from happening) say like poet
William Pillin,
    why, I thought you were a YOUNGER man...
    or like a woman I once lived with:
    said:
    I don't know, I thought you'd be more...
More WHAT?
    oh, more *fiery*! or something. I thought from reading your
poems...
    They don't understand that a man can be sitting in a chair
blinking like a staid frog   and it is a gentle seeping of the light,
in... and if you ever *do* finally throw a fit as all creatures finally
must do when the nerves are caught raw... they run to the secret
lover to tell about the beast.
    ;;;this pighead won't read; I come to grips with plenty of shit
elsewhere, and I must draw down my laws for non-shit hours so
that I may breathe.
    The boys evidently think I am something. I am amused at a
letter that I rec. today, beginning: "I am extremely pleased that
you are willing to have your poetry read at our session May 5."
    They are getting a boy to babble my words into the mike.
Fine. But they suggest I meet the "reader", if I want to. Hell, I
might as well do it myself if I have to meet some goddamned
"reader". Why I wanna meet a reader? They want buttons off

McNaughton kitty: William McNaughton (see note to SM's letter of 20
December 1960 above).

my shirt, or what? I've always been a loner, and because a few people have read my poems I am not going to skid off half-cocked and let them piss on me. If the poem bothers them enough, let them make it walk on their airwaves. I brought it out of the singular odd womb that is Buk. I will not cut the head off my poem and say it cannot go on the air, but I will not curl its hair and dress it in Sunday best for a few admirers to paw over... Where were these bastards when I was starving & freezing in Atlanta in shirtsleeves trying to get up the guts to reach over my head and touch the raw wires that hung globeless like the snakes of Hell   while I tried to put down the word? Where were they? They were slobbering up the milk from some warm mother's tit... and they still are.

Don't be mama shed slapping at my bloody mouse soul and telling me to go warble in a mike... What can I tell them when they say—

Could you give us any information you'd like used concerning publication and life history?

What can I tell them? Doesn't the poem SAY?

Jory fooled me and still does because now and then he manages to get off a poem in completely original (compared to others) vernacular.

But the hours I have watched him on my phone dialing the powers-that-be. Some editor. "This is Jory Sherman. I just got into town. I'm over at Charles Bukowski's and, etc. etc., I want to give some readings and etc. etc."

Jory never knew it. He thought it was perfectly natural. And I did not let him know   that his soul had pewked before me.

And the way he dragged me around like a lame dog when I told him I did not want it, and I finally had to say no.

And he still writes very well, at times, and I am puzzled. That is why I do not break it off completely with him. He was one time blessed by some very dark and quiet god   and it is this core of a blessing that keeps him running halfway toward a sinking sun   no matter how many times he leaps the rails. He's lucky but doesn't know it.

I took a lashing of fire to even open my eyelids.

If any half-pale god speaks through me it is because I lifted rocks and killed rattlers across my path. I am not blessed; I have been beaten witless and mumbling. I know very little besides

227

shades of light and that one man must always be one. The Jorys stun me with their easy victories.

Jory would spew his guts readily into the mike, into the assembled throng... I only WONDER what the assembled throng is??? Duty, or Pound with the term "education" always ready, or Ginsburg following the "line"—it's not god damned NEARLY ENOUGH!!!

For Sherman it would just mean more clean linen, a photograph in an honorable position, and shoes for baby. Ginsburg and Pound, of course, are rock-hard in SIGHT—that is, whatever they see

THEY SEE ROCK-HARD AND ALL THE WAY, and this is important.

But Ginsburg fails hard as H.D. fails soft. They both fail in unnatural poses, duty and the Greeks be damned. You tell me that once you were unable to understand H.D. Perhaps someday you will be able to understand C.B.   And I don't mean Christ's Balls.

There are only 2 contemporaries I look up to—Pound and Jeffers, and as the days go on, it is almost becoming a level stare. Martinelli is the most beautiful female I have ever known, and I can only place it in these simple terms.

...look here... the horror I related, I know it was wrong, but I am saved because I have others   others that have not happened to the average, and they will not know. Balls, what does it matter? What does even the poem matter? I can feel my bones now   rid of my rotten belly   my rotten mind   I can feel my bones now   straightening and sighing and what can they do with me   without their microphones and Shermans, and their Cubas to chew like tough steaks?

Shed, I have something that will amuse you. I don't know, it is the Chinese or somebody   something like that

I read sometimes but fail to get it straight.

They say this—that the way you live NOW will cause you to be what you are in reincarnation—that is, if you have been pretty tough straight baby, you prob. lion in reincar. If you pretty poor piss, maybe you end up next time   being snail   rat what have you... lowest of forms.

I do not disclaim this view any more than I disclaim boy on cross with nails. All views good to me in what they bring—I will drink beer with a capitalist or a red and fuck either of their wives when they are not looking   if it seems within the proper mainspring of unwinding, the living thing to do.

But what I am saying now   is that I see people now with the animal they are *going to be*   ALREADY TAKING SHAPE WITHIN THEM   while they are still supposed to be homo-sapiens among us.

There is one person I know that perfectly well reminds me of an ant-eater. o, it is so plain, I do wish you could see it! And another, not even an *animal*, just a fuckin' bunch of sunflower seeds in pod to be pecked dry by the passing birds. Many are not so easy to pinpoint, and the animal-god may have troubles too... segregationist troubles to make Georgia and Alabama seem   well G. and A. only. Anyhow, out at the track today it was hot and as usual I was hiding my coat over an empty counter that is never used except on Saturdays, and I noticed a little rat-face watching me. I sensed the evil there; I thought simply not much good, that one. And sure enough, after the last race, I reached for the coat and it was gone. Nothing tragic, cer-tainly. He'd even put up a little box so he could reach over and get it, short-legged nothing of a nip of nothing. And when he got it home he found out it couldn't, wdnt fit. What then? A hock shop? 2 dollars? I would not even burn this type in hell. They do not even deserve to suffer pain. Let him be just a bit of sand caught in somebody's sock in the year 5000 A.D.

I hearby consign him to return as SAND.

Sent an English teacher, dept. of Louisiana State College, your way, A and P with some pomes. Maybe he won't show. Has a tendency to be blithe and clever. Writes a strong letter but poems, so far, weak. William Corrington. Maybe you can straighten him, if he shows.

Sorry, darling, you must stand these with me.

It is a test of our love.

And he is far more idealistic than Sherman. And, I think, down under all the coating   ok if   you can shiv it away.

...I may not be able to write for a while, some bit of minor trouble, so trying to get as much out of way as possible... do not sleep off yet...

I must turn my back on H.D. because we do not fit. She started basically wrong   because she was afraid to use her real name   because Hilda Doolittle   did not sound like poetess. And other things I attempted to explain in last letter back, but maybe I had a "skinful" or you thot I had or wot   whot wot.

always have a skinfull, how you expect meee to keep moving on, woman?

...Man is not *supposed* to understand the "nature of the female". If he did   he would avoid her entirely   and nature's natural plan would go down the drain.

Perhaps you are right in saying I have never had a woman, and only the fear of Buk, but it's a buk wanting to live to see a natural daylight and not an accessory to a pair of breasts and a womb   like it seems he just got away from not so long ago, and here we are looking for another MOTHER   sucking teats, begging, slobbering...

A woman must give me BOTH flesh and spirit, and unless I am drunk, I will not take less than both.

Pascin wanted to bring the picture-frame women, the blasé pure

untouchable nudes   not only down to the end of his cock

but down to the end of his vulgar (so-called) brush

where he could say   you bastards make me sick

this motherly white god awful balloon blob surrounded by angels,

is not it... this is it   and this is love   this   is love

that modern man shall know   love running and sloppy and

unglorified   and still   for it all   when it happens

love or sex   or fire   just as GOOD az yours

your Greek white banana love   without come   or after-effect,

this is us   sloppy and lazy and filthy and real

this is us   loving   the only way we know how.

No matter that he couldn't draw hands and feet! He wasn't looking for hands and feet.

Degas ok. just going to get him a little longer to slip into the banana world, just as any new of insight against Greek-Romano Classical tradition   which you seen to uphold, and which I admire but cert. can see the cracks forming in—

the profane is the beautiful and the sacred is yesterday. You must bury your h.d's and yesterdays; only pop pound seems strong enough to advance with us... t.s.eliot a string of beans, wallace stevens just the stringing of a name across an autographed copy... only Jeffers a real buk-boy throwing on a log and saying "fuck 'em. I made a god outa crap, but they're making crap into a god."

Woman dialates from her love of man into the love and

extension of man into another man (son, offspring), and original man is singular and therefore jealous until he sees part of his own image... then all blunts because the image has been broken into three...

I took the olib. you sent me and rolled it into newspaper and smoked it. Not bad. got a vision and headache and blood-spitting. Vision mostly I was drinking water from trough. Long head and ears. I was either rabbit or donkey.

and you tell Gib that a little leaking on old car ok. It only save you oil change worry. However, if she come out too fast, valve-grind or piston-heads may be worth more than car. Rings or plugs won't help. Best deal I know is to work in a little saw-dust (very fine) into crankcase, sift it down oil-fill while listening to engine work and as sounds better and better keep adding but when starts to choke burn engine awhile until you get true soft sound

and if too much smoke from ass add proper smokeless additives, and then drive whole mess down to salesman on youused car lot, n act prop. naive so he won't pull crankcase plug.

I only say these things because the fucking guy took my coat while I was trying to nurse a 3 to one shot in with 50 on the nose.

No more drawings for a moment, Shed.

Big vultures come to pick my eyes.

love as truly as I can make it,
Buk

L.A.
May 1, 1961

Dear Sheri:

They have found me a boy to read my lines, and now the gods allow me to go ahead and do what pleases me.

L.,
Buk

231

Los Angeles, Calif.
May ?, 1961

Dear Sheri:
Enclosed more Kaja. This a little better, I think, than the others.
Also, enclosed photo Buk. You may got crows to scare away.

Love baby,
Buk

[*note on bottom in SM's hand:*] She emotes at the lowest conceit heat—

14/maggio/61   pobx 756/   half moon calif

buk/ your foto is just what yr letters say: hermit of sort; poet & man of many adventures;
    that kaja lowest yet/ quote from local newspaper: "A recent New York State police report on the typical check forger published in NY Times described him as a native white male, older than other criminals, with high intelligence & residing in an acceptable residential area. He is personally likable attractive & ingratiating & has a knack of convincing others that he is painfully pure in heart. He likes to live well & is a past master in fooling workaday merchants & well to do widows"
    sounds JUST LIKE the "kaja" female's totally UNpoetic dyed in wool, pidgeon hole mind soft shit & cold cream spew/ no thank you buk/ when we finally pin her down she'll be a runt with thick glasses on & an overly active pituatary gland/ oh shit ever since ezra pound did "portraits" via word; every crab louse that learned to write is doing them;
    well, today is peaceful darling... been in a storm pressure since ester day; this day is what ester shd have been... easter; yes that howspell/ the state bldg inspr. had the rotten elec current removed & now the cots are unlit & the suburbanite next cot cant drag our ass any more; so since the goody-goody went out of it... one is left in peace now as long before when first

232

came here; oh kid yr magic worked like a BEWteeful charm! thanks my man/ removing the electricity was THE unique solution/ it made only nature left; & we alone down here love the true place & not just sitting in with the t.v. set on & vaguely feeling "down in th' country"; darling!

This just a note... & write more when get re-settled... nobody can live here anymore... just week end cabin so we all dithered on that/ anyhow note to say kaja the bottom bucket scum & that yr foto very handsome... sort of beautiful monkey face thing...

love/sheri

L.A.
May 16, 1961

Shed mama:

much short, today. tied to rocks of all sorts but will escape.

kaja can't be all that bad, although I agree she prob. pigtail pidjin toe stumblefoot; it is the destiny of these young ladies, when unable to go to bed with a man to go to bed with a poem. reverse it and you get much of the male-half. much of the Art-world infested with the weak instead of the strong, that is why so much of it is bad...

knock on door yesterday; young man with scrabby goatee, young man simpering like tea was at door. let him in. "Mr. Bukowski, I heard your work read at radio station... we are having a reading at our church, and although I understand you are against reading your stuff, we thought..."

"I'm afraid I don't have anything that pale," I told him.

"Oh no, we're not like that. We want it strong. In fact, the reading is entitled *Voices in Rebellion...*"

Well, I let him wade through a stack of rejected poetry and through some magazines, and he stood in the doorway quite pleased with his little mass of stuff.

"Will you be our honored guest this Sunday?" he asked.

"Hell no!" I said, "and don't get caught in a strong wind." and that was that...

He's lucky he didn't catch me drunk and surly. I don't

233

think it's fair, these bastards knocking on doors, and if only they weren't so fkg raw and tender, I'd let them have it. I don't see why I don't tell them, and some day I must, to clear the boards both for myself and them. It must be, it will simply have to be...

Got a letter from Sherman; made me a bit ill. Everytime he lies or is proud, or mentions a new "in" or "contact", he begins a sentence with an offhand "O", as if it didn't matter. For example:

O I have been made advisory editor of another New Orleans magazine, *Outcry*... or

O I heard from Thorne (editor *Epos*) other day; nice letter; she sent me name of new mag. thought I'd pass on to you... it's

o o o o o o o o o o, oo oh oh god damn yes oooooooooo!!!

...good, I turned off T.V. with my hex, didn't know I was that good. Is still original hex, must be getting weak-kneed by now. Let me know if they give any more trouble and I will re-invoke full strength. I really meant it, in spirit, chicken feathers and blood at full moon, and glad it worked. I believe in everything, gods mythical and actual and unactual, Buhda, bug-gods, tree-gods, devils, angels, anything that has ever crossed the mind of man, good or evil or fanciful, is there. And you are there, my good gal Sheri, and I am very sad   now   that I did not drive up to see you when I had the chance. But I have failed before. So well.

Love,
Buk

18/ may/61   pobx 756   half moon calif

buk/ yew hopeless romantic/ "pigtail pidjin toe stumblefoot kaja"—man don't yew know a bedbug or a blood sucker when you 'SEE' one?????   & yew all wet kidttt—girls only go to bed with males because they cannot take a delight in writing poetry/ one can have any male close enough to knock down; because males will fk ANY body/ thing/ any time anywhere/ they are mere fk hops & no earthly pleasure... & one has more than a sufficient knowledge & eggsperience with pleasure... but no earthly pleasure is equal to the spasm of the mind/ not the brain but the mind/

& buk yew innocent lamb—if you'd only read a few political maz you'd know WHY a kid from a 'church' wd want to read yr poetry in church/ why didn't you tell him to read ezra pound's usury canto???? if he wanted a voice in rebellion/ the low disorganised honolulu type baptist churches have been used for a long time by the Party to help bust up the eggixting order/ yr poetry is a NATURAL to be used as such; 1/ yew aint saying anything DANGEROUS   2/ you destroy the old idea of the female being sacred & turn her into a fuck cow which is just right for the Commie boys who are operating thru yr skinny church-goer who finally feels he is livin' it up   3/ yr protests are blind stabbings out against a system which don't work for you/ IF yr poetry were employing race & its meanings; economics & its effects; true historical facts... baby they'd not show up... be aware of WHY they are using you; also you have a most interesting way of putting things & they NEED REAL artists & creators/

buk you are too conceited/ also you are in the big sleep/ the ego sleep/ i don't blame you/ it takes total lack of fear to believe that one can effect any change; i don't think i got it/ i keep trying but there are some areas i do not enter... & i KNOW enough to debunk them... but so far i have not found one single person of my own race or gods worth the trouble it will make to speak out... also what can you do???? if i sent you an american mercury it wd shake you to yr roots... but not being able to DO anything—it wd be more evil than good to wake you up

what you can do is not co-operate so well with yr female word portraits... being just what they want/ if he had knocked at my door; I wd have enlightened him as to WHY he'd been put up to hold poetry readings about pimps, whores etc (aint objectin' buk as is my subject matter at times since it is my life at times BUT why wd a church want it???? who put them up to that???) instead of a lecture or reading of some solid facts on the federal reserve system & our present economic plight... anyhow you are UNreasonable...

---

pound's usury canto: Canto 45.

american mercury: a magazine founded by H. L. Mencken in 1924 that had become extremely right-wing by the 1960s.

235

darling if you gonna have yr work read OF COURSE yr door will be knocked upon/ leave dear jory to his worldiness; he is only a lost little boy wanting pop to pat his head for good conduct... all he has is the world; the dream has not taken root in him; anyhow jory is being used as a goy out front... keep telling you you dumb pollack but you wont listen to me... jory is the nice sweet honest voiced little boet type christer they can stick out front & use to make like big art scene... meanwhile they rake in the bucks... behind der back/ jory don't see nothing but der honorary committee seat/

jory is a lackey for the party boys due to his ignorance & i cant help him... he is not worth saving; he has a scheming character/ i'd rather save the party boys as they have the better characters/ at least they are working for a dream & the kremlin/ whereas jory is out for jory/ he don't even know the united states exists/ let alone the fed res sys/ when you wake up to the fact that a race & religious & political & economic war is going on & has been going on for the past 23,000 yrs kid... then we can talk/ then you'd see jory as i see him/ a pawn/ & yr church-goer is another pawn/ a move on the board in the game...

when you get a chance to be able to speak why don't you hand them a stick of DYNAMITE instead of mere excitement verbally?????? they aint reading ezra in no watermelon communistic churches (green on outside/red on inside)... you should read the facts on them choiches... well it will all turn out somehow... it cannot be outside of nature—

yes yr hex worked swell; now please send out a charm to get clarence major down here/ i need him as a sexratary/ & i am trying to get the landlord to give him a hovel to dwell in & we'll feed him & he can run a & p & so on... I am backlog'd with work & maj wants to come out here & i NEED him plus wanting one of us to be safe of course/ gib don't mind/ he grew up over on 7th & T streets   THE street in wash d.c. & he understands the coloured paideuma/ and maj is hot to come/

ernie is back in town but we cant connect yet due to some weird circumstances... we will... he cd visit this hotel room & gib's right down the street... we cd have dinner or wotever... ernie is such a filthy beast that i already know he will want to use this room to sleep off th ship in & there goes my work shop & he is so beguiling he will find some way to make me give in &

let him stay here... oh he is a bitch... but i love him... he is so intelligent...

don't be sad buk/ you'll be up sooner r later/ landlord is thinking of making me the caretaker down there soon's the bldg spr mess blows over... then we cd have a real visit/ now moi glam/ i got to go & get zum woirk done/

lov/

shed/

Sheri

L.A.
May what what [20], 1961

Deah Shed:

large head this morning, sick...

baby, I can't get with the race war, church war, state war kick. I know that getting my balls in the wringer would give me a feeling of *usefulness* but usefulness is often a pancrea of setting down the tableknife you have been hacking away a new face you have been chipping into a stone you found in the street. Hell, I *am* a horseplayer, and I can *smell* action and manipulation, and my innocence is *chosen*, not thrust upon me. I know the church-boy's game. But here is the fact. I have written some poems. These poems may be used for other purposes than I intended, but whatever the purpose, what I have said in them remains to me true as creative fact, and if the words of my poems want to breathe in radio stations and in churches, besides the magazines, well, that is their act and their walking around and I cannot destroy them, cut their heads off. What I *can't* do, is get behind them and push them out, speak them on stages like a salesman, like a jory playing with his ego-cock.

I can't get a hard-on over what the Pope brushes his teeth with or how the Kremlin rattles the dice, or the basis of the monetary system. I have been in the economics classes and I have sat with Jewish tailors and Italian pharmacists over candlelight and plotted the overthrow of a tottering dynasty. It all creamed me well in my twenties and meant something, as the

237

tanks coming down the road in the middle of the butterflies means something, as 30 dogs and twenty men on 20 horses chasing one fox... means something. Everything means something, and if you think   you alone   Sheri Martinelli   have your sights cocked directly on TARGET   you are not alone. I met a man in a Gardena poker parlor the other night who thought the same thing.

I am going to carve my pure innocence, I am going to carve as the tanks come down the road and they will blow me to hell and my carvings to hell and they will laugh, but I will have carved what I needed to carve and sop from the Kremlin will not have ordered the laughter of my knife, or say the dictates of some halfdead facisti order hidden in some mountain-side like a tick on a hunk of capitalist cattle...

I know that men are fucklunks and will fuck anything they can get their hands on, but some women do *not* know how to put themselves *into* the hands of these fucklunks, and hence the kajas, who take it out on the poem, and not *all* poems are "spasms of the mind", some of them are just pieces of paper moaning for fucklunks and talking about something else in order to assume importance.

No, I can't bring you Major. Major is a dribbling ass, a weakling dribbling in poems and talking about poems and worried about being a nigger and worried because he is not famous, and he would really like nothing better than to write a best-selling novel, no matter how bad, so he can have some money and have people KNOW who Clarence Major is. Your boy Ernie another jerk with fuzz on his cheeks and very thin concepts. You surround yourself with decay and then try to tell me the score. Shed, baby, I love you most of the time but a lot of the time you are on some rummy road and do not know it, and it's odd, because you see clear down through sometimes; other times you just make up magic to suit your purpose and to fill the void. The latter will not do; it is not suitable; no more than the Pope in a game of craps. Love,

Bukowski

1/june/61   half moon   p.o.bx 756   calif/

buk/ re-reading a letter yrs—waiting for gib come home; grey day... never any sun this fkn calif/ yew saying people's next life already coming out in them; very amusing; usually i see 2 things in their beings; no h.d. didn't start wrong; ez thought that h.d. wd be better, they WERE only kids yew know... 15 or so when they met & it was ez who made the initials not h.d.—but royalty is represented by initials...

Pascan or Pascin howhellspelled cd not give us any other art but ghetto art because he lived there; the greeks gave us the heroic... my dear buk the purpose of Art is NOT to bury one's opinion in but to serve as a model to uplift the human animal... a world where the young ladies gazed upon his ghetto whores wd only produce more of 'em... his work is PIGnoble... you are look-ing at the pictures from a poet's point of view... he just plain wanted to DEgrade the female... to the jews we are there to grati-fy every degree of desire (not that the jews have an edge on this but ezra's conversation between ardour was higher than ernie's for ex.) and he did not love the form of the female just the parts that to him meant satisfaction of his lust; that aint even showing good character let alone fine art; it is as important to love her feet as her arse/ he was a bad artist, a good jew & not a gentleman/

that is wonderful; smoking frankenscence (olibanum) did you really get a vision??? did you get high from it??? you are the best buk; got the most love in you; gib has it but it's in a tough shell; ernie is pompous & wind-y on paper; his most valuable asset & characteristics stem from his yiddishness & he is ashamed or frightened to face being a jew; makes me mad

this time is the most dif. to pass... this 7 p.m.ish waiting...

am so bored with ezra's critics; it was the time of condens-ing many books into one book & he got the job; usually that means almost total destruction of the cultures that got their books condensed into the one & for those that got left out it means a blank for them... he chewdon all of it & they are ALL chewing on his one book... shows you his relative size/

now nears gloaming... he shd show soon...

buk i am too lonely; i am waiting for gramps to die so i can be with him... this world is silly without him

239

L.A.
June 14, 1961

Hello Princess:

Well, now, H.D. and Pascin again. Pascin I will not mention again as I see he bothers you, although I grant that many of the things you say of him are true. And H.D. H.D. may be great. I don't know. I can only say what H.D. is to me. I need more than—or perhaps *less* than the Grecio-Roman purity, the beautiful thorn. I need black bread and my own particular madness.

Some idiot has attached himself to me. They are always doing that. He's like a sucker-fish attached to my belly, drawing the life out of me. I must eventually knock him against a few rocks in order to make him see that I prefer to swim alone. Whatta sucker-fish! Well-read, spewing vocabulary and opinions against the walls like vomit, chatter chatter chatter eyes suddenly blinking shut and open in nervous spasm. He claims intelligence of the highest order but is unable to understand that he makes me ill.

Other horror stories, a bit in jail and court, but of no matter except to go along with the rest and disturb, for the time, my hacking at whatever marble sits before me.

Yet—horror upon horror finally and almost brings a plateau of calm reason in the face of anything.

Of course, the disgusting thing is that one ends up with a mop, cleaning a latrine, when the inner part is ready to walk up the sides of mountains.

But complaint is only a surly bitch crying for more and better luck, luck without the loss of pawns or blood. One cannot learn without bleeding, and by learning I do not mean education or book-lore or the correct way to pronounce; I mean when you can look at sunlight and feel the bone and tendril burning, or some such, whatever is lighting your mind at the moment, lighting out the darkness of universities and caves and the chattering ego. And particles rust and pass, without grief.

The world is not "silly" without Ez. Martinelli, you need more German in you. You do the "illuminations", baby. I love your hands and feet both and your paint better than all.

Buk

240

ps—The judge told me that I had a drinking problem. It seems to me that the main problem with my drinking is the police: if they would leave me alone when I miss a step in the street, my problem would disappear.

cb

Los Angeles, Calif.
June 22, 1961

Hoy Sheri:

Got your good letter, and I am in a bit of trouble now, but should clear, don't know; so therefore this will tend to be short, as I have horrible bulls to slay and time is needed.

Picturephoto bit of Swarm-family shows the American masses that they are not the only ones having larvae crawling across the rug, and so they feel better. The family, the nation and the church are the 3 sacred nails that hold the average man where he belongs.

Sherman and some painter in here at 2:30 am in the morning, stayed 2 hours. I was not comfortable with them but they did not know it. Painter had red beard, Rick Beck-Meyer, or some such; appeared to have more sensibility than Sherman, but they are both staying with some homosexual editor up in Hollywood, and the whole thing is less than appetizing. Jory wanted your address which I would not give him; also complained because I ran out of beer and because you did not send him a copy of last A and P.

Complainers must realize that when they invite themselves in at 3 o'clock in the morning, the host quite well might run out of beer or out of manners. The painter asked me directly, as if I were in court, "Mr. Bukowski, why do you seek isolation?" or some such. Jesus, there were 2 answers sitting before me, but I gave him an answer which was true but minor, and that was that. And so much for drab ill gossip and drab ill door-knockers. Except that J. says he is going to seek a

---

Rick Beck-Meyer: unidentified.

241

job down here; and if he does, I'm in trouble.

Sheri, I don't need friends. The old woman I know is enough; she washes my backside and squeezes my knick, and for it all, she knows more of what is true than what is false, which is also important.

I will drop H.D. a card.

My book is supposed to be out in July (new collected poems) and I sketched the covers myself when I did not care for what the artist submitted. However, I had not heard from the ed. since I told him I would accept the Metropolitan Poetry Award, but would suggest rather that he give it to a younger man, somebody who is ready to jump out of a window. I suppose I hurt him, but anybody can think up a fancy title for an award, but now it appears to me that I have told you all this before. I am getting addled. Anyhow, I will have to go on supposing the book is coming out, July, August, sometime.

Good you got one Prussian grandfather. I had one too once. I was a kid and he gave me a tin box all full of old war medals, old ribbons, copper and bronze crosses, old wars, blood on the ground, cannon, and he had a whole head of white hair and drank schnapps and he stood straight up and down and his eyes were full of things.

...yes, Mexicans corrupt to gringo because M. poor and gringo strut in land not his and think every Mexican girl a whore at his call, and so they overcharge and doublecharge, and I have been taken down there but keep quiet, for I know that then the police come and all the police know is jail until things are settled, and by settled, I mean paying them and the merchant. I once saw a sailor shot in a Mexican whorehouse and he deserved every bit of it, especially since he wasn't even drunk. I don't mean he necessarily deserved the bullet which caught up with him, but he did deserve being shot at.

Jews tend to have more love toward those they *know*, but only that.

Yes, of course it's possible to tell what kind of person by the walk. I can become almost unbearably ill when walking behind the wrong person.

Ernie is too well-read. The time comes when a man must put the book down and face the mirror of the unwritten.

My book: *Longshot Pomes for Broke Players* would appear in October.

You like to bring Ernie in, then hold him off, then bring him in again. A fish-toy. Luck. But you cannot endow him with genius simply because you know him; he will have to make his way... Ernie by Ernie... and... luck. Let him have his monkey-talk; he is trying to begin; that is what they teach young boys. It is a code: they send them up a ladder in a high wind with a bunch of balogna and if they lose the balogna and come back down, they have made it. Any other combo is failure. Jory Sherman went up with the baloney and came down with it. Pound wouldn't even mount the ladder; he laughed up and down the whole stinking ship and they threw him in irons.

The Greek wisdom does not help me now. Each thing must now be taken one at a time and combed out of its defeat. The world is continually closing in like a dirty sea full of condoms and poisons; you reach for a god or a drink or pull down the shade, and then the fuzz bangs the door and tells you it's lock-uptime for some obscure reason.

Darling, we would never get along. We are 2 bullheads, and both of us must learn more to listen; there's plenty wrong with both of us, but in growing the wrong comes along with the right, like the thorn with the rose, but of course, we ignore a lot of our own thorn, thinking we need to prick off the enemy, but what's the enemy? but our face in the mirror, a roll of fat death around the belly and side, and... assurance, stability, *Rightness...* the American gringo of the soul trying to fuck the whole Mexican girlhood of belief, lo, or what or what or what? These stringy words say so little; sometimes I think it's just the light from a globe thrown from under a dusty lamp; sometimes things are so sad, really sad, and we try to buk or buck up under them. You good gal, Shed, I don't think I'd really ever argue with you; first, I do *not* argue, and second, you burn with your *own* fire.

Sherman on phone again, wanting to come over. I am his dad, when he in trouble, come see Buk, drink beer, spill his piss before me. A formula. I told him no. I am in some trouble. He told me stuff and stuff, sharp, glib American voice, humorous, cold, energetic, undefeatable, false, money-mad, woman-mad voice... unable to sit still for a moment and watch the centuries come down in wonderful dust, the names, the ages of man, monkey-man and man-man all coming down to wistful stone; no, no, he wants assurance and talk talk talk and beer beer beer,

243

not alone, but with somebody, weak this Sherman; I have told him to take the stars and the seas out of his poems and bring in real blood, and over the phone I told him no. God damn, I am no wet-nurse for 2nd. rate poets. If Jeffers wants to drop in for a beer, I'll reconsider.

Why the hell don't we forget Pascin like we forgot Fry? I'll take your word on Pascin. But do remember, I did not make any claims for him.

The herb article I enclosed earlier was badly written by an old woman who puts out a flowerry poetry mag, but remembered you said you were looking into herbs and thot I cd. ad a wee to your gathering.

Shed, I have grown very oddly and slowly, and I feel the mounting day by day like a vine climbing up inside of me; sometimes it is knocked back down, and I try to help it a little, but it is odd, it is as if I had no choice, and no matter what I do, no matter how much wrong or opposite, the climbing continues. I am getting simpler, almost to a state of idiocy; and yet I do not mean that I condone brutality or ignorance in all sense of the word, *my* sense of the word, not theirs.

This is the danger of growing older; we think that we are growing *wiser* because we *feel* better—meaning we react less to pain: our feelers and outer limbs have been knocked off in the storms. Youths' anger must always be listened to; they see clearly because they have not been weighted—that is, they see clearly as *far* as they can see; and age which sees farther cannot see as clearly. Compose, compromise the 2 and you'll get the wisdom and the leadership—and although wisdom can do without leadership because it is one man, leadership cannot do without wisdom because it is many men.

Gib, as I've told you is a strong man. Gib steps aside for Ernie because Gib is wise and durable, either through race or self, I cannot tell you from this distance. I *can* tell you, should the situations have been reversed, Ernie would not have been strong enough to step aside for Gib. I somehow dislike Ernie, I don't know why. You may tell Gib I salute him with the iron hand, and carry on. And enough for petty names and petty gossips.

All I ask out of life is a job as a dishwasher at any greasy cafe and enough for rent and a can of fk beer, and I don't know, if any longer, I can even make that. I got 2 bucks for a poem or

244

poems the other day (*Mummy*, some S.F. pub?) but the horse ran like he had polio.

Ez should have had sense enough and strength enough to keep quiet at lawn gatherings of his when u an' Gib conversed o'r breakfast or what. It is only, and he *must* be forgiven, that genius *must* no everythin!!! And much imagination, prob. run away with conver., imag. all sorts imaginaries, commie party agents in suculent intwinement, or forevermore, the gangs and fangs or those not in immedeate forcloseure...

Ez was great but the greater you are the more doubts you have because you see how easy it has been, and then you can see how easy it can be that you will be overtaken, right, genius, or wrong.

For a short letter this has turned out to be a fucker.

Will close by quickly running over your letter: I don wana write abot white niggers. Jcrist, m[ay]b[e] the black whites, I dunno. I am sorry but the Japanese bitch is perfect; I'm quite sure by looking at her that she don't shit, piss, or whipe er hose or nose or her ass, don have too... all copper coloring from sky rusted over alfalfa hills. If a jp bitch ever gets hold of me I am finished and poetry is finished, but I have been unlucky so far. gd it, forget the Fed. Reserve for a while, will ya. Unless I can get in there the system is just that, a system to preserve rot, and what hell you want me to do, sneak in with bomb and bubble out gold bars... shit, that almost happened couple months back without bomb. Conceit wedded to vanity may make good slaves but the best slaves are those without either; the obedient humble who think a breakfast egg in a pan is Nirvanna... Yes, yes, I will send H.D. a card, but she does not know who I am, but maybe she can feel I am something, although this does not matter. It does gd bother me that one of us is in trouble. Will keep it small and simple, like unknown admirer. I am worried about how I am going to stay alive and here is one perhaps dying, and I am clawing my own personal ribs. Shit, buk, more *strength!*

I don't like to "use" people. Suckerfish or not. I'd rather

Mummy: four of CB's poems were published in an issue of *Mummy* in 1962.

white niggers: probably a reference to Norman Mailer's influential essay "The White Negro" (1957).

knock 'em lose on the rocks and swim away. The way I see it, there will not be more than 5 or 6 living people in any one century. The rest are fill-ins, dross crap. Now Hitler was living, although in the pages of righteousness and wrongness he was wrong, but it is the electric circuit that stands us up and makes us go, some little tired trickle in the blood. Hitler was born imed. with electricity; I beg time and time may trick me although I am wary. Just a job as a dishwasher until I am 50 years old. Will they let me have it?

The Irish are more superstitious than the Jews; the Grecians and Italians, both lower and upper India are more sexual than the Jews, or I might throw in the Turks or any dog with a lose bone... Please, Shed, when you make rules take in more than the light rag thrown from a singular exception so seeming to you. I take you at task to keep you clear; I do not argue, only say, you are a woman, which in the long run of history, is unfortunate.

The idea is to write the poem or the word; what happens after that is up to the dogs.

love,
Charles
BUKOWSKI

[*postcard dated by SM 27 June 1961*]

Dear Shed: they tell me I will be on the radio, my poems, that is, on KPKF FM, July 2 at 11 p.m. and July 3 at 10:45 p.m. Don't think you can catch it up there; doubt if I will listen either—no FM set. People are beginning to know that I am alive but the test comes in remaining as I am in spite of them.

There has been much interference from the practical world and I have not been able to get my card off to H.D. yet, but either tonight or tomorrow I will. ...Sherman down here remains pest, phoning at all hours of night and morning, always salty, headlong, demanding; Sherman only sees Sherman and I guess some writers are that way, but sometimes I pray for gentility, decency, courtesy, mercy... not the biblical and sugary sort, but away with the bitching and stamping of feet and snarling, and the insane lust for fame.   L.,

Buk

L.A., Sunday nite Aug 13

Hello Sheri:

Well, as you can see, I mailed card to H.D.; evidently she either died or moved or became well again.

I have been on one as usual, not feeling well. I hear from kaja and Corrington, off and on. Sherman in town, has landed something or other with the movies.

Presume you are thriving with your herbs, witchcraft and lore.

Love,

Buk

[postcard dated by SM 30 August 1961]

Princess:

gt.yrs. Hope you can locate recorder and wen u du it does not disattach us for eternity—u know that the crass and bleery-eyed Buk does not always hold poesy as holy as some of the gods wd wish, and since I do not educate the masses, only the masses of myslf that need straightenin' and laughs for my friends, I hope u take it in gd and simple order, and I think u will, wise one... You may keep tape, destroy it, or whatever; it was just meant for a moment, unimportant... Jory left town; we did not apprec. him here. There are more soul mates in Frisco to satisfy his moment-byOh every-moment hunger... Waitin' on *A & P*; still reread yr last won... and L. with capital plus 3,

Buk (no pen)

Buk

247

Los Angeles, Calif.
Sept.ending 1961

hiyo mamma:

rec. your pc. of blue paper letter; have been meaning to go ahead an' say thanks for sending H.D. issue, and in fact, did write letter, 2 pages, but an oddity or a god or an ulcer-impulse caused me to tear her up. No intent of malice or ill-will, just one of those things you do when you get a message from under the rug.

some one you know, let's say X, phoned collect other night from Frisco, coming in on jet, wanted me to pick him up at airport. He was there, another face in the crowd, operator, all a lady's man, a boy, the drivel of small things crawling his dome, worse than ever, more sunk than when I had seen him before. He radiated poison. Talk about the gods leaving; they had only thrown a shadow upon him in the first place—and now, that was gone. He slept on the couch, but not before phoning everybody in town at 12:30 a.m. outa a little black book, many women, telling them all the same thing, which is all too sick to repeat here. I dumped him off someplace the next day and then came back and closed the door, put the chain on, plugged the phone, and the walls were roses, the walls were music, and the blood began to flow back through my heart.

sometimes it is just a pleasure to stand in the center of a room and drink a glass of water without being disturbed.

it is people that kill the god. if you are by the wrong people too long he will leave. You can live for ten thousand years in a room full of stones but beware things that walk and are called human. The animals are still pure. I can stay in a room with a dog and nothing radiates but easy warmth. I am a dog myself, I know dogs, cats, tho birds and fish mystify, are out of ken. But I can feel the little round soul of a dog, I can see the sparks of it that are called paws, snout, hair. He is a too good guy, yes; we know each other. But x, x, oh, it's too sick!...

I cannot kid you. about H.D. she has her style. I am not

H.D. issue: A&P #6 was dedicated to the dying poet and contains several essays on her work by SM. CB contributed "Poem for Liz" and five pages of captioned drawings: see Appendix 2.

much of a known poet. It appears that unless you have fame, your statements are not given credence; but I do not think like H.D., her poems are too honed for me. I am slow, I am slow
it is true.
And so we go along.
If I am still around come next Feb.March, hope to come to Frisco for week or so. Should I disturb you? If not, I unnerstan'. Well, now going to open my beer. Ah.
Sure, mama.
love,
Buk

Los Angeles, Calif.
Sept. 28, no 29, 1961

Deah Shed:
just a short one, and you needn't respond... right off, only to say, no, don't want tape back, I have a machine, a bad one, true, but if I feel like making more sounds, it's there. I got it orig. to record some classical music, build a collection of sounds and what not, but since getting it, have done little. Your tape bad tape, tech. that is; Sears-Roebuck or what, and they have tendency to dry and split. Now have a couple a rolls of "mylar" which is tougher, like me. Writing this to say, due wat u wnt wit tape, but hope you got laugh.

I am up to my ass in poems and correspondence, and what with working nights and playing the ponies and drinking too much beer, I can't seem to keep up with everything, but more important is, there must be lulls of DOING NOTHING OR YOU DIE. This is important. Doing nothing is important because this is the glue that holds us: walking in the sun with things coming into the eye as it comes into the animal's eye, or on the bed with the ceiling like a blanket, nothing else, this is the glue tht holds us together. The busy BANG BANG BANG GO go go, that is Wall st. and erie tearing. Pure creation is ok, we all know that, no argument, but it's easy to be tapped and trapped by a lot of things on the edge of creation. There is always this sense of loss, loss, the draining away brought on by the self, and when you

249

add an intrusion, say, by Sherman or X, it is almost madness.

Kaja in Paris. Did I mention? She has angel, prob. Corso, tho not sure, and not my business. Gal bit depressed, walkup to room 6 floors, no window, just room, but still Paris and this keeps her going. Paris is still the magic word in cities, but not to me. I know cities are people and I know people in a way so that cities are the same. But there is a light in Kaja, I say. A good woman. She makes the mistakes we all do, we who explore beyond ordinary edges. She speaks of bringing out some of my work bi-lingual, some excerpts from letters and a couple of new poems and a few old ones. Now here she is, upset and poor, lost in a tiny room, a gamble of some sort, all melancholy, the thrill of buying a cigarette package in French about gone, and she's thinking about bringout somebody *else's* work. A good child-woman.

My 2nd. book still sitting at printers, in Pittsburg or somewhere, I think, but will out, sometime, I suppose. Also coming out in book with college prof., each of us taking about 20 pages wit pomes, only he funny college prof., cusses, and brags on me. This one might beat the other book out. Will send you both or all 3, or what the hell.

Thank you for the invite. Will drive up about March '62 but will let you know plenty time ahead about approx day arrival. I am gentle with people's property and time and am old man who does not say much and likes to look at sun. Must sleep now, all things catching up with me. I can feel small poems beginning to build in my shoulders and wrists and belly, and they need rest to form. In and out of shadows, up and down; it has been bad lately. Good to hear again, princess, my love,

Buk

ps—Kaja at, in case you feel like writing: [*address missing*]

---

book with college prof.: never published.

Dear Shed:

just heard of death of H.D., and although her poetry did not signal as much to me as it did to you, my regrets, know she was yr friend, but, lo, she did leave us a mark, and very few do that.

I must confess that I miss your letters but realize you have things to do which you consider more important than writing Bukslob. The news is thin: my x-wife has closed down her magazine, Sherman is back in Frisco, I am told, after robbing the man's apartment who befriended him, it's hot, my 2nd book still not out, drinking a little less, and that's about it. You tried leaf oregano with your eggs yet, like I told you? I thought not! Babe, sometimes ya gotta listen to me, I cannot always be incorrect, can i? aw right,

Buk

Los Angeles, Calif.
Late Oct. '61

Hello Princess:

You prob got the Autumn *Quicksilver* I asked them to send you, you probably got it now and have read my poem *Vegas*, and I have an idea you will be (are) upset. It would have been easier for me not to let you see this poem, but that is the coward's way out. First let me say that this poem was written long before the death of H.D., and second, it was written in a

---

death of H.D.: she died 27 September 1961.

x-wife ... magazine: Frye's *Harlequin*.

Vegas: rpt. in *BW* (33–34), part of which reads: "I said, there's some gal up North who used to / sleep with Pound, she's trying to tell me that H.D. / was our greatest scribe; well, Hilda gave us a few pink / Grecian gods in with the chinaware, but after reading her / I still have 140 icicles hanging from my bones."

251

humorous way with no intent at insult. That's all I can say.

My second book is out now—just got a few in the mail today—*Longshot Poems for Broke Players*, and if I find that you are not angry I will mail you a copy right away. I did the drawing on the cover and a few for the inside, and most of my latest poems are in there. I don't want to mail you a copy if you are just going to tear it up. Will wait to hear if you would like to see my head in a lion's jaws or what.

I think it fine that the H.D. issue reached her when it did; your sense of timing, of *being* there, was perfect.

It is so sad when the good ones die...

I liked very much the Pound poem for H.D., even though his mathematics are off. It is a thing of no small meaning that Ezra at his age still writes with the perfect ear and eye, where so many younger men, after a small fling at immortality have decayed.

Your vision was a true one. I had a vision once when I was very young, I mean in my early 20's. But no more. The gods have, perhaps, thrown me away.

I am rather sick tonight. No need to go into why or what. Only I must slow down a little...

Very good to hear from you, Shed.

It'll soon be March and you can cuss me to my face. Believe I will get about 3 weeks off but will only hang around a couple of days or so... don't want to be a pest... and will spend remainder of vacation in L.A. Will also try not to show up on weekend as I know that is *verbotten*...   But, then, I don't know how we stand now. This *Vegas* poem may have done me in with you...

Shed, I am rather sick really. Must stop.

Glad you liked the leaf oregano with eggs. I must go now.

      love,

       Buk

Pound poem for H.D.: a puzzling reference (there is no Pound poem for H. D. in this issue of *A&P*); perhaps a poem Pound included in his compliments on the H.D. issue, which were conveyed to SM by a mutual acquaintance.

L.A.
November 1961

Shed:

All right, I won't visit you this March as you don't wish it.
And don't worry, I won't try to search you out. I don't drop in
where I am not invited—as your "gentleman" Ernie did on me!
Talking about lawsuits, etc. How could you sue me? I don't
have anything.

My old woman was not very impressed with your Ernie's
intelligence which he tried to strut all over the place. I had to
tell him, for Christ's sake, Ernie, put the textbook down!

Well, I've met your lad now and I send him back.

Indeed.

"He tried so hard to act intelligent but he couldn't make
it," said the old lady.

The old lady said a mouthful.

You missed the point of the *Quicksilver* poem. It was not to
ruffle your hair or "expose you to the lower orders"; your part
in the poem was only *incidental* and the letter might have been
from anybody, the idea being that I was gnawing at the truckdriver, and the whole intent of the poem was humourous, not
scandalous, and if you will take time to step down from that
lofty damned perch you have built for yourself and give the
poem an impartial reading you will be able to see this.

Now, since you asked for the book, I am enclosing it and
you can do what you please with it

    BURN IT

        TEAR IT, CURSE IT

            BURY IT

        throw it in with the rest of the rubbish,
throw it to the sea, the birds, the ants, the wolves or

    GIVE THE FUCKING THING TO THE SALVATION ARMY.
I don't care.

        still,

           love,

              Buk

DeaRRRRRRRRRR Bukowski:

From mah lofty dammed perch which ah has built fo’ mahzelfffff ah dew notice (the air beingkkkkk clearer op here) that one l’l letter ob mine doth cause yew to rage mo’n one l’l poem ob yrs did cause me.

So much fo’ scientifikkk observation!

iz 8/52 a.m. just got to frisco hotel room:

now hold on kidttt—let us discuss March—the thing IS Buk that I don’t want to expose MY foibles to yr scrutiny IF I can help it—if you’d EVER get an eyeful of my PRIVATE essays as yet UNpublished & FAR more UNprintable than yrs you’d NOT want to expose yrself to MY scrutiny!

Yr Lady correct—Ernie DOES “strut” being a bantam rooster & you too; he does haul in the “textbook” /// recordi that Ernie is a provincial; a rustic who knew nothing until he hit Frisco—it is EASIER to de-louse a Tong pawn from Columbia University than to de-hick Ernie. I hev tried with no success— but that don’t mitigate the fact that he saved my life when I’d lost face with my Mezzo-slant; Ernie is responsible for me being here as I had quit it Buk & I, therefore hold him dear & his native intelligence has not to date been matched except by E.P. WITH THIS EXCEPTION   that Ernie has his racial roots to grow from & E.P. his & therein lies a worldtttt of difference which may or may not meet at some far point in Time/Destino

dear old myoptic Buk—of course I REALISE that any reference to a girl/Pound was INCIDENTAL to der truckdriver & the lower class’s approach to the different BUT THE FACT REMAINS that yr 2 hens cackled & cackled & who was irritated was me; it AGRIVATED me but I take no umbrage because Mr. Hemmingway never did & set us a model/

now to yr new publication///

A little classic / 20th c/ & you ARE a genius & I weep to think of what YOU would be IF I could ‘edit’ some of yr stuff/// you spoil the all over effect by NOT being AWARE of yr gift/// now serenetas... or serenitas or howhell anyway—Let us view

---

recordi: Italian: “remember.”
serenitas: Lat.: “brightness” (Canto 111/803).

the world you & I—as a sort of "gold fish bowl" the Yin/Yang—
it aint (space to draw it) flat
It is more as EP told me "see it like a goldfish bowl"
I CHOOSE TO REMAIN   O U T SIDE OF IT... because one
of us must & you choose to enter it & wiggle about & sculpt yr
mountain sides with portraits of what's jumpin' off inside it
specifics: re: *The Day I Kicked a Bankroll out the Window*
1/ if yr "pinch the gray out of my hair ... I'm 38"   hair is
gray @ 38 you NEED the b-complex vitamins which are easy to
get... go to health store & order a tablet DISSICATED LIVER
BREWERS YEAST PLUS LECITHIN & BONE MEAL & take 3 daily
& yr hair will return to its natural colour within 6 months to 1
yr... anyhow a drinking man should know that alcohol robs
body of its agility to use the b vitamins plus vitamin c/// all within reach dear boy. "but I'm different, baby, I can't help it..."
perfectly correct—you ARE the stuff O'Neill tried to get onto
the stage... yr drawings unique & funny
now I'm going to number the pages for sake of brevity
beginning with *State of World Affairs* etc as page 1//
p 1/ don't exhibit yr genius enough—makes reader tired:
jagged effect on total book
p/2 & 3 [*Hello, Willie Shoemaker*] classic—yr genius at work
p/4 [*Candidate Middle of Left-Right Center*] bores me—too
hit or miss
p/5 [*Prayer for Broken-Handed Lovers*] ditto
p/6 & 7/8 & 9 [*Poem for Personnel Managers*] ragged
p/10 [*The Best Way to Get Famous Is to Run Away*] a Buk
classic
p/11 [*The Life of Borodin*] Borodin incidental & yr hero worship lost on him—it is usually a mistake to kiss Gandhi's ass &
ignore our own heroes... but you will wallow in the Yin/Yang—
nobody knows ANYthing about Vivaldi's private life which IS a
better model... my godwtttt the roohoooshuns wd dream of
beating a donkey & spend all week weeping over the fact.

The Day ... out the Window: this and the following poems are from *Longshot Pomes*; titles have been supplied in brackets after SM's page
references.
roohoooshuns wd dream of beating a donkey: an allusion to Raskolnikov's
dream in Dostoevski's *Crime and Punishment* (1866).

p/12 [*Parts of an Opera...*] an attempt unresolved so far as clarity exists

p/14 [*To the Whore Who Took My Poems*] a buk classic

p/15 [*Conversation in a Cheap Room*] same

p/16 & 17 [*The Day I Kicked a Bankroll Away*] a perfect portrait of the sort of female who will never be more than a person looking for cigarette butts in the gutter & not knowing how to smoke 'em/ also a good defense of the artist.

p/18 [*Where the Hell Would Chopin Be?*] too personal to be a poem

p/19 & 20 & 21 [*What a Man I Was*] a howler; a classic; a marvel; a satire; an american satire

p/22 & 23 [*The Sun Wields Mercy*] cant read on through

p/24 [*The Loser*] beauty//

p/25 [*The Japanese Wife*] the Yawpandisease woife—for xts sake wot zentiment; man I seed dem... the bitches are totally commercial & I'm sick of the poor yiddish boys & the low white trash who get took by these business women... I am not for women who are professional women the way negroes are professional negroes & resent them as much as your resentment of college professorial critics or boets//etc etc

THE AMERICAN WOMAN IS THE MOST BEAUTIFUL & BEST & GIVINGEST IN THIS WORLD IT IS TOO BAD THAT OUR ANCIENT ENEMY WHO NOW RULES HOLLYVODTTT HAS TAKEN OVER THE BITCH MALE AMERICAN MIND & PROPAGANDISES AGAINST US & THE ASSHOLES SWALLOW THE HOLLYWOODTTT SHIT WHOLE PLUS THE NEWSPAPER PROPAGANDA—o.k. so WE'LL MARRY ORIENTALS ***THEY *KNOW* HOW TO SUCCEED FOR US & FUCK YOU BITCHES TO THE BUGGERY HELL WHERE YOU BELONG & I am currently praying for a Yiddish Hitler to be rid of you boys—we'll turn the race gold & you fuckfaces & fish eyes can whore yr ass off with yr YapanSlitherease broads/// damm you to ever lasting whore hell & rot yr dicks off in a crosseyed cunt/

As soon as I turn Ernie into a Jewish Hitler I'm going to ARM HIM & like Napoleon I know how to [m]ow something down because I know what I'm AIMING AT.

p/26–7 [*Death Wants More Death*] cant read//bores me

p/28 [*The Tragedy of the Leaves*] no sympathy—a landlady deserves her rent whether you got screwed or not

256

p/29 [*When Hugo Wolf Went Mad*—] a buk classic

p/30 [*The Ants*] this is a beauty; the orientals wd understand (including Japanese wife)... it can be compared to Hung Tzu-ch'eng of the Ming Dynasty: "When a man leisurely looks at the flies hurtling against a paper screen, he may scornfully laugh at those idiots who make obstacles for themselves..." transl. by Dr. Chao Tze-chiang in *A Chinese Garden of Serenity* Peter Pauper Press Mt. Vernon N.Y.... & Chao that stinking-stockinged oriental fake Britt said snobbishly: "do YOU have time to look at flies"??? & I said "that's ALL the time I got..." now thank gawd we have a poet who can look at ants & write a poem about it/// for which oye dank yew/

p/32 [*So Much for the Knifers...*] a minor buk classic

p/33 [*Winter Comes in a Lot of Places in August*] ditto

p/34 & 35 [*Bring Down the Beams*] a buk classic & of course that kind of rage is what makes the genius & I know it perfectly//

& 36 [*Letter from the North*] is more than a classic; it can be compared to Basil Bunting's transl. of *Chomei at Toyama* (Kamo-no-Chomei born at Kamo 1154 died at Toyama on Mt Hino 24th June 1216)

> "I am out of place in the capital
> people take me for a beggar,
> as you would be out of place in this sort of life,
> you are so—I regret it—so welded to your vulgarity..."

& much more that's pertinent but I got so much work today that I got to short cut this... but *Letter from the North* in title & poem are sheer Bukowski PERFECTION & poor Jory caught midtt his arse outdttt & pin'd down like a grub.

p/37 [*Riot*] a buk classic

38 & 39 [*Truth's a Hell of a Word*] cant read on through

I found yr p 40 & 41 [*CB's autobiographical note*] too much like a Henry Miller casual toss off but then I simply cant get you out of the Yin/Yang Buk... All in all I am proud of receiving yr book because it is literature—not classical but a classic... now encl. is $2. please send me 2 more—or better you mail out from there:

1/ Ezra Pound c/o Rachewiltz / Schloss Brunnenberg / Tirolo /
    Mereno / Italia /

257

2/ Reverend H. Swabey... no I will send out / send them to
me//
I'd like the Rev. Swabey to review for Cookson's *Agenda* &
Rev. Swabey the man wot converted Eliot to anglican choich &
UNshockable & def. one of us & yens to know what's shakin'
with us over here... so trust me & send on

& I was naturally DEElighted to discover that one small
literary effort upon my part had the power to make you far
madder than one literary effort upon yr part—alls it did was elevate moi lofty dammed perch loftier & LOFTier... & have NO
idea WHAT means "lawsuits" etc.... & my dear Bukowski IF I
had the discipline not to sue *Nation* magazine why wd I want to
sue you or ANYbody?? I do not take notice of the law for the
dogs but only the Law which governs Ladies & Gentlemen... a-
hem. & AH men.

and if you want to keep the things away from H.D.'s poetry
& leave it up to we Superiors—well that's YOUR responsibility...
I believe in educating the kids & will only offer them ambrosia
& icor... or ikor... howhellspelled

now calm down darling & tell yr Lady that she was correct
about Ernie... & didn't know he'd gone by until he wrote & of
course his portrait of you was just as irritated as yr portrait of
him—found you lacking in any appreciation of truth beauty etc
& with low morals & so forth & on... but babe he's a hick &
there are NO more moral-ists on earth than the Jews. If you tie
that up with mid-western morality you got my Ernie/

No wont give *Longshot* to Sal Army but to Yale University
where you have an audience who admires you in Mr. N. H.
Pearson even tho' he wont believe H.D. visited me day before
her departure; thank Godtt something prompted me to write an
account of it to Rev. Swabey on the day she was dying & I cdn't
have known about it; to my discredit I thought it was a head of

---

Rev. H. Swabey: Henry Swabey, an Anglican clergyman and occasional
reviewer for *Agenda*; he corresponded with Pound on Social Credit.

sue Nation magazine: SM was so incensed at David Rattray's description
of her in his *Nation* article "Weekend with Ezra Pound" (16 November
1957) that she wanted to sue him, but was talked out of it by Dorothy
Shakespear.

icor: ichor: an ethereal blood, the blood of gods (Canto 91/631).

Christ because it was so holy & mysterious & sacred...
So much for now is now 9/45 & so long Buk & we discuss yr
visit/& take yew vitamins/minerals IF yew gotta zrink pbeer/

Love//Shed

Sheri

L.A.
Nov. what? 13, 1961

Hello Shed:
Walking down the street the other night, East side of town,
there are not too many lights, I came across this body laying in
the curb and the body was dead, I know death, I have seen dead
roses and flies and moths, I have seen dead people, and his hat
was dead in the curb, and people will die anywhere, they have
no neatness, they will die on streetcars and meatmarkets, they
will die in the bath or on the pot or on their love, they will die,
they will die, and I looked at his body, the curious emptied-out
feeling, and I thought, that will be me, I will be that and then it
will be too late, I will not be able to do what I should have
done, and I walked one halfblock or so and I saw a prowl car
and waved them over, "There's a man down on the corner," I
told them and the one on the door side, thin little moustache,
too young, smiled at me knowingly and said, "Thank you, sir,"
and he thought I meant a drunk had fallen, I guess I do not talk
too excited, and I went on down the dark street and into a bar
and the place was full of angels except for the bartender who
was a bull without balls and I lifted the drink as if in a toast and
then tossed it down and he said, "Who's that for?" and I said,
"For a friend, my friend." For a friend. And I went out and the
rats were still in the gutters and a black and white dog, his tail
looped in, was eating a piece of cardboard in the parking lot,
and well. well, well, well. I walked on...
    Look, oh lofty one of the rarified air, I have enclosed 2
Longshots for which you will not be silly enough to send me 2
bucks for as if I were some grubby little merchant, but I know
you were just going through a formality there... Your tabula

259

rasa, Ernie, if he thought my morals bad, which they are and my vulgarity excellent, which it is, I am pleased, for by these
any acceptance would mean failure.
—I did not select the poems that appeared in *Longshots*. Many of them I do not care for either but I let the editors have their head and it looks as if their head were not so good, but I cannot be bothered because these poems are behind me and to slosh around in them again is only so much stale jazz on an old record, and since I am not preparing for any type of immortality they can damn fuck well do wat they please, and so. soo, so, so.

Ah, I am aware I down with the fish, and being in there I think fishthoughts and so am locked in a small area of watery whirling...

Lord, Shed, you sure got it in for the Jap broads. I think they shake it nice. Some little slanty steal a bull from ya in the far past, eh Princess? You curse classicly in your letters and I got a cigarette and a beer and my face smiles at your vocab. I've worked on the docks and the railroadyards and never heard anything like this; the only difference being that their cussing is pewkingly sickening and without soul but yours comes through like the sound of sledgehammers on the sides of a steel barn.

I do not think the 2 lonelies who printed *Vegas* in *Quicksilver* know who Sheri Martinelli is. They cannot "cackle" at what they do not know.

Jon Webb writes that the English audience especially liked my album in *Outsider* #1, and sure enough I sent some poems to an Henglish mag, *Satis*, and he took 2, and not only that, said he would run a free ad for *Longshots*, and who knows? my pub. and I might sell all 245 copies for which we might buy one small chinchilla to turn loose in the weeds.

My grey around the ears which showed at 38, left at 40, came back at 41 and then left again 2 months back. It is one hell of a thing. I am a blinking neon sign... Thanx for yr formula but seems a lot of trouble to go through. I'd rather be grey.

---

my album in Outsider #1: eleven poems were published as "A Charles Bukowski Album" in the first issue of the *Outsider* (pp. 48–53).
Satis: "A 350 Dollar Horse and a Hundred Dollar Whore" and "What Seems to Be the Trouble, Gentlemen?" were published in the Spring–Summer 1962 issue.

260

What's the difference? Some foxes (foxii?) are grey and still haven't gotten their asses trapped.

If Pearson doesn't believe H.D. visited you it means he has a strong working intelligence and you've got to hand it to him because he does not buckle down before you and buy it, but I buy it because similar things have happened to me, and although the boys try to explain it away as electricity in the air or madness, they'll have to do better than that before I'll wipe it off as nothing. And so. soo, so.

From my way of looking, you were pretty much on the mark in dis-cussing some of the poems in *Longshots*. *Letter from the North* caused some resentment from a couple of people who bothered to figure out the initials, although I changed some of them. One editoress wrote: "I don't see how you can accept information from such a shallow source. No one knows anything about our private lives except etc. etc...." Now who the hell said anything about accepting INFORMATION? I was writing about letters received that often made me physically sick. I do not accept information from a choirboy driveling at the mouth for fame.

I will say this. I did come across a few poems of Jory's in a mimeo sheet that showed some excellence, and since I judge a man more by his work than his ways, I wrote him a short note telling him this, and he is a boy, a troubled boy, but he has time.

Look, Shed, I must go out for the Racing Form and a little more beer and cigarettes. There is one good one going tomorrow that I know of. I am drinking Miller's in the pint glass bottle now and it's very good while it lasts. I have chiragra. Must stop.

love,
Buk

Los Angeles, Calif.
Nov. what, 1961

La M:

Enclosed copy of *Satis* requested. *Satis*: satis/fied, satura-tion, full, or as they explain in the inside cover—enough. Finish.

"tabula rasa, Ernie" means or equals: blank tablet, Ernie.

"I have chiragra", a stiffness or paralysis.

I told you not to send me money for *Longshots* sent unless you care to insult me. If you want *Outsider* one please send one dollar to *Outsider*, 618 Ursulines st., New Orleans, La. This is their new address. I would send you my copy but it seems as if how somebody came by and borrowed mine and I am waiting its return.

On death in gutter: D. H. Lawrence wrote a poem, don't recall title, perhaps *Ship of Death* in which he stated that one must prepare the soul for death and then its transport through the wastes into the final state of its destination.

Most men don't die. There is nothing that has lived; there is nothing to die.

The jap females are not professionally put upon us by any-body, it is only that the American male is attracted by: 1) the bone structure of the head which gives a moulded and classical look not obtained by our softer white females which have sprung out of IrishEnglishFrenchSweedishItalian putty. It is true that the outer classical look is not, in the japbitch, welded to an inner classical strength (yr boy Ernie wd use the term "inner classical beauty"). 2) the jap female attracts as an oppo-site to what we have been getting, and the darkness is not the heavy burnt coal of the niggerfemale which is really too much for us unless we simply turn the head and fuck.

You will note that the poem I wrote about the Jap female was about *another* man's reaction to same, not my own.

Yes, I am down with the fish and they are a mealy lot. Often I come home so physically ill that I can neither eat nor sleep nor think nor see; they have stung me with their snouts and fish-gabble and watery looks. Yes, it is possible to get out; it is also

---

Lawrence ... Ship of Death: written a few months before Lawrence died in 1930.

262

possible to get so FAR out that one becomes inhuman and misses the point entirely.

Editoress *Epos* upset and wrote me about Jory-poem too much opening of private window in her life but also on the other hand accepted another of my poems, *The Priest and the Matador*.

I have very bad cold and it is raining and I am drinking orange juice and shivering like a witless fink so must cut this short and get back in bed. You heard from kaja? She has sent me a couple of little paintings which are very good. Sneezing now, idiot sneezing, and out.

love,
Charles
Buk

ps—enclosed some blurbs from publisher. if you know anybody who can be dominated or influenced by this approach, mail em out, help make me rich. love. c.b.

South part of California
full of niggers, bad opera
and idiots; and almost Dec.
nineteensixtyone, all these
years after the passing of
the Lord or a part of the
Lord, 1/3, on a very bad day,
it w'd seem...

Deah Shed:
now hold!—I have seen some copies of *Agenda* that have made me feel like a crab-shucker, yes, there was won issue predicated to one long pome, a rust-fungi thing, some Frenchman in his dotage, ah, who was it? shit. mabee Shot-toe,

---

The Priest and the Matador: published in the Winter 1961 issue of *Epos*; rpt. in *BW* (41).

Agenda ... Shot-toe: Cocteau's "Leoun"; see note to CB's letter of 3 January 1961.

263

certainly something of sort, 19th. century classicism that might have looked pretty forward to Corneille, Pierre, shuffling with his grave hairs, butt to me   jus more dead horns up the asss...ya. Did Ezra O.K. this page mass of homo-cream and water-moccasin turds? Ho, lady, good fine one, I have moments when I wonder if Pound is getting alla his calories, or perhaps his systole is wrestling with some soft wormwood of the brain... But that's all right. I will allow a mistake or 2 to ol' Ez. He never did deserve the cage except for courage, or in a world's small light, swimming upstream. *Satis* is not bad, it is only that they are printing the wrong people, which I know is 9tops the battle, but I'll be in Spring Issue and everything will be looking up everywhere and people will be hollering from tops of mountains and jumping into pure blue springs of water. Ya.

The Henglo-Sexon, as ya say, Caesar's buggers, believe originally branched off from the Tuetons, which to me is one hell of a fine thing. Wen you say Tueton I get the feeling of teeth in the hair and great bug power. Present strong races are the Germans, Slavs, Russians, Chinese. Rome has really fallen off to the floppy shoed Italian of Mouth and bluff, a front-runner with a backbone of cheese. Tha Jews, as always, will endure but... their endurance is not strictly honorable. And honor is what the mind and soul sharpens its blade upon. To simply endure is not enough. The jew is correctly dispised as a nutchewer, a muncher of small foul things and a backstabber flatfalsesmiler lier for a small bag of rusted coin and nutmeg, and beside this, his god cannot make us [sic] His mind, which is one helluva thing. The Negro, as you know, is now enjoying a new recognition, but he is going stricly punchy as are the recognizers, all slober adultation in an effort to right the boards to the tune of some outside voice that commands not entirely within reality. The Nigger is rummy rampant like a child with a toy gun that he finds can shoot real bullets.

The holy order is disorder; those who survive may not be the best but they won't be the worst either. What is left over, we eventually become.

I enclose a copy of *Satis* which will not satisfy but which includes a couple a pomes by yr Wangboy, Rapheal David. I have little doubt but that his first name is really Chung but that doesn't matter. What matters is that in many of his pomes he ends up on his knees in a suculent mood, or if not that, he is

264

intent upon DEDICATING his pome to SOMEBODY. This puts him IN. IT IS A FUCKPOOR TRICK and if he ever deficates one to me I will come up there and throw him out of the nearest window. Ja, he thinks he can get in by hanging his ass out the back door, as Sherman thinks he can get in by kissing toes and noses and wrapping them in the gabble of telephone wire. I would not bother with these people at all, only it gives me some light to go on, to see them so weak, and no breach crossed. It is wrong, however, in mentioning them, I give them light. Grab garbage, dump it, forget it.

Darling, I wd not mind your SCRUTINY on any visit or anything you ever wrote about me, bad, or whatever, I am not that way, I am not that way at all, being, perhaps as Ernie told you, I am a pretty hard nut, vulgar and so forth; but, of course, u might be worried that I might spread you across the horizon in my cheap and chitty gossip column poesy, I am all and absolutely no good at all, so ya better keep me out. Still now, you will never be in my memwaws, and that is not only one helluva thing, it is just too bad.

I wrote 7 poems last night in one hour and I must retype them now and send them out, so I must be going. Caught cold standing in shirt sleeves at Los Almomitos watching them go 350 yards in 18 seconds and the beer was so green I could not drink it. Yes, I know, vitamen C. I am mixing my beer with orange juice.

love to you, my beauty,
Buk

she: small swine in pen, knotted tails,
c'd ask no more than this, c'd they?

he: I dunno, I dunno.

she: ya think the moon makes the mind
maddern' it is?

he: shit. why not?

she: how can an idiot like Man go on when he knows his sting
will run out?

265

he: didn't Shakespeare answer that for you?

she: yes, but then one wants the modern answer... Do you think it's fear of the unknown that keeps us from going there?

he: No. Some go. Early. It's that with the rest of us, we *know* we are going there... no matter, so we play out the string... knowing there's no 2nd chance here. Or, surmising as much.

29/nov/61   s.m.   pobx 217   Pacifica Calif

Buk lamb: note change pobx—it is within evening drive from frisco shd I not want to make 1 hr trip to half moon... the weather no longer nice to drive at nite... rain is here / grey today—wd be rain/fine snow back home but here just fog/rain... just got here @ 8/30 & flew about doin' this & that—stuff der lunch on der window sill in back room ally window & then come here & sit by front rm window by BUTCHER & TIEDJE Gas Station @ 4 corners—find that when my view is just 1 road going up & down I become downhearted & traced it to the one way traffic which makes me feel left out but hell when they are wizzin all over that's NO direction & I'm cool sittin' in my Private World

Now re: yr recent *Satis* wh by way has a fine "A" on it/ & yr "rough customer" note is funny... re: David Wang—he just don't understand the language he is writing INto... He cannot make up such HIGHlarious gems as "a moth just flew by doin' ½ mile an hr"—or words to in yr's recent. David is a water'd down cup of tea from the petrified records of China/// It is often called: "precious" writing or painting because it stems from a withered or petrified stalk & adds nothing new but oftime may be gemlike due to its isolation & petrification... David is no threat because he has not yr life/// the rest of yr NOT enough aint worth my brain cells

n o w   the real problem is—as po li & i discussed last night when we went to get the mail & sat in our hurricane lamp lit old country shack with the pines moaning & the sea roaring & rain pouring—a wild night much maker of thought—are we selfish to let you stay out there all alone being the only Live Person??? ought we join you instead of keeping us for the FEW??? I truly do not know Buk/// it seems to me—that no I cant figure it out—I am always working—inbetween painting & correspond. cooking & shifting papers from half moon to s.f.—working on my own book // that will appear when it's supposta... & often we write something that wd amuse 'us' (all) & if knock out some today then will enclose for yr amusement// but I do not ever go beyond that... then have I a right to complain about the LOW level of all the 'little maz'???? I just have no time to think on it//

The only thing I can do Buk—is this—send you several copies of any of the latest & if you believe it will DO SOME GOOD... either refine their ears or merry up their hearts too sober now or larn 'em somepin... then I here/now give you permission to send them out along with any of yrs... you may leave Po Li's name on his but kindly cross my name out & type in: Wishes to remain Unknown... or rather WANTS to remain UNknown—it wd be better that way// do as you please Buk// I did rather feel a coward knowing that I'd send things to you but wdn't give you any help in yr little pubs & yet insist upon criticising them// tiz a problem—I suppose I'd detest you if you hadn't sent me those drawings for the H.D. issue///

yes—all you said in yr last letter is CORRECT—

Listen you Krout Head—it aint my scrutiny on YOU that worries me but yours ON ME—I can hardly take any more of the world—no Ernie didn't tell me much in his letter—he's due here frid. or thurs. his maw very ill & he's getting out to help pay off the mortgage / I will go dithery in this small nut house of a hotel—no you bastid you aint no gottdamm gootttt when it comes to eggsposin' the vanity of der female & I aint gonna let you see me in my outdddd house... there are too many people who wd adowre a view of Sheri of the ShitHouse.

VITAMIN C CAN NOT BE GOT FROM ORANGEJUICE U N L E S S YOU PURCHASE IT FROM ORGANIC VILLE 4207 West 3rd St Los Angeles 5 Calif// where the oranges & so forth are grown without chemical sprays & poisons// I wish you'd drive over or wherever & let me know what kind of joint it is/// if you were ONLY a reliable moder-fkr I cd mail you down a list

---

my own book: never published, whatever it was.

plus some $$$ & have you get us some organically grown foods & just stick it in to the Railway Express—we'd get it inside of 2 days/// OrganicVille wants a $10. order of produce organically grown or a $2. bit for handling small orders & how in hell are Gib & I to eat $10 worth of apples oranges celery & beets & so forth in one sitting with NOwhere to keep 'em?? no ice box down country nor hotel room// 's a bitch to try to live healthy... as it is we go to a store here but the prices are high—still if you have ever eaten a vegetable grown naturally you'd never go back to the chemicals// you see my dear Buk—if you feed a vegetable chemical fertilizers & spray—the vegetable also is what it eats & when you eat it you might as well eat the chemicals & the poison because that is what you get// When you eat natural unsprayed foods you get full value/ it wd pay you to visit the store & just purchase ONE real orange or apple—the difference is mad...! I am having some vitamins sent to you—lemme know when/if they get there//

So far—you are all that LIVES in this land// Maj was alive— but the coloured folk want immediate results—they do not know that it even took Ez a whole life time—I cant make anybody rich 'n famous in a year// you have lasted... Wang has sold his arsehole for a position—Ernie goes off the main line & gets into the gotttamtist bypaths—but you Wobbling One have remained Constant/// I guess the Kaiser is fiercer than the Rabbi or the Medicine Man—but here YOU... La Druidessa hath kept pace... & there are those days not worth a nickel...

Tell yr "she" that yes the moon has an effect upon the watery parts of our brain but I do not think it controls the MIND unless it is chained to earth... Dante teaches "get past the sphere of Fortuna (MOON) to be free of Chance" Fate or whatever/// yr "he" is an ice cold turd & I would have shit one quietly & shoved it in his mackeral snapper if he answered my questions like that the narsty bitch

you are a cruel bastard bukowski but you are not a coward/// the rest are cruel AND cowardly... all but Ernie// Jory don't matter—nor Wang—they are merely "contemporaries" & Ez sez: "ya kin forget about yr contemporaries"... but last night I thought that by remaining out in my private cloud world— that I was letting you all alone with the UNamericans who do not know how to write in english & are not really what they got born because they WANT so ambitiously to write in english but

268

hear now Buk—the BEST never pay any attention to them—so actually they aint much threat—damm it all—if only the river wd part & let me see a clear path instead of trying to make each decision on my own—Gib cant help because his values aint mine

Yes—*Agenda* goes off but at least I can work with Cookson—do a cover for *Agenda*/// and who gets inside that I dig is Rev. Swabey who is a serious man// don't know what he'd think of *Satis*... maybe we shd INFILTRATE like Der Tong did—now maybe that is the way—but O! Lawd! Shall it be said of the Wilde Goose that she took off the way th' Old Blawck Vulchurss Ventttddttt???? oye Ma' Mia... it's 'nuff to make a Zaint vrummm hebben smoker der veewdttttt

now I go—it is so grey in here being only 10/10 a.m. dot I kin hardtttly zee... & thank you for *Satis* & I will ponder this new problem...

love

Shed//

Sheri

LISTEN AT THAT HEALTH STORE GET A COPY OF *PREVENTION MAGAZINE* FOR 35¢... a dec. copy & turn to p. 35 & you send for the vitamins yrself Buk/ costs 25¢ & then about $5. month for ALL NATURAL VITAMINS plus info. on them—so do it... I just thought that they wdn't let me send them to you & I already got some for my inlaws & my parents & I'll pay the $5. m.o. for them but wdn't let me send for [*illegible*]

note: it is so fkn coldttt in this unheated hotel in this cold chill rain that I just got up & fished out Gib's old army underdrawers midtt long laigs & put them on... I got on a sweater// a jumper of wool// my wool socks & my snow boots & now the long army wool drawers... look like a floradora goirl with the skirt up & a bear with the skirt down...

I mean about those vitamins// they send you a full months supply of NATURAL.... that means no coal tar nor other chemicals... vitamins for 25¢ trial of 100—then they mail you yr supply for 25¢ cheaper until you no longer want them & I got

---

Cookson: William Cookson, editor of *Agenda* and a Pound scholar.

some for my parents who cannot be educated any more than
YOU—but 1 little pill at least the dopes WILL take so I'll
send them their 100 pills which just got here this a.m. & mail
back the card saying yes I'll send the $2.25 every 2 weeks or
so—& I just realised that you'd be getting the card & you'd be
salty maybe if I stuck you for $2.25 each 2 wks.... but you sim-
ple lookin' s.o.b. & double distilled bastid THEY WILL BE A
FOOD SUPPLIMENT TO yr green beer—I hardly eat anything
now that I use the food suppliments—anyhow got no time for
it am that busy—just eat bare minimum// So get a copy of *Prevention* & send 25¢ to these people// don't be a juice square
buk//

now must go—oh mah knees are finally warm—this is the
first time I ever wore pants in mah life! It is that cold in this
joint... alls I got for heat is my little hot plate for making 2—to
heat 2 rooms—oh give me the artist life... the gay romantic
artist life... with a heart that's free as the open sea & an ass
that's coldttt as th' skies... so long buk—ah is coldttttt as a
frozen turd...

Sheri

L.A.
cold Dec. [10] 1961

Shed, girl-woman:

D.R. Wang has written one good poem that I know of.
(*Quicksilver*, Summer 1960). To wit, and with the usual senseless dedication:

> *Postscript*
> (to Max Finstein)
>
> All night long
> a mosquito
> zanzanzara
> zips and unzips
> my nerves.

270

Should I kill
kamikaze
slap   dash
ouch   goes
my soul.

now this is not a bad poem, really. And so let's give DEDI-
CATION DAVID a bow, and then let him go.

I work better alone, Princess; let's not join hands.

Rec. your enclosures and have mailed them on to Corrington.

You better keep on my good side, baby, if you want any
more drawings for any more future... whatever the long name of
your thing is.

Your Ernie will blast me from witchhazel to Sutter's Creek
but I wouldn't have it any other way.

I will run over to 4207 W. 3rd. eventually and see what's
cooking or wats not sprayed. Will give you a fullsome picture of
the proprietor and all the helty handsome rats.

Yes, you're right. Major wants so badly to be famous he
won't take time to wipe his ass. This need prob. springs partly
out of the colored thing, and it's too bad.

There is a person who wants my friendship and he dribbles
his soul upon me at every opp. It is a slimey sickening mess, but
since we spring from similar environments,
                    by learning what he wants
                    I learn what to leave alone
because I know that he is dead
by the pale shell color of his eyes.

Yes, you are right. I am cruel. It cuts away a lot of mess.
Cruelty is usually the tool of the masses. I have learned to use
this tool to gain time and solitude, 2 important factors for anybody bit with the creator-bug.

This is a bad letter and it is a bad afternoon and I am sitting
here drinking beer and smoking Salems and the menthol is too
much, and the old woman has phoned and I have said   no,
no, I can't see you   I will bring your coat and shoes over to
you, it is a bad day, I do not feel good.

Ok, she says, I know how you get.

They god damned better know because when I don't want
to be fucked with I don't want to be fucked with.

271

I am sorry I could not understand the Mancho on your letters; prob. hog-color cuss wurds by the Princess, but looked nize.

All last night I kept hearing this sound, it was like the clicking of steel marbles every 30 seconds or like the axeman swiping off a head and I thought
                    what the hell
                              oh what the merry hell now????
because I don't sleep good anyhow
and so I laid there awake all night.   if there hadda been a big
          woman cow
I coulda put my cold feet on the backs of her calves,
and I got up in the morning looking more Buk than ever
          (which is bad)
and found the sink was dripping onto a piece of wax paper,
and so today am in no mood for writing letters.

Don't know if I told you. *Satis* going to run me a free ad on *Longshots*. Also a couple of my poems in the Spring 1962 issue. Editor suggested another outfit for me in England but I don't have any more poems right now. They operate out of a basement, which I like. Good things can come from a basement that cannot come from any where else. There is something holy in poverty that makes you strong—if you know how to handle it. If you don't know how to handle it you might as well be rich because whatever god there is is wasting his benefits on you.

And now that I have poisoned your air, I'm leaving.

                    love, frum
                              krautpollock
                              Bukowski

•

Mancho: i.e., Manchu. SM apparently added Chinese ideograms (probably from Pound's *Cantos*) to some of her letters.

• 1 9 6 2 •

June wonsix2

Ya, Sheeriiie:
   it appears yr letter was mainly to see the pome I wrote
about you I wrote about pound I worked at something but it is
plainly to be seen now that the pome is gon I have destroyed it
my better judgment saying do so it is a bad poem even if it is
dedicated to Martin[elli] and so I tore it and tore it and therefore I cannot enclose it even if I wanted to. if I recall it was not
a rough pome almost a pleasant poem and not a long pome and
it was almost a love poem and it said Sheri, Pound is old and
although i am old i am not that old and I am not Pound but I
am Buk which is not as good but it is still light dark light and
Pound is in Italy and Pound is old and I am in Los Angeles and
I am not so old and so therefore why do we not reach an
approximation of love. that is about what I said in the poem.
the people said it was well written but too personal and I said it
was not well written and not even personal at all, that is was
almost laughing without meaning it, but the thing in me said
anyhow it is a bad poem so I tore it.
   Yes, somebody put a wire in the *Outsider* man Webb and
this jazz thing came out which does not reach me at all and
which may be my fault, but I have given jazz chance after
chance just like a bad whore, but it continues to lie to me. jazz,
the essence of it is too thin, too flat; it rests and tickles on the
mind, it draws out the weak and simple area of the mind. Jazz

---

Outsider ... jazz thing: a survey of jazz by several writers appeared in
issues 2 and 3 of the *Outsider*.

deflates. jazz is flesh without backbone. I would rather go to hell on a donkey.

I prefer certain classical pieces, both ancient and modern, that have not been overplayed until here too all essence is lost in hackneyed repetiveness.

Jory is in L.A. now. He knocked on door and found me in bed resting, waiting to go to track. I do wish these people would at least phone. I gave him a beer and went down to the mailbox: yr letter and another. I read them and put them in my pocket. Who? he asked. Sheri and somebody, I said. Is Sheri in San Francisco? I guess so, I said. I am on some kind of bonded word not to expose her whereabouts but I don't know her whereabouts anyhow. Will you tell her, asked Sherman, that I will be in San Francisco the second week in June? All right, I said, I will tell her.

You are hereby told. I gave him 5 dollars and he left. He is MAKING IT here in L.A. The ladies love the boy but I think he is looking for a mother. Or a father. I made a note that that would be the last of the money from me to him. I have starved in card-board shacks and on park benches and never asked a dime. But this is bitching. I do not like myself when I bitch or compare. I usually do not like myself anyhow, and this only makes it worse. Enough.

Got a notice from my x-wife in Alaska. She is marrying an eskimo. Not won dam do i giv a wit. po' po' eskimo. Mi old girl friend died 5:45 p.m. Jan. 22, 1962. It did not go well for me for quite some time and even now it is not so good, but, I am not looking for a mother.

Cuscaden writes (*Midwest Poetry Chapbooks*) that my 3rd. collection of poems *Run with the Hunted* will be out in about 2 weeks. I had more of a hand in the selection here and I think these poems are both my latter and better. But maybe not. Maybe this kroutpole head iz crumbling. o, mortal wound of nothing, o beast crying in cave, Bukowski done, Bukowski nothing, ayeeie, ayeeie!!! next page babe—

Mead is bringing out a couple of my pomes in *Satis* and

Cuscaden: R. R. Cuscaden, publisher and critic.

Satis: two of CB's poems appeared in the Spring–Summer 1962 issue, along with Cuscaden's critical essay "Charles Bukowski: Poet in a Ruined Landscape."

274

there is an article on me by Cuscaden. I do not know what the article says but I think Cuscaden is a little too overboard on me, which is all right as long as I don't go believing it, and I know all the things that are wrong with me, the things that are weak, wrong, sad. I wonder how strong a man can get? And then I wonder if a piece of steel is any longer human. The perfect sighting is the perfect art: being human and being not-human, somewhere in between there is art. So fuck it. I would rather ride a dinosour to hell.

Another too personal poem:

Remains

things are good as I am not dead yet
and the rats move in the beercans,
the papersacks shuffle like small dogs,
and her photographs are stuck onto a painting
by a dead German and she too is dead
and it took me 14 years to know her
and if they give me another 14
I will know her yet...
her photos stuck over glass
neither move nor speak,
but I even have her voice on tape
and she speaks some evenings,
her again,
so real she laughs,
says the thousand things,
the one thing I always ignored;
this will never leave me:
that I had love
and love died;
a photo and a piece of tape
is not much, I have learned late,
but give me 14 days or 14 years,—
I will kill any man
who would touch or take
whatever's left.

Remains: published in *Outcry* in 1963, rpt. in *DRA* (65).

Yes again. It is very bad. The jazz bit. It kills or distorts the whole flow of the magazine. It is like a lead in the back. A bullet.

I have much to do now. And when I mean much I mean nothing. Doing nothing. Letting the ceiling have its say. God oh jesus I am glad we eat and shit, I am glad there is music. I am glad there is rye bread; I am glad there are old dogs in the streets. I am glad there is rain and bridges and wine. And sleep.

Look, baby, don't blow yr brains out.

Or the other either.

Love,

Buk

L.A.
Friday

Dear Sheri:

Please disregard last letter. I wrote while intoxicated. I see by yrs that I might have inferred that I wanted to see you. This is child-stuff. You and I would not strike it. I mean, I am not good with people. It is so.

Enclose *Satis* in case Mead did not send. In review of my work Cuscaden does not get everything right, and in one case, *So Much for the Knifers* etc., he gets it exactly backwards. But it's all right. He's of good intent and knows that I swing the hammer around because I've got to.

I don't know if I wrote in my drunk letter what the next problem will be (except the going on, that is), and the next problem will be to keep from getting the fathead, to keep from believing the bildge about me and so forth. I have seen people like Corso and Ginsburg and Kerourac go the way of self-love, of self-importance. I think I am harder than that but I must be wary. One magazine has accepted 14 poems, another 15, another 6. This can cause trouble. The world, even the Art world, is very corrupt, rotten. They will print you if you have half a name and half a talent. They will print you if you have a big name and a little talent (or no talent at all). It is up to me not to fall into the pit.

The gods now have me up for test. They are looking down and waiting. I must not add to decay. These walls are mine.

                love,
                Buk
                Buk

[*dated by SM 7 August 1962*]

Dear Sheri:

Enclosed review from apparent liberal N.York rag and if one may defend one's self, the reviewer's idea of poetry and mine are different: he believing a poem must be fragile, "poetic", so forth, and I believing... nothing.

I am late for the god damned job and must run like any other legless worm.

No, you nedn't "expose" yrself to me   keep in yr clean light   it is best we never see each other

        we fall short
            we fall short
                we fall short

                alllove,
                BUKOWSKI

---

review: unidentified; Dorbin lists three reviews of CB's work for 1962— in *Rongwrong*, *Outcry*, and *Gallows*—but I doubt any of these could be described as a "liberal N. York rag."

277

L.A.
a Monday in August

Dear Sheri:

be calmed: I do not believe in my subject matter; it is only that I exist in this fashion and I photograph my existence... It is hard as hell to live as a Saint, the nerves give way, and then it would be tough to participate in Sainthood and find out later—like an oyster taken out of its shell—that you were wrong. If you don't put any chips on the table they can't rake them in...

Ginsburg and Corso are bothered with self-importance. They run about in various countries holding their names up above their heads while they still shine. They have taken to the worst trap and their writing—their creation—must suffer because they have taken their gift out of the mould and are using it as a wedge into something else. When I go to the race-track or to bed with a whore, I stand aside. I really do not enter. I am there to record the sounds of another world. I do things without *being* things. My x-wife found this out after 3 years of wifing: "You are nothing but a god damned puritan," was her way of expressing it. I wouldn't give her my soul to walk about in her bedroom slippers and she had thought I would be easy taking, "a dupe", after reading my poems. I am soft as air in part & then there is the hard German steel. I attempt to use these fruititians properly. God and the devil grant I am not too much in error. It would be difficult to self-impose any given laws... only there is a *very odd* thing... I am guided someplace from the back and above. Otherwise I would long ago have been gone over the rapids.

Most poets—if I may call them that—are lost in the slush and hazard of their own work. They do not know the secret and even if you told them the secret they could not use it. When Ezra said "do not worry ab't yr contemporaries" he said plenty.

Part of the secret is in having somebody in back and above. Part of the secret is in laying down the word. The word must be put on the page so that it is drilled down there, screwed-down, fucked-down, so that it will not brush away. The language must be a *basic* language that does not change. Your Kerwhoreac had an idea of this when he began but he found it too easy and he now beats on it like a drum, and as a consequence, he writes very badly. Basic language does not mean easiness. The

278

thought must seep down through, and the words without the mind are so much formula and most writers end up formula because they get tired and they write what they want them to write. When you get tired, stop writing. I stopped for ten years. I filled up enough in ten years to write for 200, maybe 2,000. Everything is so simple, and yet they cannot see. Pound saw and Jeffers saw, and the rest of the pages were wasted. T.S. Eliot got pretty and took to the bit and they cut his mouth out. The gods give us this thing and the gods get angry, pretty damned angry when they are wronged.

Somebody at Wagner College wants me to send a holograph(?) of one of my poems and a photo for somebody at Brown University, but this is a hell of a lot of work and I might pass. I don't like to be photographed and I am—in the world's eye—a very ugly man.

To publish a magazine like *Satis* would cost between 200 and 250$ for 300 copies, which means you would have to sell them all to break even. Which you don't do.

Do not become too incensed about Mead and Rutherford: their English brand of humour, ya know.

...on the job, I am cracking. I failed an examination last week and the man with the cigar roared back and laughed. My mind simply would not work at the thing, would not pick it up. But these are practicalities and just so much trash.

Good to get yr long letter and know you are trying to guide me through the rapids, and I cannot disagree with anything you say.

Tired today and sick. Drunk last night. I was on radio last night (taped), a reading of some of my poems but by the time it came on (11 p.m.) I was too far gone to listen.

May the gods be kind as possible...

love,

Buk

Mead and Rutherford: editors of *Satis*.

279

[*handwritten postcard from the Del Mar Turf Club,*
postmarked 21 August 1962]

Dear Sheri—
Telephone still in head. All good.
Drove down here (100 mi+), will prob stay 3, 4 days. Hope
they run with alacrity.
Wish I were one of your flies.
L.   *Buk*

L.A.
Sept. what? 5, 1962
or 1662 or 1442

Dear Sheri:
Death has me inside a napkin and is ready to wipe its
bloody snout face of a head and mouth, gut reaming down into
all the shit I have been stepping, making us one. hurrah.

flies walk my head,
talking about buttons.
            misery, ancient misery
            and coffeecup handles
        the sky flattens and drips
            F I R E

e.e. cummings died.
hemingway died.
Faulkner died.
Jeffers died.
J.Christ died. I am dying, I am dying, I am dying, I am dying, I
    am dying

---

cummings ... Jeffers: all of these writers died between July 1961 and September 1962.

to some of us
   sometimes
       come this thing—
that no matter what is done
it is of no matter

   things fall away finally
   and though one senses pain
   and walks as before
   and makes efforts at
       feeding
       living loving
       fucking
       paying rent
      looking for wurk
       having nightmares
but see this, essentially it has ENDED, & tho
the grass grows and the dead are buried
we see only thru motion picture eyes
the scene, as they say,
the burning soldiers marching into a golden city:
sigh.

   and o most splendid love or drums and sounds
   sheri darling image on my wrist
   speaking through frost and glass,
   how are you today?

I am not very good at love letters
   I am not very good at love
I am as old as the moss on a tourniquet,
   whatever that is.

     Ezra still breathes and if suddenly not,
     he leaves us the W(o) R K
jade-mad butterflies cuarved
     carved curved
       into the sides of rivers

I SEIZE THE INSIDE OF MYSELF AND THE WALLS BARK LIKE
  DOGS.

what are our visions worth? 29$?   ah, ha ha ha ha ha ha!

there are now
              very FEW giants left...

do you think Ginsburg can step in? iz he strong enough?
or just the clapping of tambrowines?
                              shit, who cares?

THE VOLITION IS EVERYWHERE, THE VOLITION AND THE
     VIOLATION.

I make love to an onion. I speak to it like a lady. It is pleased
and smiles. Rome was yesterday. I wonder.

              it will be good to sleep under steep hills.

              love,
                Buk

[*note with a drawing captioned
"Death-grip of everywhere—" on other side*]
9-11-62

D.Sheerii:
     The gods only allow us so many mistakes
              and then
     they burn us down.
                   (please remember.)

          L.,
            Buk

[a two-sided postcard—one handwritten, the other typed—
dated by SM 11 September 1961,
a slip for 1962 since it was probably written
the same day as the previous note
and refers to Jane Cooney Baker,
who had died in January 1962.]

The comb for you darl.
Wear it in your hair, you will be more beautiful in this fog.
She was a strong woman. She would have said yes. All the love
I have left, dear. — Buk

§

my hands behind my back in a land of hell as the mice run
along the walls
and
inside the brain—
shreds.

—B.
drunk, going down among
the rocks, not so drunk,
going among the bones
among the bones
the bones   the bones.

Love, Buk

---

6. Oct. 62   S.M.   POBX 44 Pacifica Calif

Buk: By now you are aware of the fact that I REFUSE to be wit-
nessed by YOU.
"dog howl" etc—you beech. My private life is MY private
life & that is why I wont meet you outside of literature. You are

---

"dog howl": source unknown.

a gottamed radio—just because you wear your arsehole on yr
sleeve you want us all to go about with our arses out. NO thank
you. I PREFER my privacy! If I was caught off guard enough to
tell you that I was stilling my mind's howl with the oom etc you
ought not to have spoken of it—otherwise I wd run off from
you. My art is there—I am not there—a gentleman wd see the
art—only the old fraud freud wd see the nuts & bolts.

Got a book sent me by you: *Wormwood Review* 7 // thanks
lots—it is always good to see what those on the bottom are up
to in order to prevent my conceit from making the same mistakes.

As usual you are the top of the bottom. But my godtttt.
Must you? Must you Bukowski? Be fighting & breaking glass &
staining the snow with blood??

Well your virtue is your honesty
The Anglo-saxon looks into the mouth to know the faults.
The Gaelic looks into the eye to know the virtue.
The Negroes look at price tags to learn the value.
The Jews look into the pocketbook to know the worth.
That's how come big trouble. I see the eye & totally resent hav-
ing my arse poked about by you Krout Headtss—Oye changed
studios because once my address gets out I no longer have any
privacy—thus the old phone is out as too many persons knew
it—

are you all right??????

Sheri

---

*[undated note typed at bottom of SM's previous letter
and mailed back to her]*

Dear Sheri:

Art is a private matter, life is not. I, too, desire my solitude.
Now that I have a half-fame there are more door-knockers. I
don't want to see them. I never have. But before, when I

Wormwood Review 7: includes CB's poem "Thank God for Alleys," rpt.
in *RM* (206).

284

wouldn't open the door, I was known as a "nut", now I am called a "snob". So goes it with the name-callers and door-knockers.

I am neither "snob" or "nut". I am burning with whatever burns me, and that is the story.

love,
Buk

L.A.
Mid dec. 1962

Deah Sheri

      I am in some sort of sick & tired drag
      where the feet don't want to go
      and the mind don't want to go
and the body just lays there, and when this sort of thing
      happens
it is best to ride with it, and I mean
especially if the mind don't wanna go
you don't get out and push it
           like some THING on axels
hoping it starts   so you can enter
the big race   and I don't mean the WHITE race,
I mean the old vanity race, name in lights
and the broads with mother-light in their eyes
pushing in to screw you.

    I mean, you let it go.

    I slip sometimes. I find myself running down the road like any other jackass. This is easy to do because nobody tells you anything else, and to stop running with other jackasses
          you got to slow
          and look around
          see
          where they're going,
   and it's pretty easy to see
          if you give yourself a chance,
   that they aren't going anywhere.

Webb, now he is giving me a kind of spread in *Outsider* 3, searchlights... the gods gonna be waiting to see if I crumble under to the bait. It is a good honor Webb is feeding me and I understand him this way; I do not knock if a man cares to say something well of me for I have gone long without any sayings of any sort, but I am watching the gods and the gods are watching me

and the shades flap in front of me now
and my small radio, my red radio plays
and I sit next to a bottle of MILLER High Life
and I am hungry and soon I will eat something;
I like to keep things *simple*
because that way you don't get your flapper
tangled in a lot of tinfoil and horseturds.

Anyhow, enclosed 3 submissions to yr *A & P*
(and if you never spell out the name
you ought to just call it *A & P*
because this would mean just as much
to me as the other which is not in the
dictionary—which does not mean it does not
exist.) Anyhow, got yr card, and here
3 poems and if you do not use them   need them
please return in envelope enclosed.
I eat now.
Love,
Buk

Outsider 3: three of CB's poems appeared in #3 (Spring 1963), along with a reprint of Cuscaden's essay from *Satis*: see CB's letter of 28 January 1963 below.

3 submissions: never published; *A&P* had ceased regular publication by this time.

L.A. Tuesday 18th. December 1962

Dear Sheri:

Thanks for good letter.

I made the drunk tank Monday morning—must see Judge on Wednesday and he may throw book at me—120 days—it is hard to tell.

I am getting very sick of trouble. Ankle all swollen, may be broken. Also, possible loss of job.

Pray for me, pray the gods to take away some of my trouble.

The world presses against my mind and spirit. A horror. I can hardly go on.

This is a sad letter. Perhaps, if I come through everything, I will write you something a little better.

Love,

Buk

●

• 1 9 6 3 •

L.A.
monday, mid Jan. 1963
[*dated by SM 28 January 1963*]

Dear Sheri:

My thanks for returning the poems. I had forgotten them, and as you know, I do not keep carbons. Looking at these old poems, tho, I'd say they were too involved and I'm glad I've dropped a lot of the clutter. The way I write now may not be the best for THEM but it's best for me and I'm the one who's hemmed in with the wallpaper.

Pearson sounds pretty much like a University and that's to be expected. The idea that a poem must have a certain "charge" is an old one, and is no more relevant than the fact that a streetcar should be 69 feet long. I cannot be bothered with poem-rules, as outside this door they fuck me up pretty well with their jails and ways and traps, and so I make the poem mine—any way I want it.

As to writing a novel, if I live to be 60 (which is doubtful) I MIGHT try a novel. Then I will be wide enough—if a little thinned out. Right now, I don't want to waste the paper.

You are going to have a good chance to hate my guts. Webb giving me a big spread in upcoming *Outsider* #3: photos, excerpts from letters, words from editors, a few poems and so forth. I have been named *The Outsider of the Year*, and I think,

---

a novel: CB would write his first novel, *Post Office*, seven years later.

even my picture on cover. On top of this, he's bringing out a selection, a book of my poems 1955–1963. The gods have me up for test: if I snivel or look at my bellybutton in this limelight, I am finished.

William Corrington writes me that he has heard from you in regards to one of his poems. You prob. did not know that I know Willie, and regard him as one of the better living writers of our age. There are some holes to fill where Ernie and Robinson J. and E.E. left, plus Faulkner, and Willie might do it, big order or not. He is a good man to begin with and has the talent too. These 2 factors do not always run together.

I hope that whatever pressure is upon you lifts. I will put a hex upon all lambasters, detractors and noisemakers, gloom purveyors, takers of time, pricks, fools, and so forth. Consider yourself in the clear for a while... if I have any pull with the heavens.

Now, princess, be good, sit still, very still, sense the air and the hours and the crawling of ants... and soon all will be clear.

LOVE,
Buk

Lost acres of hell
called L.A.

Feb. ten? 1:11 p.m., afternoon, some sun up, water running downstairs, ladder on grass 3 floors down, woman walking in brown skirt and mauve blouse, suddenly turns and walks back toward corner, Frost is dead but Frost was always dead, and my red radio gives me a piano that is not too interesting...

deer Sheereeeie...

---

a book of my poems: It Catches My Heart in Its Hands, published in October 1963.
Frost is dead: died 29 January 1963.

290

I hearby put into combat on your good side
upon the opening of this letter
one more god damn good hex-lifter
and my oh my
you may feel free this evening and maybe an afternoon or 2
until it rubs off. The message today being mainly
TO THINK OF RAINPIPES HANGING TO THE SIDES OF DRY
HOUSES EVERYWHERE, and this will do it, this will free you, and
you may think I am bullshitting you and I may be to an extent,
on the other hand I am not... because I never will or ever quite
say anything I do not mean, and in essence it is mainly in thinking of a stone or a frog that the rays of the long-toothed gods
are deflected FROM YOUR MIND TO THE STONE OR G.D. FROG,
or, as I would suggest today: rainpipes. The rays bounce upon
you and off of you and cannot be taken because you are thinking rainpipes and the rainpipes take the knife and since they are
dead (or seemingly dead) we get the edge on the game. Please
do not think I am insane. In simpler terms this is called
physchology, but in physchology they become lost in words and
phrases until they no longer no what the hell they damn well are
doing. Now, enough of that.

My thanks for your drawing of Sheereeie, you good baby,
and now the sun is coming up bolder and the snails and plants
climb up toward their death, and the bad piano is gone from my
red radio and I lift my cold yellow beer like a golden heart and
drink.

You are right: the Webb thing is only fateful to suckers who
buy their own shadows. I will outluck—with guts and calm-
ness—a few flashlight flickers. If you want a copy of me dancing
the fandago before the admiring eyes of the imps, let me know
and I will mail. Will be out in week or 2, and when you see you
will know the inherent dangers of fathead involved. I have been
a very lucky man in that they have allowed me to live quietly
and unbothered and I have carved small chips as it pleased me
to carve. I intend to go on doing this.

Corrington I will have a word with. He is a good man of
honor but perhaps... careless... because his mind... being fairly
young... is turning quickly, and he is drawn into too many corners and cannot cover them all. He must perhaps... be told a little... not too much, for he is grieviously clean and unusual,
albeit slack, at times, when he should be taut. It takes many

291

bricks and many years and many knives and many nights. We draw into our moulds slowly and most of our moulds are misshapen.

You've got to forgive Pearson. He is honed into a kind of logic by learning out of other men. This is called education. Take a good education and a good mind and you get a pretty good sort of man. If he thinks poetry should be thematic instead of dramatic (essentially, that is) that is only his loss because of learning. Poetry is anything I care to make it. This is my pleasure and my way of walking. Changes are wrought out of climbing. I don't give a nickel's hedgehog's belly of a damn whether my changes are accepted, only I know I've got to go this way or I will be sicker than I am now, and it has been tough lately, twice this week my horse has thrown the jock at the gate... once with a beautiful long-legged grey called *Triumph V.* and agin wit something I don't recall. They are tearing up the streets now and a crippled climbs out of the side of his little celluloid machine and stares up at me.

Death is a bug. I am ready for death. I will take it into my arms like any whore. What can it do that it has not already done?

Maybe you laugh. I went to organic foods down there at place you told me. 4 or 5 months ago. But food all dried up. Carrots dry and rotting, celery brown, everything sitting there. Not fresh. Freaks walking around, poking. Either real old people or young health faddists, idiots with bulging ugly muscles, or homosexuals, bad dream day there, did not feel well, threw things into my basket, WANTING OUT, got home, threw in refrig., forgot, never ate the lettuce, the celery, carrots, etc., forgot and later threw in garbage—maybe would *not* have, if I had oh only not seen those PEOPLE in there, did not want oh to BECOME those people, those homos, those muscles, those aging wrinkled things, tho I did eat the RADISHES AND THEY WERE GOOD, they tasted like radishes, sharp and true, tang, and that might have been worth the whole trip. But actually there is something very shabby and depressing about the store and I figured it is better for me to eat badly and drink badly than to suffer going in there.

Now the sun has gone away and a blue car comes down the street like nothing and I am suddenly cold and old, be 43 in August, but often feel more like 24 or onehundred and four at

292

same time, and red radio has fairly jazzy but not too deep tune
from musical comedy and I pause and

go get another beer
and I will put this into envelope
and go to bed and sleep
sleep
    o   sweet christ sleep
    1, 3, 2, hours
everything gone past
    and I will be like an old carrot
    stretched out in a rack in a health food store,
and they will yawn
    and walk
        past.

        love, love, love,
        Buk

[postcard dated by SM 23 February 1963]

Dear Sheri:
Feeling much better now. Hope C[orrington]. has written.
Cosmic warheads have moved off. Even wrote a poem—
bad one—the other night. Got in new supply of vitamins, beer
and comic aspecti.
The poppies grow and nod like devils and the flies look for
webs.

        L.,
        Buk

Cosmic warheads have moved off: a reference to the Cuban missile crisis.

Los Angeles
Feb. 26, 1963

Dear Sheri:

Got your last good letter, and have been sometime getting around to this... a couple of weeks of drinking, ya know, and it ripped me up. Now just tired old man looking out of a window. Some bleeding and torn parts but believe I will mend.

I appear to make my own hexes.

Would not advise attaching yourself to 6 acre lot wit attendant hoorors—as notated in yr last—but this is your business. I could not do it. I would be wacky within a week, or wackier.

Yes, god, I know the ART FILM. The broken statues, arms shooting out of sofabacks from springs, men walking through mirrors, white-bellied jackasses painting with their shirts off, people trying to QUEERLY ACT SENSITIVE... The art film. I saw a couple in the Village and came away sicker than this drunk I am coming off now. No sunlight could clean that ill away. Now I just look out my window and the sun comes in with the dull sounds of the city, I hear an airplane, I even hear some god damned birds, and I mend. I will live. But I am only allowing to mend what I TORE with a weapon they gave me (the bottle), but when I walk into one of their weapons (the art film) or one of their crowds or faces or looks or factories, it does not mend so easy because it is done mostly without my o.k.—like getting hit by a car. Somebody wrote me, a Sacramento woman with 2 children and an unhappy life, her motto is now: "Forgive them, for they know WHAT they do." Which is astute enough. But I don't think of forgiving or *not* forgiving. I just want to AVOID them. Which is not easy. So we make it, AVOID them as much as POSSIBLE. I have seen enough of the mob to draw conclusions from and about them for 10,000 years. That's why solitude is easy for me and graceful. I know that there is nothing out there in that light and sound that can help me, I mean a human help. The roads are good, the side of a hill, a bridge, I even like to look at the buildings they live in. But to search out in that mass of flesh for either love or reason is senseless.

Sacramento woman: the poet Ann Menebroker.

294

I bade Corrington write you, and you should have heard by now.

This letter is somewhat like myself today: a soft probing and mending. Not much energy. Compared to yours, nothing. You are lit by enough flames to burn us all... Webb writes *Outsider* 3 out next week. Which means 2 weeks. I will mail you a copy.

Pound read in order to find out WHAT NOT to write. Not the subject matter but the matter of approaching the subject matter. He read too much: this is a hammer upon the mind. All this work is done for one by his contemporaries. By reading them, one gleans ALL OF WHAT NOT TO DO. And it doesn't take much reading, for they all write alike. Things are quite easy. When they tell you, "you are writing badly", then you know that you are writing *well*, for you are not writing as THEM. Grass is them, and although the ego is often sick, nobody wants to be grass: we will be under it soon enough.

LOVE,
Buk

Wed. night
April 17, 1963
11:10 p.m.

Hello Mama Sheri:—

good u are not pissed and only suffering the cruxifiction bit, which is bad enough, only when we stop getting nailed
and become agreeable to the ways of the bastard masses
then, baby, we're done.
You know this.

Why you keep sending my stuff to Pearson? I want you to have it. You are more than Pearson.

When you coming to see me? I will keep you out of letter or verse or spoken word. If that's what you want. I have good honor.

Webb writes my book has good advance sales—Director of

295

Metropolitan Museum of Art ordered a copy. I am getting into high places with my crap. They are probably bored with safety. Good, good.

plenty of my love to you, princess...
Buk

[*typewritten note with large drawing dated 5 July 1963*]

Dear Sheri:
As much as you can believe me, I must tell you that the old shadows are dead, not forever, but for our lives for a certainty, and that the essence and the flower and the fire are only felt by those mostly... alive... now.

sad, yes, also,
Buk

p.s.—Love, Bukowski

[*at top are mock Chinese ideograms
and, in formal letterhead style,*
"Chinese Slave's Association of East Los Angeles";
undated, but written shortly after preceding letter.]

Sherrrrrrrrrrrrrrrrrrrrrrrrryie:
don't like to talk in riddles but I guess what I meant drunk   when I said "old shadows are dead", I was ref. to communication between people who once had communication, and essentially HARDNESS takes place in one individual   who either feels over-worldly or bored with it or sick of it   or taken up with something else   and then   the flower dies. But all this is nec. of course: one flower must die so that another may grow. So much is always nec. and I grow sad among the necessaries.

There is a horse called Yin and Yang.

My collection of poems via Webber will be out about Sept. first, and I have seen the dummy copy, and even without the poems the book would be worth 2$ because of the paper and the way he's hung it together, the design, the love, the taste of good steak and avacado, he has put his gut into the work and it is like a bell ringing or water running or stretching out on the bed and looking up at the ceiling. When Madison Ave. sees what a poor man can do with nothing they are going to learn that magic does not grow at request; it must be thought about and prayed and gambled toward.

If you see the book you will know what I mean.

It is really a time of NOT WRITING and not-doing
si, so I have not persisted upon you with letters

I am waiting for the sun and the object
to make a new shadow.

I got out the paints the other day and the tubes were so hard I could not use them; boiled them in water but no good. Finally got a little green and scarlet and did a pic. of twisted leg man with bug eyes swimming along a candle with some christ bleeding thing in upper left, the red coming down to page bottom pool. Not all that dramatic but done more in the cool half-joke, but sad. Folded in half and mailed somewhere.

Don't let them hang you, baby.

Not yet.

love,
Buk

[*handwritten postcard dated by SM 27 August 1963*]

Dear Sheri—
　　can't write with these g.d. post office pens.— Book soon out. Webb up to page 82. If you have not made arrangements— let me know and I will send one when out.
　　In the workhouse now and must get back on their clock. Let me know on the book.

　　　　　　　L.,
　　　　　　　Buk

●

• 1 9 6 4 •

10. Feb. 64   La Mart   pobx 1044 pacifica calif

open that goddamm'd door Bukowski—the Princess is home
again! Lemme IN—
   Gotcher book & you must be unconscious with love—it is a
bewt babe & I thank you with heart / loaned it to Layde of Arts
& Letters next cot[tage] & she cant live without one—hope
Webb's got a copy left & wrote him to ask—
   Been very soul sick lamb & cdn't write—cdn't do aught but
weep—terrible fit of self-pity—cdn't see the pattern for the
warp & woof—it do hurt so when they warp & woof you—but
at last—it cohered for 5 minutes so I let up yawlin'—Jez Xt
what a fit of woe—you'd have been weeping with me—Ollie
(our Layde above) says "do Y E W *k n o w* HIM?" / "who" sez
I coiyoily to drag out the moment soupreme after the rest of the
treatment of claw   barb—"OH HHHHmmmmmmm... oh of
KOURSE" (wotd else)
   My god—buk you doll—she is now a tame tigress—and yr
poetry will make her drawers wet again—if you ever came to
visit—she'd fall apart—but darling YOU would RUIN the
effect—she is seeing A HollyWoodttt Version in her mindtts
eye—wait til she reads yr work!!

---

book: *It Catches My Heart in Its Hands*—a lavishly designed production.
It had an introduction by Corrington, which SM criticizes in her next
letter.
Ollie: proprietor of a tavern near SM's cabin; Gilbert thinks her name
may have been Olivia Fort.

299

I was painting as I wept—that also prevents writing—but I got yr book & I loaned yr book out & it got a customer—and I hope you can supply her a copy / what is the price $5. ??? she is still reading my copy & I don't know.

Write thou—and what is this abt you refusing to admit one Hunter Ingalls to yr workshop sometime a while back?? Sir O Sir—this is a good man // and he can SEE La Mart without gazing through her Ezra Pound recording—

Write me darling—I MISS your touch! What is going on down there??? O my Carrot lying on the Super Mercado shelf of der Health midtt joy shop???

All good tidings—all great joy—with you Buk
love from your Princess Ra Set / i.e. La Mart

Sheri

[*an illustrated, scroll-like letter dated 14 February 1964;
CB had sent SM some of his drawings.*]

O Colourful One:
I quote:

"You mention Bukowski. Once C. B. accepted (& published?) a ½ story of mine, plus some bridge bits, in *Harlequin*, which I never saw. Which I assumed hadn't ever published me, except once someone said so. I bugged C. B. because, after acceptance, I happened to be going to L.A. on what was then business and wrote suggesting a meeting, and got a highly-defensive negative back."

Hunter Ingalls

Hunter Ingalls: (1934–), poet and later a professor of art history.

Princess Ra Set: a goddess mentioned often in the *Rock-Drill* Cantos (91/631–33, 92/638, 94/661), a conflation of two male Egyptian gods into a female divinity. SM identified with Princess Ra-Set and created both a ceramic and a painting with that title (see note to her letter of 8 February 1961 above).

300

Did you Sir upon above occasion deliver yourself of a "highly-defensive negative"?

"Workshop"—even the toilet is a work-shop. The apologists have terms but it is still a work-shop.

Your BED, Charles, is a strong, non-union, over-time, moon-lightin' second-fronted W O R K - SHOP.

The word was employed to raise yr general cultural level. Your place of work IS your work shop.

Please do NOT shout at me in flaming red or apple green.

Li: "look at the two little dogs under his bed." S.M.: "IF I know his mind-state they are two little mice or mayhap rats." Po' Li: "wow" sez he "even his mice are horses..."

Yr letter is putty as D[orothy].P[ound]. says pretty.

Yr drawing of yrself in bed is good; shows u got hold of yrself now / yr other drawings vibrated too much. Also your mountains are too point-y.

Where did you get yr black pen. I NEED a black pen like that. Where did you get yr colour pens. I *need* colour pens like that.

NOTHING in this world is worth ANYthing except a good conversation. We are all dead down here—dead & condemned—this is Hel—none of us know it except me 'n you.

You MEAN yr head *cant* get any FATrrrrr dontcha?

One has written to Webb & one will write to him again—req. another copy besides Ollie's—a copy for present for NHP @ Yale—

Yes—you shd get a certain percentage just to keep the racket from getting too twisty—"unpaid whores" & so forth...

IT *i s MISS* "Stop Weeping" to Y O U.

Is that the missing line: "Even lions dream?" Ollie has my copy & cant check buke // tell me *is* that the missing line; otherwise what?? (In clear talk man)

I thought old Corrington's words were silly & near ruined the effect of the buke. The colours were pleasing & some of yr verse also.

Maybe YOU got doors in yr head but I have not. I have nothing in MY head save the highest and most sacred ideals to

---

missing line: in "Dinner, Rain & Transport," a line ("I can prophecy evil") was dropped between lines 9–10.

waft me through this Shit River wherein ALL my brothers & sisters are wallowing delighted to have something to toss at one another. I suggest you REmove those doors in the back of your head, my dear Bukowski and go get your supply of high ideals. You should read a little more H.D. Old Creaker—it wd supply the missing link in yr chain & shut those horrid, drafty doors.

Even poets have ideals.

Now—be a good boy & eat what the neighbors send in—

Your loving Health carrot
The Princess Ra Set.
La Mart

---

24. martius. 64   s.m. po bx 1044   pacifica calif
[*another illustrated, scroll-like letter*]

dear buk

thank u for the coloured DRAW A LOT no I mean: the DRAWS A LOT—a far cry fr Lance a Lot or Gal ah had but as colourful—the colour pens have kept my bed-bug ego still for at least an hr... now I know what to look for to locate others... they lend a touch of anarchy to the hands—power mysteriously free-flowing with only a touch—

nothing happens here—not even me—ernie trys to get spinoza's words into my head but his new wife is jawlouse—yet good now got 2 middle size pups—dolls... teddybears... am v. remote today—don't know why... in orbit i guess

got yr 2 books—targets 15—gave ernie's wife one copy—& read one copy & will place one copy beneath eyes of nhp... he just got bk fr mother india

nothing o nothing new here... just love to you & encl the $ for the d r a w s — A — l o t... the new knight... am also dull today as well as remote

will sleep now in camper until time to go—dreaming's

---

targets 15: six poems by CB appear on pp. 4–20 of *Targets* #15 (September 1963).

sometimes better than thinking... not all dreams... just now &
then
   u didn't write no letter zo wut kin oye a n s w e r ? I just
drew some anarchistic pichurs forya
   now she lays her down to sleep on th camper floor and
dreams a dream... good night dear buk... right in mid-day mid-
town san francisco
   fr

   Ra Set—princess of kingdom Wu Tsi Yen

---

1. june. 64

buk/ i wondered W H E R E you were—glad to know you
are there—(I sent 2$ for colours to yr old address... hope you
rec.)
   this yang has been black—last week was b l a c k—i think it
has something to do w/the lousy music—
   no news... just walking the razor edge barefoot... painting
don't save the ass fr the fire... nor the back fr the rod
   working for an exhibit... slow grind
   life is hell... earth is hell rather & life is punishment... be
good(t) then maybe god will be kare-full... god—"the master
deceiver"
   all for now... we send love on wings—it will knock at yr
window—open & let Love Wing In—offer fragrance & flower—
and see it as the University... me 'n you at least got past grade
2—
   love, love, love,
   Sheri... cosmic scrub girl

---

old address: CB had moved from North Mariposa to De Longpre Avenue
in East Hollywood.

an exhibit: a generous selection of SM's work was exhibited in September 1964 at the Severence Center in Cleveland, her only one-woman
show.

[*postscript at top of letter:*] try to drink spring water for a while &
get some yeast tablets to put in the beer—yeast puts back the b
vits the beer removes—(*joke...* just to take)

Los Angeles, July twenty4   one9six4

Dear Sheri:

I am hung over, sitting here drinking a weak coffee, smoking a Salem which tastes too much like peppermint, and looking out the window. A woman like a cow has just walked by; a
very discouraging sight, and as I get older things simply do not
look any better. If there has been any progress in the world it is
mainly in the way I walk across a room. o, my thanks, for the
photographs of your paintings—very saintly and shining stuff in
our improper Age.

Well, listen, old man Webb is going to bring out another
collection of my wurks—all newly written ditties which have not
appeared in any of the magazines. No title yet; I seem strangely
resistant to thinking one up. Anyhow, you are supposed to tell
your friends and enemies to send 3 dollars to Jon Webb, 1109
Rue Royale, New Orleans 16, Louisiana, asking for the new
Buk book (no title). 3 bucks is the opening price, and the only
reason I huckster this way, like a shiney Jewish stockbroker, is
that the old man needs the money, and he's already shown me
paper samples and wild size outlay, and it's going to be another
beauty-mad product of format inventiveness. When the New
York Times (Rexroth) reviewed *It Catches* (July 5) he said I suffered from too good a press. This might be true: the clown may
not match the advance billing or the gaudy circus tent, but this
kind of suffering I don't quite mind too much. Rex also said
some people were comparing me to Homer and that I really
wasn't as good as Homer. I don't know where he hears this

---

new collection: *Crucifix in a Deathhand*, published in April 1965.

New York Times (Rexroth): Kenneth Rexroth reviewed CB's book (along
with those by three others) in the 5 July 1964 issue of the *New York
Times*.

304

crap. This type of literary chatter is best ignored, yet thot it might amuse you. Anyhow, *It Catches* now listed at rare book dealers at 10 dollars. Next year—the moon.

I have moved again and am down on the ground at last. If I fall out a window drunk now I am fairly safe. I am right on the street and I type by the open window with just my shorts on and the people walk by and look in at me and I look out at them in my easy disorder or beerlight and 44 year-old agony. I'll be 44 on August 16th. and it has been one hell of a ball. The real miracle is that I am still alive and continue to grind out the trash without pushing.

all right now, keep the brushes wet and a stirring in the air.

lub,
Buk

---

5. august. 64   s.m. pobx 1044 pacifica calif

hail! bukow!
the seed sprouts under the winter's snow—
re: "saintly & shining stuff in our improper age." we are at the end of black Kali Yuga—and soon it will be springtime in our cosmos—

Very well Buk—Po Li & SM will send their order (when we return) for yr Nameless Child & try to get the rest to do likewise—am glad you got a rev in NYC Times—Wax Roth and/or King Roth was being clever—"too good a press"—you do happen to be the only person on the scene who is NEAR to *saying* something when he takes his pen in hand & you have yr own way of seeing—wh is WHY yr press is good—Webb does place an odour of sanctity abt you & Wax Wrath wd not be dull enough to let it pass by his feelers—

I can see why they'd compare you to/with Homer—because of yr direct perceptions—but, as yet, your direct perceptions are

---

Kali Yuga: the fourth and most decadent of the four ages (yugas) of the Hindu world cycle.

305

telluric (earthy) whereas Mister Homer spoke of the three worlds—the written word, what is hidden in the written word & the common understanding of what the written word meant— as yet you speak of the one world wh is—or mayhap the double world—e.g. the written word & the common understanding of what the written word means—as yet, you have not spoken THROUGH the written word to those who know & understand what the written word hides that is clear only to them. If&when you are able to do this you wd very much be like Mister Homer—H.D. has to say:

"but if you do not even understand what words say
how can you pass judgement on what words conceal?"

What words reveal; what words conceal—

Homer was telling an epic tale; Homer was employing direct perceptions; Homer was using the plain speech of his day and Homer was speaking of the awful journey of the soul & its terrible temptations on its way back to its true home where its faithful & true self awaited it & what was going on with its true & original self or its missing half—To the rude soldiers it was a tale true & bold; to the learned listeners it was good literature & to those who have ears it was what it was.

And Wax Wrath knows all this too—and often employs it in his fish-wrap chats—as this reader most certainly under- stands—Yes—this "type of literary chatter" *does* "amuse me" as it is NEWS—wd like to have read his review—if they had real sense in their bone boxes they'd put you out front—they don't have ANY body else—Dylan split / Behan ditto—you are a VOICE / academicians don't really have any true ability to do anything unless they are told—YOU tell him—my reputation is the wrong colour for me to do so—but some one shd—

also glad yr bk is now worth $10. bucks—also glad you on ground floor—and 44 is when our baby teeth are being cut—@ age of one hundred and 44—we begin to know a few things for sure—

Wet brushes! man dear—Li & I put in a 10 hr work day—5

H. D. ... words conceal?": from part 8 of "The Walls Do Not Fall."
Wax Wrath ... chats: Rexroth had a regular books program on KPFA, the Berkeley-Pacifica station, which SM undoubtedly listened to.
Behan: Brendan Behan (1923–64), Irish playwright.

days a week & on the week-ends it was dawn to dusk sat & sun working like ants to get work framed / painted & packed for a big exhibit—will send you any pub soon's get any—

am right now not painting—but things very strange and neverbefore seen stir in the deep currents of the mind sea—prehistorik images taking form now... In a few weeks we 2 taking time off & making it to a wilderness & blow off the sin skins—not even any coffee! gin sing tea for brikfasta for us now—I would sacrifice my mortal self to the Most Ancient High (air)... We taking seeds / water & herbs & spending some time there—so if you hear silence fr this end—she is in retreat & meditation—40 days in the wilderness—

and YOU—behave yrself while maw is gone—I invoke and address the magical plants—plants that are red / those that are white / and the brown & black herbs... all these I do invoke

Plants & herbs of the heavens! O plants and herbs I call upon you to keep guard over Charles Bukowski while his spirit sister meditates upon her sinful desires in order to purify herself for The Most Ancient High.

O herbs your lord is Soma & you are made by Brihaspati.

With this charm Indra kill'd Vritra & smashed Asuras & is master of Heaven & Earth... Indra, Vishnu, Savitar, Rudra, Agni, Prajapati, Parameshthin, Viraj, Vaysvanara... powerful spirits stand behind this invocation for Charles Bukowski—

The Sun, the Wind, the Rain be with him; the fire guide him... Savitar the Saver guard him... the great Vayu... living Indra... Let him count a hundred summers... Svaha—let Sphota come... Yama! come! Thakur watch—Mahamaya watch... manomaya-kosha of blue light shot with gold flames... Svaha! cosi sia—

there Buk—that will keep you in ice while ah melts offrf mah snake skin—AND iffn ah sells any of my "saintly & shining stuff" ah will send YOU to the wildnerness to de-louse yo' self br'r Buk—so say yr magic prayers & incantations for this frail

***

Soma ... Svaha: all Hindu deities.
cosi sia: Italian: "so be it."

female—and encl some more shining forms for you to look at /
we send you love and a vision of the coming of the first spring
to our universe—

Sheri

●

• 1 9 6 5 •

[*undated*]

Buk moi lamb: yes please do mail me a copy of yr book—I want
to send it to Jaz Laughlin (New Directions) after I read it of
course—I wish he'd pick up on you—he cd if he wd—am glad
you are working—to be independant—or is it independent—is
the top in life—it is the edge we got on these chicken shit
boys—i wish you wd take a breather from yr Low Life and find
out who you really are—and employ yr $&¢ to print some of yr
work—to help yrself all you can—
     don't you know this is just ONE of yr lives on earth?? and
Mr. Cayce the yogi—american yogi—said that when a soul is
born with rough skin it is a sign that in a previous life that soul
was overly sexual and sensual—that is you to a T—boy—and
here you are livin' it up still! Don't you KNOW your ass will be
kicked right back? Buk you got to r e - f o r m—that is what it
means—take a NEW form—the trouble is that you are too
bloody sophisticated—lost yr original innocence—why don't
you take a stab at the Xtian Scientists??? they—no matter how
corny—are in touch with Prama—the tree sap of the universal
tree of life—which has great power to heal—and bring abt a
change of heart—you cd do so much if you'd drop ho'sez and
who'zz and juicin—leave it for the new sinner—and you get

---

yr book: *Crucifix in a Deathhand*, which would place this undated letter in
mid–1965.
Mr. Cayce: Edgar Cayce (1877–1945), American spiritualist whose
works SM would study the rest of her life.

right—get R I G H T with God(t)—save your money and DO
something for the Body of Light whence cometh forth all fruits
known of as poetry & art—
     nuff for now—but you hear—DO something—my god look
at what the blacks are doing with their little bit of light—(plus
the red fist shovin' a hot poker up their arse of cozzz) love and
re   form   buk!
     And do let me have a copy for to read & send to Laughlin/

Sheri

---

10. Nov 65   Bx 1044 Pacifica Calif

dammitALL Bukowski—where are your little set of poems that
were here yesterday?????? I cant find them—they are somewhere
here in my little desk—if they don't get included in this letter
then I will send them down presto pronto soon's they stick their
snouts up—
     I just got yr address from Veryl Rosenbaum—I sent her
photostats of the scrolls you wrote & drew upon for me as Gib
likes them & got sad at the idea of their being folded in the
mail—then I sent what rest I had of your letters—exciting to
think of a book of your letters—and its effect upon our ex-
ploding population—that'll finish 'em Buk—that's a goodttt

---

dammitALL Bukowski: cf. the opening of Pound's Canto 2: "Hang it all,
Robert Browning…" (6).
Veryl Rosenbaum: a writer who planned to publish a collection of CB's
letters (which never appeared). In April 1966 CB wrote to Rosenbaum:
"I know that the book of letters a long way away but if it ever happens,
run what you wish. only there is something I'd wish you to strike out in
reference to Sheri Martinelli. I don't know if I did, but I might have
mentioned her in other letters as 'Pound's x-whore.' she's a fine woman
but don't think she'd understand. In a sense, I am a romantic; I mean
when I call a woman a whore, I mean, in *my* language, a woman who
loves *one* man and *one* man only and I use the term in fondness to depict
faithfulness, and there is no derogatory intent involved" (*LL* 65–66).

310

kidtttt—You do reach moments of fierce clarity—inbetween your more earthy—cthonic—perceptions & observations.

A terrible experience drove me to star gaze—and I discovered astrology is right on time babe & I got my shit-hookers tight on books about it & can now cast a rudimentary horoscope—my stars were precisely in the position to jolt me & I stood inbetween life and death—and I chose life and got reborn—I was a slob before—I am now a hard boiled egg. All this leads up to:

I'd like to SEE your stars—you Star you—zo—let loose midttt der following: give me your: hour & minute of birth or thereabouts—your birth day & year & month—let me know immijit—and then I will tell you about YOU—Gib sez he's gonna buy me a tall, tall hat with a big star on top—that's how stars effect us!!!

Please do NOT see this as 'how much mist could a mist stick stick if a mist stick could stick mist'—Our charts are our report cards from our Universe-ity—Our cosmic bank accounts.

and I still cant see the poems—oh THERE they are!! I wish I were making a new *A&P*—but right now I got my hands full—I reluctantly return them suh—I know you do not make copies—

re: the 4th line of *Red Bricks in My Eyes*—"even Love, whatever that means"—the root meaning for Love is "I please"—Love pleases whenever it can truthfully—sometimes compassion moves Love—sometimes pity but that is not good—pity has envy as its opposite—whereas love has hate & Master Kung sez "only the complete person can love and hate" or words to that effect—and when we love ourselves—we please ourselves. It is the most high to Love god—but I got a sneaking suspicion—that when it is said "god is inside of YOU"—it means YOU must bring that God out—BE like that God inside... so in the long run—when we pleases our own wee selfies we iz pleasin der Godttt—

that is good "people have died before me... like tapes slipping out of a machine"—That IS the way it IS—

Red Bricks in My Eyes: unpublished.

Master Kung: Confucius (Kung Fu-tse). He is usually called Kung in *The Cantos*.

dear Buk—if you ever resorted to punctuation marks your poems will lose their sur-realism—but your edge would be harder. Your breathing is not like my breathing & I sometimes read you wrong. I.E.—"the slow horse of her body (breath s.m.l.) moves under a sheet of pink (breath s.m.l.) like carnations playing tricks with my better sense..." (breath s.m.l.) & thinks "what hell means that?? I see it reads: "the slow horse of her body moves (breath bukow) under a sheet of pink like carnations" breath bukow—see diff?? Punctuation would have caused your reader to get the proper point. Most of us are sloppy readers Buk & each one is on a different star.

"The slow horse of her body moves under a sheet of pink, like carnations; playing..." etc. It is really good Buk—it gives a sense of slow movement as if the day were hot.

The band is good also "plays as if it were an order for assassination". my god you can spell!! I cannot. But I do remember to place commas now & then between phrases.

Not with the Sunburnt Fury of a Whitman—you got the "small men" down pat. Poor lamb—incarnating as a poet in this protestant land of equality. Oh JeEzuz—the woe.

Dear Buk—you are most responsible and to Life—One moment—let me see if there is a root meaning for that word—I never looked it up before as have been too busy living it—Life means "I leave" Riṇáckti Ric (Skr.)... we should live so long just to find that out... Yes—it does mean that—our contribution to the universe—what we leave & it means that life leaves—comes & goes & it means that life must leave its electric state & become matter because "life" also has a meaning of "body"—

To return to my meaning—you are being responsible to Life who is also God as well as Love. I think—Buk—that it will get worse & what you leave those like us in the future—will be the accurate record of this flaming hell of america.

Your portrait of the bored refuge into sex of the common dog-males is terrifying—the dog-females & dog-males are horrifying. They live all around me & I have never known such could exist. It must be the heavy batter of cosmic rays out here.

The dog next cabin gets an erection at the sight of a box of candy & has to take it out on her—their lives must go—man—

Not with the Sunburnt Fury of a Whitman: also unpublished.

312

they aint people!! Good cat'likes too—God is a box of white sugar candy!!

He hates me because my experiences are larger than his & he cant own me—He gets the Hen to rush over shouting that So & So's on th' phone—I go & it's her pal & he does a long bit on "an exhibit & I'd like to have your work" but I smell a rat & anyhow I don't want my work shown with pals of the Barnyard Set so I say "NO" and then I see by their faces—that they all got together "ohhh letzz tell Sheri that Brentie's gonna have a show & she'll rush out & get all her work & then Brentie can lose it..."

I am grateful for my good stars. The Holy Ghost whispers in the ear. It flip'd them out that I had not that kind of vanity. These are my fellow country men & women—these are the whites—the catholic whites—fallen lower than whale shit (N.H.P.'s good line)—and yet—my eyes are opening Buk—before I thought all people were beautiful inside. Now I KNOW better.

Am back in office-mobile—soon I will cook lunch for the Oriental Prince. On the small swedish stove. He will have steamed rice; steamed chinese roast pork; chinese 'tea cakes' made of shrimp & pork & beef mixed with chop'd spices & vegetables & mushrooms & water chestnuts & rolled in rice dough & chop'd chinese mustard greens with lop chung (chinese duck sausage) cut up & steamed on top—then apricot pie with whip'd cream.

The l'l bastid eats like a royal king.

Thus I end this letter. I am sending out my good Jupiter rays to you & Jup will make your letters into a book that will swing—Veryl Rosenbaum is right—that'll be a book right on time. It's needed out there Buk—I'll get abt 10 or more copies if it aint too high. These ruddy crudey bloody squares need YOU—

all for now & trust all's well there & here too

your favorite star gazer

Sheri

---

office-mobile: SM did much of her work in a camper up until she died.

With me you can clearly read—The Ascendent: What I got.
The Descendent: What I aint got!
my Scorpio is my desire—to renew/to salvage—my Taurus: I
have/I possess/ to earn/to own... See what you think—I'd
incline to the Pisces/Virgo—but check—

Otherwise let me know the closest hour/minute/day/month/
year of the most important day of yr life—the kind you'd say: "if
I'd only have done that" or "if this day had never dawned I'd
never be what I am" etc—my own wd be the day I returned to
E.P. Easter 1954—from that date I'd be able to sort of see—
Scorpio rising wd make me find out everything there is to find
out—Scorp being the natural detective of the zodiac—that's
what got E.P. in so much difficulties—

You have a fab chart & you OWE it to us to do yr best to get
us the vital statistics Buk—then I'll read it for you—slowly as
this typing machine is rough & some days I just study—if you
know that most of the dough balls got their stars scattered all
over the chart you'd know that you are most unusual—if you
were born betw 8–10—you'd be in the natural House of Leo
with yr sun in Leo & Leo is the royal vib in the zodiac! I don't
know the correct degree for Jup or Merc but you lined them up
with Nept & the Sun—a decent display & good show ol' boy—
rush daughter's vital statistics—

yes—it is right to take off & rest when the body says so—we
do—try to stop—at least 1 day a month—

tell me what is your BEST HOUR through out yr life—after
sun down (I was born at 3.a.m. & when ever anything spooky
happens to me / it is at 3 a.m.) that cd be a clue—

Ask yr Uncle in Andernach. You ask "what is happening"
because "the people of the earth are tired of English professors
because english profs touch mostly books/ live a plastic life" (art
museum hogs/clogs too) E.P. "clog up the works"

---

daughter's: Marina Louise Bukowski was born 7 September 1964 to CB
and his common-law wife, Frances Elizabeth Dean (1922–).

Uncle in Andernach: Heinrich Fett, in his seventies at the time. Andernach, in northern Germany, was CB's birthplace.

O Yeast see yrself as a kind of laxitive trying to work loose the ancient dried up shit of the dough balls clogging up the divine intestinal system of our living god—we are passing from one age to another—the old petrified turds will go & the Way will be unclog'd—work hard at it—YOU may inherit the next age—

Yes—Blaz—he wrote—bright sound—I ordered yr book fr him—to use it to arouse interest with the few now got—who'd live through yr words—they are not going to LIVE any other way—

HOW DARE YOU WRITE CRITICAL ARTICLES & LONG BOOK REVIEWS without letting ME read them also?

will send this right down & send up daughter's info immediately... yes will send art & more letter... am rush[ing] this

where Andernach? what mean?

S

---

23. Dec. 65   pobx 1044 pacifica calif

I
didn't
know
yew
were/are
a real
KroutHeadtttt

Buk!!!!!

My FIRST!!!!!!

officially—

Blaz: Douglas Blazek (1941–), poet and editor of the magazine *Ole*, to which CB contributed.

yr book: *Confessions of a Man Insane Enough to Live with Beasts*, published by Blazek's Mimeo Press in August 1965. (This long story was reprinted in CB's *South of No North* [1973].)

CRITICAL ARTICLES: by this time CB was regularly writing essays and reviews in addition to poetry; see Dorbin 64–65.

315

to yr letter:

It was Gib's comment that anyone who kept yr letters with profit as the motive showed their true lack of love for the poet— I sent Veryl photostats of the letters I made scrolls of—not to crush them—& some of the rest that were still with me—I WANT you to have that book—there are at least 10 to 20 folks that I can get interested—Never cd reach them before—but astrology seems to reach them & with the door open—one can reach them deeper—yr letters wd turn them on—

the exhibit was a hell of a lot of work—Reid worked hard also—it got all my work to Ohio... then it was over—the work is still there—in a gallery that refuses to acknowledge my existence & no one there seems capable of returning the work to me without it costing $50. a case!!! I'll have to go & see what the hell goes on in the square world. I'd never DO that again. Reid was great until the exhibit was over & then this "gallery" took over & who don't know what's jumpin' off iz me! I'm so ruddy fed up with these americans Buk... they are grub-mutts—'m gonna turn my back to them—and vanish—

There is some work—I had been framing for that dead-cell gallery of Reid's but who can make love to a corpse & still be sane? I just stop'd working—but for YOU—doll—I'll hop-to & finish framing some & send them down—you'd be amused by some of them—

...last year—the 2nd worst to hit my little life—it turned me UP & OUT to the stars—astrology is fascinating—the best in gossip yet—being alone so long—8 hrs a day—seated in the camper—I read in this gloom & chill—only the chap who did *The Children of the Ghetto*—could have invented my past 7 yrs— but I did grow up—and that was a childhood aim—once you see their stars you see—

It is beautifully noble of you—to say that the work that the Gods or Daemons do through this sufferin' soul—is good nuff to hang up—'taint my work Buk—it belongs to the world—Jez Chrys' on t.v. last night—a flic on MikeAngel—they treated him worse or close tohow we iz gittin' treated—flammm—take

---

Reid: Reid B. Johnson organized SM's show.
The Children of the Ghetto: once-popular novel about Jewish life by English writer Israel Zangwill (1864–1926).

fire—these are the experiences of The Immortals!!

On days when even suicide is meaningless—because of the immortal part of us (lousy joke that & rotten luck too) I open the *I Ching* tears pouring—raining on my face & the book—& it says sugar/sugar/sugar & I beam—when the bible aint calling me a whore of babylon—it says—"if they hate you, know that they hated me before they hated you"—these books... my pals for 7 now—

MikeAngel's family at him "money—we wanna go inna business" & some manic-depressive took his statue & made a cannon of it—the pope rob'd him of his hard earned $ & then threated to wash him away unless he came back—they made him paint when he wanted to pound—it was a bitch & 1/2

and Ovid!! dear Ovid!! he sounds like Sheri Martinelli among the savages on the west coast of north america. Even Ovid wails that he'd take the easy way out but there aint no body to hip him as to whether it the final snuff or just the lousy beginning of a New Cliff Hanger—

you are The Yeast—little one—& it's yr dooty to take these dough balls & raise them up—you are The Chosen One O Innocent One—and you got to raise the dough... and then when we got the dough up high nuff—we all get baked into a heavenly loaf—the god sups & the Good of The Bread—enter his Divine Body & get new jobs... he shits out all the dross... to the chaos cess pool—and it all starts all over again—that's called Rollin' Up th Scroll. Every cell of yr body is a former friend or foe who was shit out—sent to chaos—and enters cosmos as a wee cell with a number to it—it must work for YOU—when those dough balls bug you—visualize them the size of a cell—forming a body that some one like you will come & punish the hell out of them—it is Zen/ it is Yin/ it is Yang/ it is Paradise/Purgatory/Terrestrial Paradiso all over the platz Buk—As E.P. said "a fish bowl—not flat"—it goes on all the time & all the space—I saw a hash vision of it once—if you can imagine tissue sheets hanging in close layers from one end yr room to the other—then same size tissue sheets cross sectioning the first

---

"if they hate you...": John 15:18.

Ovid: the Roman poet spent the last years of his life in exile on the coast of the Black Sea.

set—and I cd see all of them at once—that was a night worth living for—

Here's to YOU Blythe Spirit—bird thou never wert—you came right out of—a hashish yurt—(try to forgive)(I can't resist)—wdn't it be won'r'l if the national fathers revived the old time religion—and festivals could be held yearly & we'd go THERE—and see—and then we'd sit on a mt top & try to fly high on our own hi fi—O dream—I am so bored with the dog rut sluts—

How/where can these books of yrs be obtained??? Give me $&¢ listing also—you list:

Cold Dogs in the Courtyard
Crucifix in a Deathhand
Confessions of a Man Insane Enough to Live with Beasts
Poems Written before Jumping Out of an 8 Story Window
& Atomic Scribblings

get the nec info to me—where to purchase / how much cost—I can SELL some for you now—if they are not too much of course—I cdn't sell The Webb—it wd prob be too much—but any of yr books that don't cost more than $2.—I'd be able to get some sales for you—

what is the birth hour of yr daughter? what day is Labor day? hurry—immediately get me that info—I'd have to send for a book & it will cost more after end of yr—rush info to me—she must have very different stars to be YOUR daughter—think of what you will leave this little girl—a life!! the rest will get paw's automobile but you—Godling—have granted a small female spirit—the most precious gift—like E.P. did for Mary—his / a LIFE—not just survival—Of course you have complete communication with her—she chose YOU—for her hero—her doorway back into The Tear Factory—

Here's to you ... never wert: a parody of Shelley's "To a Skylark."

Cold Dogs ... Atomic Scribblings: *Cold Dogs in the Courtyard* was a poetry chapbook published in the summer of 1965. *Poems Written...*, another chapbook, was scheduled to appear in 1965 but was postponed until 1968. *Atomic Scribblings from a Maniac Age* was advertised in early 1966 as forthcoming from Border Press, but never appeared.

The Webb: the Webbs' edition of *Crucifix in a Deathhand*, priced at $7.50 when first published.

as for men & women breaking apart—not even D.P & E.P made The Scene w/out him raising a ruckus. As for me—only the direst poverty keeps me from murder or walkin'— No one can make it—maybe Jesus Christ & Mary Magdelon in the dessert—"Expect the solid from the self & the trifling from the rest & it will keep you far from Resentment"—and study astrology—inbetween— My problem has a Leo rising & his Problem has Scorpio rising—Leo is a fire sign / Scorp is a water sign—he burns me up & I sizzle him—we make Big Steam 7 yrs—it adds humour to the battle to shriek "you bloody Leo ascending" while shrieking—he mutters—

I will send Marina Louise a work of art as her birth present—

●

Mary: Mary de Rachewiltz (née Maria Rudge), Pound's daughter by his mistress Olga Rudge.

"Expect ... Resentment": source unknown.

• 1 9 6 6 •

6/Jan/ 66   s.m. to buk/

Doll— Don't answer until or unless you got *time* but get me yr
hour
    yr bel' bambina: *Virgo* in *5th House: Leo* w/*Aries ascendent.* (cd
always be incorrect because of a few degrees but fairly correct)
Pluto is in Virgo: sub-conscious force. Also conscience. Also isola-
tor of the 1-in-annihilation/ chances/individuals etc. Also Plut'
rules "the dark horse"—the unknown / also rules the beginning.
The genesis. This individual knew you IN the BEGINNING!!!!
    Virgo: to improve—to teach & I analyze, I discriminate.
    Leo: to release & I will, I rule.
    Aries: to breathe, to be & I am. *Aries:* truth/ *Leo:* harmony/
Virgo: discrimination.
    With *Pluto* in the *5th House of Leo*—this 1-in-a-million child
got her 1 in a million chance to be the daughter of a well-known
poet who may go on to real fame. It makes her home life unusual & miraculous in ways. She is born in the maternal trinity of
the zodiac—she will 'mother' you & others.
    Virgo is the Eternal Virgin—the 5th House of Leo refers to:
romance/children/educational institutions (she came to teach &
to improve—see above) pleasures/sports/speculation/creative
power.
    Pluto also represents: the collective/and institutions—she
may have come to teach the Collective or those in institutions.
    Virgo represents one's work. The 5th House is Succeedent
House related to the Fixed signs & relates to: stable qualities &
matters connected w/inner emotion. She is born in the 5th
House of Leo.
    The 6th House of Virgo: ties in w/ the "common" or

321

mutable signs & relates to mental expression/variable conditions/ inter-communications. The personal view/interest & spiritual urges are expressed through the 1st & 5th & 9th Houses/ relates to the Fire signs/ she is in 5th H. Leo. The greatest material or objective activity goes with 2nd/6th & 10th Houses & tie in with Earth signs. she is Virgo the 6th H.

The Fixed Signs (5th H. Leo) indicate the vices & virtues brought over from past lives. The Common or Mutable Signs (her Virgo is 6th H & one of such) relates to mental & spiritual gifts for future expansion & development. Fixed group: stability-permanence, WILL, solidity, dynamic energy. Mutables: flexibility, intellectuality, WISDOM, expansive energy. It represents spiritual persons / the soul.

Leo is fire (a Lion)

Virgo is earth (a Virgin)

Aries is fire (a ram). What a *trio* —Aries is her ascendent—rules her physical being—is the sign of the Ram—her birth sign is Virgo—it is an earth sign—& she is born in Leo's house—another fire sign.

That's it for right now Buk—you can see she came to DO something. What is her name???

Yr Uncle prob remembers yr birth hour.

YES of course—I want to read yr critical reviews—a small audience for yr work is slowly building through what contacts yr typist has.

Thank you for Webb address—nice comment he made & very good of you to tell me. I can count the nice things that have been said to me or about me since E.P. sailed away on the *cristoforo columbo* on one hand.

This bloody world of opposites/extremes—seems one is either NEVER left alone or left alone too much—I spend 10 hrs a day in one position—alone except for ½hr lunch w/him. It instructs one—I miss sun, air & exercise—but will break out first chance—for desert. Women represent the psychic force—but most are "wasted"—yes / the 7 deadlys waste them—the slave's plight—no—Buk—no Virgo will ever yield her temple to a sailor who "never read Walter deLaMere..." cdn't jump off... Virgo too discriminating.

Walter deLaMere: English poet and novelist Walter de la Mare (1873–1956), singled out in CB's letter of 22 April 1961 as one of "very few poets of pure aspect."

322

I made her a pearl charm yest[erday]/ it'll be encl—
YOU worry me—yr last paragraph sounds morbid—
As to "painting"—there IS a time to fish & a time to dry the
net—right now am conceiving painting seeds—they burst into
the mind & one sees them—they'll mature & break out as the
queer-ducks the dough-balls call "paintings"—right now v.
important for me to chew on astrology—a nat. food for my kind
larva—grubbie is grubbin' it up/
    you are being ordered to: take 4 brewer's yeast tablets
w/each can beer—plus vit. c.—one is not proscribing *medicine*—
that's der duckder's jobpppp—one is talking about FOOD—you
NEED it Luv—you & the beauteous young Blaz are all there is
now—he has a beautiful mind that seems to be lacking in any
malice—like yrsss doll baby—hop to & take brewer's yeast—
maybe not 4 w/each can beer—that was a faint joke—but at
least 3 times a day take 4 / w / vit c / or rose hips—go to health
food store & GET—if the customers look dingy to you imagine
them w/out their food supplements!! *The Law:* Man is made by
his own belief—the mind is everything—what you think you
become—and you Krout headtttt—you are thinking of the *not*
you—drink does not harm any / Patunjoli states that it is one
way to the god state/ Appolonius of Tyana said it merely stains
the soul—
    's o.k.—so's all of it—some more harsh than others—let it
get you high then sit back & dig the high mind—try to get there
on yr own—that's the good fight—*the way*—but don't talk abt it
causing you harm—it is powerless against the mind—state of
health—
    behave yrself Bukowski—you & Blaz—that's it—E.P.'s
hole'd up under the Green Bay Tree—his Bramin state—Keep
yr dick UP buk—it's been some busy god-rod if we're to believe
YOUR printed word—the l'l stay at home-ers are twitching their
cuntus domesticus over yr wild words—
    dawhlinkkk—the next world is a carry on of this—we got
F O R E V E R to finish all we begin down here in th hell
hole—this is where we come to DO... then we finish the job all

---

Patunjoli: i.e., Patanjali, founder of Yoga and author of the *Yogasutras*.
Appolonius of Tyana: i.e., Apollonius, Greek Neo-Pythagorean philosopher of the first century A.D., mentioned often in the *Rock-Drill* Cantos.

over our planetary system—NOT on Mt. Shasta doll but on Pluto—or Arcturus/
(interruption: 10/56 am—am downtown S.F.—sea gulls screaming & flying over camper... they my bird sign or one of my signs... something either v. good or v. wrong is/or will be jumpin' orfff... 11/05—now they are gone—)

Swedenburg said that some of the paradisial spirits when they have emptied their cosmic–bank account & must come back to work for their own good by being good for others—they weep—"oh NO, not again!!"

Be good you GOOD stud & we'll sit on our arses in paradise & read the stars from that end of the 'scope—we must either *CHANGE the world* for cosmos—or *de-range* it for chaos

SM

[followed by an elaborate handdrawn astrological chart]

Luv oye bean in big contemplatio
23 feb 1966
S.M. c/o Sloan & Co #7   74 Crestwood
Westlake   Daly City   Calif/

T/Sloans real interest in Bukowski—do write & ask 'em for their slant on Bukow—Willy Sloan has inner eye set @ degree: Buk wd also SEE
re: 'see'—this worthless thing drew a small scroll for you & will hop it on its way to you—the encl photo is it—it is Bukowski perched high on his dangerous peak... deep pine & the round moon's ray... whilst far below the slumbering huts & a winding stream gets crossed by a foot-path bridge... I have walked over the bridge & it is safe but not when storms cause rolling water to o'erflow bridge... & I have plucked the strings

---

Swedenburg: Emanuel Swedenborg (1688–1772), Swedish philosopher and mystic.
Sloans: unidentified ("of no importance," said Gilbert).

324

of the lute you hold & they were sweet true & the music notes
are edible—& the E.P. drawing was on a letter to you—I need'd
it for a while—sometimes these drawings are him & sometimes
they aint/ this one is—need for the illuminations—no one can
do illuminations until they are AT ONE ment... am on t/way—
    answer me Thou! & ask Willy Sloan whut 'e thinks 'bout yr
Confessions of a Man Insane Nuff to Live w/Beasts... he got a view
& Buk ought to see it—
    all for now Precious Fang&Claw... write & tell me... tell
me...
    Princess RA SET   *over & out to Buk*

1.a.
march eleven one9six6

Sheeerriiiieee—
    have not heard from mah German uncle, and prob. won't
now. prob. something I said in my letters either frightened or
disgusted him and so it goes and so we'll never know the hour
of my birth, but guess we'll all go on a while: Uncle, me, you.
    back from hospital last Sunday. surgery for 15 years' or
more hemorrhoids and distended intestine. sitting with very
great delicacy upon these pillows as my radio finally gives me
some decent symphony music (Mozart). you are lucky for me.
it is a painful time, of course. I wish you could hear my mono-
logue during bowel movements. you would have to laugh but I
am in dead earnest about my cusses and pronouncements during all this... shitting. I will be unable to work for from 4 to 8
weeks, which doesn't bother me at all. there is something wrong
with me: I am never bored when I am alone; I am only bored
and distressed and hammered while I am around people. take
away the physical pain and this is a pretty perfect time,
although I cannot sit at a typer too long. they tell me that my
liver is in bad shape too. my drinking days are over—if I am
able to stop, and don't *think* I'll have any trouble. it is almost a
relief, it is as if I had been carrying around a heavy stone that I
didn't need to carry at all. but, hell, no regrets, even at physical
breakdown—there were some wild great times, but now I pass

325

among the tombstones and palms and look around more gently, still seeking those things which lift me, make me complete
enough to gamble a bit longer. there's still plenty left, both of
me and of ways to get in and out of trouble, and still things to
do like paint and sleep and listen and read and not read and not
sleep and not paint, and drink water, and tangle with women,
and sun gaze and change flat tires, and spit, and walk down the
sidewalk being 4,000 years old; I can look at lettuce and eat it, I
can write Sheri Martinelli, I can drown myself or clip my finger-
nails, I can look in the mirror at this crazy chopped-up face and
laugh; I can do *nothing* with the greatest of pleasure. I am more
aware now than ever of my fingers, my nose, my feet, my ears,
my elbows, MY ASS!!—what strange things, eh?, goofy what?
there's plenty to go by, there's plenty left. sailboats. rats in the
halls. rats in clothing. I could run out of paper. I could run out
of time. I could run out of sunlight. what I mean is, Sheri, that
everything is all right. we work up and down, fall into hoary
pits, shoot past angels making love; we ride tigers and are ridden by them... we are covered with shit and clouds and energy
and unfolding.

now my ass is starting to holler and I must end this. paint it,
sweetheart, paint it blazing you good woman, I'll meet you on
the Nile, 5009 a.d., we'll eat dates with Ezra. now I am eating
lettuce and oranges and apples and all my ghosts are puzzled;
small cats peer into my windows, smile like humans, and everything is fixed o.k.

     love,
      Buk

p.s.—the Sungod Apollo is to be rebuilt in aluminum.

---

15. March 66   pobx 1044 pacifica calif

Buk:
    good for you to get 4 to 8 wks vacation—stretch it out
man—
    gave yr book to Kay Harrison & she is taking it to her lit

---

Kay Harrison: SM credited this woman with introducing her to astrology.

326

teacher here & you are being read by young painter Pat Green
& her friends—man you are traveling!!! Stay well—it will OPEN
up for you dear Buk of the opal lights—
I am making a special surprise Bukowski edition of the
A & P & it is going to be a good one—cant write much as am
banging away at stencils—but one day in mail... luv... it'll
come... and with

> l u v /
> Shed /

[*drawn around the type is a picture of a cat saying " 'allo mon" with
SM's query "This yo' cat smiles like people?"*]

---

l.a.
March oneseven, one9six6

Sheri, Sheri: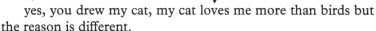
yes, you drew my cat, my cat loves me more than birds but
the reason is different.

you keep speaking of my "book" and I wonder which one:
It Catches My Heart in Its Hands, or the recent Jon Webber col-
orscope, *Crucifix in a Deathhand*. well, it doesn't matter. I wrote
both books.

you got Bukowski in your next *A & P*? you worry me, as I
don't know about myself, how can you know? well, maybe you
do. and I like your strange mystic ancient-eye classical and wisdom magazine (?) anyhow. it is like a painting, a rumbling, talking, shining bloody painting, yes. then you are busy. good. but
drink coffee, don't forget the plants, the sun, the seaweed... I
am busy too, so this must be short, I am cutting some tapes for

---

Pat Green: Gilbert thinks she may have been a member of the San Francisco Art Guild.

Bukowski edition of the A & P: issue 7, dated 20 March 1966 (but not
published until the following month), consists of astrological charts and
readings for CB, his daughter, Ezra and Dorothy Pound, H.D., and
mutual friends.

Webb who is going to put out a longplay of me talking. not
poetry. just talk. talking into the thing and hardly knowing the
why and how. no strain. like frying an egg or looking out the
window. you understand. anyhow, with the talk-record he
hopes to get enough money to get him into *Outsider* #4, the
Patchen issue, and then he's running a book by Henry Miller.
Miller gets the breaks although he seems to no longer need
them. well. anyhow, I will ship you a record when it comes out.
but right now, there's the work and pleasure and dream of *doing
it*. damn, I keep pulling back the curtain everytime a woman
walks by. they think I am nuts. they must have stuffed a lot of
cabbage into me in the hospital. these gals all dressed in their
bright colors as I sit here in the kitchen on my sore ass (had
operation on my poor ass) and drink coffee and write you. well,
anyhow, it is Los Angeles and I sit in the middle of it. tenderly,
I sit. and now the tapes, the tapes! onward! ya.

loooove,
Buk

[followed by a drawing of a cat looking back at the sun]

4-1-66

Sheri, my vury good one:
    have asked Richmond to send you his collection of poetry
Hitler Painted Roses, for which I did the foreword. as soon as it
[arrow pointing back to title] is assembled. am also sending you
Steppenwolf #1 with my review of Corrington's poetry within.
some of this stuff may not get through to you soon because of

---

a longplay of me talking: advertised as *Bukowski Talking*, it never
appeared.
Patchen: Kenneth Patchen (1911–72), American writer and painter.
Richmond ... Hitler Painted Roses: Steve Richmond's book was published
in April 1966.
Steppenwolf #1: CB reviewed Corrington's *Lines to the South and Other
Poems* (1966) under the title "Another Burial of a Once-Talent."

the train strike. I hear that only airmail is going through.

my ass coming along all right and I have 4 more weeks of loafing, powerful loafing, looking at walls, writing, writing anything that jumps into my head and feels good. even painted 3 oils which now hang in this place. painted with my palms, mostly, on plain paper because I don't like to waste time mixing colors and dipping brushes and playing at artist. not many people bothering me, so it is a good time, yes. must go see doctor in 10 minutes so this must be short but Martinelli jumped into my head right now and I go with what occurs, so here we are.

actually, today is a *down* day... I should have slept 4 more hours. sleep to me is just like getting drunk. it puts me there.

a few people angry at me now it seems, mostly because of things I have written—reviews or poems. but it is better to have enemies than a typewriter that lies. at the age of 45, I do not intend to dress in one of their precious monkey suits. have finished cutting the tapes for the record Webb has advertised. so that's that. now he can finance his Patchen issue and run his Henry Miller book. what a good boyscout I am, never asking royalties. or maybe I am a fool. but I don't want to get tangled in all that.

time certainly may not fly but it certainly does run like a young filly to my drunken advances. how's that for lousy writing? my god, if I get much worse I will be ready for *Esquire*. so then, this dead letter, to let you know that Bukowski still has his gentle and beautiful and rented walls with Bukowski inside of them, piddling, scratching, ¼ thinking, residing, waiting, jelling, mumbling, shitting and shaving; kissing his typewriter and bending a little, not too much, to the heavy gods... I know that the electric things run through you, huzzah and huzzah, good sweet sun and eggs and a way to walk, Sheri, and a way to move in a room, Sheri, and a way to stay alive with them, account of them, in spite of them and 2500 years of almost worthless culture poured over us, yes. the doctor now, the doctor, god damn him! but not

my love,
Buk

Sheri, dear—

back, a bit of Handel on radio, haven't mailed letter, prob. can't for a while. he had to find an "adhesion" to slice, so this

329

old man will be moving slowly for about 12 hours. but cigar going and the women walk past my window, so fine. maybe one of my favorite editors (x-favorite) now gives me his chilled silence because he figures I have cancer and can't go ten rounds for him anymore. but to hell with the game. I still have typer and paper. members of the human race are fitful, touchy, frightened, and a lot of the so-called leading lights seem to have antiquated Christian morals. I can't be bothered with that crew. if they want to be offended on the grounds of what I write or because I take advantage of their female friends by screwing them, then too bad. I'm going to continue writing and screwing. if there are women of love good and generous enough to lend me their bodies and I like the bodies and the spirit within, I will screw, with love, and pleasure.

went to see my little girl today, she is 18 months old, and she saw the car, the old '57 and she came running, "HANK! ANK! ANK! HANK!" (that's my name, that's my first name: Henry. middle: Charles. I write under Charles because my father's first name was also "Henry" and he was the enemy.) anyhow, she came running, laughing. we've got a pipeline going between us. we read. each other. it is so easy. I know exactly what she wants and doesn't want. she's a doll from out of the clouds, dropped by some magic hand, come to lift me out of the blues. but enough.

novacaine wearing off and old ass singing the blues a bit now but there's been worse pain than this and surely there will be worse coming. but I've got a typer and paper and I've painted 3 paintings and I'm writing Sheri Martinelli, another magic one from out of the clouds. ...o yes, something else working up in Oregon, some young madman, Bobby Watson, assembling via mimeo a book of my poems—*Poems Written Before Leaping from an 8 Story Window*. just inked him a cover. also a prose bit of a book coming out via *Ole*... about the hospital, the operation: *All the Assholes in the World and Mine*. will get this to you as soon as out but some of these things take a while because most

---

Bobby Watson: both of CB's bibliographers credit Darrell Kerr and Charles Potts with editing *Poems*, not Watson.
All the Assholes...: a chapbook published in September 1966. The story was reprinted in CB's *South of No North* (1973).

of the people putting these out, all of these people, are poor and must work between milk and eggs and sweat and squeezed hours. these are the best people; I tend to distrust the vaunted professionals.

some people have said that I am too prolific, that I might be tending to write too much and that this could be dangerous. what the hell are they talking about? I figure that I sit at this typewriter very little. I compare, say to my job where I work ten to twelve hours a night doing something that I don't care to do. do I sit at this typer ten to twelve hours? certainly not. I'd rather; I'd rather bang 12 right here. and I could. I can write forever. there's enough within me to write away 2 dozen lives and happenings. it may not be grade-A stuff but it doesn't weaken me or endanger me either, not nearly as much as the job. and they never speak of the main killer—which is the job. as usual, they miss the essentials. too many people talk without thinking; I wish they'd think without talking.

the month of March is over. I went into the hospital on the 2nd., was sliced on the 3rd., and there was a bit of horror and disbelief—locked in with the whining crowd. and their T.V. sets and many of them with imagined ills, only wanting the great Mother because society has cut their balls off and they have lost touch with the undiscovered and important gods. no souls— just mouths, bodies pewking the misery of the sell-out. the bit of pain from the knives was nothing compared to being *locked-in* with them! at least on the job, you know that in a dozen hours you will be walking down the street alone—4 a.m.—with the last of the moon sinking into your skin and bones, the quiet air giving you no con-game... you slowly fill again, you go home. the mirror is hell, but that's where you came from. but there's always that stirring inch LEFT! that something you held all the way through. a seed. a lucky charm. love. guts. spinach. you name it. you know it. but in a hospital—that's it. they've got you—(the docs and the nurses and the patients)—to talk to, fondle, slice. arrg. but I found me a little Mexican mop-up girl—all eyes and sadness, we had some laughs, corny stuff, I'd say, "Hey sweetie, you come to mop my white socks again?" "do they need it?" "oh yeah, once lightly!" and the little wench mopped my socks again! laughing. I always seem to meet these little Mexican girls working at dirty jobs, for nothing. beautiful-ly real and easy. "If I could get out of this bed I'd chase you all

331

around the room!" "why don't you try it, you might catch me!" silly stuff, I guess. she's 25 years younger than I am. old horny goat, Buk. but a lift. sure. she brought me a new pair of stockings when I left, threw them on my chest. "here! for your big stinky feet!" I didn't have the guts to ask for her whereabouts when she wasn't working. age, age, age! *Age!*

well, I've dragged on long enough here. don't write until the space arrives, until the moments juggle properly. I understand.

> the birds fly high high the drunks fall off their stools
> milkmen cry over their grey hair
> newsboys sell me death
> I hear songs so sad I want to cry
> why can't it work, why can't anything
> work? ah, maybe it
> is. cold showers. sewers. armies.
> myself shot down like a captive
> spy. great, great
> great. the waters pumping over
> everything.
> sitting on the edge of the bed
> thinking of St. Louis or oranges or
> tombs.
> ah.

> lub,
> *Buk*

[*followed by a large abstract drawing with letters of the alphabet*]

332

8. Aprille. 66   "they call this Friday good"
s.m. pobx 1044 pacifica calif.

Precious Steel Splinter:
Before me lies you review of Corrington's book of boems—
p/54—"I can lie to a hot blonde" nay Buk—there's been too
much lying to our Psyche... our seeing eye dawgs—that's how
the mess started—no lying to our hot blondes—or history—or
the invisible reader—
p/57 "because it does not come out of essence but out of
instrument"—that's THERE—"I do not write these poems from
a will but from the love that moves me to it" or words to that
effect. A quote from E.P. quoting a troubadore. Or howhellspelled.
P/58. "here in the United States we over-respect education,
the doctor, the lawyer, the professor—and we allow them to
shit all over us while we smile." THAT is how the end came with
a "whimper" not a "BANG". It is not strictly American Bukow—
it comes from our root—it's "old as th' hills" & just as dusty—
man's downfall is the worship of other men / women's too.
P/59—"We all write badly at times"—who said that? Buk—
even E.P. says that—it's a good thing once said—tell me who
said that???? You shdn't send anyone THAT honest to a
"priest/rabbi or preacher"—howly Chryst that'd corrupt such a
humble honest soul— TELL ME WHO SAID THAT I PRAY THEE.
P/60: "Art makes life" / you SAID it—nothing happens in
this shitty universe except Ye Creative Act—that was SO in the
beginning by the Prime Mover—and it's ALL we got to GO on—
The 7 Deadlys are they who stop The Process/ The Process is
like Snowflakes that make themselves as they fall—"moving
slowly like a dancer"—we catch hold of one another at the
appointed time & place—this is the meaning of heav'n & eart'—

"they call this Friday good": from Eliot's "East Coker," part 4.
Steel Splinter: in his letter of 23? July 1960, CB claimed his parents were
"splints of steel."
"whimper ... BANG": from the conclusion of Eliot's "The Hollow
Men."
"moving slowly like a dancer": cf. "move in measure, like a dancer," from
part 2 of Eliot's "Little Gidding."

(*I Ching*'s line) You'll SEE that soon's I git yr issue out—*how* we catch hold of one another to make patterns—we swirl through time like snowflakes—Pythagoras: "Time is the soul of the world"

P/61 "Christ, when are we going to BEGIN" Christ... we are going to BEGIN by reading H.D.'s *Collected Poems*—O Wilde Beaste!! Corrington has found a "respectability"—while he is here & while it is now—and he feels he can afford a "TONE"— He takes that TONE... like an echo... from H.D.'s tone / Mr. Eliot's / E. P.'s tone / James Joyce's tone "sad as a sea gull is when flying all alone" Corrington is wearing his trousers rolled/ now is when we'll SEE the real Corrington / as Abe Lincoln said "most men can endure poverty but power is the real test of them"... or words to—

Corrington now has his pat on the head & it will prove him or unprove him/ The Greeks said it too, something about Fate raising up the children of Destiny only to let them fall again— Abner Dean has a drawing—a nude male is at the top of a desperately long flight of steps & he is just about to open a door marked "appointment with Destiny" & of course the door opens to a sheer drop down to the bottom of the bin agin'— Corrington in his solitude hugs the Tone of the Masters to his naked self—He's more frightened than he ever was.

Respectability is death. His Late Late Show is a thirst that follows our most reverend Eliot's drink: "Let me disclose the gifts reserved for age"—and as usual—you are the only thing worth reading in the book/

Yr drawing of a wolf is wolfy/

Know WHY you won't read H.D. Buk?? You are afraid you'll lose your heart to her—the females you hang out with are

---

Pythagoras: Greek philosopher and mathematician of the 6th century B.C.

Joyce's ... alone": misquoted from *Chamber Music* #35: "Sad as the sea-bird is, when going / Forth alone."

Wearing his trousers rolled: from Eliot's "Love Song of J. Alfred Prufrock."

Abner Dean: American cartoonist and illustrator (1910–1982).

Eliot's ... reserved for age": from "Little Gidding," part 2.

334

wise but unpure—soft—and H.D. is wise & pure & hard—you never knew such a woman—soft as the sheen on polished jade & just as hard/ the classic woman—the ideal/

Corrington hath caught her scent—the white stag—he WANTS to be old so he too can wear his trousers rolled. Eliot "measures out his life in coffee spoons"... Cor/ says "these veins are full of tea". Cor is mellowing—but at what age???

Take a chance Buk—read H.D. as her lover—although gor' knowz (E.P.'s) H.D. would terrify you—she's a tall TALL woman. I'm not fit to wash her buddha feet with dew/

Cor uses his social backing to take a chance now—to leap OFF into the DEEP—he turns his back on his raw yout'... he has this age upon him—he can now AFFORD that distant tone—he catches from the craig where Ezra mates with his own wild kind/

You are not going to be tamed—but you must mellow—you are a plant—you will mellow—then your tone will come to us from a far place where you live—I said L I V E—

This is a world of ME *first* or *me* TOO!—the competitive dogs—we all have it—some times we compete with ourselves—most compete with the nearest person—E.P. felt this dog in us... and he wisely turned to the living Dead—Dant' / Kung / etc. E.P. lived—I lived for a brief moment on Wednesday / knew what it felt like to LIVE—not this animal decay—the stench of the filth of the world/ I see now that what I thought was LIFE was death—

And you O Buk!—that yen to shock—it's raw—Go to your mountain top... What IS your mountain top??? I found mine in D.P.—H.D. for her sacred word... and D.P. for her TONE— leave your paradisial dancing girls... your zen back alleys—and go to your mountain top—and write to us from THERE—

> "If you can hold the moon in your hands
> turning it slowly like a slightly tarnished platter
> you're there"   H.D.

Eliot ... coffee spoons": another quotation from "Prufrock."
"If you ... H. D.": from "The Moon in Your Hands" (quoted earlier in SM's letter of 19 April 1961).

Go... Buk... go... turn the moon slowly in your hands... like a slightly tarnished platter—and tell me what it was like. Only H. D. knew. If you can write "out of essence" & dissociate between essence & instrument then it's stale to write about whores & pussy—

Cant you SEE—you ARE the Life of this Place??? "Spot the rot" is good—but Buk—you are a BIG boy now—don't drag your private life to the page—just you from your mountain top—tell us from there—you are taking Corrington like a ghost in a tree & ripping him like a wild tusk'd creature.

O Savage One—write these things—then REwrite them—extracting all the private life—employ your pithy salty phrases / perceptions / insights—but mellow my Raw Whiskey—then slide into our heads like the burning bitter liquid life you ARE /

I had to 'grow UP'—to turn & rend that green ego-centric, really AWFUL monster from Greenwich Village—I had to stop cussin' and Miss Kickin' IT—egotism leads to that death of no life/ O YOU stir'd me out of the dust with yr savage boar tusk rending of the now mellow Corrington—send me   mas   mas   more   more

---

Los Angeles, Calif.
April 9, 1966

Sheri, Sheeri, Sheeeeeriii—

going through your letter, rec. this morning. regarding "I can lie to a hot blonde"—this was showmanship, clowning, to keep the audience awake. a trick but perhaps not a very good one. but speaking of lying to women, I had a piece of paper around here that I had written something on—lost it now—but it said: "the average woman loves the lie so much that she usually marries it." this is why I have preferred my certain type of whore—no fuss, no muss. I have only met and lived with one

---

stir'd me out of the dust: an echo of Pound's remark to SM in Canto 93: "You have stirred my mind out of dust" (652).

woman that I could get straight through to personally—who could hear my voice and I could hear hers. she had to die, of course. may the angels, if they are there, bless her eternally.

Leslie Wolf Hedly said "we all write badly at times." Liesly Wolf was more famous then than he is now but I fear his bad writing was more than "at times".

I *did* read H.D. you sent me a book of hers when she was dying (in Switzerland?) and asked me to write her a card. I did. I made the card as kind as possible without telling any lies.

Joyce: "sad as a seagull is when flying all alone." do you really think these lone seagulls are sad? I think that we are thinking too quickly here, picking up the first thread. I always feel that these lone gulls are *mad*, that they have popped their cork. especially at that time when the last of the sun is going into night. it's like they've spun off the wheel and when they come down over me, these lone ones, their eyes are almost torn from their heads in the agony of mad hate that seems much more than the lost hunger of sadness, and they would rip my eyes to replace theirs, they would do horrible deeds upon me there on the beach, if their devil were larger, if I were drunk, asleep, dying...

yes, most men can endure poverty; that's why they like to pretend it's brave. I have been poor most of my life because it is more comfortable—I mean that it has allowed me to do some of the things I wanted to and stopped me from doing the things I didn't want to do—like factories.

I don't know about "the mountaintop". you can't go there until you are ready and my time may not come. I know what you mean by "mountaintop". I know that it is there but I've got to work through slag, white hot slag first. the tool is good if we are true to it. but I cannot move on until I am done where I am and it may well be that my time will be finished far before I am ready. many consider that where I am now is lower than where anybody is. they think that I delight in muck, expose, talking out of class. I am only trying to find out where I am wherever that may be. and then muck is never muck, it is only called

---

Leslie Wolf Hedly: Leslie Woolf Hedley (1918–), minor American writer, editor of a magazine called *Inferno* (1950–56). CB rejected some of his poems when co-editing *Harlequin* (Sounes 39).

muck. that the moon is clean enough to behold does not mean that a whore is not a moon.

rather flattened today. wrote poetry last night from 10 p.m. to 4:30 a.m. then couldn't sleep. haven't slept yet. don't want to. must get poems typed up. Christ, come to think of it, I wrote poems from 8 a.m. to 10 p.m. also. I must be going mad. I have submissions out to 17 magazines at once.

wrote a review of Layton for some Canadian mag—*Evidence*. I told them that Layton was pretty damned good. so don't think I go around ripping and tearing because I figure ripping and tearing is easy and glorious. ah, you *know* this!

the doctor still twaddling and torturing me. but it will soon end. either that or I will break both of his arms. I tell him, "Now you get up on that table and let me work you over." "but I am not sick," he tells me. "that's not the *idea*," I tell him. "he *isss* a very *strange* man," I hear him tell the nurse as I leave. and I am thinking about them: 2 puppets on a stage, glass hunks of shit.

o, I am burned out my lovely flexible warm angel, Sheri, invisible love, listen here are parts of a long poem I wrote & you see I am still far from the mountaintop—(but don't show these lousy excerpts to any writers. some dogs have been stealing my lines... out of letters sent, out of poems submitted...)—

oh, hell no, I won't bore you (I trust you, that's not it. it's tempo, tempo & stretch & [*illegible*]. all that's important, even in letters or anywhere. sure) with my seriousness! here's a short one:

And the Moon and the Stars and the World:

long walks at night—
that's what's good for the
soul:
peeking into windows
watching tired
housewives

Layton ... Evidence: CB's review of Irving Layton's *Laughing Rooster* appeared in *Evidence* #9.

And the Moon ...: first published (with different line breaks) in 1969 in *DRA* (108).

trying to fight
off
their beer-maddned
husbands.

my oil paintings that I did with the palms of my hands with
unmixed tubes on plain large paper are about dry now. I guess
they are not exceptional but it is a spread of color and I spread
the color so it would not tire *me*, and since very few people
come to this place, that is the best way, and still would be—the
other way around.

love to you, good one,
Buk

THE LAND OF PEACE IS HERE NOW—ALL WE NEED IS A LITTLE
LUCK, BETTER DIRECTIVES, MILDER WINE...

los angles, calif.
April eleven, 19six6

sHeRi::::
10th. hour. struck down by waiting. little things in this little
cave. woman angry at me but that doesn't matter because long
ago all broken off there—physically, spiritually; but like to visit
my little girl without all her snarling. her group, her gang, has
now completely lassooed her mind. I am a loner and will not
show at their leftwing poetry readings and chatterings and
world-saving talk. I gotta save myself. wrote a foreword to a
book of poems by a young poet, Steve Richmond. *Hitler Painted
Roses.* phone just rang. talk. where was I? let's just say that her
hand-holders didn't like the foreword. I asked Richmond to
send you his book. maybe you've read it by now. anyhow, I am
playing with the girl and I can *feel* her (the woman) *bristling*, I
can feel the fangs of her ugly ⅛th. soul in the air.

---

woman: by 1966 CB had separated from Frances Elizabeth Dean.

339

"Richmond's always writing about reaching up into his ass for shit," she snarled.

"Which poem was that?"

"all his poems. in all his poems he is talking about reaching up into his ass."

"ah, yes, dirty poems," I said.

I can't haggle with them, Sheri. I don't argue in the marketplace. I learn from them. generally by *reversing* their feelings and opinions, I get the truth. people are valuable to me in this way. if they all run up one road, I know that the other road is right. why is this? what games do the gods play?

there is enough treachery, hatred, violence, absurdity in the average human being to supply any given army on any given day.

I can feel this woman slipping away, drowning, melting, dissolving into hate, into little cubicles of shoddy, 2 bit, obvious ideas. I believe she senses it too, can feel the damnation coming down, the no-light. she is drowning in the crowd. that's it—she is drowning in the crowd, and it seems so easy, it takes no resistance.

the last time she came over here she brought one of her boyfriends over with her, along with the little girl. introduced me. "this is John." fine. John was wood, 55 years of wood, the eyes drilled-out. he sat, sat. "Mr. Bukowski, I was introduced to your poetry last week." I didn't say anything. was I responsible for the fact that he was introduced to my poetry? my responsibility was over after I finished the poem.

just had a visitor. 2 hours. jesus, forgot what I was saying.

this was the guy who gave me this typer, paper, envelopes... an admirer? I am going to have to tell him I need more time. no time for chitchat. shit. you can see how he broke me off. danger. there's always this danger—people popping heads in. nice people, in a sense. but no soul. they can destroy. I've fought too long to be melted away by the handshakers. the clock is my love. going. I need words, rocks, things to carve with. bless the dead emperors. lousy letter. but will mail.

love,

Buk

340

Charles:

and I do SEE—to "keep audience awake" & that wd be legit /
and you DO "keep" them "AWAKE"—

O Buk—"the *average* woman"—if I were a Bukowski &
would put word to life describing what they have done to me—
but my way is to turn away & never employ their name nor ever
again see their face in my life—I shut them out—what crimes
they commit—no wonder E.P. laughed when I modestly said I
wanted to enlighten my sisters—the pus sacs full of 7 deadlys or
the young unpaid whores full of the most vain egotism—let us
forget the average woman—sing of the unusual females—society
is *mean* to them—only the poet retains his balance when faced
by the luminous eye of the she-male—or maybe you did well—
"the hot blonde"—(this a.m. one is not feeling even—) cause it
be a public fact that it's o.k. to lie to HER—Only it is not "the hot
blonde" who destroys our thread of life down here in The Shytte
Factory but the female maggots who feed upon our garbage
buckets like succulent maggots crawling through stale shells—
chewing away at our old turds & keeping dead shit alive with
their mouths and tongues. Give us a tombstone for that breed—

well—Hedly—but that line is full of sweet humble mod-
esty—it touched me// o.k.

YOU *D I D N ' T* read H.D. ***!!!)(' '&_%$#+"$%_&'(
)**:*)($%   you haven't digested her—Christ—begin with
H.D.—maybe your eye read her—but go to her as to a woman
needing your love—read her as if she spoke in a living voice to
YOU—Charles Bukowski—as if she were telling you her wistful
secrets—E.P. failed her—it was his early scorpio sting-tail
phase—scorpio sexiest sign of the zodiac—he cdn't over-come
that—he thought SHE failed HIM—

Don't TRY to read her with yr soul's eyes until you hit a day
when you cannot go out... when no one knows where you are
nor would you receive them if they did—when loneliness is like
a serpent with many heads tearing away at yr middle brain in
centre of body... when tears are bursting out of yr eye & inside
yr body—when no phone is near & you cannot eat... and the
windows are covered with steam & you cannot see out & what
you see in aint worth looking at—& all yr ideals have turned
into illusions... and each hero that blew in blew OUT—& there

341

is no one around for thousands of miles that you could even talk to—& when other room renters call you "th' dutchess" behind yr back because they see agony as being "stuck up"— that's the time to reach for H.D. and she puts beautiful fragrant musical silence throughout your cells & your beyond pain spirit lifts its dumb head up to gaze upon an enormous room where snails show us the way because they have a shell... built second by second—that is the "mountain top"—wait for such a day & then read H.D. "from hunger"—

I have found my mountain top—and I saw a pixie man that had his—He was walking up that street in San Francisco lined with hock shops—shorter than I—sort of roly-poly—pink face—with the merriest expression ever seen... I suspect he was not quite human—an element—and drunk as a lord—sort of floating above the ground—he was going up to The Living Dead—almost poking them in the breast bone—saying things to them—precisely pronouncing their fates to their dumb ears—he did that to me too—our eyes met—he was such FUN to see—he told me "oh *you*RRR *all* right"—my god but I am not—otherwise I would have snatched him & taken him into my life—what a fool I was... he had found his mountain top— one of the Immortals passed me by on Hock Shop Street & stupid lets him pass on!!!! O my loss bugs me right now.

Lor' man but you right—'bout Joyce & that line—I was hearing the sad lone tone—you more right—the bastids are only hungry—I guess Joyce ought to have put "sad as a sea gull seems" etc or word meaning signifying sadness rather than being sad/

O NO no one I have talked with & it includes Ye Square— thinks *that* ("delight in muck" etc)—they think that you are honest... alive with life—"muck"—that is *how* you move them—They _need_ the shock—The whores I knew in NYC were girls too intellent to subside into soupBURPia—yet cdn't wander the wilderness trusting in the Hawly Ghost—and who don't blame them iz me—They are EP's "priestess astray in the streets" or words to—

Yes—the Dogs do steal—for they are imitators—they ape— monkey see monkey do—from The Chinese:

EP's *"priestess astray in the streets"*: source unknown.

"The superior man is in HARMONY with the Process
the inferior man imitates"   competes by imitation—
They stole from E.P. & they steal from me—do not be surprised that they will also steal from you—that's also part of The
Process—It's a world of *ME FIRST*... or *ME TOO*... They
want/need that drink of life water—the first to say or do (It
starts to pall near 40) don't care doll—don't care—laugh that
last laugh that knows you snuck life into their shut skulls—
        I once saw an exhibit of the italian master of fantasy: Di
Chirico—a most clever eye had hung the show—it was Di
Chirico & some of his more famous or locally well known &
more successful competitors / they had all stolen from Di Chirico—Each one had stolen something—and Clever Eye had hung
The Imitators on each side of the wall with the original Di
Chirico in the center of the room & one's eye spun down each
opposite wall & they stealers' colours/lines/forms etc led straight
to the glowing Di Chirico! [*a drawing of the exhibit follows*] His
seed shown bright & you could see it had spread into their
minds!! They uptown artists with galleries were at that time
stealing from the poor wandering painter—alone—and that
exhibit made me laugh—
        Imitation makes the Original more bright—& Time proves
life right—But I don't blame you for being drug when others
steal what you were first on earth to SEE—
                Animus humanus amor non est sed ab ipso amor
                        procedit,
                et ideo seipso non diligit sed amore qui seipso
                        procedit"   Canto 95 EP
"The human soul is not love but love proceeds from it; therefore it does not take delight in itself but only in the love that
flows through it" or words to /
        The Muse is your Goddess & you are their God—cosi sia
(so be it) Buk / And you so right—about the tired housewives in
yr terrifying small poem!!!
        Sir Walter Releigh (orHowHellSpell) said "when others talk
or do things behind my back, I figure my tail is a good enough

---

Di Chirico: Giorgio de Chirico (1888–1978), Italian surrealist painter.
Animus ... Canto 95: actually, the epigraph to Canto 90, from Richard of
St. Victor's *Quomodo Spiritus sanctus est amor Patris et Filii.*

answer for them"—If they prefer the ass to the face—that's on them!

And as for painting—with me I cannot paint it unless I SEE it—it must be already there before this painting monkey can do it—also I find that I do more when there is that one to move to delight with the work / it is difficult to paint as a prayer—"to work is to pray"—and I find her typing / but she has a few more things to give us—right now I am seeing into my ego self and I am plumb dumbfounded/flaberghasted/aghast etc... every thing I really hate in others I am seeing in that monster who got me through Time to Here & Now—she has GOT to go man—For the simple reason that I want NO more of me around me!! Self does meet self as Edger Cayce said (but the Cayce Foundation & the Cayce-ites (the pus sacs) are not Edger Cayce any more than the xtians are J. C.) He said "Self meets self."—and this cell(f) is going to go "out th' smoke hole"... Try to make the At-one-ment scene—It is the only Life—But first to FIND the true One who is the real One of all the us of us—

Yr chicago typewriter blasts & roars O King Leo—yr growls & royal yawls are driving you to your true One—H.D. brings this one more out of all the shes within—and sometimes you can turn to yr inner pack & tell the inner dogs: "BE still & know that *I* am God"—only make sure (first if you can) that the God of you is not your own personal Devil—What I have taken as my "god'—I know see with true sadness—it was my devil form—If you want a true portrait of self—get a dog & let it live with you & then condemn it with a word "you nervous bastard" etc—dogs reflect the personality of the 'mawster'.

to a former letter:

Buk/ there's NO thing wrong with accepting payment for yr work or books called 'royalties'—ask for them & accept them—your life must go on /

am reading Swedenborg now—going on into afternoon—2:04 exact/ "willing is loving to DO"—

Fate Magazine May 1966 issue: adv/ SUBSCRIBE TO THE LITERARY TIMES has in its write up these: THE NEW IMPORTANT WORK of Charles Bukowski & others of course/ amazing to see your name in *Fate Mz*!!!!! on p/19 find one & have

---

"*to work is to pray*": an anonymous Latin saying (*laborare est orare*).

a peek @ page. *Fate* often has NEWS the blatts do not print/
along w/a lot of 'mist-stick' sticks/
17 magazines at once??!!!! It is wonderful to be occupatis-
sima—that is what kills most of those who believe they can
court boredom & not die of it/
stay—stay in the mind state of work—maybe I shd stop &
let you work / from here: good will

SM

---

l.a.
April, 13, 1966

dear Sheri:
nothing much. only we were speaking of the "female". you
know, at this lucky time of being sick, or whatever it is, I arise at
noon, drink coffee and type out whatever I put on slips of paper
the night before. then sometimes a few more poems pop up,
straight from typer. anyhow, I fiddle and diddel and diddle in
this breakfastnook, and by the time I get to the mailbox it is
5:30, 6 p.m. and the females are landing from the busses after
their scratchy day at work, and I must pass them on the sidewalk. it is the time of the sun going down, a gentle easy time for
me. I have grown a red beard out of which I spring, smoking
cigars. anyhow, the female, since the subject is her, here are a
couple of poems I wrote about her, will mail them out along
with your letter and other poems—

The Stupid Are Best at the Cruelties

beware women grown
old
who were never
anything but
young.

The Stupid ... after Work: both published in *The Eight Pager* in 1966.

345

certain devils in our heads fear
Tuesdays
as certain asses in our midst
fear devils' asses
on stormy
Thursdays,
but I'd say
the most wintry
spilled goblet of them
all
is
the ever-passing lady on the
sidewalk of the world
who won't look me
in the face
because she thinks her beauty is so
great
I'd want to rape her
if I saw
the color of her
panting
eye.

I await *A & P.* you did me honor recognizing my existence, no matter what you say... please be careful. do not let the mob burn you, trap you, fool you—if possible. my love goes with you, in your purse, in your pocket, wherever you go. you are one woman in 90 million women; please be careful, continue to live. I act tough but my sadness often gets impossible, too close in range, stomping me. sometimes a word from out of the world gives the heart a little place to look to.

Buk

l.a.
april 14, 1966

dear Sheri:
letter I wrote yesterday enclosed. Marina and Frances came by yesterday and I got held up. Marina had a cold, now I have a cold. you should see her eyes, Sheri, wild large, large with beautiful color, and now wild, either, calm, very. I was thinking— wild, in terms of life. some people say, she has your eyes. meaning me. this is quite a compliment.

went over to some editor's place last night (John Bryan) (*Notes from Underground*) but there were other people there, and everybody trying to be clever, and laughing all the time. everything is a god damned joke, nothing sacred, everything flip. cigars, grass, beer. Idolization of the hipness of Neal Cassady. I see more and more that I don't belong with the people, have got to crawl back into my hole. having to throw in a chip because I was there, I recited part of a poem I had written:

> DeMop had the siff and
> got in a rowboat and
> rowed until he was
> crazy.
> all for a piece of
> ass. France's greatest
> short story writer
> sent babbling by the
> unwashed pussy of a
> 4 foot Parisian whore!

"say, say, you come on, but you're a little *brutal*, you know?"
They always want their whipcream. yet Bryan puts out a pretty strong magazine anyhow.
Thanks for the *A & P*, which I got this morning. Marina's copy will be preserved for her until such time as she becomes

---

John Bryan: journalist and editor; CB occasionally contributed to his magazine.
Neal Cassady: Denver hipster immortalized in Kerouac's *On the Road* and *Visions of Cody*.
DeMop: Guy de Maupassant (1850–1893); poem from which this is taken unknown.

[old] enough to grasp it. Your reading of the charts sounds pretty much like the persons involved—I would say, especially Blazek. I am pretty well under, having gotten fairly high last night, and will dip more into your charts at an easier time. my many thanks for the work involved and for putting the starlight shine on my friends. By the way, Marina's chart IS VERY MUCH LIKE HER. there's got to be something to this: it seems so accurate. Richmond too. everybody. did he send you his book? I will mail you something for your amusement in next day or so (need large envelope first)—Bryan's *Peace Issue*, wherein I try to explain what PEACE is and what WAR is, what *the* ever-war is, so on. Also will send you this month's Catholic mag *Today* which has an article on one "Charles Bukowski: *Outsider No. 1*"   a priest or somebody on the magazine wrote and asked me to tell him what I thought of the article. I let him have it straight and I hope he can get in and out of his smock for a while after I finish.

got a couple of rejections this morning, and now I must read them and decide whether the writing was bad or whether the magazines simply weren't there.

stay on with us.

love,
Buk

[*handwritten at top:*]
Buk—came 'cross this... was in dif mind... maybe U enjoy—yesss? SM

21. June 66

BukO:
Blaz sends me *Ole* w/yr poem in: *Drunk Again & Wondering, Wondering...* Wang Shou-jen: "the mind of man is Heaven" and Hell—this fr *The Way of Chinese Painting*—& E.P. has it in

---

Today ... No. 1 ": a brief article written by Jay Robert Nash.
Ole ... Wondering: in *Ole* #3 (November 1965); see *SB* 169–71.
Wang Shou-jen ... The Way of Chinese Painting: Chinese philsopher (1472–1528); the book is unidentified.

the Cantos that Kati said "a man's paradise is his own good nature"—& Artie Richer said it "but first we must invent paradise" in order to go there/ I know the mind-state you were in that evoked the poem—it is cheerless—HOW to reach this paradisial mind-state where we know that we, ourselves, are 'god' / atomic parts of the aforesaid. That way we can only blame us—murder in your own self what you hate in the others... that's the ONLY way—& for the REST of the Woe—I guess the Chinese is best: "SEE no evil/ hear no evil/ speak no evil"—

& this coming from this person who could have been seen this a.m. early walking in the wet salt sea barefoot along the cold dark sand, weeping salt tears (very wet) praying to the Nereids who live in the sea caves (H.D. says "Nereids who dwell in wet caves..." she also gives us a handle to hold onto in the Burning Pot: "and each god-like name spoken is as a shrine in a godless place.")

There are times when my shoe-laces are falling apart at the seams upstairs when I shreik at the Dough Balls: "Bukowski UNDERSTANDS"—Blessed are the Dough Balls that can be shrieked at—and cursed be they who are too evil for even a whisper to pass out of the mouth—Buk—it is better to say ANY name that is sacred to you than to cuss God(tt) but you better tell me too 'countta I slip in low gear especially in the early a.m.

life—jeezzz chriss—it "aint possible"—I think most of our agony comes from our lousy society that is spiritually dead—on the other hand—if we are its antaenne!!! the tip top of it!!! what a thought...

The chinese idea that when we draw paint or write we are keeping this 'god' or this 'heaven' alive in us is a joyous mind-state to enter—When you wrote you so-sad poem I wept bitterly—& you wrung this letter from my soul—and I enclose a letter (lost some how but will find & send on) I was scribbling to you & as I draw I recall Dr. Wm Carlos Williams at St Liz watching me draw E. P. saying in a cool, clear voice over my shoulder... "ah! I'm GLAD you gave him such *n i c e* whiskers... he has SUCH *AN* UNNNNNN fortunate CHIN"

Kati ... good nature": the Egyptian king's aphorism is quoted at the beginning of Canto 93.

Artie Richer: a poet and painter who contributed to *A&P*.

H.D. ... godless place": from "Acon" and "Sea Heroes," respectively.

The big boys—so gentle & amusing in their ego digs—somehow The RoughHouse Set dont come off—but YOU—I understand you—*but* only as a person—I find I do not understand the male or female part of the person—it seems to me that it is more a conditioning than a real being—and a thing we must get the hell OUT of—follow the Light moth & you'll fly—
all for now—

S

●

· 1 9 6 7 ·

10 March 1967

Bukowski:

the Steve Richmond sent one an edition of *Earth* 2 containing a 'poem' (?) (is it?? of yours??) untitled/unsigned... these lines: "are you Charles Bukowski" & ending "I was Charles Somebody"

Did YOU write that one? or is it a take-off on one of yrs?? MUST you cackle over yr cock Bukowski?? What's worse you've got them all off cackling o'er their cocks. That's arse backwards//

> "The human soul is not love but love proceeds from it
> therefore it does not take delight in itself but only in
> the love flowing from it."

YOU'd make some telephone luv'... you'd be so busy cackling "I'm talking, I'm Charles Somebody" that no goddessa could get through.

I'd like to read more in praise of love & less in praise of your battle-stick Charles. my 12 dogs all feel the same way 'bout same subject matter as you do... why ought one read above poem when one can get a really straightforward account from observing the dog population?? only the dogs display such a

---

Earth 2 ... Charles Somebody": a polemic entitled "In Defense of a Certain Type of Poetry, a Certain Type of Life, a Certain Type of Blood-Filled Creature Who Will Someday Die—."

"The human soul ... from it": an English translation of the Latin epigraph to Canto 90 (625); see SM's letter of 12 April 1966 and note.

sense of responsibility to Doll or Nikki (their wives)—there's
none of this hop-to @ first op to—

O! Telo Rigido! or how th' dickens EP spells / an orgasm is
not ecstasy—ecstasy has power to elevate the soma weightless-
ly... every cell participates... th' cock is a local stop... Love 'e
forma di Filosofia'

You lead the female down the Ego-path when you move her
mind towards thinking she SO irresistible that the Grit Poet
loses his will power @ sight of HER—the Gods are very different
in their Way of Love than you poets (said she)

Yr photos looking tall & otherwise good day to you Charles

4-16-67
3 a.m.
[*handwritten letter*]

Sherrieee:

You keep picking at the Word!

When I said that Pound "knew too much" I meant that he
studied too much & that when a man is studying he cannot be
doing something else.

Now, of course, your *next* move will be to tell me to be *exact*
with the language, that you don't have the time to play around
with half-words, you have WORK to do!

All right, do your work & stop being cranky with me.

I never received the painting you promised. But did rec. a
photo. That's all right. Photo's all right. Do you want me to
ship ya won a mine paintings? I paint too, tho not very good
they tell me. But if I listen to them they will stop the flow of all
my natural movements, including shitting, eating, fucking, so
forth. I do what I do and what I do is nec. for me.

Telo Rigido: Italian: "with rigid javelin" (a sexual reference), from Canto
20 (91).

'*e forma di Filosophia*': Italian: "is the form of philosophy," from Canto
93 (646).

352

Met an intellectual, one John Thomas X, who has letters from Pound and claims you couldn't have known Pound at St. Liz and for me to tell you so. I have done so.

I don't know how in in the hell I get in the middle.

From my *heart-instinct* I *know* you knew Pound. I tell him this.

Yet, still, he is a good man, tho heavy-brained & kool toward individual pain toward singular & mass objects.

So much for that.

As for me, I am writing better as I get older. I used to run all over the page—now I can say the same 100 words in ten. And I am more *in* myself & *out* of myself than before. I once said that if I could live to be 55 that I would be able to write. I said that when I was 30 years old, I had 25 years to go. Now I have 8, *if* I make it. But, of course, *being* 55 won't make it; one has to *arrive* at 55 in a certain form & shape. So far, sweetie, I am pure as melted butter. There have been little slips & slides but all to the good.

Any word for John Thomas? He lives at 2245 Lakeshore, Los Angeles. We sit around his place listening to the Horse Vessell Song or however you spell it, and when I leave he hands me little pictures of Hitler dead at the bunker, Goring after suicide, so forth, I don't know if he is joking or not. The whole thing seems a little melancholy & depressive to me. John is supported by a beautiful woman while I must work for a living—and even tho I might be the better poet, his is the happier life.

I hope you can read this. I am yours when you need me. Please keep alive & doing what is needed.

Love,

Buk

John Thomas: a poet CB hung out with at the time. An avid drug user, Thomas introduced CB to yage and LSD. See his memoir *Bukowski in the Bathtub*, ed. Philomene Long (Raven, 1997).

Horse Vessell Song: "The Horst Wessel Song" was a popular Nazi anthem.

Goring: Hermann Göring, Hitler's chief of the Luftwaffe; he committed suicide in jail in 1946.

[SM's response to the preceding letter is undated and unsigned.
She later identified the final sentence
as a piece of advice Pound once gave her.]

One awaits a seal & once properly 'seal'd' yr chinese scroll will be sent down to you/ as it is it aint yet THERE / patience.

one refuses to be drawn into any political discussions @ degree of yr acquaintance... her only comment: gentlemen most especially american gentlemen do not "doubt" without representation. There exists (unfortunately) TOO many printed proofs as to those days. Tell him to go look them up in the library and/or book marts. As E. P. wd state: "he aint got 'is 'omework done." Dismissed.

Yr letter does *not* sound like YOU—the spirit of it is wrong— as if it were you being motivated. Never in this long correspondence have you EVER presumed what this person wd do/say/write!! "Now, of course, your *next* move etc" Just dont understand that tone.

AND such a seal is not easy to get—am trying—only got saturdays to look for such—you can be certain that one will find a seal OR make one her self & then your little scroll will bashfully stand before yr eye/ yr inner eye/

all for now—and one rarely writes letters these days... as He said "to very old friends or very new"... & friends are persons who are friendly/ friend: fr old A.S. word meaning: to love /

Have nothing to do w/the affairs of t/world

●

354

Appendix 1
Martinelli's review of *A Signature of Charles Bukowski*

[*This appeared in* A&P #5 *(January 1961) immediately following Clarence Major's review of* Flower, Fist and Bestial Wail *and three other books. Major's subsequent review, promised in the first paragraph, never appeared.*]

Targets #4—*A Signature of Charles Bukowski* (arrived too late to airmail to Mr. Major so the typist must do it & she is not going to "cock" Mr. Bukowski "up with kisses." As a matter of fact she is reviewing one poem only & the rest will be reviewed by Mr. Major next issue of the *Anagogic & Paideumic Review*).
Page 19: *Horse on Fire* wherein Mr. Bukowski has Mr. Ezra Pound saying:
"one of the greatest love poems ever written"
He did NOT say *that*; he said "*AMONG* the best love poems in the language"
Mr. Bukowski has Mr. Pound described:
"many kinds of traitors of which the political are the least."
Mr. Pound was *not* guilty of any political treason. Mr. Pound's *own* statement:
"*W H A T I WD HAVE BEEN GUILTY OF IF I HAD NOT SPOKEN*"
(Of Misprision of Treason/*European* '59)
covers his conduct.
It was a grim jest to call Mr. Pound a "traitor" & it is a traitorous act to release him in the care of his wife, a British lady, however correct she may be & of high class & the best dressed lady in the world (I mean the tie dots matching the hat feather & glove stripe—that degree of knowing. Whispering in the artist's ear: "that lipstick's the WRONG colour for that dress") *b u t* Ezra *is* an American & he ought to be free to come to us if he wants & he cannot because it needs his wife to bring him & she's "*been* here" & that was enough for her.
We'd need reform ourselves overnight to be good enough

for a lady who wore a black silk top-coat/ a river-mist grey knit fez-hat glittering with silver sequins/ a jewel'd ring matching the colour of her strip'd scarf & grey'd tone'd stockings of silk matching her grey'd tone'd silk gloves/ a scarf pin whose colour fit the colour of her eyes & underneath a dress of forest green to match her shoes that she's put black narrow ribands under th arch & tied criss-cross up her ankles, ballet fashion... on the hottest day of the hottest town in the midi—the swamptown heat of Washington D.C. traveling to St. Liz on a bus full of half-naked red-skins—Mrs. Dorothy Shakespear Pound was a miracle of civilisation & all by herself; without writing any Cantos "you've *no* idea how these tawrsome paradises bowre me" she could have raised our general cultural level & uplifted our society from "it's goddamn'd dry on these rocks" [Canto 93/643] on toward a proper civilisation.

The look of pain in Allen Ginsberg's eyes when the typist said: "he read me Dante translating as he went along & Guido the same & Ovid's *Metamorphosis* and his own *Cantos* starting from XX to spare me Hell"... Allen needs to have his Dante read to him. We all need him: Mr. Major needs him:

> "all of us who do not know what it means to ever have had a Guru or a means to go into ourselves quietly & find the beautiful boundless area of what we call Heaven—we find Hell every time."

What good did it do to release him from St. Liz & sign him over to our British cousins?

A recording of an artist reading his poetry is *not* it. That is for the mass mind & ALL they got; but any who are of the caste of artists—the muse worshippers ought to stand in the Presence of the Throne & be Knighted. There is a power; there is a living reality & you aint going to get it from any recording of a human voice—the monkey mind is forever concerned with mass production.

The typist has uncovered evidence of enough intelligence alive & at work in the U.S. to warrant saying: there *are* men here who are men in their own right & they shd be in the presence of the living reality of a Dante walking the earth. They are being *cheated* of their right to equality—what good does it do to make the grocer's clerk equal when our best men must resort to plastic recordings of something that is theirs by right of proximity—our best red-skin poets forced down to the factory level. It

356

is a political & ethical crime to cheat a boy of sensititvity & intelligence as Peter Orlofsky of his cultural heritage as a fellow republican & citizen of a free nation. Poor Pete, beautiful of mind & body & ignorant as a goldfish—his inborn love of arts & letters is pitiful in its poverty but persistent beauty: "Sheri, today I was at Sutro Park & I saw a 'painted ship upon a painted ocean'" & "wheredja get th' blues?" (forget-me-nots plucked in Sutro Park for Diana striding white in moon ray) How are we EVER going to reach the level of Europe & the Orient? Our one international success has been sold into slavery. O! Go down Moses & pull our Ezra up so's Pete can sing: "Leafdi Diana, leove Diana, Heye Diana..." [Canto 91/632–33] & Michael Grieg can test his dry, double distill'd wit upon the master of wit & Rob't Stock can see first-hand the out-go-er sea-farer & know its likeness to the in-go-er sea-rougher... remove the eyes of pain from Allen Ginsberg—hasn't he had ENOUGH Hell?

O Ezra who art in Italy—tho' scandalized be thy name—our renaissance is come & thy word got through in the United States as it did in Europe—Give us this day our daily Ezra & fo'give him his sins as we forgive those who sin'd agin' him & o let Ezra lead us into Ovid's temptations & deliver us into delushus evils of the flesh for Pete Orlofsky's sake & Ez we do have a Kingdom of Kulch & Ez we do have a Power of sorts & if we are let we'll bring glory—O National Treasure which cannot be changed on th' market... so long's we exist as a nation... ah! *men*! (wot bug jobs they are.)

Mr. Bukowski's been told but Mr. Bukowski will persist in his un-doing—that sort of art work on cover, to a very busy person doing research up there ahead of us in the 21st onward centuries, will signify to our busy future scholar that Mr. Bukowski's book aint worth readin' because its Art Work'll serve as a sign post saying: LATE LATE VICTORIAN ERA SCHOOL OF PICKARSSS-O & the ugly kind of drawing will disqualify Mr. Bukowski's poetry from being read by those who come after us & Mr. Bukowski HAS GOT A SUBJECT MATTER: A POINT OF VIEW HOWEVER DOWNWARD IT IS CAST: A POINT OF PERCEPTION & WORDS OF MULTI-COLOR THAT HE USES TO INDICATE THE INNER SPACE WHERE THE MOON REALLY IS. *IF* Mr. Ezra Pound had read *his* Charles Bukowski he would NOT have EVER attempted to "save th' United State of Murka."

The printing of *Targets* is elegant & its only *real* art work. Egg-shell white with black print is the cover/ inside cover is sea-foam white & a half-page handsomely prints Mr. Bukowski's signature so we may judge his character in his brush strokes. The half-page colour is brown-egg-shell tan & sits on the inner pages whose colour is gold diluted to its thinnest yellow & little decorations of strange nature exist on each page.

Mr. Bukowski: "Write it
so'z a man on th' West Coast a
Africa could
understand ut";

The "man on the West Coast of Africa" looking at his English-African Dictionary trying to translate—wd want to know WHAT MEANS "DECORATIONS OF STRANGE" etc—well, the first one is a goat with eyes under his horn's root & a tongue like a mechanical part from an automobile carburator & polka dots under his eyes & ears like Babylonian wedge marks/ his horns are like a clown's hat & his fur has lightening crossing it & he's big's a U.S. 25¢ piece of silver. A silly-strange but effective decoration/ I mean when the Aztecs use this kind of fantastic animal it hath an arcane meaning but this arcane animal is meaningless in any religious or artistic sense & is a silly but effective dec.

The little horse used on page with *Horse on Fire* is not a serious horse & I will not take him seriously/ Mr. Bukowski is warning Mr. Pound that:

"self appraisal of poetry & love has proved more fools
than rebels"

which is harsh but correct with this exception: IF WE CANNOT EVALUATE OUR OWN SELVES' WORTH WHO IN THE HELL IS GOING TO DO IT WHILST WE WALK THIS EARTH?

DOES MR. BUKOWSKI WANT MR. POUND TO WAIT SEVERAL AGES TO HEAR SOME DRY BONE UP THERE SAY WHAT MR. HOT BLOOD RIGHT NOW KNOWS TO BE TRUE? THAT IT *IS* "AMONG THE BEST LOVE POEMS IN THE LANGUAGE" (CANTO 90)

MR. POUND HAS THE MAP OF LOVE POETRY INSIDE HIS HEAD & KNOWS IMMEDIATELY WHERE A LOVE POEM STANDS IN RELATION TO THE RACE OF LOVE POETRY.

Mr. Bukowski says: "and he proceeded to write the *Cantos*
full of dead languages..."

Doesn't Mr. Bukowski understand that "Our Man on the West

Coast of Africa" hath a love of culture? Cannot Mr. Bukowski imagine him seated in the boring heat & dither calmly translating the *Cantos* from his various dictionaries & when he gets to the Egyptian hieroglyphics of Kati's that the princess Ra Set got into the book—Our Man will be caused to write a letter to an European Egyptologist or mayhap an American Egyptologist & peace on earth, at least among the cultured, shall be the rule of the day. Language is important. The Hebrew language kept the Jews together as a clan more than any one MAN could ever do; men come & go but the symbol is eternal. Dr. Lovell says the "Torah" of the Jews was also the "Tara" of the Irish. Mr. E. P. Walker asks "what does the word 'tara' *mean* to a contemporary of the Irishry?"

It is a SOUND & it brings a rush of emotion; wild battle cries & hilaritas of dealing directly with one's foes; when the Irishry cannot die fighting & wildly singing or laughing... then it is their proud disdain of the "dog's life" that they'll die drinking & be in their imagined world of wild strange sounds like "TARA" & I do hope that answers Mr. Walker's question.

Mr. Bukowski wd rather Mr. Pound write about "straight things in bird-light the terror of a mouse..." I have NO idea what Our Man on the West Coast of Africa wd translate that as because we have no "bird light" far's I know. Of course "mouse terror" is world-wide/ This is a good place as any to record: the cat plays with the mouse because he forces his captured victim to teach him more about how to catch other mice/ the female wd do her cause well to play with the male like that/ free him & see which way he runs & then she'd know better how to catch another male—of course they CAN run faster/ there's a danger!

Mr. Bukowski says:

"the terror of a mouse reaches dormitory levels"

One has no idea what that signifies here OR on the West Coast of Africa.

Mr. Bukowski records:

"and reading Canto 90 he put the paper down
Ez did (both their eyes were wet)"

Canto 90 when properly read hath power to wet the eye from the terrible blast of its heated force rising upward. *The Cantos* will be more intelligible to Our man than Mr. Bukowski's poem on the subject.

The back drawing on the cover is the female form divine

359

seen through a pair of eyes that wobbled & done by a pair of hands that shook. The drawing a rivoting machine wd make cd it draw. NYC hog-wash: "but don't you think Botticelli is TOO beautiful?" No, one did NOT but one does think this set of drawings on Bukowski's book are TOO UGLY & that is much worse than being too beautiful. Those collecting CONTEMPO-RARY AMERICANA are advised to snatch up this book—the price is 50¢ & one orders them from EDITORS/TARGET: Casabuelo, Sandia Park/N.M. or Bukowski: 1623 N. Mariposa Ave/Los Angeles 27/Calif.

SM

●

Appendix 2

Bukowski's Contributions to
the *Anagogic & Paideumic Review*

[*The first four poems appeared in* A&P #5 *(January 1961); "Poem for Liz" and the series of drawings appeared in #6 (September 1961)*]

I GET ALL THE BREAKS

I burnt my hand, he said, trying to light a cigarette
with an ox's tail, and so your book won't be out
for a couple of more weeks yet, but you've been
very patient;: of course, I'm having trouble with my
printer and it's possible that O SO MORE GREESE
by Ricardo Willinsi and DAWN BOWN GRITTING by
Alan Roach will be out before yours; printer only
mailed half your pages (postal regulations) and
when the other half came, they were wrong sequenced
so I had to send them back, then had auto accident
but sent my brother down with your covers and
Villinsi's, and any day now you should be getting
something in the mail. I know that 2 years
have been a long time and you've been very patient
and I'm going to be proud to have your book
in my series, but, of course, unless sales increase
I may have to drop the entire project, although
I do hope to get yours out. As you may know,
this is a one-man operation coming out of my own
pocket, my own time and effort, and, if you'll reflect,
you will realise that we have been more than
hospitable to you.

dog walking intestine through days of dog dream
not hearing the scheming of cornhusks in Nebraska
or a dirty river with a big name,
or a dirty name for love,
not seeing angels with diamonds on their wings
winking at clouds,
not reading about Dostoievsky
the guy who kept trying to figure out
new ways to beat roulette;
not bothered with trying to like Dylan Thomas
when you really don't,
or a wife who wants to all night;
my dog, you have never stared at alligators
trying to find your name,
or watched the roaches walk the walls all night,
falling from the ceiling onto your whore--
a fat scream--while you tried to figure
Hemmingway's bulls, right or wrong,
or trying to play it smart:
marrying rich, trying to hang onto cold bedsheets
that freeze in your hands like dead knowledge;
friend dog, I walk you now,
you and I, alone,
pattering up the leave-torn sidewalks,
and although you haven't read Kafka,
and until you do--
no woman will share
our bone.

casuistics and memory, a magdalen hospital
swinging on the end of beads; scaglia and dream,
odd dream: birds and pistols; and so I think we write
now in order to capsize self and reality down to reason.
reason and finally, disintegration; the salina of our tears
really has dried; families have fallen like a brush before a roller,
maps have been torn down like posters:

> quick little men
> in offices of gold
> drink down cups
> half-poisoned, peering
> at walls of clouds and
> rockets like the sides
> of elephants that will
> not forget; and Nothing
> nods Its head and smiles,
> scaled like a fish, put
> in a Sunday pocket, patted,
> forgotten;--yet the stress
> is gone and the halfcrazy
> dead knit the earth, but

but wait, Miss Smith, god damm it, where's the report from Holcomb?
and figs grow in the valley, sticky as love, and each of us,
day-drowned, sits in a cafe, a nightcap in a blue necktie,
drink it like you mean it; Holcomb was drunk, didn't
send in report; Miss Smith cried; you will either
have to give her a raise, fire her or reach beneath her dress; the bombers are nearly over
Brazil now; boys still steal watermelons
later to become nothing but seeds, but
suffuse the discophora: at half-past
nine, some night, some morning, it
will rain a good one, cups all
spilled over the old maps,
Miss Smith, scaled like a
fish I reach beneath
your dress.   I say::
don't cry, it's
only 8:30.

A DISORGANISED POEM ON A DISORGANISED DAY, WITH WOMEN
RUNNING IN AND OUT AND THE PRICE OF BEER UP 2¢ A CAN.

los angeles. . . Sunday mostly, gloom necktie, rot grass,
unenchanted lake,
                        and she has just taken the towel from
her magic hips and hung it across the screen door
like a drape,
and it is dark and it is Doomday,
5 o'clock.

there is more fucking in the graves.

monolete lorda all the big guys built bigger than God
meant them to be
bringing in the music
while the eggs fry in their simple pans.

birds fall out of sky heavy with golden rock.
tend the mizzen, sing: o ye, o ye go damm.

girls so keep running in and out of doors downstairs
changing bathing suits, putting little blue ribbons
in their hair, donning china kimonoes, and there are
little dogs whirling like fleas, one or two roses
hang the fence, and an old man sits on the edge of his
chair like a cliff, afraid to fall.

rondo brilliant with Peter Haydn doing Mendy,
dog feet running grass and keys/ door slams,
birds everywhere bleep bleep they have atom bomb
dreams that struss their feathers.

(I died for you many a night feeding my love
my goofy love into your writhing
when I should have held a poem in my hand
like a sword
                and cut you in half)

now they are torturing a little girl and fighting over
a dog: fucks of the future to drive a man crazy
to burn his hair when he sleeps and write his name
on the bottom of a vase. . . Cleopatras, your blue ribbons:

cheesbait for micemen/   I am cracking another beer
like a walnut.

turkeyneck and lorca, poet smiling upon his fingernails
on Melrose Ave., weak lights, fat cats of blackbirds,
shoes always old, cops always young, spiders filled with
blood and moonlight. . . a poem is love even when it hates,
and Mr. Phillin, I want to tell you:
a poet has one fist of steel and one fist
of love/   manolete on the horn before the crowd,
the sunshine coming out red. . .
even the flies and pebbles are stunned,
and the bull
the bull is manolete now   and this poem
                                       hopes it finds
                                       some undead.

POEM FOR LIZ:

the bumblebee of our meaning
is less than a stack of
potatoe chips,
and growling and groaning
through barbs
searchlights shining into eyes,
I think of the good whore
who wouldn't even
god damm easy take money
and when you slipped it into her purse
would find it
and slap it back
like the worst of insults,
but she saved you from the law
and your own razor
only meant to shave with
to find her dead later
in a three dollar and fifty cent a week room,
stiff as anything you can stiffen,
never having complained

365

starved and laughing
only wanting one more drink
and one less man
only wanting one small child
as any woman would
coming across the kitchen floor toward her,
everything done up in ribbons and sunshine,

and when the man next to the barstool
that sat next to mine
heard about Liz
he said,
"Too bad, god damm, she was a fine piece."

No wonder a whore is a whore.

Liz, I know, and although I'd like to see you
now
I'm glad
you're dead.

NO TITLE: by   Charles Bukowski

I

This is a picture of a man ⌣ adriving home at 4:30 PM. He usually
arrives at 6:30 PM. It can ⌣ be any man. Any 2 men & a woman. Or any
2 women & a man. Or it can be 3 women. Or 3 men. But, for Christ's sake,
let's keep it simple—as of above.
If the drawing is poor: he is carrying flowers in his left hand. If he is
poor he probably didn't buy them, but stealing flowers makes sense because they usually die quicker than people.

II

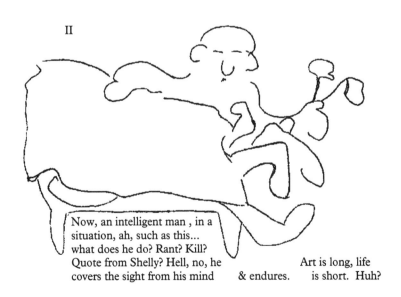

Now, an intelligent man , in a
situation, ah, such as this...
what does he do? Rant? Kill?
Quote from Shelly? Hell, no, he   Art is long, life
covers the sight from his mind   & endures.   is short. Huh?

367

III Contemplation is the birth of the
mind's tragedy
in the vise...

vice?

who said likker was quicker?
sometimes these fks seem to last
h o u r s !

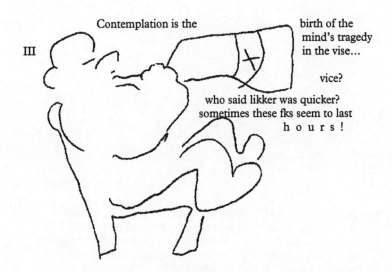

IV The congratulatory palm to the victor. When the swallows
came over Capistrano, it was nothing like this....

Lie is an
intransitive verb
& means to
recline;
lay
is an intransi-
tive verb &
means to put
down. The
principle parts
of Woman are:
lie , lay , lain ,
lay , laid , LAID.
Women & intransitive
verbs are a great
deal alike ; you
might as well shake
hands with any
sentence they bring
upon you.

368

V: Well, so here we go...once again to the library..to attempt to read once again ...Tolstoy's WAR & PEACE. Maybe the old boy knew something & stuck it in near the end ; the END , of the book. This time we'll read it backwards, & let the *lover* pay the rent as we ride off under watchet skies... endure, endure Beelzebub & Atlantis..the Earl of Chester-field wd have scoffed into a pink hanky at the animalistic infidel ity of our soul-mares. I still keep thinking, the as the wheels turn, & the library nears ..I shda sure as shit left-hook'd him, belly-deep, & when he bent, the old right, uppercut, & then the knee to the magic nuts..but wait.. TOLSTOY, TOLSTOY %)O SHIT#$% T O L S T O Y !!!

1.
This in case you cant make it out..is a jock beating hell out of a horse, down the stretch. He's supposed to win. They're all supposed to WIN. But sometimes there are 12 h0rses in a race, so every body gets a beating, including the winner; but wait... I lost 85$ today, but I still think horses might be good for something & beatings too, but right now I am listening to: SHEEP MAY SAFELY GRAZE by Bach.

369

2. This is a man beating hell out of the subspecies. In California a common-law wife owns one half of what you have after one year of being under a common roof. Even if you dont own anything. I think this is a vicious law.

We're never gonna cross the Jordan at this rate.

Aut Caesar aut nullus... why fk around?

Bukowski contemplating his future..We do not expect pity here in the dirty socks & the unwashed of the mind; but sometimes thinking is a game wherein the hounds bound ahead of the fox, & it's better in a downpour of pad-lock & silence; or if this is too fancy...it's better sometimes to get drunk & fall down among the old racing forms & love letters # than attempt to be C.P. Snow or Lionel Trilling . . .

370

####### Pound and Hux argueing hell outs each other at St. Liz.

They both knew St. Liz was nothing and #### Pound and #### Hux wuz something.....

This was a moment in history only known to the gods, and god damm those...the jailors, the white steeples and domes of Liberty; god damm those who let Van Gogh take life out of the world with a borrowed shotgun, and #3 Melpomene is the muse of tragedy, and America is tradgedy without muse, and I am dying like a yellow leaf in a shaking wind...

I do, supp0se tho, that we might be exaggerating a little. It is our lot to make sounds in a vacumn.

And drawings. And darlings in the dawn.

Index

Bukowski, Henry (CB's father), 7, 9, 43, 56
Bukowski, Marina Louise, 314, 318–19, 321–22, 327, 330, 347–48
Bunting, Basil, 257
Burnett, Whit, 91, 165
Burns, Robert, 12, 222

Capone, Al, 162
Carpenter, Humphrey, 23
Cassady, Neal, 347
Castro, Fidel, 104, 108, 112, 189
Cavalcanti, Guido, 18, 20, 53, 356
Cayce, Edgar, 25, 309, 344
Chamberlain, Safford, 205
Chaucer, Geoffrey, 88, 222
Chao Tze-chiang, 257
Charles, Ray, 173
Chekhov, Anton, 59
Chesterfield, Earl of, 369
Chirico, Giorgio de, 343
Chopin, Frédéric, 37, 39, 40, 42, 71, 256
Churchill, Winston, 50
Cocteau, Jean, 143, 263–64
Coke, Sir Edward, 159
Coleridge, Samuel T., 222
Confucius, 161, 311
Cookson, William, 24, 258, 268
Cooney, Seamus, 29
Corneille, Pierre, 264
Corrington, John William, 167–68, 183, 196, 229, 247, 271, 290–93, 295, 301, 328, 333–36
Corso, Gregory, 61, 205, 250, 276, 278
Crane, Hart, 222
Crews, Judson, 187
Cummings, E. E., 11, 92, 95, 120, 222, 280, 290
Cuscaden, R. R., 274–76, 286

Dante Alighieri, 19, 50, 53, 94, 268, 335, 356

Dean, Abner, 334
Dean, Frances Elizabeth, 339, 347
Debussy, Claude, 76
Degas, Edgar, 223, 230
De la Mare, Walter, 222, 322
Deren, Maya, 12, 14
Dillinger, John, 92
Disraeli, Benjmain, 155
Donne, John, 74, 222
Doolittle, Hilda. *See* H.D.
Dos Passos, John, 8, 168
Dostoevski, Fyodor, 9, 50, 59, 168, 255, 362
Dreiser, Theodore, 8
Dryden, John, 222

Earth, 351
Eberhart, Richard, 222
Edge, 113
Eight Pager, 345
Einstein, Albert, 137
Einstein, Charles, 159
Eliot, T. S., 11, 18, 23, 28, 38, 86, 92, 95, 143, 222, 230, 258, 279, 333–35
Epos, 11, 43, 68, 82, 84, 102, 108, 112, 234, 263
Ernie; see Walker, E. P.
Esquire, 329
Evidence, 338

Fante, John, 8
Fate, 344–45
Faulkner, William, 72, 149, 168, 280, 290
Ferlinghetti, Lawrence, 25, 57, 193, 197
Fett, Heinrich, 314, 325
Fett, Katharina, 7
Flory, Wendy Stallard, 17
Fort, Olivia, 299–301
Franck, César, 46, 81
Frobenius, Leo, 24, 121
Frost, Robert, 149, 167, 171, 222, 290

Frye, Barbara, 10, 46, 51–53, 55, 60, 65, 68, 69, 73, 75, 81, 85, 118, 198, 251, 274, 278

Gaddis, William, 11, 14, 18
Gandhi, Mahatma, 255
Gaudier-Brzeska, Henri, 216–17
Gib; see Lee, Gilbert
Ginsberg, Allen, 11, 25–26, 27, 30, 61, 67, 98, 104, 108, 112, 113, 117, 156, 161–62, 189, 193, 197–98, 205, 222, 228, 276, 278, 282, 356–57
Giotto, 17
Göring, Hermann, 353
Gould, Stanley, 119
Graves, Robert, 59, 71–72, 222
Greco, El, 211
Greek Anthology, 11, 38
Green, Pat, 327
Grieg, Michael, 159, 357
Griffith, E. V., 10, 41, 78, 109
Gumbiner, Richard, 172

Handel, George Frederick, 165–66, 329
Harlequin, 10, 85, 300, 337
Harrison, Kay, 326
Haydn, Peter, 364
Hayter, Stanley W., 14, 51
H.D. (Hilda Doolittle), 11, 22–23, 147, 181–84, 194, 198, 203–04, 212, 215–17, 222–25, 228–29, 239–40, 242, 245–49, 251–52, 258, 261, 306, 327, 334–37, 341–42, 344, 349
Hearse, 10, 41, 78
Heckel, Erich, 43
Hedley, Leslie Woolf, 333, 337, 341
Hemingway, Ernest, 8, 71–72, 149, 168, 280, 290, 362
Henley, William, 222
Hitchcock, George, 49
Hitler, Adolf, 151, 165, 191, 209, 246, 256, 353

Hokusai, 159
Homer, 19, 50, 304–06
Hope, Bob, 47, 161–62, 205
Horace, 95
Hung Tzu-ch'eng, 257
Huxley, Aldous, 92, 371

Ibsen, Henrik, 75
I Ching, 28, 317, 334
Ingalls, Hunter, 300

James, Henry, 117
Jeffers, Robinson, 28, 61, 92, 127–30, 133–35, 149–50, 154, 155, 158, 163, 167, 170, 193–94, 207, 222, 228, 230, 279, 280, 290
Jefferson, Thomas, 43, 51, 63
Johnson, Reid B., 25, 316
Jones, James, 117
Joyce, James, 18, 334, 337, 342

Kafka, Franz, 362
Kaja (Kaye Johnson), 180–81, 183, 194–95, 208, 232–34, 247, 250, 263
Kamo no Chomei, 257
Karpman, Dr., 112
Kati, 349, 359
Kaufman, Bob, 25, 115
Keats, John, 28, 92, 222
Kennedy, John F., 167, 179
Kenyon Review, 59, 144, 164
Kerouac, Jack, 23, 25, 61, 72, 276, 278
Kodály, Zoltán, 76
Koestler, Arthur, 43, 168
Kuan-tzu, 53

Lamantia, Philip, 25
Larsen, Carl, 204
Laughlin, James, 17, 19, 20, 123–24, 130, 158, 309–10
Lawrence, D. H., 8, 43, 46, 47, 62–63, 92, 149, 222, 262
Layton, Irving, 338

376

379

Printed April 2001 in Santa Barbara &
Ann Arbor for the Black Sparrow Press by
Mackintosh Typography & Edwards Brothers Inc.
Text set in Plantin by Words Worth.
Design by Barbara Martin.
This first edition is published in paper wrappers;
there are 750 hardcover trade copies;
& there are 526 numbered & lettered copies
handbound in boards by Earle Gray
each containing an original serigraph print
by Charles Bukowski.

CHARLES BUKOWSKI is one of America's best-known contemporary writers of poetry and prose and, many would claim, its most influential and imitated poet. He was born in Andernach, Germany to an American soldier father and a German mother in 1920, and brought to the United States at the age of three. He was raised in Los Angeles and lived there for fifty years. He published his first story in 1944 when he was twenty-four and began writing poetry at the age of thirty-five. He died in San Pedro, California on March 9, 1994 at the age of seventy-three, shortly after completing his last novel, *Pulp* (1994).

During his lifetime he published more than forty-five books of poetry and prose, including the novels *Post Office* (1971), *Factotum* (1975), *Women* (1978), *Ham on Rye* (1982), and *Hollywood* (1989). His most recent books are the posthumous collections *What Matters Most Is How Well You Walk Through the Fire* (1999), *Open All Night: New Poems* (2000), and *Beerspit Night and Cursing: The Correspondence of Charles Bukowski & Sheri Martinelli, 1960–1967* (2001).

All of his books have now been published in translation in over a dozen languages and his worldwide popularity remains undiminished. In the years to come Black Sparrow will publish additional volumes of previously uncollected poetry and letters.

SHERI MARTINELLI (1918–1996) was an artist, writer, model, and magazine editor. She studied ceramics at the Philadelphia School of Arts, engraving at Atelier 17, and literature with Ezra Pound at St. Elizabeths Federal Hospital for the Insane. Reproductions of some of her paintings were published in *La Martinelli* (1956), with an introduction by Pound. She edited the *Anagogic & Paideumic Review* (1959–70) and privately published numerous booklets of prose, poetry, and drawings.

STEVEN MOORE is the author/editor of five previous books— three on William Gaddis, one on Ronald Firbank, and an anthology of vampire poetry—and has contributed numerous essays on modern literature to a variety of periodicals. He knew Sheri Martinelli during the last dozen years of her life.